TORTURED LOGIC

ALSO BY JOSEPH RUSSOMANNO

*Speaking Our Minds: Conversations with the People Behind
Landmark Amendment Cases*, author

*Defending the First: Commentary on First Amendment
Issues and Cases*, editor

The Law of Journalism and Mass Communication 2nd ed., coauthor

RELATED TITLES FROM POTOMAC BOOKS, INC.

Wanting War: Why the Bush Administration Invaded Iraq
—Jeffrey Record

Overcoming the Bush Legacy in Iraq and Afghanistan
—Deepak Tripathi

*Getting Away with Torture:
Secret Government, War Crimes, and the Rule of Law*
—Christopher H. Pyle

*The Secrets of Abu Ghraib Revealed:
American Soldiers on Trial*
—Christopher Graveline and Michael Clemens

*The Quotable Founding Fathers: A Treasury of 2,500 Wise and Witty
Quotations from the Men and Women Who Created America*
—Buckner F. Melton Jr.

*The Mythology of American Politics:
A Critical Response to Fundamental Questions*
—John T. Bookman

TORTURED LOGIC

A Verbatim Critique of the George W. Bush Presidency

EDITED BY

JOSEPH RUSSOMANNO

Foreword by Jonathan Alter

Potomac Books, Inc.
Washington, D.C.

The editorial cartoon in the front matter, "We Don't Torture," by Mike Keefe, was originally published in the Denver Post (October 10, 2007). Reprinted with permission.

Library of Congress Cataloging-in-Publication Data
Russomanno, Joseph.
 Tortured logic : a verbatim critique of the George W. Bush presidency / Joseph Russomanno ; foreword by Jonathan Alter. — 1st ed.
    p. cm.
 Includes bibliographical references and index.
 ISBN 978-1-59797-513-1 (hardcover : alk. paper)
 1. Executive power—United States—History—21st century. 2. Presidents—United States—History—21st century. 3. Bush, George W. (George Walker), 1946- 4. United States—Politics and government—2001-2009. I. Title.
 JK516.R87 2010
 973.931092—dc22
                                                                    2010037860

Printed in the United States of America on acid-free paper that meets the American National Standards Institute Z39-48 Standard.

Potomac Books, Inc.
22841 Quicksilver Drive
Dulles, Virginia 20166

First Edition

10 9 8 7 6 5 4 3 2 1

To those who
seek truth, reveal truth, and speak truth to power.

———◆———

Special thanks to Cody Shotwell.

CONTENTS

FOREWORD

The Bush administration is only a few years old in historical terms but it sometimes feels like another age, with the details already hazy and the awful implications fading into the mists of time. Was it really true that the American government issued a constant barrage of lies? Did we actually come so close to losing our most precious constitutional protections? Were we in fact led into war under false pretenses? The answer to these questions is yes, but without documented proof these established historical facts still feel like exaggerations. No more. This book offers not just opinions but rock solid evidence.

Historical amnesia is a dangerous thing. It might feel better not to revisit the abuses of another time, but forgetting or even just "moving on" inevitably increase the chances of such abuses occurring again. The surest antidote to this natural human tendency to put the painful past to rest is a vigorous effort to remind the public of what it felt like to live through a dark time. Conventional narrative history or the analytical tools of political science usually do this.

In recent years a new approach has been undertaken, one that still doesn't have a name. It consists of linking together quotes from journalists and policymakers of the time to create a pattern of history, usually with a sharp point. The slow accretion of facts, perspectives, and cogent analysis creates a pointillist painting of history. Sometimes the aim is literary, as Nicholson Baker showed when he strung together short newspaper accounts about the origins of World War II in *Human Smoke*.

Now Joseph Russomanno has applied the technique to the Bush administration's post-9/11 "war on terror" and path to war in Iraq. The result is a deeply informative pastiche of reporting and analysis that add up to a new history of our recent past. It's a postmodern approach that allows the reader to experience the primary and secondary sources directly. Russomanno has a clear point of view and has selected the quotations to advance his argument but he lets his sources do the talking, which adds force and credibility to his work.

This mode is like a Spanish *tapas* bar—a series of tiny dishes that offer the reader a sampling of the tangiest fare available anywhere. The quotes come from a Who's Who of the best reporters, analysts, and sources of the era, including Bob Woodward, Seymour Hersh, Richard Clarke, Michael Isikoff, Al Gore, James Fallows, Tom Ricks, Maureen Dowd, Tyler Drumheller, Frank Rich, Anthony Zinni, Scott McClellan, and hundreds more. Sometimes the quotes come straight from the horse's mouth—George W. Bush, Dick Cheney, Colin Powell, Donald Rumsfeld, Mohamed ElBararedei, Sandra Day O'Connor. And sometimes they belong to the ages—John Stuart Mill, John Locke, Thomas Jefferson, Abraham Lincoln, Oliver Wendell Holmes.

To give you a few appetizers:

"What's in the newspapers worth worrying about? I glance at the headlines just to kind of [get] a flavor of what's moving . . . I rarely read the stories. I get briefed by people who have probably read the news themselves."

—George W. Bush

"Bin Laden Determined to Strike in the U.S."

—title of the President's Daily Briefing, August 6, 2001

"President Bush . . . made 232 false statements about weapons of mass destruction in Iraq and another 28 false statements about Iraq's links to Al Qaeda."

—Charles Lewis and Mark Reading-Smith, Center for Public Integrity

"I saw what was discussed. I saw it in spades. From Addington to the other lawyers at the White House. They said the President of the United States can do whatever he damn pleases. People were arguing for a new interpretation of the Constitution. It negates Article One, Section Eight, that lays out all the powers of Congress, including the right to declare war, raise militias, make laws and oversee the common defense of the nation."

—Lawrence Wilkerson, chief of staff to Colin Powell

"The enemy of the moment always represented absolute evil, and it followed that any past or future agreement with him was impossible."

—George Orwell

Russomanno's layering of these quotes has a cumulative power that brings home the story of the Bush era in a fresh and often terrifying way. What follows is more than superb source material for future historians; it's a compelling history in its own right, of interest to anyone who cares about a twisted time in the life of the nation.

—Jonathan Alter, *Newsweek* columnist and author,
The Promise: President Obama, Year One and
The Defining Moment: Franklin Roosevelt and the First Hundred Days
June 2010

INTRODUCTION

It wasn't just that it was wrong. They lied.[1]
—*Carl Ford, U.S. State Department*

Alexander Meiklejohn, a twentieth-century philosopher and free-speech advocate, once wrote that the First Amendment is primarily a shield against the "mutilation of the thinking process of the community."[2] Simple logic suggests by extension that when the thinking process of the community is mutilated through lying, deception, dishonesty, trickery, and the distortion of facts, the First Amendment has been violated. George W. Bush and his cronies twisted and tortured that logic.

The reasons are many and varied. They largely revolve around the effort to take and expand power, thus embracing the notion of the Imperial Presidency. At the heart of this effort to establish an American monarchy—ignoring the separation of, and limitations on, powers established in the Constitution—was not merely the desire to control information, but also to distort and manipulate it. Administration officials hid the truth, and did so in a number of ways. In short, as the pages that follow illustrate, the hallmark of the Bush Imperial Presidency was lying. Bush and his minions took perhaps the most vital ingredients of American democracy—truth and being truthful with the citizenry—and deliberately trampled them. They readily acknowledged attempting to create new realities. The truth was what they said it was. As Ron Suskind wrote, it was "an age when assertion tends to overwhelm evidence, when claim so easily trumps fact."[3] "Truthiness"[4] found a home in the White House.

A report by the Center for Public Integrity released in 2007 concluded that Bush and top administration officials made at least 935 false statements about national security in the two years following September 11, 2001.[5]

The administration—freed so utterly, from 9/11 forward, from the traditional dictates of transparency—had an undiscovered country of judgments and actions to hide, from torture to illegal wiretaps to breathtaking mishaps in the so-called war on terror, as well as certain troubling convictions that actually drove policy.[6]

It is posited here that the stream of lies and half-truths emanating from the Bush administration lasted not just two years, but until Bush left office. In the narrative that follows, the players include: Bush administration officials; political philosophers and statesmen; and journalists, authors, and commentators.

The words are their own, verbatim. As with a jigsaw puzzle, by putting the pieces together, they collectively reveal a picture—and hopefully one that is greater than the sum of its parts. Part One examines the Imperial Presidency. It must be acknowledged that an irony (and challenge) exists in devoting only one part of this volume specifically to Bush's imperial presidency. The entire Bush-Cheney presidency was imperialistic. Imperialism permeated every fiber, poking its head into every dark corner of the two Bush terms. Nevertheless, the effort has been made to parse this curious presidency by examining imperial-specific topics apart from global issues.

Part Two looks at Bush's self-proclaimed War Presidency. As indicated above, the focus is on how the Bush administration handled information—facts, ideas and theories so vital in any democracy, but particularly in one considering, then fighting, a war. What emerges is a group of ideologues that treated information and its control as one of many paths to ever-increasing power. Rather than sharing information with citizens, the administration hoarded it. Rather than considering all ideas, those at the top of the government accepted only those which corresponded to their preconceived notions and ideology, rejecting others. Rather than embracing and seriously considering dissenting opinions, officials discarded such ideas and often ostracized those with the audacity of mentioning them in the first place. As Meiklejohn suggested, by deliberately controlling information thinking is in turn controlled, even manipulated. The Orwellian extremes to which the Bush administration practiced this deception were unprecedented.

Part One

THE IMPERIAL PRESIDENCY

We may not have realized it at the time, but in the period from
late 2001–January 19, 2009, this country was a dictatorship.
The constitutional rights we learned about in high school civics were
suspended. That was thanks to secret memos crafted deep inside the Justice
Department that effectively trashed the Constitution.[1]
—Scott Horton, national security lawyer

The *Imperial Presidency* is a term coined by historian Arthur M. Schlesinger
Jr. It is used to describe either a specific U.S. presidency, or the office in general, when it pushes or exceeds the limits stipulated by the Constitution. "When
the constitutional balance is upset in favor of presidential power and at the
expense of presidential accountability," Schlesinger wrote, "the presidency can
be said to become imperial."[2] In fact, an imperial presidency is largely defined
by its inclination to ignore and circumvent those constitutional checks and
balances. At the heart of these presidencies is the belief that any requirement
to recognize and deal with Congress and the courts as coequal branches of
government is not only unnecessary, but burdensome. During these periods,
the operation of the federal government begins to model the very forms of
governments the Framers opposed, mistrusted, and sought to lay to rest—a
dictatorial monarchy. Though imperialism is not limited to the global arena,
Schlesinger noted that its "perennial threat" to constitutional balance at least
tends to arise in the field of foreign affairs.[3]

1

The rise of the Imperial Presidency ran against the original intent of the constitutional framers. With the war-making propensities of absolute monarchs in mind, the framers of the Constitution took care to assign the vital foreign policy powers exclusively to Congress. Article I gave Congress not only the appropriations power—itself a potent instrument of control—but also the power to declare war, to raise and support armies, to provide and maintain a navy, to regulate commerce, and to grant letters of marque and reprisal.[4]

It is not uncommon for U.S. presidents to conclude that the office has much less power than they assumed prior to entering the Oval Office. An administration may respond to the frustrations that naturally surface when its leaders feel relatively powerless in a way that leads it into the realm of an imperial presidency. Rather than compromising and respecting Congress and the courts and adhering to their decisions, a belief that those institutions are merely obstacles to the executive's "rightful" supremacy is a step in the direction of imperialism. The checks and balances established by the Constitution's authors, say the imperialists, are unnecessary and cumbersome, especially given the unique circumstances that exist at a particular time. According to this approach, those circumstances—e.g., being at war—may actually warrant or even demand violating laws and interpreting constitutional principles in favor of the executive.

In many respects, the Bush administration became the textbook example of the imperial presidency. While other presidencies (e.g., Richard Nixon's) may have quintessentially represented the imperial presidency, the first presidency of the twenty-first century exceeded its monarchical rivals in virtually every way. No less of an authority than former Nixon White House counsel John Dean made the convincing case in his book, *Worse Than Watergate*. The "constitutionally contrarian style"[5] of Bush and Vice President Dick Cheney, Dean notes, endangered not just the United States but had global implications as well. One of their weapons, according to Dean, was information. Bush and his lieutenants are "men whose obsession with control of information, and spin, is so strong that they are willing to subvert the democratic process for their own short-term personal political gain."[6]

Imperialism permeated virtually every aspect of the Bush administration, including those areas considered in Part Two of this book. Part One looks at some of the tactics used by Bush and other administration officials to secure and safeguard power within the executive branch. In turn, the acquisition of power resulted in viewing the constitutionally mandated separation of powers as an inconvenience. The Bush administration's repeated failure to acknowledge that the executive is but one of three separate, coequal branches of the U.S. government—and that the powers of each branch are distinct—signaled imperialism at work.

An imperial presidency also acts according to political and ideological goals, rather than by principle. Under George W. Bush, this surfaced in several ways, including the politicization of the one federal department, perhaps more than any other, that must operate objectively and according to principle. Instead, the Bush Justice Department became an instrument of politics, selecting targets to prosecute in order to advance the Bush political agenda and Karl Rove's strategy for a permanent Republican majority. When some U.S. attorneys refused to take part in the political gambit, they were fired.

The Bush administration's efforts to expand presidential power also included disregard for the rule of law, the concept that stipulates that no one is above the law. Laws apply equally to every citizen, regardless of position, rank, title or status. Accepting the rule of law is generally regarded as a prerequisite for democracy. High-ranking government officials who reject the concept and believe that their positions grant them special considerations are typically in the midst of a power grab.

There may be no greater act of defiance of the rule of law than the signing statement—a presidential addendum, of sorts, to legislation that has been passed by both houses of Congress and signed by the president. President Bush, however, often tagged those laws with his own statement declaring (1) whether to follow the law was his prerogative (in spite of having just signed it), or (2) that he could interpret the law as he (and his legal team) saw fit. Moreover, these statements were often issued in secret. Unlike a presidential veto that kills a law (absent a congressional override), these signing statements muddle the law and generate questions: Is the law what the bill says it is? Or is it something else that will only be known once it is seen how the president ultimately interprets it? Does it defy the rule of law by insisting that, due to the president's position, he is immune from the law?[7]

Another aspect of the Bush imperial presidency was secrecy. Operating covertly meant not having to account for actions, questionable or otherwise.

A lack of transparency left those in the Bush administration unanswerable, largely because would-be questioners were unaware. That is, it is difficult to investigate particular actions or policies when they are unknown because they were kept secret. Secrecy describes not only a belief system that characterized the Bush presidency,[8] it was at the heart of specific practices. In what seemed to be a rebirth of Orwellian vernacular, this included detention by "extraordinary rendition," establishing prisons and "black sites" to house "enemy combatants" in order to conduct "enhanced interrogation."

When some of the Bush administration's stealth operations were revealed, the need for them was attributed to living in a post-9/11 world. Yet, many of the maneuvers in question were planned or had been launched prior to the terrorist attacks. In yet another homage to Orwell, spying, eavesdropping, and wiretapping were executed either by ignoring applicable laws, rewriting laws, or interpreting them so that various acts would be within the law's boundaries.

The Bush administration's view of the supreme executive—sometimes referred to as the unitary executive[9]—also emerged through its efforts to create its own realities. Facts were often secondary to ideology. Political goals took precedence. Dissent was discouraged and dissenting voices were marginalized,[10] loyalty was valued over truth, and propaganda techniques were used to sell both false claims and half-truths.

—1—

Presidential Power

It is love of power for its own sake that is the
original sin of this presidency.[1]
—Al Gore

Time and again, President Bush and his team have assured Americans that they needed new powers to prevent another attack by an implacable enemy. Time and again, Americans have discovered that these powers were not being used to make them safer, but in the service of Vice President Dick Cheney's vision of a presidency so powerful that Congress and the courts are irrelevant.[2]

—*New York Times* editorial

[T]he administration has already gone so far as to say they can commit torture to gather foreign intelligence if the president thinks it's necessary. It's hard to imagine any broader power that can be asserted under the Constitution.[3]

—Bruce Fein, constitutional law expert

[T]he Bush administration's abuses extended from environmental policy to voting rights. And most of the abuses involved using the power of government to reward political friends and punish political enemies.[4]

—Paul Krugman, columnist

[Cheney] turns everything on its head and he *becomes* the power. And he does it through his network. This is a guy who's an absolute genius at bureaucracy and an absolute genius at not displaying his genius at bureaucracy. He's always quiet.[5]

—Lawrence Wilkerson, chief of staff to Colin Powell

[I]t was almost as if they were interested in expanding executive power for its own sake.[6]

—Jack Goldsmith, former government lawyer

The Party seeks power entirely for its own sake. We are not interested in the good of others; we are interested solely in power. Not wealth or luxury or long life or happiness; only power.[7]

—George Orwell

There is no question that this administration has been involved in a very carefully thought-out, systematic process of expanding presidential power at the expense of the other branches of government. This is really big, very expansive, and very significant.[8]

—Phillip Cooper, professor

And lurking behind it all remained the magic man, Vice President Cheney. No one knew better how to orchestrate what was happening from behind the curtain while the grand production was playing out on stage. Quietly slipping in and out of internal deliberations, his influence and wand waving barely discernable to the outside world, Cheney rarely showed all his cards and never disclosed how he made things happen. Yet somehow, in every policy area he cared about, from the invasion of Iraq to expansion of presidential power to the treatment of detainees and the use of surveillance against terror suspects, Cheney always seemed to get his way. He viewed the world as an ominous place where evil has to be fought by any means necessary—including some that are decidedly unpleasant.[9]

—Scott McClellan, former Bush press secretary

He became vice president well before George Bush picked him. And he began to manipulate things from that point on, knowing that he was going to be able to convince this guy to pick him, knowing that he was then going to be able to wade into the vacuums that existed around George Bush—personality vacuum, character vacuum, details vacuum, experience vacuum.[10]

—Lawrence Wilkerson, chief of staff to Colin Powell

This administration has very systematically and from the beginning acted in a way to interpret its executive powers as broadly as possible and to interpret the power of Congress as narrowly as possible as compared to the executive.[11]

—Phillip Cooper, professor

[U]nlike previous war presidents—Lincoln, FDR—who bent the Constitution in order to save it, and took responsibility for doing so, the Bush administration stonewalled, as if public ignorance were the best way, in many cases, to give the president the powers he needed.[12]

—Christopher Dickey, journalist

If men were angels, no government would be necessary. If angels were to govern men, neither external nor internal controls on government would be necessary. In framing a government, which is to be administered by men over men, the great difficulty lies in this: you must first enable the government to control the governed; and in the next place, oblige it to control itself.[13]

—James Madison

[The Framers] thus designed a Constitution based on insight that men are not angels, and are not more inclined to be so in time of emergency.[14]

—Frederick A. O. Schwarz Jr. and Aziz Z. Huq, lawyers

Next January, when I put my hand on the Bible, I will swear not only to uphold the laws of our land, I will swear to uphold the honor and dignity of the office to which I have been elected, so help me God.[15]

—George W. Bush

And will to the best of my ability, preserve, protect, and defend the Constitution of the United States.[16]

—George W. Bush

[T]he oath [of office] is more than a political gimmick; for the founding generation it was a solemn pledge, designed to bind the officeholder to the country and the Constitution he serves. Throughout his tenure, President Bush has repeatedly dishonored that pledge.[17]

—Gene Healy and Timothy Lynch, lawyers

[Y]ou have a president who's not recognizing a fundamental tenet of our constitutional system that he constitutionally took an oath to protect.[18]

—Jonathan Turley, law professor

Fidelity to the constitutional oath of office should be a central factor in judging Presidents.[19]

—Gene Healy and Timothy Lynch, lawyers

It is not wisdom but Authority that makes a law.[20]

—Thomas Hobbes

[T]he right-wing presidency of George W. Bush and Richard B. Cheney has taken positions that are in open defiance of international treaties or blatant violations of domestic laws, while pushing the limits of presidential power beyond the parameters of the Constitution.[21]

—John Dean, former White House counsel

The right of nature . . . is the liberty each man hath to use his own power, as he will himself, for the preservation of his own nature; that is to say, of his own life.[22]

—Thomas Hobbes

The top-heavy focus on dominance as a goal for the U.S. role in the world is exactly paralleled by this administration's aspiration for the role of the president to completely dominate our constitutional system. The goal of dominance necessitates a focus on power, even absolute power.[23]

—Al Gore

Nip the shoots of arbitrary power in the bud, is the only maxim which can ever preserve the liberties of any people.[24]

—John Adams

President Bush's constitutional vision is, in short, sharply at odds with the text, history, and structure of our Constitution, which authorizes a government of limited powers.[25]

—Gene Healy and Timothy Lynch, lawyers

The great question which in all ages has disturbed mankind, and brought on them the greatest part of those mischiefs which have ruined cities, depopulated countries, and disordered the peace of the world, has been, not whether there be power in the world, nor whence it came, but who should have it.[26]

—John Locke

The essence of Government is power; and power, lodged as it must be in human hands, will ever be liable to abuse.[27]

—James Madison

The jaws of power are always open to devour, and her arm is always stretched out, if possible, to destroy the freedom of thinking, speaking, and writing.[28]

—John Adams

The purpose of the Constitution was not only to grant power, but to keep it from getting out of hand.[29]

—Robert Jackson, U.S. Supreme Court

[N]o one can love freedom heartily, but good men; the rest love not freedom, but license, which never hath more scope or more indulgence than under tyrants.[30]

—John Milton

There ought to be limits to freedom.[31]

—George W. Bush

No man who knows aught can be so stupid to deny that all men naturally were born free.[32]

—John Milton

Our enemies are innovative and resourceful, and so are we. They never stop thinking about new ways to harm our country, and neither do we.[33]

—George W. Bush

You may give a Man an office, but you cannot give him discretion.[34]

—Benjamin Franklin

I think anybody who doesn't think I'm smart enough to handle the job is misunderestimating.[35]

—George W. Bush

Only two things are infinite: the universe and human stupidity; and I'm not sure about the universe.[36]

—Albert Einstein

I am the commander, see? I do not need to explain why I say things. That's the interesting thing about being the President. Maybe somebody needs to explain to me why they say something, but I don't feel like I owe anybody an explanation.[37]

—George W. Bush

The Bush administration has operated on an entirely different concept of power that relies on minimal deliberation, unilateral action and legalistic defense. This approach largely eschews politics: the need to explain, to justify, to convince, to get people on board, to compromise.[38]

—Jack Goldsmith, former government lawyer

Being ignorant is not so much a shame as being unwilling to learn.[39]

—Benjamin Franklin

Nothing in all the world is more dangerous than sincere ignorance and conscientious stupidity.[40]

—Martin Luther King Jr.

What is strength without a double share of wisdom?[41]

—John Milton

The example of such unlimited executive power that must have most impressed the forefathers was the prerogative exercised by George III, and the description of its evils in the Declaration of Independence leads me to doubt that they were creating their new Executive in his image.[42]

—Robert Jackson, U.S. Supreme Court

Bruce Fein, a Republican legal activist, who voted for Bush in both Presidential elections, and who served as associate deputy attorney general in the Reagan Justice Department, said that [Cheney counsel David] Addington and other Presidential legal advisers had "staked out powers that are a universe beyond any other Administration. This President has made claims that are really quite alarming. He's said that there are no restraints on his ability, as he sees it, to collect intelligence, to open mail, to commit torture, and to use electronic surveillance."[43]

—Jane Mayer, journalist

[I]n the first place, I put for a general inclination of all mankind, a perpetual and rest-less desire of power after power, that ceaseth only in death.[44]

—Thomas Hobbes

History may ultimately hold Bush in the greatest contempt for expanding the powers of the presidency beyond the limits laid down by the U.S. Constitution.[45]

—Sean Wilentz, historian

Don't interfere with anything in the Constitution. That must be maintained, for it is the only safeguard of our liberties.[46]

—Abraham Lincoln

The Founders really understood the history of what people *did* with power, going back to Greek and Roman and Biblical times. Our political heritage is to be skeptical of executive power, because, in particular, there was skepticism of King George III. But Cheney and Addington are not students of history. If they were, they'd know that the Founding Fathers would be shocked by what they've done.[47]

—Bruce Fein, constitutional law expert

The highest priority for the Karl Rove–driven presidency is . . . to preserve its own power at all costs. With this gang, political victory and the propaganda needed to secure it always trump principles, even conservative principles, let alone the truth.[48]

—Frank Rich, columnist

Liberty lies in the hearts of men and women; when it dies there, no constitution, no law, no court can save it.[49]

—Learned Hand, judge

[The imperial presidency] is certainly exactly what the founders of our country rejected from the outset. They did not want to have an elected monarch.[50]

—John Dean, former White House counsel

[T]heir experience under the British crown led the Founding Fathers to favor less cen-tralization of authority than they perceived in the British monarchy. As the victims of what they considered a royal tyrannical prerogative, they were determined to fashion themselves a Presidency that would be strong but still limited.[51]

—Arthur Schlesinger, historian

[T]he founders who had recently fought a revolution against a king named George would tell you that monarchical behavior, the behavior of a king, acting like a king, is an impeachable offense. You need not look for specific laws or statutes. What you need to look for is a pattern of behavior that says that the presidency is superior not merely to Congress but to the laws of the land, to the rules of law.[52]

—John Nichols, journalist

Wherever the real power in a government lies, there is the danger of oppression. In our Governments the real power lies in the majority of the Community. . . . Wherever there is an interest and power to do wrong, wrong will generally be done.[53]

—James Madison

The great genius of the founding fathers, their revolutionary idea, with the chief mission of the state is to make you and them free to pursue their ambitions and faculties. Not to build empires, not to aggrandize government. That's the mission of the state, to make them free, to think, to chart their own destiny. And the burden is on government to give really good explanations as to why they're taking these extraordinary measures. And on that score, Bush has flunked on every single occasion.[54]

—Bruce Fein, constitutional law expert

Give me the liberty to know, to utter, and to argue freely according to conscience, above all liberties.[55]

—John Milton

Give me liberty, or give me death.[56]

—Patrick Henry

[T]his president has an obsession with this concept of an absolute ruler, the absolute president.[57]

—Jonathan Turley, law professor

Those who would give up essential liberty to purchase a little temporary safety, deserve neither liberty nor safety.[58]

—Benjamin Franklin

Nations sometimes lose their bearings when confronted by an enemy.[59]

—Ishmael Reed, journalist

[T]he Office of Legal Counsel issued a memo declaring that the President had inherent constitutional authority to take whatever military action he deemed necessary, not just in response to the September 11th attacks but also in the prevention of any future attacks from terrorist groups, whether they were linked to Al Qaeda or not. The memo's broad definition of the enemy went beyond that of Congress, which, on September 14th, had passed legislation authorizing the President to use military force against "nations, organizations, or persons" directly linked to the attacks.[60]

—Jane Mayer, journalist

Now, presidents can evade responsibility a new way: they just say their lawyer said it was legal.[61]

—Frederick A. O. Schwarz Jr. and Aziz Z. Huq, lawyers

Bruce Fein said that the Bush legal team was strikingly unsophisticated. "There is no one of legal stature, certainly no one like Bork, or Scalia, or Elliot Richardson, or Archibald Cox," he said. "It's frightening. No one knows the Constitution—certainly not Cheney."[62]

—Jane Mayer, journalist

The layman's constitutional view is that what he likes is constitutional and that which he doesn't like is unconstitutional.[63]

—Hugo Black, U.S. Supreme Court

The powers delegated by the proposed Constitution to the federal government are few and defined. Those which are to remain in the State governments are numerous and indefinite.[64]

—James Madison

All the powers of government, legislative, executive, and judiciary, result to the legislative body. The concentrating these in the same hands is precisely the definition of despotic government. . . . An *elective despotism* was not the government we fought for.[65]

—Thomas Jefferson

In a 1977 interview with David Frost, Richard Nixon described his view of the president's national security authority, "Well, when the President does it, that means it is not illegal." In the arguments it has advanced, both publicly and privately, for untrammeled executive power, the Bush administration comes perilously close to that view.[66]

—Gene Healy and Timothy Lynch, lawyers

It was Richard Nixon who said, "When the president does it, that means that it is not illegal." George W. Bush and Dick Cheney, operating behind the mammoth fig leaf of national security, took this theoretical absurdity to heart and put it into widespread practice.[67]

—Bob Herbert, journalist

Bush has so outdone Nixon that Nixon almost looks innocent in this area. We're now reaching into such broad scale and widespread programs with just utter in-your-face defiance of the law that even Nixon himself didn't push the envelope nearly as far as this administration is.[68]

—John Dean, former White House counsel

Cheney sought to make the office way beyond Nixon's imperial presidency, which they had accomplished by the end of the first term.[69]

—John Dean, former White House counsel

It so happened that administration lawyers had for months been incubating theories about how to expand presidential power. The ideas were originally seeded by the Vice President, a believer, since his harrowing days in the death throes of the Nixon administration, that executive power had been dangerously diminished.[70]

—Ron Suskind, journalist

The president and the vice president, it appears, believe the lesson of Watergate was not to stay within the law, but rather to not get caught. And if you do get caught, claim that the president can do whatever he thinks necessary in the name of national security. Bush and Cheney have also insulated and isolated themselves so that when they break the law—which they have done repeatedly—they have already built their defense. To protect themselves, they have structured their White House as La Cosa Nostra might have recommended, and surrounded themselves with men who owe their careers to their bosses. All of the key staff people close to Bush and Cheney have very long relationships with them. These have been mutually beneficial relationships. Stated differently, Bush and Cheney are protected by staff who will take a bullet for them.[71]

—John Dean, former White House counsel

Few [in the late 1970s] accepted Nixon's blunt assertion that "when the president does it, that means that it is not illegal." But his claim was not forgotten. Ten years later, in 1987, the same claim reappeared in the minority section of a congressional report about the Iran-Contra scandal. According to the minority report, "the Chief Executive will on occasion feel duty bound to assert monarchical notions of prerogative that will permit him to exceed the laws." The leading congressional advocate of this view was a new representative from Wyoming by the name of Richard Cheney.[72]

—Frederick A. O. Schwarz Jr. and Aziz Z. Huq, lawyers

He and his Republican colleagues showed a remarkable facility very early, decades ago, to really ignore facts and then to reinterpret the law. . . . [He] also shows very clearly how a man, the higher he rises in office, doesn't change, but he reveals himself even further.[73]

—John Dean, former White House counsel

Cheney rejected the majority report of the Iran-Contra committee's investigation, which said that the common elements of both "the Iran and Contra policies were secrecy, deception and disdain for the law" and that the entire affair "was characterized by pervasive dishonesty and inordinate secrecy." Cheney was not the least bit concerned by either the secrecy or lawbreaking, and said so when filing a minority report. . . . Cheney's attitude about the Congress vis-à-vis the president has changed little since 1987.[74]

—John Dean, former White House counsel

Bush's two most influential advisers—Dick Cheney and Donald Rumsfeld—both worked very closely with President Nixon when he was in the Oval Office. . . . It is no secret that both men looked at the rollback of unexamined presidential authority after Watergate with abhorrence.[75]

—Al Gore

Cheney's overriding goal was enlargement of presidential authority. Since the mid-1970s, he believed, power grabs by Congress and courts had intruded on the dominion of the executive.[76]

—Barton Gellman, journalist

Cheney, it seems, had been traumatized as Ford's chief of staff when the Congress began dismantling Nixon's imperial presidency.[77]

—John Dean, former White House counsel

In the aftermath of Vietnam and Watergate . . . there was a concerted effort to place limits and restrictions on presidential authority . . . the decisions that were aimed at the time trying to avoid a repeat of things like Vietnam or . . . Watergate. . . . I thought they were misguided then, and have believed that given the world that we live in, that the president needs to have unimpaired executive authority.[78]

—Dick Cheney

During the Reagan years, the Iran-Contra conspirators violated the Constitution in the name of national security. But the first President Bush pardoned the major male-factors. . . . [T]he second Bush administration picked up right where the Iran-Contra conspirators left off—which isn't too surprising when you bear in mind that Mr. Bush actually hired some of those conspirators.[79]

—Paul Krugman, columnist

Rummy, a Ford chief of staff who became defense secretary, and his protégé, Cheney, who succeeded him as chief of staff, felt diminished by the post-Watergate laws and reforms that reduced the executive branch's ability to be secretive and unilateral, tilting power back toward Congress. . . . So these two crusty pals spent 30 years dreaming of inflating the deflated presidential muscularity. Cheney christened himself vice president and brought in Rummy for the most ridiculously pumped-up presidency ever. All this was fine with W., whose family motto is: "We know best. Trust us."[80]

—Maureen Dowd, journalist

I do believe that, especially in the day and age we live in, the nature of the threats we face, it was true during the cold war, as well as I think what is true now, the president of the United States needs to have his constitutional powers unimpaired, if you will, in terms of the conduct of national security policy.[81]

—Dick Cheney

[T]he Bush administration—in seeking to restore what Cheney, a Nixon administration veteran, has called "the legitimate authority of the presidency"—threatens to overturn the Framers' healthy tension in favor of presidential absolutism.[82]

—Sean Wilentz, historian

The [unitary executive] theory is not a response to 9/11, but, as the 1987 minority report suggests, has long been nurtured by the leaders of today's Bush Administration.[83]

—Frederick A. O. Schwarz Jr. and Aziz Z. Huq, lawyers

Armed with legal findings by his attorney general (and personal lawyer) Alberto Gonzales, the Bush White House has declared that the president's powers as commander in chief in wartime are limitless. No previous wartime president has come close to making so grandiose a claim. More specifically, this administration has asserted that the president is perfectly free to violate federal laws on such matters as domestic surveillance and the torture of detainees.[84]

—Sean Wilentz, historian

It has been remarked that there is a tendency in all Governments to an augmentation of power at the expense of liberty.[85]

—James Madison

A people who proclaim their civil liberties, but extend them only to preferred groups start down the path to totalitarianism.[86]

—William O. Douglas, U.S. Supreme Court

If the ground of democracy is truth, the ground of dictatorship is assertion. In a dictatorship, reality belongs to whoever has the greatest power to assert.[87]

—Naomi Wolf, author

If this were a dictatorship, it'd be a heck of a lot easier, just so long as I'm the dictator.[88]

—George W. Bush

Power is not a means; it is an end. One does not establish a dictatorship in order to safeguard a revolution; one makes a revolution in order to establish the dictatorship. The object of persecution is persecution. The object of torture is torture. The object of power is power.[89]

—George Orwell

This is a totalitarian system in which there are no checks or balances on the executive. The president can do whatever he wants, acting as a dictator. In this system the courts have no independent function and can't protect anybody's rights. [With Military Order No. 1,[90] Bush] issued a military order giving himself the power to run the country as a general.[91]

—Naomi Wolf, author

Under military order No 1, issued by President Bush in November 2001, the president gave himself the right, in defiance of national and international law, to detain indefinitely any non-U.S. citizen anywhere in the world. Many ended up in Guantánamo where at least some of their names were discovered. Others simply vanished.[92]

—Isabel Hilton, journalist

Military Commission Order No. 1 . . . exceeds limits that certain statutes, duly enacted by Congress, have placed on the President's authority to convene military courts.[93]

—Stephen Breyer, U.S. Supreme Court

The truth is that all men having power ought to be mistrusted.[94]

—James Madison

A fondness for power is implanted, in most men, and it is natural to abuse it, when acquired. This maxim, drawn from the experience of all ages, makes it the height of folly to entrust any set of men with power which is not under every possible control.[95]

—Alexander Hamilton

Power must never be trusted without a check.[96]

—John Adams

[T]hose in power need checks and restraints lest they come to identify the common good for their own tastes and desires, and their continuation in office as essential to the preservation of the nation.[97]

—William O. Douglas, U.S. Supreme Court

The accretion of dangerous power does not come in a day. It does come, however slowly, from the generative force of unchecked disregard of the restrictions that fence in even the most disinterested assertion of authority.[98]

—Felix Frankfurter, U.S. Supreme Court

Power naturally grows. Why? Because human passions are insatiable.[99]

—John Adams

Whoever undertakes to set himself up as a judge of Truth and Knowledge is shipwrecked by the laughter of the gods.[100]

—Albert Einstein

[L]iberty may be endangered by the abuses of liberty, as well as by the abuses of power.[101]

—James Madison

[A] long and violent abuse of power, is generally the Means of calling the right of it in question.[102]

—Thomas Paine

The Founding Fathers, who feared despotism and had an entirely realistic view of human nature, were quite prepared to believe that Presidents might abuse their power and were therefore determined to provide the new republic with a way of removing any who did.[103]

—Arthur Schlesinger, historian

The potential for the disastrous rise of misplaced power exists and will persist.[104]

—Dwight Eisenhower

The resistance to giving a "single man," even if he were President of the United States, the unilateral power to decide on war pervaded the contemporaneous literature.[105]

—Arthur Schlesinger, historian

Uncontrolled power, in the hands of an incensed, imperious and rapacious conqueror, is an engine of dreadful execution; and woe be to that country over which it can be exercised.[106]

—Thomas Paine

The monarchical executive theory was not simply a response to 9/11. It was a realization of the vision first articulated in the Iran-Contra minority report headlined by then-congressman Dick Cheney. Within weeks of the 9/11 attacks, Vice President Cheney and his senior legal advisor David Addington, who had been at Cheney's side in the Iran-Contra investigation, urged that the Administration ignore prohibitions on government searches contained in the Constitution's Fourth Amendment and in a host of federal prohibitions and start intercepting Americans' e-mails and telephone calls. Similar logic was also soon used to justify extraordinary rendition and indefinite detention without trial.[107]

—Frederick A. O. Schwarz Jr. and Aziz Z. Huq, lawyers

I saw what was discussed. I saw it in spades. From Addington to the other lawyers at the White House. They said the President of the United States can do whatever he damn pleases. People were arguing for a new interpretation of the Constitution. It negates Article One, Section Eight, that lays out all the powers of Congress, including the right to declare war, raise militias, make laws, and oversee the common defense of the nation.[108]

—Lawrence Wilkerson, chief of staff to Colin Powell

This preceded 9/11. . . . [T]he idea of reducing Congress to a cipher was already in play. It was Cheney and Addington's political agenda.[109]

—Bruce Fein, constitutional law expert

Cheney, say those who know him, has always had a Hobbesian view of life. The world is a dangerous place; war is the natural state of mankind; enemies lurk. The national-security state must be strong, vigilant and wary. . . . Cheney is a strong believer in the necessity of government secrecy as well as more broadly the need to preserve and protect the power of the executive branch.[110]

—Mark Hosenball, Michael Isikoff, and Evan Thomas, journalists

The condition of man . . . is a condition of war of everyone against everyone.[111]

—Thomas Hobbes

For Cheney, the 9/11 attack was *not* a transforming event; rather it was further confirmation of his long-held Hobbesian perception of the world's likely state of perpetual war. Those close to Cheney say of 9/11, "It wasn't an epiphany, it wasn't a sudden eureka moment; it was an evolution, but one that was primed by what he had done and seen at the end of the Cold War". . . . Indeed, it was not only an evolution, it was an opportunity.[112]

—John Dean, former White House counsel

The White House, handed an opportunity and a mandate by the shocking events of 9/11, unfurled a brilliantly produced scenario to accomplish a variety of ends, the most unambiguous of which was to amass power and hold on to it.[113]

—Frank Rich, columnist

Bush and Cheney saw 9/11 as an excuse to indulge their natural authoritarian and conservative instincts. In doing so, they have brought out the worst in conservatism: They have justified and rationalized their increasing use of authoritarian tactics in the name of fighting terrorism.[114]

—John Dean, former White House counsel

The Bush Administration has parlayed national security into a partisan issue, stifling and polarizing debate.[115]

—Frederick A. O. Schwarz Jr. and Aziz Z. Huq, lawyers

Ideas are hatched in the White House, for political or ideological reasons, then are thrust on the bureaucracy, "not for analysis, but for sale."[116]

—Bruce Bartlett, government official

[T]his president's theory of his power is now, I think, so extreme that it's unprecedented. He believes that he has the inherent authority to violate federal law. He has said that. . . . [P]residents, when they acquire power, rarely return it to the people. And so we have to be very concerned. This country is changing in a very significant way, and it's something that citizens have to think about, because if there is a war on terror—and I believe that we must fight terror, obviously—but we're trying to defend that Constitution. And we're really at a point where the president is arguing about his own presidential power in ways that are the antithesis of that Constitution and the values that it contains.[117]

—Jonathan Turley, law professor

Bush instructed his insubordinates that the laws [requiring that information be provided to Congress] were unconstitutional constraints on his own inherent power as commander in chief and as head of the "unitary" executive branch and thus need not be obeyed as written.[118]

—Charlie Savage, journalist

The administration asserts that the president has the sole authority to supervise and direct executive officers, and that Congress and the courts cannot interfere. This theory, which has no support in American history or the Constitution, is a formula for autocracy.[119]

—*New York Times* editorial

In the aftermath of the 9/11 attacks, the Justice Department secretly gave the green light for the U.S. military to attack apartment buildings and office complexes inside the United States, deploy high-tech surveillance against U.S. citizens and potentially suspend First Amendment freedom-of-the-press rights in order to combat the terror threat. . . .[120]

—Michael Isikoff, journalist

■ ■ ■

In an Oct. 23, 2001, memo, John C. Yoo, then a Justice Department lawyer, explained how Mr. Bush could ignore the Fourth Amendment and the Posse Comitatus Act and deploy the military within the United States in "anti-terrorist operations."[121]

—*New York Times* editorial

First Amendment speech and press rights may also be subordinated to the overriding need to wage war successfully.[122]

—John C. Yoo and Robert J. Delahunty, Bush administration attorneys

In October 2001, they were trying to construct a legal regime that would basically have allowed for the imposition of martial law.[123]

—Kate Martin, Center for National Security Studies

We conclude that the President has ample constitutional and statutory authority to deploy the military against international or foreign terrorists operating within the United States. We further believe that the use of such military force generally is consistent with constitutional standards, and that it need not follow the exact procedures that govern law enforcement operations.[124]

—John C. Yoo and Robert J. Delahunty, Bush administration attorneys

The opinions reflected a broad interpretation of presidential authority, asserting as well that the president could unilaterally abrogate foreign treaties, ignore any guidance from

Congress in dealing with detainees suspected of terrorism, and conduct a program of domestic eavesdropping without warrants.[125]

—Neil Lewis, journalist

Yoo was dismissive of the claims of international law and institutions, instead championing the need for America to assert its supremacy without apology or hindrance in the world. Yoo's specialty was the area of presidential power during war. Unlike most mainstream academics, he likened the president's powers to that of British kings, arguing that America's founders had meant for presidents to be able to wage war almost unilaterally. Yoo's views were not widely accepted. Critics accused him of "fictionalizing the founding" history of the country.[126]

—Jane Mayer, journalist

But the memo from the Justice Department's Office of Legal Counsel . . . illustrates with new details the extraordinary post-9/11 powers asserted by Bush administration lawyers. Those assertions ultimately led to such controversial policies as allowing the waterboarding of terror suspects and permitting warrantless wiretapping of U.S. citizens.[127]

—Michael Isikoff, journalist

[T]aken together, the opinions disclosed Monday were the clearest illustration to date of the broad definition of presidential power approved by government lawyers in the months after the Sept. 11 attacks.[128]

—Neil Lewis, journalist

The released memos were written by the Justice Department's Office of Legal Counsel [OLC], which is supposed to ensure policies comply with the Constitution and the law. They make it chillingly clear how quickly that office was rededicated to finding ways for Mr. Bush to evade, twist or ignore both.[129]

—*New York Times* editorial

I've been drilling into OLC for some time now. I have described it as Dick Cheney's little shop of legal horrors. This recent disclosure only makes it worse. The difference between America, a country of laws, and some tin pot dictatorship, where everybody does what the generalissimo tells them, is institutions like the Office of Legal Counsel, which are supposed to do their duty, which are supposed to follow the law, which are supposed to be driven by principles higher than the urgencies of the moment. For them to have rolled over and allowed themselves to be told what to say and to do so in ways that just are flagrantly apart from any defensible legal theory, really shows how bad things got.[130]

—Sen. Sheldon Whitehouse

These memos provide the very definition of tyranny. These memos include everything that a petty despot would want from the domestic use of the military in searches and seizures, suspension of free press, free speech, arrests of individuals without legal process. The amazing thing is that this is the blueprint of our government, not the people we were fighting.[131]

—Jonathan Turley, law professor

The most controversial, and best known, of Yoo's legal opinions was his Aug. 1, 2002, memo that effectively approved the president's right to disregard a federal law banning torture in ordering the interrogation of terror suspects. An accompanying (and still unreleased) memo from the same day approved the CIA's authority to use "waterboarding" (or simulated drowning) against terror suspects.[132]

—Michael Isikoff, journalist

These memoranda are extensive. They have lengthy historical discussions. I would say, looking at them, they look an awful lot like law review articles and books that have been written by John Yoo. It looks like John Yoo has found an opportunity to turn his nutty legal theories into opinions of the attorney general. That's what he did.[133]

—Scott Horton, national security lawyer

It really does show, I think, the great tragedy of a very bright individual working very, very hard to satisfy the president and to tell him what he wanted to hear.[134]

—Jonathan Turley, law professor

On Jan. 15, 2009, five days before Mr. Bush left office, Steven G. Bradbury, the head of the counsel's office in Mr. Bush's second term, repudiated the earlier memos and tried to excuse them by saying they were made "in a time of great danger and under extraordinary time pressure." They were, but that should have led honest lawyers to exercise extra prudence, not to rush into sweeping away this country's most cherished rights.[135]

—New York Times editorial

What's really pathetic is the memo on January 15th, where Bradbury finally just says we don't believe most of this stuff. This is just something that can't be sustained. And so you've got eight years of Constitutional terror for civil libertarians, followed by five days of legal contrition. And it's really quite pathetic. It's basically an effort of Bush lawyers to say, we want to go back into the Bar, despite the fact that for the last eight years, we have been saying we can suspend every element of a free nation.[136]

—Jonathan Turley, law professor

THE SEPARATION OF POWERS

The accumulation of all powers, legislative, executive, and judiciary, in the same hands, whether of one, a few, or many, and whether hereditary, self-appointed, or elective, may justly be pronounced the very definition of tyranny.[137]

—James Madison

Reflecting Madison's insights, the Constitution does not simply divide government power among three separate branches—a lawmaking part in Congress; a law-executing part in the president and his departments and agencies; and an adjudicative part in the federal courts—it also fashions a system of separate institutions *sharing* power, thus restraining each other from power's abuse.[138]

—Frederick A. O. Schwarz Jr. and Aziz Z. Huq, lawyers

I think that [Bush] has acted precisely as Madison feared. He has taken powers unto himself that were never intended to be in the executive. And, frankly, that when an executive uses them, in the way that this president has, you actually undermine the process of uniting the country and really focusing the country on the issues that need to be dealt with.[139]

—John Nichols, journalist

[T]he executive remains the dominant, almost exclusive, branch of government choosing and wielding national security tools in response to terrorist threats. President George W. Bush acts with little deference to or collaboration with Congress or the federal courts on matters he considers relevant to national security.[140]

—Frederick A. O. Schwarz Jr. and Aziz Z. Huq, lawyers

The doctrine of the separation of powers was adopted by the Convention of 1787, not to promote efficiency but to preclude the exercise of arbitrary power. The purpose was, not to avoid friction, but, by means of the inevitable friction incident to the distribution of the governmental powers among three departments, to save the people from autocracy.[141]

—Louis Brandeis, U.S. Supreme Court

George Bush seemed at war from the minute he took the first oath with the concept of the separation of powers. And even before 9/11, he really chafed at the idea of sharing power and it continued to his very last day.[142]

—Jonathan Turley, law professor

The preservation of a free Government requires not merely, that the metes and bounds which separate each department of power be invariably maintained; but more especially that neither of them be suffered to overlap the great Barrier which defends the rights of the people.[143]

—James Madison

The impact of 9/11 and of the overhanging terrorist threat gives more power than ever to the Imperial Presidency and places the separation of powers ordained by the Constitution under unprecedented, and at times unbearable, strain.[144]

—Arthur Schlesinger, historian

The dignity and stability of government in all its branches, the morals of the people, and every blessing of society depend so much upon an upright and skillful administration of justice, that the judicial power ought to be distinct from both the legislative and executive, and independent upon both, that so it may be a check upon both, as both should be checks upon that.[145]

—John Adams

[A] nation that loses control in the check on its commander-in-chief is something other than a democracy.[146]

—John Dean, former White House counsel

The Constitution says that Congress and the White House are co-equal branches of government, but Mr. Bush and his people aren't big on constitutional niceties.[147]

—Paul Krugman, columnist

I have a duty to protect the executive branch from legislative encroachment.[148]

—George W. Bush

In the framework of our Constitution, the President's power to see that the laws are faithfully executed refutes the idea that he is to be a lawmaker. The Constitution limits his functions in the lawmaking process to the recommending of laws he thinks wise and the vetoing of laws he thinks bad. And the Constitution is neither silent nor equivocal about who shall make laws which the President is to execute. The first section of the first article says that "All legislative Powers herein granted shall be vested in a Congress of the United States . . . ." After granting many powers to the Congress, Article I goes on to provide that Congress may "make all Laws which shall be necessary and proper for carrying into Execution the foregoing Powers, and all other Powers vested by this Constitution in the Government of the United States, or in any Department or Officer thereof."[149]

—Hugo Black, U.S. Supreme Court

Vice President Dick Cheney sets the gold standard, placing himself not just above Congress and the courts but above Mr. Bush himself. For the last four years, he has been defying a presidential order requiring executive branch agencies to account for the classified information they handle. When the agency that enforces this rule tried to do its job, Mr. Cheney proposed abolishing the agency.[150]

—Michael Duffy, journalist

Congress must recognize that effective foreign policy requires, and the Constitution mandates, the President to be the country's foreign policy leader.[151]

—Dick Cheney

[T]he vice-president of the United States believes that Congress shouldn't even be a part of the foreign policy debate.[152]

—John Nichols, journalist

According to the Bush-Cheney Doctrine, executive powers trump the constitutional doctrine of separation of powers.[153]

—Sen. John Kerry

The massive Bush campaign machine was integrally woven into his White House governance, without adequate controls or corresponding checks and balances.[154]

—Scott McClellan, former Bush press secretary

They clearly have no regard for the checks and balances.[155]

—John Nichols, journalist

Cheney's actions are part of an effort to weaken Congress, which is one of many building blocks in returning to a Nixonian imperial presidency.[156]

—John Dean, former White House counsel

Our government was founded by a delicate balance of powers—whereby one branch carefully checks the other branches to prevent a dangerous consolidation of power. The actions of this White House have totally destroyed this careful balance. Without these checks and balances, a president could run roughshod over any law and turn us into a nation where wars can be waged based on lies and laws can be rewritten without the input of Congress or the American people.[157]

—Rep. Robert Wexler

[Overreaching with executive power] means asserting powers and claiming that there are no other branches that have the authority to question it. Take, for instance, the assertion that [Bush has] made that when he is out to collect foreign intelligence, no other branch can tell him what to do. That means he can intercept your e-mails, your phone calls, open your regular mail, he can break and enter your home. He can even kidnap you, claiming I am seeking foreign intelligence and there's no other branch— Congress can't say it's illegal, judges can't say this is illegal. I can do anything I want. That is overreaching. When he says that all of the world, all of the United States is a military battlefield because Osama bin Laden says he wants to kill us there, and I can then use the military to go into your homes and kill anyone there who I think is al-Qaeda or drop a rocket, that is overreaching. That is a claim even King George III didn't make.[158]

—Bruce Fein, constitutional law expert

Mr. Cheney seems unconcerned about little things like checks and balances and traditional American notions of judicial process. At one point, he gave himself the power to
selectively declassify documents and selectively leak them to reporters.[159]

—*New York Times* editorial

The system of checks and balances . . . serves a high purpose in diluting the power of
each branch of government, making it subject to restraint by the other branches.[160]

—William O. Douglas, U.S. Supreme Court

As a matter of constitutional theory, we should be very nervous about unilateral executive pronouncements that don't rest on firm authority. As a matter of politics, it's always
better for presidents to seek consent.[161]

—Jack Rakove, history professor

[W]henever power is unchecked and unaccountable, it almost inevitably leads to mistakes and abuses. In the absence of rigorous accountability, incompetence flourishes.
Dishonesty is encouraged and rewarded.[162]

—Al Gore

[W]hen government responds to security threats by ignoring the Constitution's checks
and balances, America's security, its moral luster, and its standing in the world are all
diminished.[163]

—Frederick A. O. Schwarz Jr. and Aziz Z. Huq, lawyers

For Cheney and his like-minded associates, 9/11 was a perfect storm, a moment they
had even anticipated when looking earlier for a catalyst necessary to accomplish their
broader goals.[164]

—John Dean, former White House counsel

[T]he President seems to have been pursuing policies chosen in advance of the facts—
policies designed to benefit friends and supporters—and has used tactics that deprived
the American people of any opportunity to effectively subject his arguments to the
kind of informed scrutiny that is essential in our system of checks and balances.[165]

—Al Gore

Mr. Cheney is the driving force behind the Bush administration's theory of the "unitary executive," which holds that no one, including Congress and the courts, has the
power to supervise or regulate the actions of the president. Just as he pays little attention to old-fangled notions of the separation of powers, Mr. Cheney does not overly
bother himself about the bright line that should exist between his last job as chief of the
energy giant Halliburton and his current one on the public payroll.[166]

—*New York Times* editorial

In the wake of the invasion, they were able to terrify the American people, subjugate the American people, drive through a series of laws that dismantled key checks and balances, allowed overreaching executive power, and completely eviscerated what the founders set in place, thus weakening America.[167]

—Naomi Wolf, author

[T]he constitution did not contemplate that the title Commander-in-Chief of the Army and Navy [would make the president] also Commander-in-Chief of the country, its industries, and its inhabitants. [A president] has no monopoly of "war powers," whatever they are.[168]

—Robert Jackson, U.S. Supreme Court

[I]n a representative republic, where the executive magistracy is carefully limited, both in the extent and the duration of its power; and where the legislative power is exercised by an assembly, which is inspired by a supposed influence over the people with an intrepid confidence in its own strength. . . . The legislative department derives a superiority in our governments from other circumstances.[169]

—James Madison

That military powers of the Commander in Chief were not to supersede representative government of internal affairs seems obvious from the Constitution and from elementary American history.[170]

—Robert Jackson, U.S. Supreme Court

Unitary executive theory returned, reinvigorated and in a new form, after 9/11 to justify the executive branch's use of torture, detention, and spying in violation of federal law. Executive branch lawyers asserted a novel "suspension" theory. The president, they argued, has the same power as the old English kings to "suspend" laws. The lawyers were not describing just an emergency power that could be used only in the interval between a crisis and Congress's subsequent meeting. Rather, executive branch lawyers described an ongoing authority to set aside legal checks imposed by Congress.[171]

—Frederick A. O. Schwarz Jr. and Aziz Z. Huq, lawyers

The Founders were determined to deny the American President what [Sir William] Blackstone[172] had assigned to the British King—"the sole prerogative of making war and peace." Even Hamilton, the most consistent advocate of executive centralization, proposed in the Constitution that the Senate "have the sole power of declaring war" with the executive to "have the direction of war when authorized or begun."[173]

—Arthur Schlesinger, historian

Alexander Hamilton—one of the most ardent defenders of executive power, also starkly rejected the comparison between the English monarchy and the office of president.[174]

—Frederick A. O. Schwarz Jr. and Aziz Z. Huq, lawyers

The history of human conduct does not warrant that exalted opinion of human virtue which could make it wise in a nation to commit interests of so delicate and momentous a kind, as those which concern its intercourse with the rest of the world, to the sole disposal of a magistrate created and circumstanced as would be a President of the United States.[175]

—Alexander Hamilton

In *Federalist* 69, Hamilton compared a monarch and the new president, asking, "What answer shall we give to those who persuade us that things so unlike resemble each other?" The same answer one would give, explained Hamilton, to one who would take the U.S. Constitution to establish, "an aristocracy, a monarchy, and a despotism."[176]

—Frederick A. O. Schwarz Jr. and Aziz Z. Huq, lawyers

The President is to be commander-in-chief of the army and navy of the United States. In this respect his authority would be nominally the same with that of the king of Great Britain, but in substance much inferior to it. It would amount to nothing more than the supreme command and direction of the military and naval forces, as first General and admiral of the Confederacy; while that of the British king extends to the *declaring* of war and to the *raising* and *regulating* of fleets and armies—all which, by the Constitution under consideration, would appertain to the legislature.[177]

—Alexander Hamilton

The Founding Fathers did not have to give unconditional power to declare war to Congress. They might have said, in language they used elsewhere in the Constitution, that war could be declared by the President with the advice and consent of the Congress, or by Congress with the recommendation of the President. But they chose not to mention the President at all in connection with the war-making power.[178]

—Arthur Schlesinger, historian

The Constitution's drafters were intent on balancing power so no one branch could drift toward despotism. The system of checks and balances that runs through the document divides the war power between the president and Congress.[179]

—Adam Cohen, journalist

In some nations that power is entrusted to the executive branch as a matter of course or in case of emergencies. We chose another course. We chose to place the legislative power of the Federal Government in the Congress. The language of the Constitution is not ambiguous or qualified. It places not some legislative power in the Congress; Article I, Section 1 says "All legislative Powers herein granted shall be vested in a Congress of the United States, which shall consist of a Senate and House of Representatives.[180]

—William O. Douglas, U.S. Supreme Court

The Constitution supposes, what the history of all Governments demonstrates, that the Executive is the branch of power most interested in war, & most prone to it. It has accordingly with studied care vested the question of war in the Legislature.[181]

—James Madison

The Bush administration insists that if Congress tries to manage the Iraq war, it will leave the commander in chief with too little authority. But the greater danger is the one Madison recognized at the nation's founding—that all the power will be left with the person "most interested in war, and most prone to it."[182]

—Adam Cohen, journalist

Nothing in our Constitution is plainer than that declaration of a war is entrusted only to Congress. Of course, a state of war may in fact exist without a formal declaration. But no doctrine that the Court could promulgate would seem to me more sinister and alarming than that a President whose conduct of foreign affairs is so largely uncontrolled, and often even is unknown, can vastly enlarge his mastery over the internal affairs of the country by his own commitment of the Nation's armed forces to some foreign venture.[183]

—Robert Jackson, U.S. Supreme Court

The Europeans used to have an expression for this, which was all too well earned from their own experiences. They noted that "War is the sport of kings." This is precisely why America's Founders so feared the concentration of political power that they created a system devoted to spreading that power out, through checks and balances, through federalism, and through guaranteed civil liberties. Often those institutional obstacles have been successful at preventing presidents from acting like kings, but sometimes not. During the George W. Bush presidency, Congress has been a side-show, and many of America's Bill of Rights–provided civil liberties have been shredded.[184]

—David Michael Green, political science professor

The constant aim is to divide and arrange the several offices in such a manner as that each may be a check on the other—that the private interest of every individual may be a sentinel over the public rights.[185]

—James Madison

This "monarchical executive" argument is deployed to many ends: for example, to defeat laws barring both torture and cruel or degrading treatment; to underwrite the "outsourcing" of torture to other countries, such as Syria and Egypt; to detain individuals, including Americans, indefinitely without any due process; to spy on Americans' telephone calls and e-mails in violation of federal statutes and, at times, the Fourth

Amendment; and to infiltrate and keep watch on domestic groups protesting government policy.[186]

—Frederick A. O. Schwarz Jr. and Aziz Z. Huq, lawyers

The constitution vests the power of declaring war in Congress; therefore no offensive expedition of importance can be undertaken until after they shall have deliberated upon the subject and authorized such a measure.[187]

—George Washington

The men who prepared and ratified the Constitution lived most of their lives as subjects to a British king and were steeped in British constitutional history. This history, however, provided a powerful warning *against* vesting the executive branch with an open-ended power to set aside statutory provisions.[188]

—Frederick A. O. Schwarz Jr. and Aziz Z. Huq, lawyers

What recurred regularly in various arguments as the Constitution and Bill of Rights took shape was the widespread fear of an unchecked executive. It's not surprising that these patriots would so deeply fear a single man invested with too much power. They had just freed themselves from being subjugated to George III, an abusive, not to mention mentally ill, monarch.[189]

—Naomi Wolf, author

A dependence on the people is, no doubt, the primary control on the government; but experience has taught mankind the necessity of auxiliary precautions.[190]

— James Madison

There can be but one supreme power, which is the legislative, to which all the rest are and must be subordinate. [The executive] is both ministerial and subordinate to the legislative.[191]

—John Locke

Powers properly belonging to one of the departments ought not to be directly and completely administered by either of the other departments. . . . It will not be denied, that power is of an encroaching nature and that it ought to be effectually restrained from passing the limits assigned to it.[192]

—James Madison

The executive, except for recommendation and veto, has no legislative power. . . . With all its defects, delays and inconveniences, men have discovered no technique for long preserving free government except that the law be made be parliamentary deliberations.[193]

—Robert Jackson, U.S. Supreme Court

The administration's legal position can be summed up starkly: When we're at war, anything goes, and the president gets to decide when we're at war.[194]

—Gene Healy and Timothy Lynch, lawyers

We do not lose our right to condemn either measures or men because the country is at war.[195]

—Francis Biddle, former U.S. attorney general

Power should be a check to power.[196]

—Montesquieu

This is a president who still remains uncomfortable within that constitutional skin. He just has a hard time playing well with the other branches. . . . [Y]ou have a president who's not recognizing a fundamental tenet of our constitutional system that he constitutionally took an oath to protect. . . . [T]hat has led a lot of people to wonder what's really behind some of these things. And there's a lot of us who have become cynics in the last few years. We believe—at least, I believe—that there's a great deal of illegality that's occurred under this administration, including possible crimes.[197]

—Jonathan Turley, law professor

The White House is charged with deliberately lying to Congress and the American people and manipulating intelligence regarding weapons of mass destruction in Iraq; ordering the illegal use of torture; firing U.S. attorneys for political purposes; denying the legitimate Constitutional powers of Congressional oversight by blatantly ignoring subpoenas; among countless other crimes. Never before in the history of this nation has an administration so successfully diminished the Constitutional powers of the legislative branch. It is unacceptable, and it must not stand. This is not how our Founders so carefully and delicately designed our democracy.[198]

—Rep. Robert Wexler

—2—

The Rule of Law

For as in absolute governments the king is law, so in free countries
the law ought to be king and there ought to be no other.[1]
—Thomas Paine

Only by fully understanding what Mr. Bush has done over eight years to distort the rule of law and violate civil liberties and human rights can Americans ever hope to repair the damage and ensure it does not happen again.[2]

—*New York Times* editorial

This is a president who believes that he can define what the law is or ignore it. He's also a president that created his own judicial system just on the other side of the border, and he says that he can try people by his own rules and execute them. Well, that combines the legislative, judicial, and executive powers of this government in one person.[3]

—Jonathan Turley, law professor

"Equal rights to all and special privileges to none" is the maxim which should control in all departments of government.[4]

—Williams Jennings Bryan

It is fundamental to the rule of law that all citizens stand before the bar of justice as equals.[5]

—Patrick Fitzgerald, U.S. attorney

Americans have lost trust in a White House which refuses to brief Congress and insists it is above the law.[6]

—Rep. Jane Harman

The clearest way to show what the rule of law means to us in everyday life is to recall what has happened when there is no rule of law.[7]

—Dwight Eisenhower

For the first time in American history, the executive branch claims authority under the Constitution to set aside laws permanently—including prohibitions on torture and warrantless eavesdropping on Americans. A frightening idea decisively rejected at America's birth—that a president, like a king, can do no wrong—has reemerged to justify torture and indefinite presidential detention.[8]

—Frederick A. O. Schwarz Jr. and Aziz Z. Huq, lawyers

Known as the New Paradigm, this strategy rests on a reading of the Constitution that few legal scholars share—namely, that the President, as Commander-in-Chief, has the authority to disregard virtually all previously known legal boundaries, if national security demands it.[9]

—Jane Mayer, journalist

A federal judge in Detroit ruled yesterday that the National Security Agency's warrantless surveillance program is unconstitutional, delivering the first decision that the Bush administration's effort to monitor communications without court oversight runs afoul of the Bill of Rights and federal law.[10]

—Dan Eggen and Dafna Linzer, journalists

There are no hereditary kings in America and no powers not created by the Constitution.[11]

—Anna Diggs Taylor, judge

[W]ith a careful, thoroughly grounded opinion, one judge in Michigan has done what 535 members of Congress have so abysmally failed to do. She has reasserted the rule of law over a lawless administration and shown why issues of this kind belong within the constitutional process created more than two centuries ago to handle them.[12]

—*New York Times* editorial

It was never the intent of the framers to give the president such unfettered control, particularly when his actions blatantly disregard the parameters clearly enumerated in the Bill of Rights. The three separate branches of government were developed as a check and balance for one another.[13]

—Anna Diggs Taylor, judge

[W]hen the court sets aside civil liberties and defers to the president, it acts out of fear; when the court checks the president and reaffirms those liberties, it acts out of strength.[14]

—Jonathan Mahler, journalist

The people of these United States are the rightful masters of both Congresses and courts not to overthrow the constitution, but to overthrow the men that pervert that constitution.[15]

—Abraham Lincoln

Laws are a dead letter without courts to expound and define their true meaning and operation.[16]

—Alexander Hamilton

[T]he Bush constitutional record . . . is overwhelmingly one of contempt for constitutional limits.[17]

—Gene Healy and Timothy Lynch, lawyers

Top Bush administration officials in 2002 debated testing the Constitution by sending American troops into the suburbs of Buffalo to arrest a group of men suspected of plotting with Al Qaeda, according to former administration officials. Some of the advisers to President George W. Bush, including Vice President Dick Cheney, argued that a president had the power to use the military on domestic soil to sweep up the terrorism suspects, who came to be known as the Lackawanna Six, and declare them enemy combatants. . . . A decision to dispatch troops into the streets to make arrests has few precedents in American history, as both the Constitution and subsequent laws restrict the military from being used to conduct domestic raids and seize property.[18]

—Mark Mazzetti and David Johnston, journalists

Bush and his people have tried to turn flouting the law into a virtue if it's a law they find inconvenient.[19]

—Eugene Robinson, columnist

This president decides that he and not the law must prevail.[20]

—Keith Olbermann, political commentator

I sincerely wish . . . we could see our government so secured as to depend less on the character of the person in whose hands it is trusted. Bad men will sometimes get in and with such an immense patronage may make great progress in corrupting the public mind and principles. This is a subject with which wisdom and patriotism should be occupied.[21]

—Thomas Jefferson

The Bush administration has tried to expand the power of the executive branch by undermining and bypassing this constitutional framework.[22]

—Gene Healy and Timothy Lynch, lawyers

[L]et me make this pledge to you all. I'm going to make respect for federalism a priority in this administration. Respect for federalism begins with an understanding of its philosophy. The framers of the Constitution did not believe in an all-knowing, all-powerful federal government. They believed that our freedom is best preserved when power is dispersed. That is why they limited and enumerated the federal government's powers, and reserved the remaining functions of government to the states.[23]

—George W. Bush

[F]ar from making "respect for federalism a priority" in his administration, President Bush has broken that pledge repeatedly. Six years into his tenure in office, the president's record on federalism is depressingly clear. It is one of consistent disdain for the constitutional role of the states and for limits on federal power.[24]

—Gene Healy and Timothy Lynch, lawyers

Throughout his tenure, President Bush has repeatedly intruded into areas constitutionally reserved to the states.[25]

—Gene Healy and Timothy Lynch, lawyers

It is not enough to know that the men applying the standard are honorable and devoted men. This is a government of laws, not of men. . . . It is not without significance that most of the provisions of the Bill of Rights are procedural. It is procedure that spells much of the difference between rule by law and rule by whim or caprice.[26]

—William O. Douglas, U.S. Supreme Court

This is not, and has never been, a debate over whether the United States should conduct effective surveillance of terrorists and their supporters. It is over whether we are a nation ruled by law, or the whims of men in power. Mr. Bush faced that choice and made the wrong one.[27]

—*New York Times* editorial

After 9/11 they and other top officials in the administration dealt with FISA [Foreign Services Intelligence ACT] and the way they dealt with other laws they didn't like: they blew through them in secret based on flimsy legal opinions that they guarded closely so no one could question the legal basis for the operations.[28]

—Jack Goldsmith, former government lawyer

Bush is totally heedless of any honor for law and accountability, that he has special rules for him and his cabinet.[29]

—Bruce Fein, constitutional law expert

[Bush] is a man who thinks that defending the rule of law is a partisan matter.[30]

—Katrina VanDen Heuvel, journalist

Mr. [Alberto] Gonzales and Mr. Bush have not shown the slightest interest in upholding constitutional principles or following legislative guidelines that they do not find ideologically or politically expedient.[31]

—*New York Times* editorial

Throughout his tenure, Gonzales has tried the impossible: to use the legal system to acquire extralegal powers. . . . Like President Bush, Gonzales often ignores the easier alternative of working within the constitutional system to achieve the same objectives.[32]

—Jonathan Turley, law professor

Attorney General Alberto Gonzales . . . was in the thick of President George W. Bush's most damaging attacks on the rule of law. As White House counsel, he helped to justify torture and illegal wiretapping. As attorney general, he politicized the Justice Department. And he misled Congress in both jobs.[33]

—*New York Times* editorial

It is impossible to calculate the moral mischief, if I may so express it, that mental lying has produced in society. When a man has so far corrupted and prostituted the chastity of his mind, as to subscribe his professional belief to things he does not believe, he has prepared himself for the commission of every other crime.[34]

—Thomas Paine

For more than seven decades, civilized nations have adhered to minimum standards of decent behavior toward prisoners of war—agreed to in the Geneva Conventions. They were respected by 12 presidents and generations of military leaders because they reflected this nation's principles and gave Americans some protection if they were captured in wartime. It took the Bush administration to make the world doubt Washington's fidelity to the rules.[35]

—*New York Times* editorial

[W]hat emerged through the two [Bush] terms was that people who seemed to be accused of violating the law had a rapid ascent in this administration. And one has to wonder whether this is suddenly a criteria, that the president likes people who are willing to go to the edge of the law and beyond it to achieve what he believes is a worthy purpose.[36]

—Jonathan Turley, law professor

After each perceived security crisis ended, the United States has remorsefully realized that the abrogation of civil liberties was unnecessary. But it has proven unable to prevent itself from repeating the error when the next crisis came along.[37]

—William Brennan, U.S. Supreme Court

It is a universal truth that the loss of liberty at home is to be charged to the provisions against danger, real or perceived, from abroad.[38]

—James Madison

If ours were a parliamentary democracy, the entire Bush team would be out of office by now, and deservedly so.[39]

—Thomas L. Friedman, journalist

If George W. Bush could have been removed from office for being a bad president, he would have been sent back to his ranch a long time ago.[40]

—Bob Herbert, journalist

The end of law is not to abolish or restrain, but to preserve and enlarge freedom.[41]

—John Locke

[A] Constitution of Government once changed from Freedom, can never be restored. Liberty lost is lost forever.[42]

—John Adams

Civil liberties are a very precious commodity. When you lose them, it tends to run out of your hand like sand, and it's hard to get it back.[43]

—Jonathan Turley, law professor

Liberals must stop saying President Bush hasn't asked Americans to sacrifice for the war on terror. On the contrary, he's asked us to sacrifice something enormous. Our civil rights.[44]

—Bill Maher, political commentator

Mr. Bush and his team say they have safeguards to protect civil liberties, meaning surveillance will be reviewed by the attorney general, the director of national intelligence and the inspectors general of the Justice Department and the Central Intelligence Agency. There are two enormous flaws in that. The Constitution is based on the rule of law, not individuals; giving such power to any president would be un-American. And this one long ago showed he cannot be trusted.[45]

—*New York Times* editorial

The administration must start obeying the law now, rather than waiting for yet another court to declare that it has trampled on far too many people's rights.[46]

—*New York Times* editorial

SIGNING STATEMENTS: "SOMETHING BETTER THAN A VETO"

The signing statements are documents that earlier presidents generally used to trumpet their pleasure at signing a law, or to explain how it would be enforced. More than any of his predecessors, the current chief executive has used the pronouncements in a passive-aggressive way to undermine the power of Congress.[47]

—*New York Times* editorial

Bush has used more signing statements than any other president. The way Bush is using signing statements essentially relegates Congress to an advisory role. This abuse lets the President choose what laws he wishes to enforce or not, overruling Congress and the people. So Americans are living under laws their representatives never passed. Signing statements put the president above the law.[48]

—Naomi Wolf, author

Unlike the presidential veto, use of a signing statement of noncompliance is not a high-profile act . . . and has previously not carried heavy political costs even when the president took extraordinary measures.[49]

—Frederick A. O. Schwarz Jr. and Aziz Z. Huq, lawyers

The A.B.A. [American Bar Association] called Mr. Bush's use of presidential signing statements "contrary to the rule of law and our constitutional system of separation of powers" and recommended that Congress enact legislation clarifying the issue.[50]

—*New York Times* editorial

President Bush has quietly claimed the authority to disobey more than 750 laws enacted since he took office, asserting that he has the power to set aside any statute passed by Congress when it conflicts with his interpretation of the Constitution.[51]

—Charlie Savage, journalist

Freedom of men under government is to have a standing rule to live by, common to every one of that society, and made by the legislative power vested in it; a liberty to follow my own will in all things, when the rule prescribes not, and not to be subject to the inconstant, unknown, arbitrary will of another man.[52]

—John Locke

A president who tries to void laws he doesn't like by encumbering them with "signing statements" and who regards the Geneva Conventions as a nonbinding technicality isn't going to start playing by the rules now.[53]

—Frank Rich, columnist

Federal law is not some buffet line where the president can pick parts of some laws to follow and others to reject.[54]

—Sen. Robert Byrd

The Constitution is clear in assigning to Congress the power to write the laws and to the president a duty "to take care that the laws be faithfully executed." Bush, however, has repeatedly declared that he does not need to "execute" a law he believes is unconstitutional. . . . Far more than any predecessor, Bush has been aggressive about declaring his right to ignore vast swaths of laws—many of which he says infringe on power he believes the Constitution assigns to him alone as the head of the executive branch or the commander in chief of the military.[55]

—Charlie Savage, journalist

The abusive use of signing statements to circumvent the Founders' design of checks and balances is part of a broader effort by the administration to concentrate virtually all power in the hands of the executive branch. Indeed, the current administration came to power in the thrall of a legal theory that aims to convince us that this excessive concentration of presidential authority is exactly what our Constitution intended.[56]

—Al Gore

Many laws Bush has asserted he can bypass involve requirements to give information about government activity to congressional oversight committees.[57]

—Charlie Savage, journalist

It's about accountability. If you veto something, everyone knows where you stand. But this President wants to do it sotto voce. He wants to give the image that he's accommodating on torture, and then reserves the right to torture anyway.[58]

—Bruce Fein, constitutional law expert

Bush's legal team was using signing statements as something better than a veto—something close to a line-item veto. . . . Moreover, it was an absolute power because, unlike when there is a regular veto, Congress had no opportunity to override his illegal judgments.[59]

—Charlie Savage, journalist

Rather than vetoing legislation when it arrives at the White House, the White House (read: Cheney and his staff) issues a brief statement giving its interpretation of the new law as it relates to presidential powers. These statements are consistently different from the intent of Congress, so Bush and Cheney have, in effect, told Congress to go to hell on the few occasions when the Republican Congress has stood up to the White House.[60]

—John Dean, former White House counsel

Where you have a president who is willing to declare vast quantities of the legislation that is passed during his term unconstitutional, it implies that he also thinks a very significant amount of the other laws that were already on the books before he became president are also unconstitutional.[61]

—David Golove, law professor

The White House put out two statements that day about the new spending package. The first statement was meant for public consumption. . . . But around 8 p.m., the White House issued another statement about the bill. Given almost exactly the same title, this second document was not meant for public consumption, although it would be entered in the Federal Register. Written in dense legalistic language, and making frequent references to bill sections identified only by number, this "signing statement" contained instructions for the CIA and military interrogators about how they were to interpret the new torture ban law: "The executive branch shall construe [the torture ban] in a manner consistent with the constitutional authority of the President to supervise the unitary executive branch and as Commander in Chief and consistent with the constitutional limitations on judicial power, which will assist in achieving the shared objective of the Congress and the President . . . of protecting the American people from further terrorist attacks."[62]

—Charlie Savage, journalist

[A]fter members of Congress and reporters had left, Bush issued a signing statement declaring that he did not consider himself bound to obey the new oversight requirements.

Despite the law's mandatory provisions that the executive branch regularly give Congress a complete accounting of how the FBI was using the Patriot Act, that its disclosure would be undesirable."[63]

—Charlie Savage, journalist

Mr. Bush has drawn intense scrutiny and criticism from Democrats and groups like the American Bar Association for issuing signing statements reserving the right to disregard more than 800 selected provisions of measures that he signed into law, often on the grounds that they represented an unconstitutional infringement on executive authority.[64]

—Eric Lichtblau, journalist

The American Bar Association and members of Congress have said Bush uses signing statements excessively as a way to expand his power.[65]

—Associated Press

This is an attempt by the president to have the final word on his own constitutional powers, which eliminates the checks and balances that keep the country a democracy. There is no way for an independent judiciary to check his assertions of power, and Congress isn't doing it, either. So this is moving us toward an unlimited executive power.[66]

—Bruce Fein, constitutional law expert

In October 2004, five months after the Abu Ghraib torture scandal in Iraq came to light, Congress passed a bill containing a series of new rules and regulations for military prisons. Bush signed the bill, turning each of the sections into laws, and then he said he could ignore them all.[67]

—Charlie Savage, journalist

The gap between the legal claims in the Bush-Cheney signing statements and mainstream understandings of the Constitution threw new light on a potentially enormous problem lurking in the Constitution: If a president has the power to instruct the government not to *enforce* laws that he alone has declared to be unconstitutional, then he can free himself from the need to *obey* laws that he alone says restrict his actions unconstitutionally—even when the Supreme Court, were it given an opportunity to review his theory, would be unlikely to agree with it.[68]

—Charlie Savage, journalist

The president's constitutional duty is to enforce laws he has signed into being, unless and until they are held unconstitutional by the Supreme Court. The Constitution is not what the president says it is.[69]

—American Bar Association report

President Bush, again defying Congress, says he has the power to edit the Homeland Security Department's reports about whether it obeys privacy rules while handling back-

ground checks, ID cards and watchlists. . . . But Bush, in a signing statement attached
to the agency's 2007 spending bill, said he will interpret that section "in a manner consistent with the President's constitutional authority to supervise the unitary executive
branch."[70]

—Associated Press

Also last month, Mr. Bush issued another of his infamous "presidential signing statements," which he has used scores of times to make clear he does not intend to respect
the requirements of a particular law—in this case a little-noticed Postal Service bill. The
statement suggested that Mr. Bush does not believe the government must obtain a court
order before opening Americans' first-class mail. It said the administration had the right
to "conduct searches in exigent circumstances," which include not only protecting lives,
but also unspecified "foreign intelligence collection." The law is clear on this. A warrant
is required to open Americans' mail under a statute that was passed to stop just this sort
of abuse using just this sort of pretext. But then again, the law is also clear on the need
to obtain a warrant before intercepting Americans' telephone calls and e-mail. Mr. Bush
began openly defying that law after Sept. 11, 2001, authorizing the National Security
Agency to eavesdrop without a court order on calls and e-mail between the United States
and other countries.[71]

—*New York Times* editorial

He's not interpreting the Constitution when he's rewriting these laws. The Constitution
is perfectly clear. It's not subject to interpretation on this point. Congress writes the law.
He can veto it, but he can't rewrite it. . . . [A]mbiguity really breeds mischief, and this
president has shown that.[72]

—Jonathan Turley, law professor

The American Bar Association said Sunday that President Bush was flouting the Constitution and undermining the rule of law by claiming the power to disregard selected
provisions of bills that he signed. . . . If the president deems a bill unconstitutional,
he can veto it, the panel said, but "signing statements should not be a substitute for a
presidential veto."[73]

—Robert Pear, journalist

No error is more certain than the one proceeding from a hasty and superficial view of
the subject.[74]

—James Madison

Some of Mr. Bush's signing statements have become notorious, like the one in which he
said he didn't feel bound by the new law against torturing prisoners. Others were more
obscure, like the one in which he said he would not follow a law forbidding the White

House to censor or withhold scientific data requested by Congress. . . . The Bush administration often says the president is just trying to stop Congress from interfering with his ability to keep the nation safe, and that other presidents also included constitutional objections in their signing statements. That's just smoke.[75]

—*New York Times* editorial

The American Bar Association claims President Bush has violated [his] oath [of office] by issuing hundreds of "signing statements" to disregard selected provisions of the laws that Congress passed and he signed. A bipartisan, 11-member panel of the ABA found that President Bush is not only disregarding laws but using such signing statements far more than any president in history. In fact, Bush has used signing statements to raise constitutional objections to more than 800 provisions in more than 100 laws. All of the presidents combined before 2001 had issued only 600. . . . [I]t stands as a metaphor for a 21st century America that is no longer secure in the claim to be a nation of laws.[76]

—Lou Dobbs, TV anchor

The amazing thing about that signing picture of all these legislators grinning as [the president] signs a law that he is in the very process of rewriting, and saying, "I don't have to do any of this." And that's part of the problem. We have a system that has survived this long, because it's stable, it has this divided government, these shared powers. . . . By having signing statements like this, the president preserves the argument that he was acting on the color of law, that he all along read this in a particular way, even though nobody else did. And so there's a suspicion that just before the Democrats started to investigate, the signing statements are continuing to lay some plausible deniability that they didn't violate the law knowingly.[77]

—Jonathan Turley, law professor

Over the last seven years, Mr. Bush has issued hundreds of these insidious documents declaring that he had no intention of obeying a law that he had just signed. This is not just constitutional theory. Remember the detainee treatment act, which Mr. Bush signed and then proceeded to ignore, as he told CIA interrogators that they could go on mistreating detainees?[78]

—*New York Times* editorial

Every time we have looked under the rug, we have seen this president going to the edge of law and beyond it. And that is consistent with his view that he can violate federal law when he believes it's in the nation's interest. And that's not just national security laws. In his signing statement controversies, he has taken the same position, on domestic laws that range from environmental to affirmative action.[79]

—Jonathan Turley, law professor

"ENEMY COMBATANTS" AND THE LAW

The Bush Administration created a category it called "enemy combatants," who could be detained indefinitely at the President's discretion via exercise of his war powers. The term "enemy combatant" might sound as if it comes from the laws of war, but the term has no historical grounding or fixed meaning. Hence the government can invoke it to justify a sweeping power to detain civilians indefinitely without any possible test of whether their claimed connections to terrorism are real. Once more, creative legal maneuvering yielded new, effectively unchecked, powers to the executive.[80]

—Frederick A. O. Schwarz Jr. and Aziz Z. Huq, lawyers

Injustice anywhere is a threat to justice everywhere.[81]

—Martin Luther King Jr.

It takes a lot of degeneration before a country falls into dictatorship, but we should avoid these ends by avoiding these beginnings.[82]

—Sandra Day O'Connor, U.S. Supreme Court

The administration doesn't want to call the detainees prisoners of war, because that would accord them some rights under international law, and it doesn't want to treat them as criminal suspects since that would give them rights under U.S. law. So they remain "enemy combatants" for whom the rules seem to be whatever we decide at any given time.[83]

—Eugene Robinson, columnist

The U.S. Supreme Court repudiated a central legal doctrine of the Bush administration's antiterrorism efforts yesterday, saying U.S. citizens and foreigners being held as enemy combatants must be allowed to challenge their imprisonment in federal courts. In strong language warning of a "system of unchecked detention" that "carries the potential to become a means for oppression," the justices said Yaser Esam Hamdi, a U.S. citizen captured while fighting for the enemy in Afghanistan, must have a lawyer and a chance to assert his claim to innocence before a judge.[84]

—Stephen Henderson, journalist

A state of war is not a blank check for the President when it comes to the rights of the Nation's citizens. . . . Whatever power the United States Constitution envisages for the Executive in its exchanges with other nations or with enemy organizations in time of conflict, it most assuredly envisages a role for all branches when individual liberties are at stake.[85]

—Sandra Day O'Connor, U.S. Supreme Court

This is how tyranny is defined. It's the ability of a single individual to strip someone of their right to counsel, access to court, and to hold them indefinitely at their own whim.[86]

—Jonathan Turley, law professor

The very core of liberty secured by our Anglo-Saxon system of separated powers has been freedom from indefinite imprisonment at the will of the Executive.[87]

—Antonin Scalia, U.S. Supreme Court

An American citizen and a former Chicago gang member, Mr. [Jose] Padilla was arrested in May 2002 when he arrived at O'Hare International Airport in Chicago. He was soon declared an "enemy combatant."[88]

—David Stout, journalist

We must support our rights or lose our character, and with it, perhaps, our liberties.[89]

—James Monroe

The administration long resisted charging Mr. Padilla in a civilian court, preferring to hold him without charges in the Navy brig.[90]

—David Stout, journalist

He that would make his own liberty secure, must guard even his enemy from oppression; for if he violates this duty, he establishes a precedent that will reach to himself.[91]

—Thomas Paine

The administration did bring charges, accusing him of being part of a terrorist cell. But those charges contained no mention of a radioactive-bomb plot.[92]

—David Stout, journalist

The intent of that move was clear: to avoid what appeared to be an inevitable showdown in the Supreme Court over Mr. Bush's imperial vision of executive authority. And it worked. Shifting Mr. Padilla to a civilian court rendered the issue of the president's detention powers "at least for now, hypothetical."[93]

—*New York Times* editorial

[The Bush administration's] claims about Padilla's dirty bomb, known to be false, were a means of advancing their claims about executive power. When confronted with the possibility of losing on those claims, they pulled him back to the criminal courts so as not to lose powers they'd already won.[94]

—Dahlia Lithwick, journalist

If any fundamental assumption underlies our system, it is that guilt is personal and not inheritable.[95]

—Robert Jackson, U.S. Supreme Court

[Padilla] was even denied access to a lawyer until court pressure forced the administration to back off. . . . Fortunately, the court did not hand a total victory to the administration. Justice Kennedy made it clear that the case raises "fundamental issues respecting the separation of powers."[96]

—*New York Times* editorial

And even though Justice Stevens found today that the Padilla case need not be considered now, he declared at an earlier stage in the case that "at stake in this case is nothing less than the essence of a free society."[97]

—David Stout, journalist

▮ ▮ ▮

The Supreme Court's Guantanamo ruling on Thursday was the most significant setback yet for the Bush administration's contention that the Sept. 11 attacks and their aftermath have justified one of the broadest expansions of presidential power in American history. . . . For Mr. Bush, this is not the first such setback. The court ruled two years ago that the giant prison at Guantanamo Bay, Cuba, was not beyond the reach of American courts and that prisoners there had some minimal rights.[98]

—David E. Sanger and Scott Shane, journalists

The Supreme Court's decision striking down the military tribunals set up to try the detainees being held in Guantanamo Bay is far more than a narrow ruling on the issue of military courts. It is an important and welcome reaffirmation that even in times of war, the law is what the Constitution, the statute books and the Geneva Conventions say it is—not what the president wants it to be.[99]

—*New York Times* editorial

What this decision says is, "No, Mr. President, you can be bound by treaties and statutes. If you need to have these changed, you can go to Congress." This idea of a coronated president instead of an inaugurated president has been dealt a sharp rebuke.[100]

—Bruce Fein, constitutional law expert

In a recent commencement address, [Cheney] declaimed against prisoners who had the gall to "demand the protections of the Geneva Convention and the Constitution of the United States."[101]

—*New York Times* editorial

How easy it is to abuse truth and language, when men, by habitual wickedness, have learned to set justice at defiance.[102]

—Thomas Paine

President Bush waged war as he saw fit. If intelligence officers needed to eavesdrop on overseas telephone calls without warrants, he authorized it. If the military wanted to hold terrorism suspects without trial, he let it. . . . [T]he decision echoed not simply as a matter of law but as a rebuke of a governing philosophy of a leader who at repeated turns has operated on the principle that it is better to act than to ask permission. . . .

Bush came to office intent on expanding executive power even before Sept. 11, 2001, encouraged in particular by Vice President Cheney, who has long been convinced that presidential authority was improperly diminished after Watergate.[103]

—Peter Baker and Michael Abramowitz, journalists

President Bush and his lawyers say that terrorists are "enemy combatants" and that enemy combatants are not entitled to the protections of the Bill of Rights. The defect in the president's claim is circularity. A primary function of the trial process is to sort through conflicting evidence in order to find the truth. Anyone who *assumes* that a person who has merely been accused of being an unlawful combatant is, in fact, an enemy combatant, can understandably maintain that such a person is not entitled to the protection of our constitutional safeguards. The flaw, however, is that that argument begs the very question under consideration. . . . The Constitution does not confer on the U.S. government a general police power, allowing it to legislate on all matters affecting the health, safety, and welfare of the American people.[104]

—Gene Healy and Timothy Lynch, lawyers

"[U]nlawful enemy combatant." Those are the magic words. If the president alone decides that those words accurately describe someone, then that person can be immediately locked up and held incommunicado for as long as the president wants, with no court having the right to determine whether the facts actually justify his imprisonment. . . . Now, if the president makes a mistake, or is given faulty information by somebody working for him, and locks up the wrong person, then it's almost impossible for that person to prove his or her innocence—because he or she can't talk to a lawyer or family or anyone else. The prisoner doesn't even have the right to know what specific crime he is accused of committing. So a constitutional right to liberty and the pursuit of happiness that we used to think of in an old-fashioned way as "inalienable" can now be instantly stripped from any American by the president with no meaningful review by any other branch of government.[105]

—Al Gore

Like his predecessor [John] Ashcroft, [Alberto] Gonzales gamed the system: misleading or lying to Congress, continually changing positions in the courts, moving around detainees and defendants to avoid judicial review.[106]

—Jonathan Turley, law professor

Having claimed the right to label enemy combatants and detain them indefinitely without charges, the Bush administration cannot retreat from that position without ceding ground. The president is as much a prisoner of Guantanamo Bay as the detainees are.[107]

—Dahlia Lithwick, journalist

The most odious of all oppressions are those which mask as justice.[108]

—Robert Jackson, U.S. Supreme Court

The Supreme Court declared Thursday that President Bush had overstepped his authority in the war against terrorism, ruling he does not have the power to set up special military trials at Guantanamo Bay without the approval of Congress. In a 5–3 decision, the high court said the planned military tribunals lacked the basic standards of fairness required by the nation's Uniform Code of Military Justice and by the Geneva Convention.[109]

—David G. Savage, journalist

President Bush has declared that he has heretofore unrecognized inherent power to seize and imprison any American citizen whom he alone determines to be a threat to our nation—without an arrest warrant, without notifying them of what charges have been filed against them, and without even informing their families that they have been imprisoned. The president claims that he can simply snatch an American citizen off the street and keep him or her locked up indefinitely—even for the rest of his or her life—and refuse to allow that citizen the right to make a phone call or talk to a lawyer—even to argue that the president or his appointees have made a mistake and imprisoned the wrong person.[110]

—Al Gore

[The] case has now become a much larger battle over the principle of habeas corpus, which is embedded in the Constitution and says that a prisoner cannot be denied the right to challenge his detention. Mr. Bush's decision after 9/11 that he had the power to put prisoners beyond the reach of the law at his choosing was the first attempt to suspend habeas corpus on American territory since the Civil War.[111]

—*New York Times* editorial

It seemed almost too much to hope for, but the Supreme Court finally called George W. Bush onto the carpet yesterday and asked him the obvious question: What part of "rule of law" do you not understand? The justices rejected the kangaroo-court tribunals the administration had planned for the detainees who have been held for years without charges at Guantanamo Bay—proceedings engineered to have the appearance of due process but not the substance. . . . Despite his outrageous claims of virtually unlimited presidential power, the self-proclaimed Decider doesn't get to decide everything. . . . He has been told that he is still a president, not an emperor.[112]

—Eugene Robinson, columnist

In undertaking to try Hamdan and subject him to criminal punishment, the Executive is bound to comply with the Rule of Law that prevails in this jurisdiction.[113]

—John Paul Stevens, U.S. Supreme Court

The opinion in *Hamdan* is really historic. On the one hand, it tells the executive branch that it will not be free to act as it chooses, which means to act lawlessly. At the same time, it acknowledges as part of American law certain international minimums of decency, morality and ethics, and those are encompassed in Common Article 3. . . . It's important for the American people to know that this has been done in their name so that they can disavow it, disclaim it. We have to hold ourselves up to a mirror. We have to see what we have done. And at that point, we have to say, "Oh my god, we can't do this anymore."[114]

—Bill Goodman, lawyer

Where, as here, no emergency prevents consultation with Congress, judicial insistence upon that consultation does not weaken our Nation's ability to deal with danger. To the contrary, that insistence strengthens the Nation's ability to determine—through democratic means—how best to do so. The Constitution places its faith in those democratic means. Our Court today simply does the same.[115]

—Stephen Breyer, U.S. Supreme Court

The court declared unconstitutional a provision of the Military Commissions Act of 2006 that, at the administration's behest, stripped the federal courts of jurisdiction to hear habeas corpus petitions from the detainees seeking to challenge their designation as enemy combatants.[116]

—Linda Greenhouse, journalist

The right of habeas corpus is so central to the American legal system that it has its own clause in the Constitution: it cannot be suspended except "when in cases of rebellion or invasion the public safety may require it." Despite this, the Bush administration repeatedly tried to strip away habeas rights.[117]

—*New York Times* editorial

It shouldn't be necessary for the Supreme Court to tell the president that he can't have individuals taken into custody, spirited to a remote prison camp and held indefinitely, with no legal right to argue that they've been unjustly imprisoned—not even on grounds of mistaken identity. But the president in question, sigh, is George W. Bush, who has taken a chain saw to the rule of law with the same manic gusto he displays in clearing brush at his Texas ranch.[118]

—Eugene Robinson, columnist

The laws and the Constitution are designed to survive, and remain in force, in extraordinary times. Liberty and security can be reconciled; and in our system they are reconciled within the framework of the law. The Framers decided that habeas corpus, a right of first importance, must be a part of that framework, a part of that law.[119]

—Anthony Kennedy, U.S. Supreme Court

That reference to "extraordinary times" takes care of a specious argument that Bush and his legal minions have consistently tried to make—that when the nation is at war, as it has been since the 9/11 attacks, the president has extraordinary powers that allow him to do, well, basically anything he wants.[120]

—Eugene Robinson, columnist

The Supreme Court has now made clear that while justice and honor may be mere inconveniences for George W. Bush, they remain essential components of our national identity.[121]

—Eugene Robinson, columnist

I think what we really gained here is credibility. That is, we show the world that having an idiot-proof system doesn't mean you don't have idiots. It means you can transcend them. It means that you have a legal system that can be better than its leaders.[122]

—Jonathan Turley, law professor

JUSTICE: "PURGE AND PUNISH"

[T]he Justice Department really never lived up to its name. It was not the Department of Justice—it was often the Department of Litigation Risk, and they saw everything through the perspective of whether a decision might result in some kind of liability, whether someone might get sued or prosecuted. But that's not the only role of the lawyer. The role of the lawyer is also to exercise good judgment and to look at long-term consequences, and ultimately to do what's the ethically and morally correct thing.[123]

—John Bellinger III, lawyer

After Republicans lost control of Congress last year, newly empowered Democrats promised to launch a series of tough investigations on everything from the Iraq war to Medicare and high energy prices. But since taking charge on Capitol Hill in January, a series of unexpected new issues have captured their attention, none potentially more damaging to the Bush Administration than the controversy over alleged political influence in the firing of eight Republican U.S. attorneys last Dec. 7, in an episode that some of its victims have already taken to calling the "Pearl Harbor Day Massacre."[124]

—Adam Zagorn, journalist

[W]hile the Bush team has been lecturing the Iraqi Shiites to limit de-Baathification in Baghdad, it was carrying out its own de-Democratization in the Justice Department in Washington.[125]

—Thomas L. Friedman, journalist

We do know that it's standard practice for this administration to purge and punish dissenters and opponents.[126]

—Frank Rich, columnist

The Bush Justice Department hired lawyers on the basis of political affiliation, brought cases to help the Republican Party win elections and endorsed torture, among other serious misdeeds.[127]

—New York Times editorial

Justice is the end of government. It is the end of civil society. It ever has been and ever will be pursued until it be obtained, or until liberty be lost in the pursuit.[128]

—James Madison

[W]hat we need to look at is the pattern of subverting the Constitution—which last I checked was not a partisan document—and politicizing, deprofessionalizing and purging federal agencies. And the Justice Department has been part of that process, and this president has been part of subverting the Constitution and the rule of law for this last six years of his administration.[129]

—Katrina VanDen Heuvel, journalist

[P]romoting little lies seems to have been one of the main things U.S. attorneys, as loyal Bushies, were expected to do. For example, David Iglesias, the U.S. Attorney in New Mexico, appears to have been fired because he wouldn't bring unwarranted charges of voter fraud.[130]

—Paul Krugman, columnist

I knew that U.S. attorneys were only asked to resign essentially for misconduct, and I knew I hadn't committed any misconduct. I knew my office was doing well by the Justice Department's internal metrics. Logically that only left one possibility, which was politics.[131]

—David Iglesias, U.S. attorney

It is vital that Congress get to the truth about these firings. Last week, the Republican National Committee threw up another roadblock, claiming it had lost four years' worth of e-mail messages by Karl Rove that were sent on a Republican Party account. Those messages, officials admitted, could include some about the United States attorneys. It is virtually impossible to erase e-mail messages fully, and the claims that they are gone are not credible.[132]

—New York Times editorial

There's something happening here, and what it is seems completely clear: the Bush administration is trying to protect itself by purging independent-minded prosecutors. . . . Since the day it took power this administration has shown nothing but contempt for the normal principles of good government. For six years ethical problems and conflicts of interest have been the rule, not the exception.[133]

—Paul Krugman, columnist

It is hard to call what's happening anything other than a political purge. And it's another shameful example of how in the Bush administration, everything—from rebuilding a hurricane-ravaged city to allocating homeland security dollars to invading Iraq—is sacrificed to partisan politics and winning elections.[134]

—Adam Cohen, journalist

[T]here are a lot of career people at Justice that are very unhappy with what's happened to the Justice Department. You know, the Justice Department has always really sold itself as independent of the president. They're not the president's lawyer. There are a lot of career lawyers over there, and there's been a lot of complaints that they've been politicized under this administration.[135]

—Jonathan Turley, law professor

There are two types of attorney generals, those who are yes men or those that are yes or no depending on what the law says. We have an Attorney General here who's clearly been sent there to protect the White House.[136]

—John Dean, former White House counsel

We opposed Mr. Gonzales's nomination as attorney general. His résumé was weak, centered around producing legal briefs for Mr. Bush that assured him that the law said what he wanted it to say. More than anyone in the administration, except perhaps Vice President Dick Cheney, Mr. Gonzales symbolizes Mr. Bush's disdain for the separation of powers, civil liberties and the rule of law. . . . [Gonzales] has never stopped being consigliere to Mr. Bush's imperial presidency.[137]

—New York Times editorial

Attorney General Alberto R. Gonzales was "extremely upset" that his deputy told Congress last month that a federal prosecutor had been fired for no reason, according to e-mail released Monday by the Justice Department. . . . Agency officials said the documents showed the dismissals had been over performance, not politics, as critics have charged.[138]

—David Johnston and John M. Broder, journalists

It was Mr. Gonzales, after all, who repeatedly defended Mr. Bush's decision to authorize warrantless eavesdropping on Americans' international calls and e-mail. He was an eager public champion of the absurd notion that as commander in chief during a time of war, Mr. Bush can ignore laws that he thinks get in his way. Mr. Gonzales was disdainful of any attempt by Congress to examine the spying program, let alone control it. The attorney general helped formulate and later defended the policies that repudiated the Geneva Conventions in the war against terror, and that sanctioned the use of kidnapping, secret detentions, abuse and torture. He has been central to the administration's assault on the courts, which he recently said had no right to judge national security policies, and on the constitutional separation of powers.[139]

—New York Times editorial

Honestly, I don't see how anybody can suggest that this administration has not had an unprecedented level of politicalization of the Justice Department. I mean, some of these people were obviously fired for raw politics. And, in fact, the last defense raised by Gonzales is that we really can fire people for purely raw political reasons, and that apparently is why they did it. There [were] no real performance problems. One guy was fired just to give Karl Rove's assistant a job. So, you know, I think at this point, that issue is already settled. . . . People should understand how serious this is. The Justice Department has always been protected from this type of political influence, that even political appointees were seasoned prosecutors or seasoned criminal law experts. And here you have a memo with two people with no appreciable experience to speak of, who were told to basically get rid of experienced attorneys if they don't meet their criteria. That criteria, for these two, clearly is political loyalty to the president and to the party.[140]

—Jonathan Turley, law professor

The very thing that made Gonzales appealing to Bush proved his undoing as attorney general. He acted more as an enabler than as an attorney for Bush. When the president wanted rough methods to be used on detainees, Gonzales was there with a pen in hand to sign a memo defending the use of acts viewed as torture under international law. When Bush wanted to override Justice Department officials who viewed his domestic surveillance programs as unconstitutional, it was Gonzales who appeared at the hospital bed of [then-attorney general John] Ashcroft to coerce a signature. When Bush wanted to declare citizens enemy combatants and strip them of their constitutional rights, Gonzales assured the president that he had the power. When Congress demanded answers to embarrassing questions, the attorney general gave evasive answers and then conveniently claimed dozens of lapsed memories to avoid further questions. Bush's favorite lawyers tend to follow this same model of treating the law as simply one means to an end rather than the end itself. The fact is that if Gonzales had been a little more attorney than general in this war on terror, he would have been a much better attorney general.[141]

—Jonathan Turley, law professor

This was the attorney general of the United States speaking, yet another straight man for an administration that has raised governing to new heights of witlessness. Watching the Bush administration in action would be hilarious, if its ineptitude and brutally misguided policies didn't end so often in needless suffering and sorrow.[142]

—Bob Herbert, journalist

[A] fight over the Office of Administration's status is part of a larger battle over access to an estimated five million e-mail messages that have mysteriously disappeared from White House computers. The missing messages are important evidence in the scandal over the firing of nine United States attorneys, apparently because they refused to use their positions to help Republicans win elections. . . . What exactly does the administration want to hide? It is certainly acting as if the e-mail messages would confirm suspicions that the White House coordinated the prosecutors' firings and that it may have broken laws. It is hard to believe the administration's constant refrain that there is nothing to the prosecutor scandal when it is working so hard to avoid letting the facts about it get out.[143]

—New York Times editorial

Mr. Gonzales, [his chief of staff,] Mr. [Kyle] Sampson and the others have given so many conflicting, barely credible stories for the firings that it is impossible not to suspect a cover-up.[144]

—New York Times editorial

President Bush's excesses in the name of fighting terrorism are legion. To avoid accountability, his administration has repeatedly sought early dismissal of lawsuits that might finally expose government misconduct, brandishing flimsy claims that going forward would put national security secrets at risk. . . . As a result, victims of serious abuse have been denied justice, fundamental rights have been violated and the constitutional system of checks and balances has been grievously undermined.[145]

—New York Times editorial

The Bush administration has been acting lawlessly in refusing to hand over information that Congress needs to carry out its responsibility to oversee the executive branch and investigate its actions when needed.[146]

—New York Times editorial

Instead of answering these questions, the administration has done its best to ensure that everyone stays confused. It has refused repeated requests by Senator Jay Rockefeller, the Democratic chairman of the Senate Intelligence Committee, for documents relating to the president's order creating the spying program, and the Justice Department's legal justifications for it.[147]

—New York Times editorial

Over the last eight years, political manipulation and influence from partisan political operatives in the White House have undercut the Department of Justice in its mission, severely undermined the morale of its career professionals, and shaken public confidence in our Federal justice system.[148]

—Sen. Patrick Leahy

There was an unbroken rule, embodied in law, regulation and department policy, that no political questions would be asked of those who wanted to serve in career—as opposed to political—positions in the department. We demanded of our Justice Department, in its core prosecutorial and adjudicative functions, that it be separate from politics. Until the Bush administration.[149]

—Jamie Gorelick, journalist

[T]he president has once again forced a constitutional crisis. He's basically telling Congress that "even if I did politicize the Justice Department, even if there are crimes here, I can tell people not to give you evidence." And we have now this long list of people that are refusing to testify upon orders of the president.[150]

—Jonathan Turley, law professor

Senior aides to former Attorney General Alberto R. Gonzales broke Civil Service laws by using politics to guide their hiring decisions, picking less-qualified applicants for important nonpolitical positions, slowing the hiring process at critical times and damaging the department's credibility, an internal report concluded on Monday. . . . According to the report, officials at the White House first developed a method of searching the Internet to glean the political leanings of a candidate and introduced it at a White House seminar called The Thorough Process of Investigation. Justice Department officials then began using the technique to search for key phrases or words in an applicant's background, like "abortion," "homosexual," "Florida recount," or "guns."[151]

—Eric Lichtblau, journalist

Justice Department officials illegally used "political or ideological" factors in elite recruiting programs in recent years, tapping law school graduates with Federalist Society membership or other conservative credentials over more qualified candidates with liberal-sounding résumés, an internal report found Tuesday. The report, prepared by the Justice Department's own inspector general and its ethics office, portrays a clumsy effort by senior Justice Department screeners to weed out candidates for career positions whom they considered "leftists," using Internet search engines to look for incriminating information or evidence of possible liberal bias.[152]

—Eric Lichtblau, journalist

U.S. President George W. Bush's Justice Department improperly injected politics into hiring programs, a department investigation released on Tuesday found. A report by the department's inspector general and office of professional responsibility said members of a screening committee were asked to weed out "wackos" and ideological "extremists" who sought work in a competitive honors program for entry-level attorneys or as summer interns. It said the committee rejected applicants with liberal or Democratic affiliations at a much higher rate than those with Republican, conservative or politically neutral backgrounds.[153]

—Randall Mikkelsen, journalist

At the Justice Department, for example, political appointees illegally reserved nonpolitical positions for "right-thinking Americans"—their term, not mine—and there's strong evidence that officials used their positions both to undermine the protection of minority voting rights and to persecute Democratic politicians.[154]

—Paul Krugman, columnist

A former senior official at the Justice Department routinely hired conservatives, Republicans and so-called RTA's—"Right-Thinking Americans"—for what were supposed to be apolitical posts and gave them plum assignments on important civil rights cases, an internal report found Tuesday. . . . The investigation, conducted by the department's inspector general and its office of professional responsibility, is the fourth and last in a series of reports since last year detailing the use of improper political considerations in hiring decisions at the department. The investigations grew out of the controversy over the firings of eight Unted States attorneys, which led to the 2007 resignation of Attorney General Alberto R. Gonzales.[155]

—Eric Lichtblau, journalist

During the occupation of Iraq—an occupation whose success was supposedly essential to national security—applicants were judged by their politics, their personal loyalty to President Bush and, according to some reports, by their views on Roe v. Wade, rather than by their ability to do the job.[156]

—Paul Krugman, columnist

What we're talking about here is the use of politics for career people, people who are supposed to be selected on the basis of their talent. You know, this administration's been accused of incompetence from Katrina, to Iraq, to various other scandals. And it's beginning to appear that the reason is because they're not hiring people for their competence. They're hiring them like they're Ba'athists, like they're loyal to some supreme leader, and not looking at how good they are as lawyers. . . . [W]hen it comes to doing the public's business, we're supposed to pick the best people, not the people most loyal to President Bush or Karl Rove or anyone else.[157]

—Jonathan Turley, law professor

Bush administration hacks forced out accomplished career attorneys and packed the department with lawyers selected for their dedication to a right-wing political agenda rather than to enforcing the law.[158]

—*New York Times* editorial

Last month, we learned that political functionaries deputized by Attorneys General John Ashcroft and Alberto R. Gonzales had screened the best and the brightest coming out of law schools, judicial clerkships and other positions to weed out those who appeared to be Democrats or who might hold liberal ideas; favor was shown to Republicans, members of the Federalist Society, and those considered to be good and loyal conservatives. As the department's inspector general and its Office of Professional Responsibility noted, this is illegal. It also breaks the promise of justice that is above politics and undermines the department's best values. Now, an equally graphic report by the same two offices concludes that in 2003, the apolitical process for selecting immigration judges and prosecutors was stood on its head. A chief aide to Attorney General Ashcroft (and later to Attorney General Gonzales) "outlined a new process for hiring [immigration judges] that listed the White House as the sole source for generating candidates."[159]

—Jamie Gorelick, journalist

It was hardly news that President Bush's Justice Department has been illegally politicized, but it was important that the Justice Department finally owned up to that sorry state of affairs. An internal investigation released on Monday found that the department's top staff routinely took politics and ideology into account in filling nonpolitical positions—and lied about it.[160]

—*New York Times* editorial

[I]t is neither permissible nor acceptable to consider political affiliations in the hiring of career Department employees. . . . But not every wrong, or even every violation of the law, is a crime. In this instance, the two joint reports found only violations of the civil service laws. That does not mean, as some people have suggested, that those officials who were found by the joint reports to have committed misconduct have suffered no consequences. Far from it. The officials most directly implicated in the misconduct left the Department to the accompaniment of substantial negative publicity.[161]

—Michael Mukasey, former U.S. attorney general

We wish we'd been surprised to learn that the White House was deeply involved in the politically motivated firing of eight United States attorneys, but the news had the unmistakable whiff of inevitability. This disaster is just part of the Bush administration's sordid history of waving the bloody bullhorn of 9/11 for the basest of motives: the perpetuation of power for power's sake. . . . [T]hese firings had nothing to do with national security—or officials' claims that the attorneys were fired for poor performance. This looks like a political purge, pure and simple, and President Bush and his White House are in the thick of it.[162]

—*New York Times* editorial

This is how President Bush keeps his promise to deal with Congress in good faith on issues of national security and the balance of powers: He sends the attorney general to the
Senate Judiciary Committee to stonewall, obfuscate and spin fairy tales.[163]

—*New York Times* editorial

When Bush's violations of federal law have come to light, as over domestic surveillance,
the White House has devised a novel solution: Stonewall any investigation into the violations and bid a compliant Congress simply to rewrite the laws.[164]

—Sean Wilentz, historian

President Bush directed two former aides today to defy congressional subpoenas and
refuse to testify about the dismissals of nine U.S. attorneys, asserting executive privilege for the second time in two weeks amid rising partisan tensions between the White
House and Capitol Hill.[165]

—Peter Baker, journalist

This is more stonewalling from a White House that believes it can unilaterally control
the other co-equal branches of government. It raises the question: What is the White
House trying to hide by refusing to turn over evidence? . . . The White House continues
to try to have it both ways, but at the end of the day it cannot. It cannot block Congress from obtaining the relevant evidence and credibly assert that nothing improper
occurred.[166]

—Sen. Patrick Leahy

—3—

Secrecy and "Vice"

Secrecy, being an instrument of conspiracy, ought never to be
the system of a regular government.[1]
—Jeremy Bentham, English philosopher

George W. Bush will go down in the annals of history as "The Secrecy President." No president in modern times has done more to conceal the workings of government from the people. Not just with regard to national security information, but on every front Bush has rolled back public access to government records and has tried to shield records from the people.[2]

—David Vladeck, law professor

There's no end to President Bush's slyness in subverting new Congressional law and clinging to the secrecy that has been the administration's executive cloak.[3]

—*New York Times* editorial

In my administration, we will ask not only what is legal but also what is right, not just what the lawyers allow but what the public deserves. In my administration, we will make it clear there is the controlling legal authority of conscience.[4]

—George W. Bush

For those who believe that democracy can flourish only with open and accountable government, the Bush administration has been a nightmare.[5]

—David Vladeck, law professor

A government or an administration, who means and acts honestly, has nothing to fear, and consequently has nothing to conceal.[6]

—Thomas Paine

One of the core principles of our democracy is that government should be open and accountable.[7]

—Congressional Report

The Central Intelligence Agency withheld information about a secret counterterrorism program from Congress for eight years on direct orders from former Vice President Dick Cheney. . . . The report that Mr. Cheney was behind the decision to conceal the still-unidentified program from Congress deepened the mystery surrounding it, suggesting that the Bush administration had put a high priority on the program and its secrecy.[8]

—Scott Shane, journalist

George W. Bush and Richard B. Cheney have created the most secretive presidency of my lifetime. Their secrecy is far worse than during Watergate, and it bodes even more serious consequences. Their secrecy is extreme—not merely unjustified and excessive but obsessive.[9]

—John Dean, former White House counsel

When people are not informed, they cannot hold government accountable when it is incompetent, corrupt, or both.[10]

—Al Gore

Secrecy—the first refuge of incompetents—must be at bare minimum in a democratic society, for a fully informed public is the basis of self-government. Those elected or appointed to positions of executive authority must recognize that government, in a democracy, cannot be wiser than the people.[11]

—Congressional Report

The people never give up their liberties but under some delusion.[12]

—Edmund Burke

Whenever the people are well-informed, they can be trusted with their own government.[13]

—Thomas Jefferson

It is universally admitted that a well-instructed people alone can be a permanently free people.[14]

—James Madison

We are born weak, we need strength; helpless, we need aid; foolish, we need reason. All that we lack at birth, all that we need when we come to man's estate, is the gift of education.[15]

—Jean-Jacques Rousseau

The only truly self-governing people is that people which discusses and interrogates its administration.[16]

—Woodrow Wilson

People without information cannot question, influence, or even understand secret government policy, and when they do, they no longer have any choice or voice.[17]

—John Dean, former White House counsel

When the government fears the people, there is liberty; when the people fear the government, there is tyranny.[18]

—Thomas Jefferson

Tyranny and anarchy are never far asunder.[19]

—Jeremy Bentham, English philosopher

[T]here has been a 95 percent increase in classified material under Bush and Cheney, with almost 20 million documents now being classified annually. This increase is not because of the needs of the war on terror.[20]

—John Dean, former White House counsel

With Cheney's guidance, documents were being classified at twice the rate of the previous administration.[21]

—Ron Suskind, journalist

The liberties of the people never were nor ever will be secure when transactions of their rulers may be concealed from them.[22]

—Patrick Henry

What seems to be coming out of the [Bush-Cheney] administration is the idea that public information is a dangerous thing.[23]

—Tom Connors, archivist

[T]he Administration's actions represent an unparalleled assault on the principle of open and accountable government.[24]

—Congressional Report

The [Bush] Administration controls the spigots of public information.[25]

—Frederick A. O. Schwarz Jr. and Aziz Z. Huq, lawyers

The constitutional right of free speech has been declared to be the same in peace and war.[26]

—Louis Brandeis, U.S. Supreme Court

A nation under a well regulated government should permit none to remain uninstructed. It is monarchical and aristocratical government only that requires ignorance for its support.[27]

—Thomas Paine

The pervasive secrecy threatened the First Amendment's guarantee of free speech.[28]

—Christopher Dickey, journalist

The people shall not be deprived or abridged of their right to speak, to write, or to publish their sentiments; and the freedom of the press, as one of the great bulwarks of liberty, shall be inviolable.[29]

—James Madison

Open and accountable government is one of the bedrock principles of our democracy. Yet virtually since inauguration day, questions have been raised about the Bush Administration's commitment to this principle.[30]

—Congressional Report

A popular government without popular information or the means of acquiring it, is but a prologue to a farce, or a tragedy, or perhaps both.[31]

—James Madison

[T]he system of presidential lawmaking combines with an excessive fondness for secrecy. And it is not only operational details that are kept from the public and congressional sight. A president, using his power to issue directives and then classify them against the scrutiny of legislators and the public, can undermine constitutional protections. . . . Indeed, on initial examination, it seems that any presidential lawmaking is antithetical to the Constitution. The Constitution's first words, after its preamble, explains that, "*All legislative Powers herein granted shall be vested in a Congress.*"[32]

—Frederick A. O. Schwarz Jr. and Aziz Z. Huq, lawyers

The American presidency has come to see itself in messianic terms as the appointed savior of the world whose unpredictable dangers call for rapid and incessant deployment of men, arms, and decisions behind a wall of secrecy. This view seems hard to reconcile with the American Constitution.[33]

—Arthur Schlesinger, historian

Instead of working within new laws, the executive branch mined the laws' ambiguities to grab powers Congress never intended to grant. The Administration secretly sidestepped checks Congress inserted into law. And once more, the exercise of unchecked presidential power led to abusive mission creep and to inefficient, abusive use of intelligence powers.[34]

—Frederick A. O. Schwarz Jr. and Aziz Z. Huq, lawyers

The greatest dangers to liberty lurk in the insidious encroachment by men of zeal, well-meaning but without understanding.[35]

—Louis Brandeis, U.S. Supreme Court

The Bush administration has been one of the most secretive in history, aided by a Congress controlled by loyal allies engaged in virtually no oversight of the executive branch. Those facts leave no doubt that there is a whole universe of Bush administration actions that remain concealed.[36]

—Glenn Greenwald, lawyer/journalist

The Bush gaps of missing e-mails run into hundreds of thousands during some of the most sensitive political moments. Key gaps coincide with the lead-up to the Iraq war—and the White House's manipulation of intelligence—as well as the destruction of videotapes of CIA interrogations and the outing of the CIA operative Valerie Plame Wilson. Missing e-mails include entire blank days at the offices of President Bush and Vice President Cheney. Also mysteriously wiped from the record are e-mails from Karl Rove, the president's political guru, and dozens of other White House workers who improperly conducted government business on Republican Party e-mail accounts.[37]

—*New York Times* editorial

After watching wholesale lots of the Bush administration's most important e-mails go mysteriously missing, Congress is trying to legislate against any further damage to history. The secrecy-obsessed White House is, of course, threatening a veto—one more effort to deny Americans their rightful access to the truth about how their leaders govern or misgovern.[38]

—*New York Times* editorial

A government for the people and by the people should be transparent *to* the people. Yet the Bush administration seems to prefer making policy in secret, based on information that is not available to the public and in a process that is insulated from any meaningful participation by Congress or the American people. When Congress' approval is required under our current Constitution, it is to be given without meaningful debate.[39]

—Al Gore

The Bush Administration believes only the executive, or a small coterie within the executive, should determine key policies, acting largely in secret.[40]

—Frederick A. O. Schwarz Jr. and Aziz Z. Huq, lawyers

Undue secrecy not only is undemocratic, denying the public its right to know, but also schools scandal by concealing and protecting errors, excesses, and all manner of impropriety.[41]

—John Dean, former White House counsel

The executive branch has many means at its disposal to put the monarchical executive theory into action. Inevitably, executive branch lawyers must interpret the laws when they apply them. This gives the Administration an opportunity to exploit ambiguities or simply sidestep legal obligations. Post-9/11, the Department of Justice crafted legal opinions that reinterpreted the laws in unreasonable, and clearly erroneous, ways. Government lawyers also argued that the president could ignore the law simply by invoking unspecified "national security" concerns. These legal opinions remained secret—so neither Congress nor the public knew of the laws being set aside.[42]

—Frederick A. O. Schwarz Jr. and Aziz Z. Huq, lawyers

They know what they're doing, using secrecy and its handmaidens—obfuscation, deception, stonewalling, and lying—to remain unaccountable, when possible, which is merely
further evidence of dissonance between the man and his high office.[43]

—John Dean, former White House counsel

The executive branch has followed a determined strategy of obfuscating, delaying, withholding information, appearing to yield but then refusing to do so, and dissembling in
order to frustrate the efforts of the legislative and judicial branches to restore our constitutional balance. After all, the other branches can't check an abuse on power if they
don't know it is happening.[44]

—Al Gore

The government being the public's business, it necessarily follows that its operation
should be at all times open to the public view.[45]

—William Jennings Bryan

I think they have an overreliance on the utility of secrecy. They don't seem to realize
secrecy is a two-edge sword that cuts you as well as protects you.[46]

—Steven Garfinkel, lawyer

[Cheney's agenda] is the most likely to remain unknown, because of Cheney's personality and his penchant for secrecy. He may be driven by a desire to finish the job he started
as defense secretary in 1991.[47]

—Scott McClellan, former Bush press secretary

Bush and Cheney seek to reverse [the] trend toward open government. They are once
again closing government, and their practice and policy started long before the September 11, 2001, terror attacks.[48]

—John Dean, former White House counsel

The Bush-Cheney administration seized the atmosphere of emergency and uncertainty
that followed 9/11 to dramatically expand the zone of secrecy surrounding the executive
branch. It broke the ice by seizing greater secrecy powers in matters directly related to
terrorism investigations. Later, however, the clampdown moved into other areas that . . .
had nothing to do with national security.[49]

—Charlie Savage, journalist

Bush administration officials often cite the September 11 attacks as the reason for the
enhanced secrecy. But as the Inauguration Day directive from [White House chief of
staff Andy] Card indicates, the initiative to wall off records and information previously
in the public domain began from Day 1.[50]

—Christopher Schmitt and Edward Pound, journalists

Mr. Cheney's office ordered the Secret Service last September to destroy all records of visitors to the official vice presidential mansion—right after *The Washington Post* sued for access to the logs. That move was made in secret, naturally.[51]

—*New York Times* editorial

Even supporters of the administration, many of whom agree that security needed to be bolstered after the attacks, say Bush and his inner circle have been unusually assertive in their commitment to increased government secrecy.[52]

—Christopher Schmitt and Edward Pound, journalists

Tightly controlling information, from the White House on down, has been the hallmark of this administration.[53]

—Roger Pilon, lawyer

We have a commander-in-chief who believes that anything in the name of fighting terrorism he has the authority to do.[54]

—John Dean, former White House counsel

Educate and inform the whole mass of the people. . . . They are the only sure reliance for the preservation of our liberty.[55]

—Thomas Jefferson

Our defense is in the preservation of the spirit which prizes liberty as a heritage of all men, in all lands, everywhere. Destroy this spirit and you have planted the seeds of despotism around your own doors.[56]

—Abraham Lincoln

The Government Reform Committee revealed "a consistent pattern in the Administration's actions: laws that are designed to promote public access to information have been undermined, while laws that authorize the government to withhold information or to operate in secret have repeatedly been expanded. The cumulative result is an unprecedented assault on the principle of open government."[57]

—Congressional Report

Those who won our independence believed . . . that public discussion is a political duty; and that this should be a fundamental principle of the American government.[58]

—Louis Brandeis, U.S. Supreme Court

[The] Bush Administration has systematically sought to limit disclosure of government records while expanding its authority to operate in secret.[59]

—Congressional Report

As one Republican columnist told me, "These guys are more inbred, secretive, and vindictive than the Mafia."[60]

—Richard Clarke, former White House counterterrorism expert

Contrary to the open government principles, the Bush Administration has often pursued policies that limit public access to information and allow more secret government operations.[61]

—Congressional Report

The free communication of thoughts and opinions is one of the most precious rights of man.[62]

—The Declaration of the Rights of Man

All government is a trust. Every branch of government is a trust, and immemorially acknowledged to be so.[63]

—Jeremy Bentham, English philosopher

President Bush quietly signed an executive order making sweeping changes to federal guidelines for classifying information. . . . Bush's executive order also made it easier for the government to create new classified secrets.[64]

—Charlie Savage, journalist

Bush's March 2003 executive order also gave the vice president, for the first time in U.S. history, the highest power to classify and declassify documents across the entire government.[65]

—Charlie Savage, journalist

Bush—without justification—is sweeping much of his secrecy into national security-classified material, where it may reside for countless decades before becoming publicly available.[66]

—John Dean, former White House counsel

When government officials can select which fragments of information reach the public, they can shape public opinion in a way that will improve their chances of being returned to office. Conversely, a freer flow of information about what the government is doing serves as one of the most sweeping checks on abuses by those in power.[67]

—Charlie Savage, journalist

Sunlight is said to be the best of disinfectants; electric light the most efficient policeman.[68]

—Louis Brandeis, U.S. Supreme Court

Darkness cannot drive out darkness; only light can do that.[69]

—Martin Luther King Jr.

Truth will ultimately prevail where there is pains to bring it to light.[70]

—George Washington

Cheney . . . believed that transparency limited the quality of the advice that the president received before making a decision. The executive branch needed to be able to keep its internal dealings hidden from Congress and the public so that the president's advisers felt free to be candid. To advance this principle, Cheney fostered a culture of secrecy in the administration, denounced leaks, and used the energy task force case and then 9/11 to expand the shield of confidentiality around the White House.[71]

—Charlie Savage, journalist

Beginning with the fight over the energy task force records, the Bush-Cheney administration systematically set out to expand government secrecy wherever it found an opportunity for doing so. Although 9/11 would be invoked as justification for the administration's efforts to seize greater control over information, the curtain of secrecy had begun to descend across the federal government long before the terrorist attacks.[72]

—Charlie Savage, journalist

His new position that he's in the legislative branch is in direct contradiction to the position he took when he met in secret with oil executives developing an energy policy, when he then said he wasn't going to turn over those documents because he was a member of the executive branch. . . . [T]his is all an attempt to be unaccountable and act like he's above the law. . . . [W]hen it came to knowing about his secret meetings with the energy executives and designing policy that would affect the country, he said, "You can't know that information, because I have the—I'm a part of the executive branch of government." This is all about his secrecy, all about being not accountable, and all acting like he's above the law.[73]

—Rep. Rahm Emanuel

Across the board, the vice president's office goes to unusual lengths to avoid transparency. Cheney declines to disclose the names or even the size of his staff, generally releases no public calendar and ordered the Secret Service to destroy his visitor logs. His general counsel has asserted that "the vice presidency is a unique office that is neither a part of the executive branch nor a part of the legislative branch," and is therefore exempt from rules governing either. Cheney is refusing to observe an executive order on the handling of national security secrets, and he proposed to abolish a federal office that insisted on auditing his compliance.[74]

—Barton Gellman and Jo Becker, journalists

This disdain for accountability is distressing, but not surprising. Mr. Cheney has had it on display from his first days in office, when he refused to name the energy-industry executives who met with him behind closed doors to draft an energy policy.[75]

—*New York Times* editorial

If a nation expects to be ignorant and free, in a state of civilization, it expects what never was and never will be.[76]

—Thomas Jefferson

Knowledge will forever govern ignorance; and a people who mean to be their own governors must arm themselves with the power which knowledge gives.[77]

—James Madison

Give me the liberty to know, to utter, and to argue freely according to conscience, above all liberties.[78]

—John Milton

[Cheney] also sent an example by his own conduct. Any investigator seeking to uncover what Cheney was up to would find few writings by the vice president. Four years into the Bush-Cheney presidency, Cheney would remark that because of Watergate, he refused to keep a diary or engage in correspondence and barely wrote anything down—he didn't even use e-mail.[79]

—Charlie Savage, journalist

Abuse thrives on secrecy. . . . Knowledge is the key to control. Secrecy should no longer be allowed to shield the existence of constitutional, legal and moral problems from the scrutiny of all three branches of government or from the American people themselves.[80]

—Congressional Report

The advancement and diffusion of knowledge is the only guardian of true liberty.[81]

—James Madison

Vice President Cheney's office has refused to comply with an executive order governing the handling of classified information for the past four years and recently tried to abolish the office that sought to enforce those rules, according to documents released by a congressional committee yesterday. . . . Cheney's office argued that it is exempt from the rules in this case because it is not strictly an executive branch agency.[82]

—Peter Baker, journalist

Bush also said he could bypass laws requiring him to tell Congress before diverting money from an authorized program in order to start a secret operation, such as funding for new "black sites," where suspected terrorists were secretly imprisoned around the world.[83]

—Charlie Savage, journalist

According to the Bush-Cheney Doctrine, alliances and international institutions are now disposable—and international institutions are dispensable or even despicable.[84]

—Sen. John Kerry

If you can control the flow of information, you often can control the process itself. I think they believe that's the most effective way to govern, and so that's what they sought to do.[85]

—Peter Weitzel, open government advocate

The priceless heritage of our society is the unrestricted constitutional right of each member to think as he will. Thought control is a copyright of totalitarianism, and we have no claim to it.[86]

—Robert Jackson, U.S. Supreme Court

Governments have to keep secrets. But this administration has grossly abused that trust, routinely using claims of national security to hide policies that are immoral and almost certainly illegal, to avoid embarrassment, and to pursue Mr. Bush's dreams of an imperial presidency.[87]

—*New York Times* editorial

We perpetuated the endless investigations and scandals we'd vowed to move beyond by engaging in spin, stonewalling, hedging, evasion, denial, noncommunication, and deceit by omission. . . . When candor could have helped minimize the political fallout from the unraveling of the chief rationale for war, spin and evasion were instead what we employed.[88]

—Scott McClellan, former Bush press secretary

[Cheney's] philosophy is that the president and the vice president and the people around the president decide what's secret and what's not.[89]

— Kathryn Olmsted, history professor

It's hard to think of a president and an administration more devoted to secrecy than President Bush and his team.[90]

—*New York Times* editorial

The people at the top are getting scared, that's what's going on. The fog of secrecy is lifting, and the Bush administration is frightened to death that it will eventually have to pay a heavy price for the human rights abuses it has ordered or condoned in its so-called war on terror. . . . Torture? Secret prisons? Capital trials in which key evidence is kept from the accused? That's the stuff of Kafka, not Madison and Jefferson.[91]

—Bob Herbert, journalist

There are more instances of the abridgement of the freedom of the people by the gradual and silent encroachments of those in power, than by violent and sudden usurpations.[92]

—James Madison

Enlighten the people generally, and tyranny and oppressions of body and mind will vanish like evil spirits at the dawn of day.[93]

—Thomas Jefferson

Without Freedom of Thought, there can be no such thing as Wisdom; and no such thing as publick Liberty, without Freedom of Speech, which is the right of every man.[94]

—Cato

Freedom of thought, and speech . . . is the matrix, the indispensable condition, of nearly every other form of freedom.[95]

—Benjamin Cardozo, U.S. Supreme Court

Freedom is never voluntarily given by the oppressor; it must be demanded by the oppressed.[96]

—Martin Luther King Jr.

As nightfall does not come at once, neither does oppression. In both instances, there's a twilight where everything remains seemingly unchanged, and it is in such twilight that we must be aware of change in the air, however slight, lest we become unwitting victims of the darkness.[97]

—William O. Douglas, U.S. Supreme Court

I've always been troubled to the extent which our government keeps things secret from the American people. It is amazing what some agencies think is secret. As a culture, we need to be careful not to be so wrapped up in secrecy that we lose track of our core values and laws.[98]

—Leonie Brinkema, judge

In 1966 Congress passed the Freedom of Information Act based on the proposition that disclosure should be the rule, not the exception, and that the burden should be on government to justify the withholding of records. This was a most beneficial law until [John] Ashcroft got hold of it. Rejecting the spirit of the law, the attorney general advised federal officials that when they "decide to withhold records, in whole or in part, you can be assured that the Department of Justice will defend your decisions."[99]

—Arthur Schlesinger, historian

A just completed study by the Coalition of Journalists for Open Government shows that federal departments and agencies have made little if any progress in responding to Freedom of Information Act requests, despite a two-year-old presidential order to improve service.[100]

—Coalition of Journalists for Open Government

Congress on Tuesday struck back at the Bush administration's trend toward secrecy since the 2001 terrorist attacks, passing legislation to toughen the Freedom of Information Act and increasing penalties on agencies that don't comply. . . . It would be the first makeover of the FOIA in a decade, among other things bringing nonproprietary information held by government contractors under the law. The legislation also is aimed at reversing an order by former Attorney General John Ashcroft in the wake of the attacks, in which he instructed agencies to lean against releasing information when there was uncertainty about how doing so would affect national security.[101]

—Laurie Kellman, journalist

The Bush administration's obsession with secrecy took another absurd turn this week. The administration is claiming that the White House Office of Administration is not covered by the Freedom of Information Act, even though there are some compelling reasons to think it is. Like the fact that the office has its own FOIA officer. And it responded to 65 FOIA requests last year. And the White House's own Web site, as of yesterday, insisted the office is covered by FOIA. The administration's logic-free claim about the Office of Administration follows fast on the heels of Vice President Dick Cheney's laughable claim that he was immune to an open-government law because his office supposedly was not an executive agency.[102]

—New York Times editorial

Did President Bush think nobody was looking when he effectively neutered a law seeking enforcement of the Freedom of Information Act? If so, he underestimates open-government advocates, who notice stunts like that. At issue is a law Bush just signed before the new year, establishing an ombudsman in the National Archives and Records Administration. But in his budget request this week, the president proposed eliminating the new Office of Government Information Services and assigning its functions to the Justice Department. That's like letting the fox guard the henhouse. Justice is the department that defends the federal government when its agencies want to withhold information. The FOIA requests, by contrast, seek to make information public. Can you say "conflict of interest?"[103]

—Honolulu Advertiser editorial

For four years, Vice President Dick Cheney has resisted routine oversight of his office's handling of classified information, and when the National Archives unit that monitors classification in the executive branch objected, the vice president's office suggested abolishing the oversight unit, according to documents released yesterday by a Democratic congressman.[104]

—Scott Shane, journalist

Vice President Dick Cheney has been resisting even his own Executive Branch's efforts to find out what kind of secret material his office has been stashing away over the last four years. . . . Cheney's dustup with the normally non-controversial National Archives and Records Administration is the latest reminder that Cheney believes he can play by his own rules. And it probably secures for Cheney a place alongside Richard Nixon in the Washington pantheon of secret-keepers.[105]

—Michael Duffy, journalist

[T]he obsession with secrecy and refusal to accept public scrutiny have made a tragic mess of national security policy.[106]

—New York Times editorial

The administration's refusal to comply with open-government laws is ultimately more important than any single scandal. The Freedom of Information Act and other right-to-know laws were passed because government transparency is vital to a democracy. The American people cannot monitor their elected officials, and ensure that they act in the public interest, if government is allowed to operate under a veil of secrecy.[107]

—*New York Times* editorial

Democracies die behind closed doors. The First Amendment, through a free press, protects the people's right to know that their government acts fairly, lawfully, and accurately in deportation proceedings. When government begins closing doors, it selectively controls information rightfully belonging to the people. Selective information is misinformation. The Framers of the First Amendment "did not trust any government to separate the true from the false for us. They protected the people against secret government."[108]

—Damon J. Keith, judge

In its instrumental aspect, the First Amendment serves to foster the values of democratic self-government. This is true in several senses. The First Amendment bars the state from imposing upon its citizens an authoritative vision of truth. It prohibits the state from interfering with the communicative processes through which its citizens exercise and prepare to exercise their rights of self-government. And the Amendment shields those who would censure the state or expose its abuses.[109]

—William Brennan, U.S. Supreme Court

It must be seen that no two principles can be either more indefensible in reason, or more dangerous in practice—than that 1. arbitrary denunciations may punish, what the law permits, & what the Legislature has no right, by law, to prohibit—and that 2. the Government may stifle all censures whatever on its misdoings; for if it be itself the Judge it will never allow any censures to be just, and if it can suppress censures flowing from one lawful source it may those flowing from any other—from the press and from individuals as well as from Societies.[110]

—James Madison

The vice president, who believes in unwarranted, unlimited snooping, is so pathologically secretive that if you use Google Earth's database to see his official residence, the view is scrambled and obscured. You can view satellite photos of the White House, the Pentagon and the Capitol—but not of the Lord of the Underworld's lair. Vice is literally a shadow president. He's obsessive about privacy—but, unfortunately, only his own.[111]

—Maureen Dowd, columnist

Stealth is among Cheney's most effective tools. Man-size Mosler safes, used elsewhere in government for classified secrets, store the workaday business of the office of the vice president. Even talking points for reporters are sometimes stamped "Treated As: Top Secret/SCI." Experts in and out of government said Cheney's office appears to have invented that designation, which alludes to "sensitive compartmented information," the most closely guarded category of government secrets. By adding the words "treated as," they said, Cheney seeks to protect unclassified work as though its disclosure would cause "exceptionally grave damage to national security."[112]

—Barton Gellman and Jo Becker, journalists

Cheney has dulled political accountability and concocted theories for evading the law and Constitution that would have embarrassed King George III. . . . The legal precedent set by Cheney would justify a decision by Russian President Vladimir Putin to kidnap American tourists in Paris and to dispatch them to dungeons in Belarus if they were suspected of Chechen sympathies. . . . [I]t's quite a leap to go from hiding in a secure, undisclosed location in the capital to hiding in a secure, undisclosed location in the Constitution.[113]

—Maureen Dowd, columnist

The government's assault on truth and liberty is joined with a government assault on openness and an insistence on secrecy.[114]

—Michael Traynor, lawyer

[W]hat has brought us up from savagery is a loyalty to truth, and truth cannot emerge unless it is subjected to the utmost scrutiny.[115]

—Learned Hand, judge

A foolish faith in authority is the worst enemy of truth.[116]

—Albert Einstein

Authoritarianism and secrecy breed incompetence; the two feed on each other. It's a vicious cycle. Government with authoritarian tendencies point to what is in fact their own incompetence as the rationale for giving them yet more power.[117]

—Joshua Marshall, journalist

Americans have always believed that we the people have a right to know the truth and that the truth will set us free. The very idea of self-government depends upon honest and open debate as the preferred method for pursuing the truth—and a shared respect for the Rule of Reason as the best way to establish the truth. The Bush Administration routinely shows disrespect for that whole basic process, and I think it's partly because they feel as if they already know the truth and aren't very curious to learn about any facts that might contradict it. They and the members of groups that belong to their ideological coalition are true believers in each other's agendas.[118]

—Al Gore

The mark of a truly civilized man is confidence in the strength and security derived from the inquiring mind.[119]

—Felix Frankfurter, U.S. Supreme Court

For the past three years, the Bush administration has quietly but efficiently dropped a shroud of secrecy across many critical operations of the federal government—cloaking its own affairs from scrutiny and removing from the public domain important information on health, safety, and environmental matters. The result has been a reversal of a decades-long trend of openness in government while making increasing amounts of information unavailable to the taxpayers who pay for its collection and analysis.[120]

—Christopher Schmitt and Edward Pound, journalists

[T]he real policy debates about the "war on terror" were, after all, conducted in secret, killing off reasoned, fact-based public discourse precisely at the time the president suddenly presided over a nation in need of clarity. The White House message machine worked overtime, without any expectation of having ever to provide underlying evidence to support what it said.[121]

—Ron Suskind, journalist

Cheney formed what is, in effect, a shadow NSC. . . . This shadow operation, while informally integrated, actually has its own agenda as well as the power to realize it through the vice president's clout. It is a secret government—beyond the reach of Congress, and everyone else as well.[122]

—John Dean, former White House counsel

The White House yesterday blocked a House committee's attempt to obtain internal FBI reports about the leak of a CIA officer's identity, asserting that notes from interviews of Vice President Cheney and other administration officials are protected by executive privilege.[123]

—Dan Eggen, journalist

This unfounded assertion of executive privilege does not protect a principle; it protects a person. If the vice president did nothing wrong, what is there to hide?[124]

—Rep. Henry Waxman

SPIES LIKE U.S.

[T]his administration has read your phone records, credit card statements, mail, Internet logs. . . . I mail myself a copy of the Constitution every morning just on the hope they'll open it and see what it says.[125]

—Bill Maher, political commentator

The political uproar over President Bush's secret domestic spying program escalated yesterday as the president denied overstepping his constitutional bounds while congressional critics from both parties stepped up their attack and vowed a full investigation. Bush mounted a vigorous defense of his order authorizing warrantless eavesdropping on overseas telephone calls and e-mail of U.S. citizens with suspected ties to terrorists. He contended that his "obligation to protect you" against attack justified a circumvention of the traditional process in a fast-moving, high-tech battle with a shadowy enemy.[126]

—Peter Baker and Charles Babington, journalists

We brought in the chairman and the ranking member, House and Senate, and briefed them a number of times up until—this was—be from late '01 up until '04 when there was additional controversy concerning the program. At that point, we brought in what I describe as the big nine—not only the intel people but also the speaker, the majority and minority leaders of the House and Senate, and brought them into the situation room in the basement of the White House. I presided over the meeting. We briefed them on the program, and what we'd achieved, and how it worked, and asked them, "Should we continue the program?" They were unanimous, Republican and Democrat alike. All agreed—absolutely essential to continue the program.[127]

—Dick Cheney

[T]he administration never afforded members briefed on the program an opportunity to either approve or disapprove [of the eavesdropping program, conducted by the National Security Agency].[128]

—Sen. Jay Rockefeller

Sen. John Rockefeller, D-W.Va., and former Sen. Tom Daschle, D-S.D., said they had objected to Bush's plan, but had no way to stop it without exposing classified information. Rockefeller, the top Democrat on the Senate Intelligence Committee, produced a 2003 letter he wrote to Vice President Dick Cheney listing his objections.[129]

—Ron Hutcheson, journalist

Given the security restrictions associated with this information and my inability to consult with staff or counsel on my own, I feel unable to fully evaluate, much less endorse these activities.[130]

—Sen. Jay Rockefeller

It was one of the more outrageous moments in the story of the Bush administration's illegal domestic wiretapping. Almost a year ago, Congressional Democrats called for a review of the Justice Department's role in the program. But the department investigators assigned to do the job were unable to proceed because the White House, at President Bush's personal direction, refused to give them the necessary security clearance.[131]

—New York Times editorial

Months after the Sept. 11 attacks, President Bush secretly authorized the National Security Agency [NSA] to eavesdrop on Americans and others inside the United States to search for evidence of terrorist activity without the court-approved warrants ordinarily required for domestic spying, according to government officials.[132]

—James Risen and Eric Lichtblau, journalists

President Bush today defended his administration's decision to collect information on tens of millions of domestic phone calls, saying the National Security Agency program was legal, protects the privacy of Americans and helps guard the nation against terrorist attacks.[133]

—Kathy Kiley and Andrea Stone, journalists

The government does not listen to domestic phone calls without court approval. We are not trolling through the personal lives of millions of innocent Americans. Our efforts are focused on links to al Qaeda terrorists and its affiliates who want to harm the American people.[134]

—George W. Bush

The Bush administration has swept aside nearly thirty years of rules and regulations and has secretly brought the NSA back into the business of domestic espionage. The NSA is now eavesdropping on as many as five hundred people in the United States at any given time and it potentially has access to the phone calls and e-mails of millions more. It does this without court-approved search warrants and with little independent oversight.[135]

—James Risen, journalist

Man is born free, and everywhere he is in chains.[136]

—Jean-Jacques Rousseau

Of the many ways that President Bush has trampled civil liberties and the balance of powers since the 9/11 attacks, one of the most egregious was his decision to order wiretaps of Americans' international calls and e-mail without court approval.[137]

—*New York Times* editorial

For the first time since the Watergate-era abuses, the NSA is spying on Americans again, and on a large scale.[138]

—James Risen, journalist

According to the Bush-Cheney Doctrine, unwarranted secrecy and illegal spying are now absolute imperatives of our national security.[139]

—Sen. John Kerry

NSA Domestic Surveillance Began 7 Months Before 9/11, Convicted Qwest CEO Claims[140]

—Wired.com headline

Congress passed a law in 1978 that required search warrants, approved by a secret court, for domestic wiretaps in national security cases. That law, the Foreign Intelligence Surveillance Act (FISA), along with other new rules and regulations imposed on the intelligence community in the 1970s and 1980s, effectively ended the NSA's role in domestic surveillance operations.[141]

—James Risen, journalist

Mr. Bush decided after 9/11 that he was no longer going to obey [FISA]. He authorized the National Security Agency to intercept international telephone calls and e-mail messages of Americans and other residents of this country without a court order. He told the public nothing and Congress next to nothing about what he was doing, until *The Times* disclosed the spying in December 2005.[142]

—*New York Times* editorial

This is a different era, a different war. People are changing phone numbers and phone calls, and they're moving quick. And we've got to be able to detect and prevent. I keep saying that, but this . . . requires quick action.[143]

—George W. Bush

A state of war only serves as an excuse for domestic tyranny.[144]

—Aleksandr Solzhenitsyn, Soviet author

Mr. Bush claimed that FISA did not allow the United States to act quickly enough to stop terrorists. That was nonsense. FISA always gave the government the power to start listening and then get a warrant—a grace period that has been extended since Sept. 11. More fundamental, Mr. Bush's powers do not supersede laws passed by Congress or the Constitution's protections against unreasonable searches and seizures.[145]

—*New York Times* editorial

In 2002, President Bush signed a secret presidential order authorizing NSA surveillance in the homeland, akin to the order used to set the extraordinary rendition program in motion.[146]

—Frederick A. O. Schwarz Jr. and Aziz Z. Huq, lawyers

Under a presidential order signed in 2002, the intelligence agency has monitored the international telephone calls and international e-mail messages of hundreds, perhaps thousands, of people inside the United States without warrants over the past three years in an effort to track possible "dirty numbers" linked to Al Qaeda, the officials said. The agency, they said, still seeks warrants to monitor entirely domestic communications.[147]

—James Risen and Eric Lichtblau, journalists

The previously undisclosed decision to permit some eavesdropping inside the country without court approval was a major shift in American intelligence-gathering practices, particularly for the National Security Agency, whose mission is to spy on communications abroad. As a result, some officials familiar with the continuing operation have questioned whether the surveillance has stretched, if not crossed, constitutional limits on legal searches.[148]

—James Risen and Eric Lichtblau, journalists

With its direct access to the U.S. telecommunications system, there seems to be no physical or logistical obstacle to prevent the NSA from eavesdropping on anyone in the United States that it chooses.[149]

—James Risen, journalist

Following President Bush's order, U.S. intelligence officials secretly arranged with top officials of major telecommunications companies to gain access to large telecommunications switches carrying the bulk of America's phone calls. The NSA also gained access to the vast majority of American e-mail traffic that flows through the U.S. telecommunications system.[150]

—James Risen, journalist

Bush has so outdone Nixon that Nixon almost looks innocent in this area. We're now reaching into such broad scale and widespread programs with just utter in-your-face defiance of the law that even Nixon himself didn't push the envelope nearly as far as this administration is.[151]

—John Dean, former White House counsel

That same month, October, Bush signed a secret presidential order allowing NSA, with its telecom helpers, to carry forward what had already begun and continue to eavesdrop on U.S. citizens.[152]

—Ron Suskind, journalist

President Bush claims that he can bypass the warrant application process and surveil the e-mail and phone conversations of Americans because he is the commander in chief of the U.S. military. . . . Indeed, the president's lawyers have already informed the federal judiciary that they regard the entire world, including every inch of U.S. territory, a "battlefield." . . . Unfortunately, the president appears to believe that he is the ultimate arbiter of what is legal and what is illegal—at least in matters relating to national security.[153]

—Gene Healy and Timothy Lynch, lawyers

The FBI secretly sought information last year on 3,501 U.S. citizens and legal residents from their banks and credit card, telephone and Internet companies without a court's approval, the Justice Department said Friday. It was the first time the Bush administration has publicly disclosed how often it uses the administrative subpoena known as a National Security Letter, which allows the executive branch of government to obtain records about people in terrorism and espionage investigations without a judge's approval or a grand jury subpoena. . . . Ann Beeson, the associate legal counsel for the American Civil Liberties Union, said the report to Congress "confirms our fear all along that National Security Letters are being used to get the records of thousands of innocent Americans without court approval."[154]

—Associated Press

The volume of information harvested from telecommunication data and voice networks, *without court-approved warrants* [emphasis added], is much larger than the White House has acknowledged, the officials said. It was collected by tapping directly into some of the American telecommunication system's main arteries, they said.[155]

—Eric Lichtblau and James Risen, journalists

We know that the administration . . . is keeping track of the phone calls of millions of citizens who have nothing at all to do with terrorism. Bush has tried to convince us that the overwhelming majority of Americans are not affected by domestic surveillance, but now we know that the opposite is true: The overwhelming majority of us are.[156]

—Eugene Robinson, columnist

The National Security Agency has been secretly collecting the phone call records of tens of millions of Americans, using data provided by AT&T, Verizon and BellSouth, people with direct knowledge of the arrangement told *USA Today*. The NSA program reaches into homes and businesses across the nation by amassing information about the calls of ordinary Americans—most of whom aren't suspected of any crime.[157]

—Leslie Cauley, journalist

Both the attorney general and the president have lied to the American people about the scope and nature of the NSA's program. It's clearly not focused on international calls and clearly not just focused on terrorists.[158]

—Anthony Romero, lawyer

At least now we know that the Bush administration's name for spying on Americans without first seeking court approval—the "terrorist surveillance program"—isn't an exercise in Orwellian doublespeak after all. It's just a bald-faced lie.[159]

—Eugene Robinson, columnist

Bush made an unscheduled appearance before White House reporters and sought to shape perceptions about the surveillance while declining to acknowledge that it is taking place. He said that "the intelligence activities I authorized are lawful," but specified no source of statutory or constitutional authority. He denied forcefully that his administration is "mining or trolling through the personal lives of millions of innocent Americans."[160]

—Barton Gellman and Arshad Mohammed, journalists

What we have here is a clandestine surveillance program of enormous size, which is being operated by members of the administration who are subject to no limits or scrutiny beyond what they deem to impose on one another. If the White House had gotten its way, the program would have run secretly until the war on terror ended —that is, forever.[161]

—*New York Times* editorial

You'll recall that when it was revealed last year that the NSA was eavesdropping on phone calls and reading e-mails without first going to court for a warrant, the president said his "terrorist surveillance program" targeted international communications in which at least one party was overseas, and then only when at least one party was suspected of some terrorist involvement. Thus no one but terrorists had anything to worry about. Not remotely true, it turns out.[162]

—Eugene Robinson, columnist

Seeking congressional approval was viewed as politically risky because the proposal would be certain to face intense opposition from civil liberties groups. In order to support the White House decision not to seek new legislation to support the NSA operation, administration lawyers secretly argued that new laws were unnecessary because the post-9/11 congressional resolution on the war on terror provided ample authorization.[163]

—James Risen, journalist

With access to records of billions of domestic calls, the NSA has gained a secret window into the communications habits of millions of Americans. Customers' names, street addresses and other personal information are not being handed over as part of NSA's domestic program, the sources said. But the phone numbers the NSA collects can easily be cross-checked with other databases to obtain that information.[164]

—Leslie Cauley, journalist

One of the most worrisome aspects of the NSA's move into domestic surveillance is that it appears to be part of a broader series of policies and procedures put in place by the Bush administration that threaten to erode civil liberties in the United States. Across the administration, many questionable actions taken in the heat of the moment after the September 11 attacks have quietly become more permanent, lowering the bar on what is acceptable when it comes to the government's ability to intrude into the personal lives of average Americans.[165]

—James Risen, journalist

The domestic and international call-tracking programs have things in common, according to the sources. Both are being conducted without warrants and without the approval of the FISA court. The Bush administration has argued that FISA's procedures are too slow in some cases. Officials, including Gonzales, also make the case that the USA Patriot Act gives them broad authority to protect the safety of the nation's citizens.[166]

—Leslie Cauley, journalist

It is now clear that the White House went through the motions of the public debate over the (2001) Patriot Act, all the while knowing that the intelligence community was secretly conducting a far more aggressive domestic surveillance campaign. "This goes way beyond the Patriot Act," said one former official familiar with the NSA operation.[167]

—James Risen, journalist

In order to overturn the system established by FISA in 1978, and bring the NSA back into domestic wiretaps without court approval, administration lawyers have issued a series of secret legal opinions, similar to those written in support of the harsh interrogation tactics used on detainees captured in Iraq and Afghanistan.[168]

—James Risen, journalist

Bush violated FISA . . . because he *wanted to violate the law* in order to establish the general "principle" that he was not bound by the law, to show that he has the power to break the law, that he is more powerful than the law.[169]

—Glenn Greenwald, lawyer/journalist

It is a wholesale destruction of the privacy of the American people.[170]

—Rep. Edward Markey

We have lost count of the number of times he has said Americans have to choose between protecting the nation precisely the way he wants, and not protecting it at all. On Friday, President Bush posed a choice between ignoring the law on wiretaps, and simply not keeping tabs on terrorists.[171]

—*New York Times* editorial

The president continues to insist . . . that he can spy on Americans without warrants irrespective of what a statute says, that he has constitutional authority to override whatever Congress may do, so that all of this maneuvering over the statute really is just a charade.[172]

—Bruce Fein, constitutional law expert

Kate Martin, executive director of the Center for National Security Studies, said the new disclosures show that [attorney general Alberto] Gonzales and other administration officials have "repeatedly misled the Congress and the American public" about the extent of NSA surveillance efforts. "They have repeatedly tried to give the false impression that the surveillance was narrow and justified," Martin said.[173]

—Dan Eggen, journalist

The Pentagon counsel with responsibility for supervising the NSA, Richard Shiffrin, only learned of the warrantless domestic spying in December 2005, when he read about it in *The New York Times*. The Vice President and his counsel had simply bypassed Shiffrin and gone straight to [then-NSA chief Michael] Hayden.[174]

—Frederick A. O. Schwarz Jr. and Aziz Z. Huq, lawyers

The White House approached some in Congress after the executive branch started spying illegally without warrants. Told it could not get a statute passed, the Administration kept on doing what it had been doing regardless of the lack of statutory authority.[175]

—Frederick A. O. Schwarz Jr. and Aziz Z. Huq, lawyers

President Bush has turned the executive branch into a two-way mirror. They get to see everything Americans do: our telephone calls, e-mail, and all manner of personal information. And we get to see nothing about what they do. Everyone knows this administration has disdained openness and accountability since its first days. That is about the only thing it does not hide. But recent weeks have produced disturbing disclosures about just how far Mr. Bush's team is willing to go to keep lawmakers and the public in the dark. That applies to big issues—like the CIA's secret prisons—and to things that would seem too small-bore to order up a cover-up.[176]

—Michael Duffy, journalist

The joke, history may note, is that even as Mr. Bush deludes himself that he is bringing "democracy" to Iraq, he is flouting democracy at home.[177]

—Frank Rich, columnist

—4—

Creating Realities

We're an empire now, and when we act, we create our own reality. And while
you're studying that reality—judiciously, as you will—we'll act again, creating
other new realities, which you can study, too, and that's how things will sort out.
We're history's actors . . . and you, all of you, will be left to just study what we do.[1]
—an aide to George W. Bush

The administration set out to create its own reality, whether approaching the Bill of Rights like a classified document to be redacted or girding itself for war in Iraq with a steady diet of dubious intelligence.[2]

—Christopher Dickey, journalist

We have nothing to fear from the demoralizing reasonings of some, if others are left free to demonstrate their errors and especially when the law stands ready to punish the first criminal act produced by the false reasonings; these are safer corrections than the conscience of the judge.[3]

—Thomas Jefferson

Bush and Cheney . . . cherish secrecy, they deplore constraint and they sneer at dissent, so nothing and nobody can dissuade them from their chosen course. Reality checks are not allowed.[4]

—Christopher Dickey, journalist

Those who won our independence believed that the final end of the State was to make men free to develop their faculties; and that in its government the deliberative forces should prevail over the arbitrary. They valued liberty both as an end and as a means. . . .

They believed that freedom to think as you will and to speak as you think are means indispensable to the discovery and spread of political truth; that without free speech and assembly discussion would be futile; that with them, discussion affords ordinarily adequate protection against the dissemination of noxious doctrine; that the greatest menace to freedom is an inert people; that public discussion is a political duty; and that this should be a fundamental principle of the American government.[5]

—Louis Brandeis, U.S. Supreme Court

All ideas having even the slightest redeeming social importance—unorthodox ideas, controversial ideas, even ideas hateful to the prevailing climate of opinion, have the full protection of the guaranties [of the First Amendment].[6]

—William Brennan, U.S. Supreme Court

Freedom of expression is the well-spring of our civilization. . . . The history of civilization is in considerable measure the displacement of error which once held sway as official truth by beliefs which in turn have yielded to other truths. Therefore the liberty of man to search for truth ought not to be fettered, no matter what orthodoxies he may challenge.[7]

—Felix Frankfurter, U.S. Supreme Court

The general proposition that freedom of expression upon public questions is secured by the First Amendment has long been settled by our decisions. The constitutional safeguard, we have said, "was fashioned to assure unfettered interchange of ideas for the bringing about of political and social changes desired by the people."[8]

—William Brennan, U.S. Supreme Court

The will of the people is the only legitimate foundation of any government, and to protect its free expression should be our first object.[9]

—Thomas Jefferson

If there is any fixed star in our constitutional constellation, it is that no official, high or petty, can prescribe what shall be orthodox in politics, nationalism, religion, or other matters of opinion or force citizens to confess by word or act their faith therein.[10]

—Robert Jackson, U.S. Supreme Court

DISSENT AND "DISLOYALTY"

This was an administration that not only didn't tolerate dissent, it worked ways in the system and the decision-making system that dissent could be shuttled aside so that their single opinion could be carried out in terms of execution. It's . . . a unique situation. It has no parallel in our history.[11]

—Lawrence Wilkerson, chief of staff to Colin Powell

[H]istory tells us that the degree to which dissent is tolerated is a measure of a government's strength, not its weakness.[12]

—Jon Meacham, journalist

It is dangerous to be right when the government is wrong.[13]

—Voltaire

I am one of those who think the best friend of a nation is he who most faithfully rebukes her for her sins—and he her worst enemy, who, under the specious and popular garb of patriotism, seeks to excuse, palliate, and defend them.[14]

—Frederick Douglass

Dissent is the highest form of patriotism.[15]

—Howard Zinn, historian

Speaking truth to power is actually a form of loyalty. It is the best and at times only way to make sure that government (or any organization) lives up to its potential.[16]

—Richard Haass, State Department adviser

We are not afraid to follow truth wherever it may lead, nor to tolerate any error so long as reason is left free to combat it.[17]

—Thomas Jefferson

The president's contempt for dissent is notorious.[18]

—Glenn Greenwald, lawyer/journalist

[C]ommentators from across the political spectrum have recognized that at the very core of the First Amendment lies the right to criticize elected officeholders. Unfortunately, President Bush has failed to protect that right.[19]

—Gene Healy and Timothy Lynch, lawyers

[O]nce Bush set a course in action, it was rarely questioned. That is what Bush expected and made known to his top advisers.[20]

—Scott McClellan, former Bush press secretary

Bush can be petulant about dissent; he equates disagreement with disloyalty. After five years in office, he is surrounded largely by people who agree with him.[21]

—Evan Thomas, journalist

Dismissing dissent is not only wrong, but dangerous when America's leadership is unwilling to admit mistakes, unwilling to engage in honest discussion of the nation's direction, and unwilling to hold itself accountable for the consequences of decisions made without genuine disclosure, or genuine debate.[22]

—Sen. John Kerry

[W]hen Truth and Error have fair Play, the former is always an overmatch for the latter.[23]

—Benjamin Franklin

The protection given speech and press was fashioned to assure unfettered interchange of ideas for the bringing about of political and social changes desired by the people.[24]

—William Brennan, U.S. Supreme Court

A former top Bush Administration lawyer, reflecting on the mind-set, said, "They were living in a fantasyland. They were just not welcoming of other views. It was almost like instead of arriving at an opinion, they were writing briefs—one-sided adversarial arguments. If you're sure you're right, you only want to hear what conforms with what you think."[25]

—Jane Mayer, journalist

[H]e's surrounded himself with fairly radical law professors who told him what he wanted to hear, that you could take a citizen off the street, unilaterally strip him of all of his rights, hold him until you wanted to release him, if at all.[26]

—Jonathan Turley, law professor

It seemed, suddenly, that there were no let's-look-at-the-facts brokers in any of the key White House positions.[27]

—Ron Suskind, journalist

[M]en may differ widely as to what loyalty to our country demands, and an intolerant majority, swayed by passion or by fear, may be prone in the future, as it has been in the past, to stamp as disloyal opinions with which it disagrees.[28]

—Louis Brandeis, U.S. Supreme Court

He doesn't want to hear from anyone who doubts him.[29]

—Jim Wallis, pastor

Compulsory unification of opinion achieves only the unanimity of the graveyard.[30]

—Robert Jackson, U.S. Supreme Court

If all mankind minus one, were of one opinion, and only one person were of the contrary opinion, mankind would be no more justified in silencing that one person, than he, if he had the power, would be justified in silencing mankind.[31]

—John Stuart Mill

The real value of freedom is not to the minority that wants to talk but to the majority that does not want to listen.[32]

—Zechariah Chaffee, judicial philosopher

[T]he Bush team believes in loyalty over expertise. When ideology always trumps reality, loyalty always trumps expertise. . . . I understand that loyalty is important, but what good is it to have loyal crew members when the ship is sinking? So they can sing your praises on the way down to the ocean floor?[33]

—Thomas Friedman, journalist

The U.S. government is being stalked by an invisible bandit, the Crony Fairy, who visits key agencies by dead of night, snatches away qualified people and replaces them with unqualified political appointees. There's no way to catch or stop the Crony Fairy, so our only hope is to change the agencies' names. That way she might get confused, and leave our government able to function.[34]

—Paul Krugman, columnist

What's being lost in the Beltway uproar is the extent to which the lying, cronyism and arrogance showcased by the current scandals are of a piece with the lying, cronyism and arrogance that led to all the military funerals that Mr. Bush dares not attend. Having slept through the fraudulent selling of the war, Washington is still having trouble confronting the big picture of the Bush White House. Its dense web of deceit is the deliberate product of its amoral culture, not a haphazard potpourri of individual blunders.[35]

—Frank Rich, columnist

After the fall of Saddam Hussein's government in April 2003, the opportunity to participate in the U.S.-led effort to reconstruct Iraq attracted all manner of Americans—restless professionals, Arabic-speaking academics, development specialists and war-zone adventurers. But before they could go to Baghdad, they had to get past Jim O'Beirne's office in the Pentagon. To pass muster with O'Beirne, a political appointee who screens prospective political appointees for Defense Department posts, applicants didn't need to be experts in the Middle East or in post-conflict reconstruction. What seemed most important was loyalty to the Bush administration.[36]

—Rajiv Chandrasekaran, journalist

Republican operatives and conservative ideologues flooded in Baghdad to work for the CPA [Coalition Provisional Authority]. They sought to turn Iraq into a laboratory for conservative ideas that they had not yet been able to sell in the United States. But while they were fiddling with their pet projects, Baghdad was starting to burn.[37]

—James Risen, journalist

A people that values its privileges above its principles soon loses both.[38]

—Dwight Eisenhower

[Bush operated] continually in campaign mode: never explaining, never apologizing, never retreating. Unfortunately that strategy also has had less justifiable repercussions: never reflecting, never reconsidering, never compromising. Especially not where Iraq was concerned.[39]

—Scott McClellan, former Bush press secretary

[The president's] inability to admit mistakes or take responsibility for failure approaches the pathological. He surrounds himself with subordinates who share his aversion to facing unpleasant realities. And as long as his appointees remain personally loyal, he defends their performance, no matter how incompetent. After all, to do otherwise would be to admit that he made a mistake in choosing them.[40]

—Paul Krugman, columnist

At this point, nobody should have any illusions about Mr. Bush's character. To put it bluntly, he's an insecure bully who believes that owning up to a mistake, any mistake, would undermine his manhood—and who therefore lives in a dream world in which all of his policies are succeeding and all of his officials are doing a heckuva job.[41]

—Paul Krugman, columnist

President Bush has such an absolute certainty in the validity of his rigid right-wing ideology that he does not feel the same desire that many of us would in gathering facts relevant to the questions at had. As a result, he ignores the warnings of his own experts, forbids dissent, and often refuses to test his assumptions against the best available evidence.[42]

—Al Gore

The spirit of liberty is the spirit which is not too sure that it is right; the spirit of liberty is the spirit which seeks to understand the mind of other men and women; the spirit of liberty is the spirit which weighs their interests alongside its own without bias.[43]

—Learned Hand, judge

To refuse a hearing to an opinion, because they are sure that it is false, is to assume that their certainty is the same thing as absolute certainty. All silencing of discussion is an assumption of infallibility.[44]

—John Stuart Mill

Persecution for the expression of opinions seems to me perfectly logical. If you have no doubt of your premises or your power and want a certain result with all your heart you naturally express your wishes in law and sweep away all opposition.[45]

—Oliver Wendell Holmes Jr., U.S. Supreme Court

We can never be sure that the opinion we are endeavoring to stifle is a false opinion, and if we were sure, stifling it would be an evil still.[46]

—John Stuart Mill

Our system is premised on citizens' having information about their leaders, including their actions and their intentions, so they can express consent or dissent.[47]

—John Dean, former White House counsel

Where there is much desire to learn, there of necessity will be much arguing, much writing, many opinions; for opinions in good men is but knowledge in the making.[48]

—John Milton

Liberty cannot be preserved without a general knowledge among the people.[49]

—John Adams

Our forefathers found the evils of free thinking more to be endured than the evils of inquest or suppression. This is not only because individual thinking represents no danger to society, but because thoughtful, bold and independent minds are essential to wise and considered self-government.[50]

—Robert Jackson, U.S. Supreme Court

All tyranny needs to gain a foothold is for people of good conscience to remain silent.[51]

—Thomas Jefferson

Allowing contrary opinions to be expressed is the only way to give ourselves the opportunity to reject the received opinion when the received opinion is false. A policy of suppressing false beliefs will in fact suppress some true ones, and therefore a policy of suppression impedes the search for truth.[52]

—John Stuart Mill

As the framers stressed, widespread error is likely to result when likeminded people, insulated from others, deliberate on their own.[53]

—Cass Sunstein, legal scholar

In the end it is worse to suppress dissent than to run the risk of heresy.[54]

—Learned Hand, judge

[D]efamation of the government is an impossible notion for a democracy.[55]

—Harry Kalven Jr., legal scholar

Whatever the immediate gains and losses, the dangers to our safety arising from political suppression are always greater than the dangers to the safety resulting from political freedom. Suppression is always foolish. Freedom is always wise.[56]

—Alexander Meiklejohn, free speech advocate

Over time, the president's staff has become increasingly monolithic and loyal to the president's worldview and core convictions, and correspondingly less burdened by dissent.[57]

—Glenn Greenwald, lawyer/journalist

To announce that there must be no criticism of the president, or that we are to stand by the president, right or wrong, is not only unpatriotic and servile, but is morally treasonable to the American public.[58]

—Theodore Roosevelt

All Americans . . . need to watch what they say, watch what they do.[59]

—Ari Fleischer, former Bush press secretary

To those who scare peace-loving people with phantoms of lost liberty, my message is this. Your tactics only aid terrorists, for they erode our national unity and diminish our resolve. They give ammunition to America's enemies, and pause to America's friends. They encourage people of good will to remain silent in the face of evil.[60]

—John Ashcroft, former U.S. attorney general

Those who challenged his policies, he declared, would "only aid terrorists" and "give ammunition to America's enemies." . . . [A] line had been drawn: Americans who were not "with" the administration might just be "with" the terrorists.[61]

—Frank Rich, columnist

[A]n intolerant majority swayed by passion or by fear, may be prone . . . to stamp out disloyal opinions with which it disagrees. Convictions such as these, besides abridging freedom of speech, threaten freedom of thought and of belief.[62]

—Louis Brandeis, U.S. Supreme Court

■ ■ ■

September 15, 2002: In an interview with *The Wall Street Journal*, the assistant to the president for economic policy, Lawrence Lindsey, estimates the cost of a war with Iraq to be in the neighborhood of $100 billion to $200 billion. . . . Defense Secretary Rumsfeld calls Lindsey's estimate "baloney."[63]

—Cullen Murphy and Todd S. Purdum, journalists

Within four months, Larry was gone, having "resigned from the administration as part of a reshaping of the president's economic team."[64]

—Scott McClellan, former Bush press secretary

Those who begin coercive elimination of dissent soon find themselves exterminating dissenters.[65]

—Robert Jackson, U.S. Supreme Court

Lindsey's biggest mistake wasn't the size of the figures he chose to cite. It was citing any figures at all. Talking about the projected cost of a potential war wasn't part of the script, especially not when the White House was in the crucial early stages of building broad public support. In fact, none of the possible consequences of war—casualties, economic effects, geopolitical risks, diplomatic repercussions—were part of the message. . . . Citing or discussing potential costs, financial or human, only played into arguments our critics and opponents of war were raising. Lindsey had violated the first rule of the disciplined, on-message Bush White House: don't make news unless you're authorized to do so.[66]

—Scott McClellan, former Bush press secretary

Dissenters within the executive branch were excluded from decision making; some were pushed out of government.[67]

—Frederick A. O. Schwarz Jr. and Aziz Z. Huq, lawyers

It is better to leave a few of [speech's] noxious branches to their luxuriant growth, than by pruning them away, to injure the vigour of those yielding the proper fruits.[68]

—James Madison

It was part of a pattern. "The people who were running things and the people who were getting promoted were politically responsive" to the administration, said one CIA source.[69]

—James Risen, journalist

[Michael Hayden] is a Cheney pal who stood up for the White House's right to be unconstitutional, going along with the heinous warrantless snooping. That makes him one of the team and ready for a promotion, or a Medal of Freedom.[70]

—Maureen Dowd, columnist

President Bush yesterday nominated Air Force Gen. Michael V. Hayden to be the new director of the CIA. . . . Mr. Bush said Gen. Hayden, currently the deputy director of national intelligence and former head of the National Security Agency (NSA), is "supremely qualified" for the top CIA position.[71]

—Stephen Dinanand and Christina Bellantoni, journalists

Medals of Freedom [were awarded] to George Tenet, who said Saddam had WMD, Tommy Franks, who failed to secure Iraq, and Paul Bremer, who botched the occupation.[72]

—Paul Krugman, columnist

[T]he peculiar evil of silencing the expression of an opinion is, that it is robbing the human race . . . those who dissent from the opinion, still more than those who hold it.[73]

—John Stuart Mill

New opinions are always suspected, and usually opposed, without any other reason but because they are not already common.[74]

—John Locke

Mr. Bush has gone further than any previous president—even Richard Nixon—in attacking the patriotism of anyone who criticizes him or his policies.[75]

—Paul Krugman, columnist

Ultimately all the questions boil down to one—Whether we as a people will try fearfully and futilely to preserve democracy by adopting totalitarian methods, or whether in accordance with out traditions, and our constitution we will have the confidence and courage to be free.[76]

—Hugo L. Black, U.S. Supreme Court

The hope of a secure and livable world lies with disciplined nonconformists who are dedicated to justice, peace and brotherhood.[77]

—Martin Luther King Jr.

One longtime former Republican official, who held senior posts in both the first and second Bush administrations, was bluntest of all: "My question is," this former official told me, "does he expose himself to people who respectfully disagree, or thoughtfully disagree, or may have a legitimate suggestion? Not a lot, no."[78]

—Todd Purdum, journalist

The White House was so desperate to maintain its crumbling narrative that it often lost track of where the reality that it created ended and the reality recognized by the "reality-based community" and, for that matter, anyone outside the administration's bubble, began.[79]

—Frank Rich, columnist

[T]he longer you remain inside the White House bubble, the harder it becomes to see things clearly and objectively.[80]

—Scott McClellan, former Bush press secretary

"What's in the newspapers worth worrying about? I glance at the headlines just to kind of [get] a flavor of what's moving . . . I rarely read the stories . . . [I get] briefed by people who have probably read the news themselves."[81]

—George W. Bush

"I'm not a textbook player. I'm a gut player."[82]

—George W. Bush

"I don't watch the nightly newscasts on TV . . . nor do I watch the endless hours of people giving their opinion about things. I don't read the editorial pages; I don't read the columnists. It can be a frustrating experience to pay attention to somebody's false opinion."[83]

—George W. Bush

"I appreciate people's opinions, but I'm more interested in news. And the best way to get the news is from objective sources. And the most objective sources I have are the people on my staff who tell me what's happening in the world."[84]

—George W. Bush

Demands of rigid loyalty, along with a "kill the messenger" attitude toward bearers of news that undermines beliefs, are particularly dangerous for a president such as George Bush, who, by his own reckoning, depends so heavily on aides—not only for advice and counsel but also for basic information about what is going on in the world.[85]

—Glenn Greenwald, lawyer/journalist

A foreign diplomat who declined to be identified was startled when Secretary of State Rice warned him not to lay bad news on the president. "Don't upset him," she said.[86]

—Evan Thomas and Richard Wolffe, journalists

[Bush] was insulated from the reality of events on the ground and consequently began falling into the trap of believing his own spin. He failed to spend enough time seeking independent input from a broad range of outside experts, those beyond the White House bubble who had firsthand experience on the ground in Iraq, and—perhaps most important—those with differing points of view, including those who disagreed with his policies.[87]

—Scott McClellan, former Bush press secretary

Being ignorant is not so much a shame as being unwilling to learn.[88]

—Benjamin Franklin

The president of the United States is not a fact checker.[89]

—Dan Bartlett, Bush communications director

The contrast with having briefed his father and Clinton and Gore was so marked. And to be told, frankly, early in the administration, by Condi Rice and [her deputy] Steve Hadley, you know, Don't give the president a lot of long memos, he's not a big reader— well, shit. I mean, the president of the United States is not a big reader?[90]

—Richard Clarke, former White House counterterrorism expert

This is one key feature of the faith-based presidency: open dialogue, based on facts, is not seen as something of inherent value. It may, in fact, create doubt, which undercuts faith. It could result in a loss of confidence in the decision-maker and, just as important, by the decision-maker.[91]

—Ron Suskind, journalist

When you have people with a strong ideological position, and you hear from only one side, you can pretty much predict the outcome.[92]

—Paul O'Neill, former Secretary of the Treasury

A continual circulation of lies among those who are not much in the way of hearing them contradicted, will in time pass for the truth; and the crime lies not in the believer but the inventor.[93]

—Thomas Paine

The President was caught in an echo chamber of his own making, cut off from everyone other than a circle around him that's tiny and getting smaller and in concert on everything—a circle that conceals him from the one thing he needs most: honest, disinterested perspectives about what's real and what the hell he might do about it.[94]

—Ron Suskind, journalist

A nation or civilization that continues to produce soft-minded men purchases its own spiritual death on the installment plan.[95]

—Martin Luther King Jr.

Since his ideology teaches him contempt for the very notion of "the public interest," he actually prefers to rely on biased information prepared by sources of questionable reliability. . . . The president has, in effect, outsourced the truth.[96]

—Al Gore

[A] situation [had developed] in which right-minded people, *en masse*, all deviate downward toward a state of panic. "No one says, 'There's no proof!'" the CIA manager exhorted. . . . "There is no judgment in the system. No one is saying, 'Based on my experience, this person is a lying dog.' No one is saying, 'These reports are completely without any foundation.'"[97]

—Ron Suskind, journalist

[W]hat lies at the heart of the Bush presidency is an absolutist worldview capable of understanding all issues and challenges only in the moralistic, overly simplistic, and often inapplicable terms of "Good vs. Evil." The president is driven by his core conviction that he has found the Good, that he is a crusader of it, and that anything which impedes his decision-making is, by definition, a deliberate or unwitting ally of Evil.[98]

—Glenn Greenwald, lawyer/journalist

Those who were not squarely behind the president's crusade for Good were suspected, and frequently declared guilty, of siding with Evil. Attempting to impede the president's policies or, worse, the president himself, subjected one to accusations of harboring sympathy for terrorists, or at least of a reckless indifference to the danger the enemy presented.[99]

—Ron Suskind, journalist

An unconditional right to say what one pleases about public affairs is what I consider to be the minimum guarantee of the First Amendment.[100]

—Hugo L. Black, U.S. Supreme Court

Speech concerning public affairs is more than self-expression; it is the essence of self-government.[101]

—William Brennan, U.S. Supreme Court

After Bush squeaked out a victory in the 2004 election, he replaced those officials who had exhibited even minimal independence of mind, such as Colin Powell and John Ashcroft, with the supremely loyal Condoleezza Rice and Alberto Gonzales. And when Bush's Republican party lost its House and Senate majorities in the 2006 election, Bush quickly acted *not* by seeking out different counsel, but by further purging dissent from his inner circle.[102]

—Glenn Greenwald, lawyer/journalist

Bush's discomfort with change makes it difficult for him to step back from the bonds he develops and make clear-eyed decisions about what is best.[103]

—Scott McClellan, former Bush press secretary

[N]o change of doctrine or in political alignment can ever be admitted. For to change one's mind, or even one's policy, is a confession of weakness.[104]

—George Orwell

The louder the reports of failures on this president's watch, the louder he tries to drown them out by boasting that he has done everything "within the law" to keep America safe and by implying that his critics are unpatriotic, if not outright treasonous.[105]

—Frank Rich, columnist

[O]ne can reasonably conclude that how they think, their policies, and their style of governing are based to an alarming extent on their own authoritarian personalities, which tolerate no dissent, use dissembling as their standard modus operandi, and have pushed their governing authority beyond the law and the Constitution.[106]

—John Dean, former White House counsel

The president and his supporters locate new "enemies" continuously, in every corner and seemingly on a daily basis, and vow heightened wars against them, because they must.[107]

—Glenn Greenwald, lawyer/journalist

[Ron] Suskind quotes [Treasury Secretary Paul] O'Neill as describing a *pre*-9/11 National Security Council meeting where the invasion of Iraq was discussed with virtually no dissent.[108]

—Glenn Greenwald, lawyer/journalist

[T]hose who merely raised concerns about invading Iraq—let alone those who emphatically opposed it—were accused by the president's supporters, first implicitly and then overtly, of opposing efforts to stop terrorism and even siding with the terrorists and acting as their allies.[109]

—Glenn Greenwald, lawyer/journalist

September 11 gave them the opportunity to implement this long-cherished vision, and a chance to slander and scare opponents with the smear of disloyalty.[110]

—Frederick A. O. Schwarz Jr. and Aziz Z. Huq, lawyers

Gradually, Rumsfeld succeeded in replacing those officers in senior Joint Staff positions who challenged his view. "All the Joint Staff people now are handpicked, and churn out products to make the Secretary of Defense happy," the planner said.[111]

—Seymour Hersh, journalist

Policy makers also fought to ensure that internal dissenters, who did not toe the preferred line of unlimited presidential power, were simply cut out of the decision-making process.[112]

—Frederick A. O. Schwarz Jr. and Aziz Z. Huq, lawyers

[CIA] officials who appeared to be unenthusiastic about Iraq soon mysteriously found themselves sidelined, while their more eager and ambitious colleagues began to rise, both within the Directorate of Operations and in the Directorate of Intelligence, the analytical arm. The pressure from the Bush administration was being transmitted directly into the ranks of the nation's intelligence community, affecting careers and lives.[113]

—James Risen, journalist

[N]ot all lawyers in the OLC [Office of Legal Counsel] of the executive branch agreed with [Cheney's] vision. Some expressed their discomfort and disagreement, and found themselves edged out of decision-making roles. Lawyers with a long history of advocating expansive visions of presidential power occupied the driver's seat.[114]

—Frederick A. O. Schwarz Jr. and Aziz Z. Huq, lawyers

[Cheney counsel] David Addington . . . "generally excluded dissenters" and used the post-9/11 environment as an opportunity to put into practice his and Cheney's cherished ideals of executive branch unilateralism.[115]

—Frederick A. O. Schwarz Jr. and Aziz Z. Huq, lawyers

War opponents were demonized and dismissed as guilty, not only of poor judgment but also of poor character.[116]

—Glenn Greenwald, lawyer/journalist

It became evident to officers in the field that intelligence reports raising questions about the conduct of the war and the problems being encountered in Baghdad because of the Bush administration's policies—or lack of policies—were not welcome in Washington.[117]

—James Risen, journalist

[Within the White House there was a] reckless vindictiveness against anyone questioning the war.[118]

—Frank Rich, columnist

In contrast to prior administrations, the Bush administration has marched in virtual lockstep. . . . Dissident officials who stray from the president's views have been inexorably excised from power.[119]

—Glenn Greenwald, lawyer/journalist

According to [onetime Bush speechwriter] David Frum, the president purposely staffs the White House with capable but less-than-brilliant individuals, precisely because he seeks those who will loyally carryout instructions rather than those who will prod, question, and deviate from predetermined policies.[120]

—Glenn Greenwald, lawyer/journalist

In meetings, I'd ask if there were any facts to support our case. And for that, I was accused of disloyalty![121]

—Christine Todd Whitman, former EPA administrator

When traveling in the United States, Bush also uses his advance men and the Secret Service to remove demonstrators from his sight. . . . Bush's White House has revived this unconstitutional practice by claiming, as did the Nixon White House, that it is necessary for presidential protection. . . . This is criminalization of dissent.[122]

—John Dean, former White House counsel

What country can preserve its liberties if its rulers are not warned from time to time that their people preserve the spirit of resistance?[123]

—Thomas Jefferson

The Bush administration has also allowed restrictions on the rights of Americans to criticize the government on the streets of our cities and towns. In case after case, when President Bush makes a public appearance, nonviolent protesters have been harassed by law enforcement—either Secret Service agents or local police operating at their request—and forced out of the president's line of sight, to a designated protest area known as the "free-speech zone."[124]

—Gene Healy and Timothy Lynch, lawyers

Discussion cannot be denied and the right, as well as the duty, of criticism must not be stifled.[125]

—Felix Frankfurter, U.S. Supreme Court

[R]ight conclusions are more likely to be gathered out of a multitude of tongues, than through any kind of authoritative selection.[126]

—Learned Hand, judge

Returning to his 2000 campaign playbook, President Bush is now staging "Ask President Bush" forums once or twice a week around the country. These aren't stereotypical town hall-style meetings, where politicians take questions from all comers. Bush's events are elaborately scripted, with prescreened questioners selected for their adoration and ability to help the President make his case on everything from tax cuts to the war in Iraq.[127]

—Kenneth R. Bazinet, journalist

As you know, these are open forums: you're able to come and listen to what I have to say.[128]

—George W. Bush

[T]he State may not, consistently with the spirit of the First Amendment, contract the spectrum of available knowledge.[129]

—William O. Douglas, U.S. Supreme Court

Those who deny freedom to others deserve it not for themselves.[130]

—Abraham Lincoln

The most formidable weapon against errors of every kind is reason.[131]

—Thomas Paine

The spirit of resistance to government is so valuable on certain occasions that I wish it to be always kept alive. It will often be exercised when wrong, but better so than not to be exercised at all.[132]

—Thomas Jefferson

James Madison, Thomas Jefferson, and others had established a national tradition of open discussion; weaker twentieth-century descendants insulted their memory by choking off discussion.[133]

—Zechariah Chaffee, judicial philosopher

With a sort of Orwellian logic, the message to Americans by Bush supporters is clear: "You have the constitutional right to protest. So, you should be grateful for that right and show your gratefulness by not protesting, no matter how questionable your government's actions might be."[134]

—Colleen Redman, writer

The very purpose of a Bill of Rights was to withdraw certain subjects from the vicissitudes of political controversy, to place them beyond the reach of majorities and officials and to establish them as legal principles to be applied by the courts. One's right to life, liberty, and property, to free speech, a free press, freedom of worship and assembly, and other fundamental rights may not be submitted to vote; they depend on the outcome of no elections.[135]

—Robert Jackson, U.S. Supreme Court

During the 2004 re-election campaign, presidential advance teams expelled from public events anyone they suspected might not quietly toe the party line. Since then, Bush has rarely appeared before any group, big or small, whose loyalties and questions were not pre-screened and pre-approved.[136]

—Todd Purdum, journalist

If there is a bedrock principle of the First Amendment, it is that the government may not prohibit the expression of an idea simply because society finds the idea itself offensive or disagreeable.[137]

—William Brennan, U.S. Supreme Court

[T]he ultimate good desired is better reached by free trade in ideas—that the best test of truth is the power of the thought to get itself accepted in the competition of the market.[138]

—Oliver Wendell Holmes Jr., U.S. Supreme Court

Though all the winds of doctrine were let loose to play upon the earth, so Truth be in the field, we do ingloriously, by licensing and prohibiting, to misdoubt her strength. Let her and Falsehood grapple: who ever knew Truth put to the worse in a free and open encounter?[139]

—John Milton

Critics, unable to access source material to make informed arguments, could offer only scattershot critiques of U.S. policy. When they did, they were criticized for giving comfort to the enemy.[140]

—Ron Suskind, journalist

[T]he history of the Bush administration, from the botched reconstruction of Iraq to the botched start-up of the prescription drug program, shows that a president who isn't serious about governing, who prizes loyalty and personal connections over competence, can quickly reduce the government of the world's most powerful nation to third-world levels of ineffectiveness.[141]

—Paul Krugman, columnist

I wrote my "Areopagitica" . . . in order to deliver the press from the restraints with which it is encumbered; that the power of determining what was true and what was false, what ought to be published and what to be suppressed, might no longer be entrusted to a few illiterate and illiberal invidivuals.[142]

—John Milton

The national security bureaucracy is maddeningly slow, lacks creativity, and is risk averse. . . . Yet this creaking process does serve one purpose: it tends to weed out really stupid or dangerous ideas, unethical and even immoral ideas; ideas that could get people killed or could even start wars. After 9/11, the moderating influences of the slow-moving bureaucracy were stripped away. The president and his principals—Don Rumsfeld, Colin Powell, Condi Rice, and a handful of others—held almost constant, crisis-atmosphere making decisions on the fly. Instead of proposals gradually rising up through the normal layers of the government, they were introduced and imposed from above. Debate was short-circuited.[143]

—James Risen, journalist

When a question of policy is before the house, free men choose to meet it not with their eyes shut, but with their eyes open. To be afraid of ideas, of any idea, is to be unfit for self-government. Any such suppression of ideas about the common good the First

Amendment condemns with its absolute disapproval. The freedom of ideas shall not be abridged.[144]

—Alexander Meiklejohn, free speech advocate

After invoking the language and symbols of religion to bypass reason and convince the country to go to war, Bush found it increasingly necessary to disdain and dispute inconvenient facts that began to surface in public discussions. . . . This same pattern has characterized the effort to silence dissenting views *within* the executive branch, to censor information that may be inconsistent with its stated ideological goals, and to demand conformity from all executive branch employees.[145]

—Al Gore

Political freedom ends when government can use its powers to silence its critics.[146]

—Harry Kalven Jr., legal scholar

It is not the function of our Government to keep the citizen from falling into error; it is the function of the citizen to keep the Government from falling into error.[147]

—Robert Jackson, U.S. Supreme Court

It would give public servants an unjustified preference over the public they serve, if critics of official conduct did not have a fair equivalent of the immunity granted to the officials themselves.[148]

—William Brennan, U.S. Supreme Court

Fear of serious injury cannot alone justify suppression of free speech and assembly. Men feared witches and burnt women. It is the function of speech to free men from the bondage of irrational fears. To justify suppression of free speech there must be reasonable ground to fear that serious evil will result if free speech is practiced. There must be reasonable ground to believe that the danger apprehended is imminent.[149]

—Louis Brandeis, U.S. Supreme Court

■ ■ ■

In Feburary 2003, before the war began, Army Chief of Staff General Eric Shinseki told Congress that the occupation could require several hundred thousand troops, but the White House had already decided that a much smaller force was adequate. Rather than engaging in a reasoned debate on the question, they undercut Shinseki for disagreeing with their preconceived notion—even though he was an expert and they were not. The other generals and admirals got the message and stopped expressing disagreement with the White House. Shinseki had been right, of course, and most of the uniformed officers at the upper echelons of the Pentagon knew he was right. But the decision-making process was one that did not allow for principled differences. As a result, the policy selected was not informed by the collective wisdom.[150]

—Al Gore

The idea that the war might be a painful drain on the military was heresy. Shinseki was pushed aside. The message was not lost on other American military commanders: don't complain about the resources available for the war in Iraq if you want to keep your job. Bush and Rumsfeld would later both claim that they were always prepared to send more troops to Iraq if commanders in the field requested them. But the generals learned not to ask.[151]

—James Risen, journalist

I saw at a minimum, true dereliction, negligence and irresponsibility, at worst, lying, incompetence and corruption; false rationales presented as justification, a flawed strategy, lack of planning, the unnecessary distraction from real threats, and the unbearable strain dumped on our overstretched military. All of these caused me to speak out, and I was called a traitor and a turncoat by civilian Pentagon officials.[152]

—Gen. Anthony Zinni

Those generals who disagreed with the White House policy were undercut and sidelined. Those who supported it enthusiastically were promoted—even though it has been a catastrophic failure at every turn.[153]

—Al Gore

[S]uppression promotes inflexibility and stultification, preventing society from adapting to changing circumstances and developing new ideas.[154]

—Thomas Emerson, legal scholar

[M]ost [generals] had soured on [Rumsfeld] before the public did. . . . Though some of the generals had complained while on active duty about Rumsfeld's handling of the war—and, they believe, were penalized for their candor—each had to overcome a lifetime of reticence before calling for him to be replaced.[155]

—David Margolick, journalist

The Pentagon officials were at odds with the leaders of the State Department, who were far more restrained in their planning, and accused Pentagon leadership of confusing dissent with disloyalty.[156]

—Seymour Hersh, journalist

A man who participated in high-level planning for both Afghanistan and Iraq . . . told me, "There was absolutely no debate in the normal sense. There are only six or eight of them who make the decisions, and they only talk to each other. And if you disagree with them in public, they'll come after you, the way they did with Shinseki."[157]

—James Fallows, journalist

I think a lot of the problem the president had is: people around him were doing what he said, and nobody was doing the analytical questioning of the things we were doing where you could do all the puts and takes and say, "O.K., Mr. President, here's all the pros to do this and here's all the cons to do this, and here's the likely outcome. Now, let's make a decision." I don't think that ever happened. I never saw anything like that.[158]

—Jay Garner, former Iraq reconstruction director

The point is not that [chairman of the Joint Chiefs of Staff Richard] Myers or his successor Peter Pace should ever have spoken disrespectfully of decisions made by their commander in chief. But to many watching from lower down the chain of command, their example suggested that political loyalty counted for more than independent professional judgment at the military's top rank.[159]

—James Fallows, journalist

In 2004, case officers stationed in Baghdad told their colleagues that they were frequently ordered to revise intelligence reports that were considered "negative" about Iraq. And in late 2004, when a new CIA station chief—the successor to the officer pulled in December 2003—wrote another [brief] reporting on the deadly conditions in Iraq, his political allegiances were quickly questioned by the White House, the CIA officials later learned.[160]

—James Risen, journalist

[M]any CIA officials . . . knew before the war that they lacked sufficient evidence to make the case for the existence of Iraq's weapons programs. Those doubts were stifled because of the enormous pressure that officials at the CIA and other agencies felt to support the administration.[161]

—James Risen, journalist

Some CIA officials who were skeptical were shunted to the side by CIA management.[162]

—James Risen, journalist

The Right of all members of society to form their own beliefs and communicate them freely to others must be regarded as an essential principle of a democratically organized society.[163]

—Thomas Emerson, legal scholar

The top U.S. commander in the Middle East, whose views on Iran and the region in general have sometimes conflicted with the Bush administration's outlook, abruptly resigned on Tuesday. Adm. William Fallon, who headed the U.S. Central Command, said recent news reports that showed him to be out of step with the Bush administration had become a distraction.[164]

—Aamer Madhani, journalist

Fallon's backers in and out of the Pentagon said his departure simply proves that the Administration brooks no dissent on matters of war and peace. "Bush says he'll listen to commanders in the field," one retired admiral says, "unless they say something he doesn't like, and then he fires them."[165]

—Mark Thompson, journalist

[S]uppression of expression conceals the real problems confronting a society and diverts public attention from the critical issues. It is likely to result in neglect of the grievances which are the actual basis of the unrest, and thus prevents their correction.[166]

—Thomas Emerson, legal scholar

[Before the 9/11 Commission hearings began,] Bush's aides were trying to deliver a political message to [Commission cochair Tom] Kean, although he would not fully understand it until later. . . . "We want you to stand up. You've got to stand up." "You've got to have courage." "We don't want a runaway commission." . . . Kean would realize later how naïve he had been. After months of tense negotiations with the White House as it tried to block the commission's access to secret documents and interviews, he would think back to those first meetings at the White House in 2002. He realized that he was not being told by the White House to stand up for what was right. . . . When Bush's aides told him to "stand up," what they meant was that Kean and the commission needed to "stand up for the president," [but] not necessarily for the truth. The truth was secondary. "You've got to stand up for the president, and you've got to protect him in the process. That's what they meant."[167]

—Phillip Shenon, journalist

According to the Bush-Cheney Doctrine, those who question the abuse of power question America itself.[168]

—Sen. John Kerry

■ ■ ■

A bill of rights is what the people are entitled to against every government on earth.[169]

—Thomas Jefferson

Thomas Jefferson's initial reaction to the proposed Constitution was negative, for, as he wrote to James Madison, he feared the possibility of the rise of an American tyrant: "Roman emperors, popes, German emperors, deys of the Ottoman dependencies, and Polish kings—all were elective in some sense."[170]

—Naomi Wolf, writer

I have sworn upon the altar of God eternal hostility against every form of tyranny over the mind of man.[171]

—Thomas Jefferson

[T]he Framers of the Bill of Rights did not purport to "create" rights. Rather they designed the Bill of Rights to prohibit our Government from infringing rights and liberties
presumed to be preexisting.[172]

—William Brennan, U.S. Supreme Court

The fabric of American empire ought to rest on the solid basis of the consent of the
people. The streams of national power ought to flow immediately from that pure, original fountain of all legitimate authority.[173]

—Alexander Hamilton

No man is good enough to govern another man without that other's consent.[174]

—Abraham Lincoln

[T]he people are the only legitimate fountain of power, and it is from them that the constitutional charter, under which the several branches of government hold their power,
is derived.[175]

—James Madison

The Court has emphasized that the central meaning of the free expression guarantee is
that the body politic of this Nation shall be entitled to the communications necessary
for self-governance, and that to place restraints on the exercise of expression is to deny
the instrumental means required in order that the citizenry exercise that ultimate sovereignty reposed in its collective judgment by the Constitution.[176]

—William Brennan, U.S. Supreme Court

Jefferson and Franklin and Washington had messages they prized, and repeated often,
displaying firmly held beliefs. But those favorite phrases were distillates of a sort, the
product of lives ordered by experience, and study, fierce debate, and a search for what
was known and knowable—the end of a process, not the starting point. Nowadays, an
appropriate message—shallow but wide—is often the first consideration.[177]

—Ron Suskind, journalist

Knowledge is in every country the surest basis of happiness.[178]

—George Washington

But confronted by presidential initiatives in foreign affairs, Congress and the courts,
along with the press and the citizenry, often lack confidence in their own information
and judgment and are likely to be intimidated by executive authority.[179]

—Arthur Schlesinger, historian

Those who won our independence by revolution were not cowards. They did not fear
political change. They did not exalt order at the cost of liberty. To courageous, self-
reliant men, with confidence in the power of free and fearless reasoning applied through
the processes of popular government, no danger flowing from speech can be deemed

clear and present, unless the incidence of the evil apprehended is so imminent that it may befall before there is opportunity for full discussion.[180]

—Louis Brandeis, U.S. Supreme Court

Free speech has occupied an exalted position because of the high service it has given our society. Its protection is essential to the very existence of a democracy. The airing of ideas releases pressures which otherwise might become destructive. When ideas compete in the market for acceptance, full and free discussion exposes the false and they gain few adherents. Full and free discussion even of ideas we hate encourages the testing of our own prejudices and preconceptions. Full and free discussion keeps a society from becoming stagnant and unprepared for the stresses and strains that work to tear all civilizations apart.[181]

—William O. Douglas, U.S. Supreme Court

[There exists] a profound national commitment to the principle that debate on public issues should be uninhibited, robust, and wide-open, and that it may well include vehement, caustic, and sometimes unpleasantly sharp attacks on government and public officials.[182]

—William Brennan, U.S. Supreme Court

The Age of Reason ideals upon which the country was founded, championed open, rigorous, fact-based debate—even reserving constitutional seats for unruly freedoms such as speech, press, and assembly—to form a counterweight to faith, a titanic force, no matter how judiciously the founders attempted to circumscribe it; and to fear, so often born of ignorance, or dread of what is not known.[183]

—Ron Suskind, journalist

The very idea of self-government depends on open and honest debate as the preferred method of pursuing the truth—a shared respect for the rule of reason as the best way to establish the truth.[184]

—Al Gore

[T]he campaign mentality at times led the president and his chief advisers to spin, hide, shade and exaggerate the truth, obscuring nuances and ignoring the caveats that should have accompanied their arguments. Rather than choosing to be forthright and candid, they chose to sell the war, and in so doing they did a disservice to the American people and to our democracy.[185]

—Scott McClellan, former Bush press secretary

Democracy depends on a social agreement that is so obvious to us that it usually goes unspoken: There is such thing as truth. In an open society, we know facts may be hedged and spun in the back-and-forth of debate, but truth is the ground from which the edging or spinning begin. Democracy depends upon accountability; accountability requires us to be able to tell truth from lies; and to be able to tell truth from lies, we all first must agree that truth matters.[186]

—Naomi Wolf, writer

To inform the minds of the people, and to follow their will, is the chief duty of those placed at their head.[187]

—Thomas Jefferson

■ ■ ■

The demand for loyalty is itself a by-product of his faith-based certainty. Certitude that one is right will naturally reduce, if not eliminate, a tolerance for those who question what has been accorded the status of unquestionable Truth.[188]

—Bruce Bartlett, government official

[F]aith has also shaped his presidency in profound, nonreligious ways. The president has demanded unquestioning faith from his followers, his staff, his senior aides and his kindred in the Republican Party. Once he makes a decision—often swiftly, based on a creed or moral position—he expects complete faith in its rightness. . . . The faith-based presidency is a with-us-or-against-us model that has been enormously effective at, among other things, keeping the workings and temperament of the Bush White House a kind of state secret.[189]

—Ron Suskind, journalist

His arrogance and certitude were less a reflection of hard-right ideology than of his soft character, which was in turn the product of a biography full of easy landings.[190]

—Frank Rich, columnist

Hubris is, in its way, a loss of context. Those with hubristic clarity of their rightness view even small setbacks as a profound affront, and attack on one's gilded integrity. Opposing points of view shrink to invisibility.[191]

—Ron Suskind, journalist

[W]hat Jefferson warned against was not faith itself—nor even organized religion itself. He was warning us against the combination of religious dogma and government power.[192]

—Al Gore

The Bush presidency, awash in moralistic rhetoric, has ushered in some of the most extremist, previously unthinkable and profoundly un-American practices—from indefinite, lawless detentions, to the use of torture, to bloody preventative wars of choice, to the abductions of innocent people literally off the street or from their homes, to radical new theories designed to vest in the president the power to break the law. These measures were pursued not despite the moralistic roots of the president's agenda, but *because* of them. . . . As the president ceaselessly proclaimed the Goodness at the heart of America's destiny and its role in the world, his actions have resulted in an almost full-scale destruction of America's moral credibility in almost every country and on every continent. The same president who has insisted that core moralism drives him has brought America to its lowest moral standing in history.[193]

—Glenn Greenwald, lawyer/journalist

In our country are evangelists and zealots of many different political, economic and religious persuasions whose fanatical conviction is that all thought is divinely classified into two kinds—that which is their own and that which is false and dangerous.[194]

—Robert Jackson, U.S. Supreme Court

This is why [Bush] dispenses with people who confront him with inconvenient facts. He truly believes he's on a mission from God. Absolute faith like that overwhelms a need for analysis. The whole thing about faith is to believe things for which there is no empirical evidence. But you can't run the world on faith.[195]

—Ron Suskind, journalist

[T]he president's core view [is] that the world can be understood as an overarching conflict between the forces of Good and Evil, and that America is "called upon" to defend the former from the latter. . . . Such a philosophy is centrally predicated on the certainty that government leaders can divine God's will—not with regard to specific issues and policies but in the generalized moral sense—and can therefore confidently enlist and expand the awesome power of the American government in service to universal moral dictates.[196]

—Glenn Greenwald, lawyer/journalist

If men are so wicked with religion, what would they be without it?[197]

—Benjamin Franklin

The binary view of Good and Evil came not merely to define every significant political issue but to engulf all political debate. One was presented with a false choice—embrace and actively support the president's policies to wage war on Evil or side with Evil, either deliberately or by default. With these dualistic premises underlying virtually the entire national political discussion, Supreme Court justices who ruled against the president on national security matters were accused of being tyrants, traitors, and pro-terrorist.[198]

—Glenn Greenwald, lawyer/journalist

It has for some time been a question with me whether a commonwealth suffers more by hypocritical pretenders to religion or by the openly profane. But some late thoughts of this nature have inclined me to think that the hypocrite is the most dangerous person of the two, especially if he sustains a post in government.[199]

—Benjamin Franklin

[The battle between Good and Evil] subordinates all other considerations and never gives way to any conflicting or inconsistent goals.[200]

—Glenn Greenwald, lawyer/journalist

[The president was] clearly signing on to strong ideological positions that had not been fully thought through. But, of course, that's the nature of ideology. Thinking it through is the last thing an ideologue wants to do.[201]

—Paul O'Neill, former Secretary of the Treasury

By some measures it has been the most politically motivated presidency of modern times, with policy on issues from science to taxes dictated by considerations of partisan advantage and ideological dogma.[202]

—Todd Purdum, journalist

I think an ideology comes out of feelings and it tends to be non-thinking. A philosophy, on the other hand, can have a structured thought base. One would hope that a philosophy, which is always a work in progress, is influenced by the facts. So there is a constant interplay between *what do I think* and *why do I think it*. . . . Now, if you gather more facts and have more experience, especially with things that have gone wrong—those are especially good learning tools—then you reshape your philosophy, because the facts tell you you've got to. . . . Ideology is a lot easier, because you don't have to know anything or search for anything. You already know the answer to everything. It's not penetrable by facts. It's absolutism.[203]

—Paul O'Neill, former Secretary of the Treasury

There is no precedent in any modern White House for what is going on in this one: a complete lack of a policy apparatus. What you've got is everything—and I mean everything—being run by the political arm. Everything—and I mean everything—is being run by the Mayberry Machiavellis.[204]

—John J. DiIulio Jr., Bush administration official

A PROPAGANDA COMPANY

See, in my line of work, you got to keep repeating things over and over and over again for the truth to sink in, to kind of catapult the propaganda.[205]

—George W. Bush

The nation's freedoms are under assault by an administration's policies that can do us as much damage as al Qaeda. The nation's marketplace of ideas is being poisoned by a propaganda company so blatant that Tokyo Rose would have quit.[206]

—Keith Olbermann, political commentator

[The president's] seeming contempt for the rule of reason and his early successes in persuading people to believe in his dogma-driven view of the world apparently tempted him to the hubristic and deeply dangerous illusion that reality itself, has become a commodity that can be created and sold with clever propaganda and public relation skills.[207]

—Al Gore

The Bush administration unloads coffins of dead American soldiers from planes at night and has forbidden photographers to take pictures of coffins.[208]

—Naomi Wolf, writer

The move to block the release of pictures from Dover drew a rebuke from Rep. Jim McDermott, a Washington Democrat who served in the navy during the Vietnam War. "This is not about privacy," McDermott told reporters. "This is about trying to keep the country from facing the reality of war."[209]

—Charlie Savage, journalist

The administration tries to play down any sense of individual loss; the president has not attended a single funeral, and the government banned pictures of their returning coffins.[210]

—Maureen Dowd, columnist

From the start, the Bush team has tried to keep the Iraq war "off the books" both financially and emotionally.[211]

—Thomas Friedman, journalist

Half the truth is often a great lie.[212]

—Benjamin Franklin

The administration's enforcement of a prohibition on photographs of coffins returning from Iraq was the first policy manifestation of the hide-the-carnage strategy. . . . Out of sight, out of mind was the game plan, and it has been enforced down to the tiniest instances.[213]

—Frank Rich, columnist

This is how the war planners wanted it, of course. No new taxes, no draft, no photos of coffins, no inconveniences that might compel voters to ask tough questions. This strategy would have worked if the war had been the promised cakewalk. But now it has backfired. A home front that has not been asked to invest directly in a war, that has subcontracted it to a relatively small group of volunteers, can hardly be expected to feel it has a stake in the outcome five stalemated years on.[214]

—Frank Rich, columnist

[H]e who knows nothing is nearer to truth than he whose mind is filled with falsehoods & errors.[215]

—Thomas Jefferson

The simple truth is that the Bush crowd, busy trying to hide the costs of the president's $2 trillion tragedy in Iraq, can't find the money to pay for all the care that's needed by the legions of wounded and mentally disabled troops who are coming home. . . . The administration has tried its best to keep the reality of the war away from the public at large, to keep as much of the carnage as possible behind the scenes.[216]

—Bob Herbert, journalist

In short, 9/11 allowed for preparation to meet opportunity. . . . In the wide, diffuse, "war on terror," so much of it occurring in the shadows—with no transparency and only perfunctory oversight—the administration could say anything it wanted to say. That was a blazing insight of this period. The administration could create whatever reality was convenient.[217]

—Ron Suskind, journalist

Falsity is susceptible of infinite combinations, whereas truth has only one manner of being.[218]

—Jean-Jacques Rousseau

Before 9/11, however, the right-wing noise machine mainly relied on little lies. And now it has returned to its roots. . . . Even in the post-9/11 environment, little lies never went away. . . . The G.O.P.'s reversion to the Little Lie technique is a symptom of political weakness, of a party reduced to trivial smears because it has nothing else to offer.[219]

—Paul Krugman, columnist

[A] lie cannot endure forever.[220]

—Thomas Carlyle

[Neoconservatives] believe lying is necessary for the state to survive. They believe certain facts should be known only by the political elite, and withheld from the general public. . . . They view civil liberties with suspicion, as unnecessary restrictions on the federal government. They despise libertarians, and dismiss any arguments based on constitutional grounds.[221]

—John Dean, former White House counsel

There are a lot of people who lie and get away with it.[222]

—Donald Rumsfeld

President George W. Bush and seven of his administration's top officials, including Vice President Dick Cheney, National Security Adviser Condoleezza Rice, and Defense Secretary Donald Rumsfeld, made at least 935 false statements in the two years following September 11, 2001, about the national security threat posed by Saddam Hussein's Iraq. Nearly five years after the U.S. invasion of Iraq, an exhaustive examination of the record shows that the statements were part of an orchestrated campaign that effectively galvanized public opinion and, in the process, led the nation to war under decidedly false pretenses. . . . This concerted effort was the underpinning of the Bush administration's case for war.[223]

—Charles Lewis and Mark Reading-Smith, Center for Public Integrity

The administration has developed a highly effective propaganda machine to imbed in the public mind mythologies that grow out of the one central doctrine that all of the special interests agree on, which—in its purest form—is that government is very bad and should be done away with as much as possible—except the parts of it that redirect money through big contracts to industries that have won their way into the inner circle.[224]

—Al Gore

[H]e who permits himself to tell a lie once, finds it much easier to do a second and third time, till at length it becomes habitual; he tells lies without attending to it, and truths without the world believing him. This falsehood of the tongue leads to that of the heart, and in time depraves all its good dispositions.[225]

—Thomas Jefferson

Once you accomplish this flooding of the plain of discourse with lies, you are much closer to closing down an open society. If citizens can't be sure you are telling the truth or not, you can manipulate people into supporting almost anything the state wants to undertake; and it is also much more difficult for citizens to advocate or mobilize on their own behalf: How can they be sure what is right and what is wrong?[226]

—Naomi Wolf, writer

Tricks and treachery are the practice of fools that have not wit enough to be honest.[227]

—Benjamin Franklin

Instead of embracing candor and honesty when they were most needed and using them to his advantage, the president decided to avoid them for fear of political damage.[228]

—Scott McClellan, former Bush press secretary

The first of qualities for a great statesman is to be honest.[229]

—John Adams

When [the] painful reality [of failure in Iraq] began to displace illusion in the public mind, the president made increasingly strenuous efforts to silence the messengers of truth and create his own version of reality.[230]

—Al Gore

In *Nineteen-Eighty-Four* a continual bombardment of propaganda—or Newspeak—from the Ministry of Truth produced a form of amnesia and thought constriction among the subjects of Orwell's dystopia. Integral to this form of mind control was the ability of the state to rewrite the news and history in ways that suited the shifting needs of Big Brother.[231]

—Scott O'Reilly, writer

Every record has been destroyed or falsified, every book has been rewritten, every picture has been repainted, every statue and street and building has been renamed, every date has been altered. And that process is continuing day by day and minute by minute. History has stopped. Nothing exists except an endless present in which the Party is always right.[232]

—George Orwell

Orwell described that people who want to close down an open society don't just lie, they make lies the grounds of the discourse. There is this extraordinary fudging of reality, not just to change the record, but to disorient us. I think that we have to get it that what they are up to is not just about abuses of democratic process. It's about an end run *around* the democratic process.[233]

—Naomi Wolf, writer

To tell deliberate lies when genuinely believing them, to forget any fact that has become inconvenient, and then, when it becomes necessary again, to draw it back from oblivion for just so long as it is needed, to deny the existence of objective reality and all the while to take account of the reality which one denies—all this is indispensably necessary.[234]

—George Orwell

You, [President Bush], have now given us chaos and called it order. You, sir, have now imposed subjugation and called it freedom. . . . For the most vital, the most urgent, the most inescapable of reasons. We have handed a blank check drawn against our freedom, to a man who may now, if he so decides, declare not merely any non-American citizens "unlawful enemy combatants" and ship them somewhere, anywhere, but may now, if he so decides, declare you an "unlawful enemy combatant" and ship you somewhere, anywhere. He lied to get it. He lied as he received it. . . . Your words are lies, Sir. They are lies that imperil us all.[235]

—Keith Olbermann, political commentator

There are many who believe George Bush is a liar, a President who knowingly and deliberately twists facts for political gain. But lying would indicate an understanding of what is desired, what is possible, and how best to get there. A more plausible explanation is that words have no meaning for this President beyond the immediate moment, and so he believes that his mere utterance of the phrases makes them real. It is a terrifying possibility.[236]

—Seymour Hersh, journalist

Four years into a war fought to eliminate a nonexistent threat, we all have renewed appreciation for the power of the Big Lie: people tend to believe false official claims about big issues, because they can't picture their leaders being dishonest about such things. But there's another political lesson I don't think has sunk in: the power of the Little Lie—the small accusation invented out of thin air, followed by another, and another, and another. Little Lies aren't meant to have staying power. Instead, they create a sort of background hum, a sense that the person facing all these accusations must have done something wrong.[237]

—Paul Krugman, columnist

Perhaps the barrage of lies serves a more substantial purpose than simply advancing a certain position. Sending a current of lies into the information stream is part of classic psychological operations to generate a larger shift—a new reality in which the truth *can no longer be ascertained and no longer counts.* In this reality citizens no longer feel empowered or able to establish the truth on either side—and therefore give up their agency. At this point people can be manipulated into supporting almost any state action. For how can citizens know what is right? Truth itself has been cheapened, made subjective and internal, not absolute and external.[238]

—Naomi Wolf, writer

The lie about a connection between al-Qaeda and Iraq was also the key to justifying the constitutional power grab by the president. And in the end, for this administration, it is all about power. As long as their big, flamboyant lie remained an established fact in the public's mind, President Bush was seen by the majority as justified in taking for himself the power to make war on his whim. He was seen as justified in suspending many civil liberties at his personal discretion. And he could continue to distort the political reality experienced by the American people.[239]

—Al Gore

The administration's propaganda machinery encompassed not just the usual government flacks disseminating misleading information but also hidden and elaborate fake news factory, complete with its own fake "journalists," all of it paid for by taxpayers. . . . Two "reporters" named Karen Ryan and Alberto Garcia had appeared in TV spots distributed to local news stations around the country to promote the administration's new Medicare prescription-drug benefit as the best thing to happen to America's elderly since Social Security. . . . A government spokesperson defended the fake news with pure Orwell-speak: "Anyone who has questions about this practice needs to do some research on modern public information tools."[240]

—Frank Rich, columnist

Armstrong Williams, a conservative commentator, talk-show host, and newspaper columnist (for *The Washington Times* and *Detroit Free Press*, among others), was unmasked
as the front man for a scheme by which $240,000 of taxpayers' money was quietly
siphoned through the Department of Education and a private PR firm to Williams so
that he would "regularly comment" upon (translation: shill for) the Bush administration's No Child Left Behind program in various media venues during the election year.[241]

—Frank Rich, columnist

Under the Bush administration, the federal government has aggressively used a well-
established tool of public relations: the prepackaged, ready-to-serve news report that
major corporations have long distributed to TV stations to pitch everything from head-
ache remedies to auto insurance. . . . The reports themselves, though, are designed to fit
seamlessly into the typical local news broadcast. In most cases, the "reporters" are careful
not to state in the segment that they work for the government. Their reports generally
avoid overt ideological appeals. Instead, the government's news-making apparatus has
produced a quiet drumbeat of broadcasts describing a vigilant and compassionate administration.[242]

—David Barstow and Robin Stein, journalists

[We saw] a White House press secretary month after month turning for softball questions to "Jeff Gannon," a fake reporter for a fake news organization ultimately unmasked as a G.O.P. activist's propaganda site.[243]

—Frank Rich, columnist

By my count, "Jeff Gannon" is now at least the sixth "journalist" (four of whom have
been unmasked so far this year) to have been a propagandist on the payroll of either the
Bush administration or a barely arms-length ally like Talon News while simultaneously
appearing in print or broadcast forums that purport to be real news. Of these six, two
have been syndicated newspaper columnists paid by the Department of Health and Human Services to promote the administration's "marriage" initiatives. The other four have
played real newsmen on TV.[244]

—Frank Rich, columnist

Bruce Bartlett, a White House veteran of the Reagan-Bush I era, said that "if Gannon
was using an alias, the White House staff had to be involved in maintaining his cover."[245]

—Frank Rich, columnist

In 2006, the GAO [Government Accounting Office] said that the Bush administration
had spent $1.6 billion on advertising and public relations just from 2003 through the
second quarter of 2005. Even that figure understated the extent of the propaganda.

There was no way to quantify the fictionalizing in every corner of the administration, much of which came to light after the 2004 election.[246]

—Frank Rich, columnist

Even now, we know that the fake news generated by the six known shills is only a small piece of the administration's overall propaganda effort. President Bush wasn't entirely joking when he called the notoriously meek March 6, 2003, White House press conference on the eve of the Iraq invasion "scripted" while it was still going on. (And "Jeff Gannon" apparently wasn't even at that one). Everything is scripted.[247]

—Frank Rich, columnist

Rumsfeld had given his own stamp of approval, applauding the fake news as a "nontraditional means" of providing "accurate information" to the Iraqi people. He did not explain how placing camouflaged American propaganda in Iraqi papers could be squared with the professed American mission of exporting democratic freedoms, including that of a free and independent press.[248]

—Frank Rich, columnist

[F]reedom of expression in the political realm is usually a necessary condition for securing freedom elsewhere.[249]

—Thomas Emerson, legal scholar

Everything that is really great and inspiring is created by the individual who can labor in freedom.[250]

—Albert Einstein

There is so much about this presidency that we don't know, and may never learn.[251]

—Seymour Hersh, journalist

Part Two

THE WAR PRESIDENT

I'm a war president. I make decisions here in the Oval Office in
foreign policy matters with war on my mind.[1]
—George W. Bush

War was on the mind of George W. Bush much sooner than many had imagined. It is clear that remaking the Middle East was on the Bush agenda well before his presidency began. Invading and occupying an "easy" to conquer nation in the region was merely one option—but the option that rose to the top of his list.

But the neoconservative dream of Middle Eastern democracy—first by imposition in one nation, then, as if by magic, spreading to others—would never be a sufficient justification to sell the American citizenry on war. No, a greater trigger would be needed, one that would resonate throughout America, allowing the war to be sold.

Of course, 9/11 was that trigger. Saddam Hussein's Iraq was a convenient target. But it had achieved target status even prior to the tragedies of September 2001. Still, without a clear link between the terrorist attacks and Iraq, more was needed for the necessary groundswell of support to achieve regime change. To achieve its goals, Bush administration officials would again resort to the same sort of manipulation and distortion of information—and sometimes outright lying—that they utilized to acquire and abuse power.

As with aspects of the law explored in Part One, Part Two of this volume reveals a group of officials who believed the law is what they say it is. Akin to the Nixonian mantra, "if the president does it, it's not illegal," Bush officials molded a belief system to suit their needs. The practice became routine and manifested itself within the war on terror. That included Iraq, of course, but especially acquired traction in the treatment of detainees and ultimately the torture of some. By re-defining torture in a manner inconsistent with the Geneva Conventions, the White House's Office of Legal Counsel gave the president and vice-president what they wanted—a virtual blank check. "By the end of the Bush years," writes Jane Mayer, "America's reputation as a lead defender of democracy and human rights was in tatters."[2] Moreover, questions arose whether torture was used only to extract terror-related information, or if coercing statements about an al Qaeda-Iraq link was a goal, so as to more easily sell the American public on invasion—an invasion that seems to have been pre-determined.

■ ■ ■

[T]hey had one hypothesis. And when you only have one hypothesis, you tend to see things which fit it. I think everyone would agree that Saddam was a threat and a problem that had to be dealt with. The Bush administration elected to deal with him by getting rid of him by force. And they had to sell that to the American people, and they had to sell that in a way that would make it worth an enormous cost.[3]

—Charles Duelfer, Iraq Survey Group

Bush wanted to go to war in Iraq from the very first days he was in office. Nothing was going to stop that.[4]

—Rob Richer, CIA

It is, in retrospect, no great surprise that the first National Security council meeting in January 2001 dealt with the overthrow of Saddam Hussein. And so did the second. It was a matter of *how*, not *whether*.[5]

—Ron Suskind, journalist

Actually, I was hoping to solve the Iraqi issue diplomatically. That's why I went to the United Nations and worked with the United Nations Security Council, which unanimously passed a resolution that said disclose, disarm or face serious consequences. That was the message, the clear message to Saddam Hussein. He chose the course. . . . It was his decision to make.[6]

—George W. Bush

Let's see, we have learned that Iraq had no weapons of mass destruction. That means Bush is claiming that Saddam Hussein "chose" the invasion—and, ultimately, his own death—by not showing us what he didn't have.[7]

—Eugene Robinson, columnist

Bullying and intimidation are not acceptable ways to conduct foreign policy in the 21st century.[8]

—George W. Bush

A year from now, I'll be very surprised if there is not some grand square in Baghdad that is named after President Bush. There is no doubt that, with the exception of a very small number of people close to a vicious regime, the people of Iraq have been liberated and they understand that they've been liberated. And it is getting easier every day for Iraqis to express that sense of liberation.[9]

—Richard Perle, neoconservative

At the spot where U.S. forces helped Iraqis topple a statue of Saddam Hussein in 2003, protesters Friday tore down an effigy of President Bush and set it afire during a demonstration over plans to keep American troops in Iraq through 2011.[10]

—Tina Susman and Caesar Ahmed, journalists

One of the major theaters against al Qaeda turns out to have been Iraq. This is where al Qaeda said they were going to take their stand.

—George W. Bush

But not until after the U.S. invaded.

—Martha Raddatz, journalist

Yeah, that's right. So what?[11]

—George W. Bush

—5—

September 11 Run-Up

"Bin Laden Determined to Strike in the U.S."[1]

—title of the President's Daily Briefing, August 6, 2001

Bush was specifically warned of a possible attack in an item on [CIA director George] Tenet's daily briefing of August 6, 2001, which was entitled: "Bin Laden Determined to Strike in US." The briefing also spoke of FBI awareness of "patterns of suspicious activity consistent with preparations for hijackings or other types of attacks, including recent surveillance of federal buildings in New York."[2]

—Tyler Drumheller, CIA

All right. You've covered your ass, now.[3]

—George W. Bush (dismissing a CIA briefer who was trying to emphasize the importance of the 8-6-01 PDB)

I don't think anybody could have predicted that these people would take an airplane and slam it into the World Trade Center, take another one and slam it into the Pentagon— that they would try to use an airplane as a missile.[4]

—Condoleezza Rice

[I]n 1994 Algerians hijacked an Air France airliner with the intention of crashing it into the Eiffel Tower.[5]

—David Plotz, journalist

In 1995, police in the Philippines uncovered an al-Qaida plot to fly a plane into CIA headquarters. (One of the plotters: Khalid Sheikh Mohammed.)[6]

—David Plotz, journalist

There wasn't any way then we could have anticipated what was about to happen, of course, on 9/11.[7]

—Dick Cheney

[T]he FBI indicates patterns of suspicious activity in the United States consistent with preparations for hijacking.[8]

—President's Daily Brief, August 6, 2001

These terrorists had burrowed in our country for over two years. They were well organized. They were well planned. They struck in a way that was unimaginable."[9]

—George W. Bush

An FBI agent in Minneapolis, Minnesota, writes a memo suggesting Zacarias Moussaoui is training to learn to fly planes into buildings. The agent "mentioned the possibility of Moussaoui being that type of person that could fly something into the World Trade Center," FBI Director Robert Mueller later tells Congress. The FBI notifies the CIA about Moussaoui, but neither agency tells the White House Counterterrorism Security Group. The Federal Aviation Administration, also told about Moussaoui, decides not to warn airlines about a possible threat, an FAA official says.[10]

—FBI memo

When Clinton left office many people, including the incoming Bush administration leadership, thought that he and his administration were overly obsessed with al Qaeda. . . . Why was Clinton so worked up about al Qaeda and why did he talk to President-elect Bush about it and have Sandy Berger raise it with his successor as National Security Advisor, Condi Rice?[11]

—Richard Clarke, former White House counterterrorism expert

Some counterterrorism officials think there is another reason for the Bush Administration's dilatory response. Clarke's paper, says an official, "was a Clinton proposal." Keeping Clarke around was one thing; buying into the analysis of an Administration that the Bush team considered feckless and naive was quite another. So Rice instructed Clarke to initiate a new "policy review process" on the terrorism threat. Clarke dived into yet another round of meetings. And his proposals were nibbled nearly to death.[12]

—Michael Elliot, journalist

We were not left a comprehensive strategy to fight al Qaeda.[13]

—Condoleezza Rice

In January 2001, Clarke forwarded a strategy paper to Rice warning that al Qaeda had a presence in the United States.[14]

—9/11 Commission report

It was, Clarke wrote, "Developed by the last administration to give to you, incorporating diplomatic, economic, military, public diplomacy, and intelligence tools." Clarke's memo requested a follow-up cabinet-level meeting to address time-sensitive questions about al Qaeda. But President Bush had downgraded counterterrorism from a cabinet-level job, so Clarke now dealt instead with deputy secretaries.[15]

—Keith Olbermann, political commentator

We *urgently* need . . . a principals level review on the al Qaeda network. . . . [Al Qaeda] is not some narrow little terrorist issue that needs to be included in broader regional policy.[16]

—Richard Clarke, former White House counterterrorism expert

We've certainly established, definitively, that the 9/11 Commission was briefed in a secret session by George Tenet, the former CIA director, the CIA director at the time, that [Rice] was briefed before 9/11 about the possibility of an attack. She said today that it is incomprehensible that she would have ignored such a warning, but it's very clear that she was warned. The interpretation of how she took that—apparently some of the people who were present at the briefing from the CIA felt she did take it very seriously indeed.[17]

—Andrea Mitchell, journalist

[I]n April 2001, Richard Clarke, then the White House counterterrorism adviser, talked about the urgent need to go after bin Laden and the al-Qaeda leadership in Afghanistan, according to Clarke's memoirs. [Paul] Wolfowitz was dismissive. "Well, I just don't understand why we are beginning by talking about this one man, bin Laden," he replied. Wolfowitz tried to switch the subject to "Iraqi terrorism."[18]

—Michael Isikoff and David Corn, journalists

I think it is fair to say that, at the higher level, at the strategic level, there wasn't the level of engagement that you would expect at the most senior levels of the administration on taking down al Qaeda. Richard Clarke teed up a strategy for the administration to take a look at, and, if you will, we stepped in line behind everybody else that had something that needed to be reviewed by the most senior levels of the administration.[19]

—Paul Kurtz, National Security Council

The proposals Clarke developed in the winter of 2000–01 were not given another hearing by top decision makers until late April, and then spent another four months making their laborious way through the bureaucracy before they were readied for approval by President Bush. It is quite true that nobody predicted Sept. 11—that nobody guessed in advance how and when the attacks would come. But other things are true, too. By last summer, many of those in the know—the spooks, the buttoned-down bureaucrats, the law-enforcement professionals in a dozen countries—were almost frantic with worry that a major terrorist attack against American interests was imminent. It wasn't averted because 2001 saw a systematic collapse in the ability of Washington's national-security apparatus to handle the terrorist threat.[20]

—Michael Elliot, journalist

This administration, while it listened to me, either didn't believe me that there was an urgent problem or was unprepared to act as though there were an urgent problem.[21]

—Richard Clarke, White House counterterrorism expert

Great spirits have always encountered opposition from mediocre minds.[22]

—Albert Einstein

I think it is fair to say that, at the higher level, at the strategic level, there wasn't the level of engagement that you would expect at the most senior levels of the administration on taking down al Qaeda.[23]

—Paul Kurtz, National Security Council

Bush had told [journalist] Bob Woodward that his blood was "not so boiling" and he felt no "sense of urgency" about bin Laden before 9/11.[24]

—Phillip Shenon, journalist

[Rice] was warned. I mean, there was a meeting. It was George Tenet, Dick Clarke, another individual from the agency, Cofer Black, and Steve Hadley. [It was] a briefing for Dr. Rice that was similar to a briefing the CIA gave to us in the situation room about a week before, laying out the information, the intelligence, laying out the sense of urgency. And it was pretty much given to Dr. Rice and Steve Hadley in pretty stark terms.[25]

—Roger Cressey, National Security Council

A review of White House records has determined that George J. Tenet, then the director of central intelligence, did brief Condoleezza Rice and other top officials on July 10, 2001, about the looming threat from Al Qaeda, a State Department spokesman said Monday. The account by the spokesman, Sean McCormack, came hours after Ms. Rice, the secretary of state, told reporters aboard her airplane that she did not recall the specific meeting on July 10, noting that she had met repeatedly with Mr. Tenet that summer about terrorist threats. Ms. Rice, the national security adviser at the time, said it was "incomprehensible" to suggest she had ignored dire terrorist threats two months before the Sept. 11 attacks.[26]

—Philip Shenon and Mark Mazzetti, journalists

We agreed that Tenet would insure that the president's daily briefings would continue to be replete with threat information on al Qaeda. President Bush, reading the intelligence every day and noticing that there was a lot about al Qaeda, asked Condi Rice why it was that we couldn't stop "swatting flies" and eliminate al Qaeda. Rice told me about the conversation and asked how the plan to get al Qaeda was coming in the Deputies'

Committee. "It can be presented to the Principals in two days, whenever we can get a meeting," I pressed. Rice promised to get to it soon. Time passed.[27]

—Richard Clarke, former White House counterterrorism expert

I just don't understand why she keeps denying what has actually happened, because there's really—there's no good reason for it. The 9/11 Commission had it right about the summer of 2001 . . . which was there was an overwhelming body of evidence, but there was not that sense of urgency in the West Wing of the White House to be proactive and aggressive in going after al Qaeda and taking proactive steps, and directing the interagency to do so.[28]

—Roger Cressey, National Security Council

On September 4, 2001, the Principals Committee meeting on al Qaeda that I had called for "urgently" on January 25 finally met. . . . Rumsfeld, who looked distracted throughout the session, took the Wolfowitz line that there were other terrorist concerns, like Iraq, and whatever we did on this al Qaeda business, we had to deal with other sources of terrorism.[29]

—Richard Clarke, former White House counterterrorism expert

They didn't give a shit about al-Qaeda. They had priorities. The priorities were lower taxes, ballistic missiles, and the defense thereof.[30]

—Lawrence Wilkerson, chief of staff to Colin Powell

[Clarke testified] how the president and Rice had all but ignored the terrorism threats in 2001. How Rice rebuffed his requests to brief Bush on al-Qaeda throughout that year. How he had been demoted in the first weeks of the presidency. He said that Rice and her deputy Stephen Hadley had seemed determined instead to focus on their "vestigial cold war concerns" like the Anti-Ballistic Missile Treaty with Russia.[31]

—Phillip Shenon, journalist

■ ■ ■

The President did not—not—receive information about the use of airplanes as missiles by suicide bombers. This was a new type of attack that had not been foreseen.[32]

—Ari Fleischer, former Bush press secretary

Ari Fleischer, the White House spokesman, said Friday that the title of the president's intelligence brief that day was "Bin Laden Determined to Strike the United States."[33]

—Bob Drogin, journalist

In addition, a new controversy flared yesterday about a classified presidential briefing delivered to Bush on Aug. 6, 2001. The briefing, titled "Bin Laden Determined to Strike

Inside U.S.," has long been characterized by Rice and other Bush officials as a historical summary of suspected al Qaeda plots. But several Democratic commissioners said in yesterday's hearing that the briefing also includes significant details about suspected al Qaeda sleeper cells and their plans to carry out domestic hijackings.[34]

—Dan Eggen and Walter Pincus, journalists

Rice's news conference came eight months after the attacks. Yet she was suggesting that in all that time, no one had bothered to tell her that there were indeed several reports prepared within the CIA, the FAA, and elsewhere in the government about the threat of planes as missiles. Was she really suggesting that no one informed her that in the Moussaoui case, an FBI agent had warned specifically in August 2001 that he might be involved in a plot to "crash a plane into the World Trade Center?" Had no one told her in all those months that the Department of Defense had conducted drills for the possibility of a plane-as-missile attack on the Pentagon? Had she forgotten that when she and Bush attended the G-8 summit in Italy in July 2001, the airspace was closed because of the threat of an aerial suicide attack by al-Qaeda?[35]

—Phillip Shenon, journalist

Condoleezza Rice, President Bush's national security adviser, testified Thursday that Mr. Bush was warned a month before the Sept. 11 terror attacks that the FBI had detected "suspicious activity" that suggested terrorists might be planning a domestic hijacking. She said he was also told that the bureau was conducting 70 investigations of possible terrorist cells connected to Al Qaeda operating within American borders.[36]

—Phillip Shenon, journalist

Isn't it a fact, Dr. Rice, that the August 6 PDB warned against possible attacks in this country? And I ask whether you recall the title of that PDB?

—Richard Ben-Veniste, 9/11 Commission member

I believe the title was, "Bin Laden Determined to Attack Inside the United States."[37]

—Condoleezza Rice

[Rice] acknowledged that the August 6 intelligence briefing that said that Islamic militants in bin Laden's camp might hijack American airlines.[38]

—Frank Rich, columnist

From what they had learned about the PDB, the [9/11] commission's staff knew that Rice had been misstating its contents for the better part of a year. They knew that despite her claims, it did contain some fresh intelligence in 2001 to suggest an ongoing al-Qaeda hijacking plot, possibly one directed at buildings in New York. . . . In hindsight, the transcript is a remarkable document. To many of the commission's staff, it offered proof of how, to Condoleezza Rice, everything is semantics. A threat is not a threat, a warning is not a warning, unless she says it is.[39]

—Phillip Shenon, journalist

We went into a period in June [2001] where the tempo of intelligence about an impending large-scale attack went up a lot, to the kind of cycle that we'd only seen once or twice before. And we told Condi that. She didn't do anything. She said, Well, make sure you're coordinating with the agencies, which, of course, I was doing. By August, I was saying to Condi and to the agencies that the intelligence isn't coming in at such a rapid rate anymore as it was in the June-July time frame. But that doesn't mean the attack isn't going to happen. It just means that they may be in place.[40]

—Richard Clarke, former White House counterterrorism expert

To my knowledge there was no warning, no alert as to suicide attackers in airplanes.[41]

—Donald Rumsfeld

Make no mistake about it, if we had known that the enemy was going to fly airplanes into our buildings, we would have done everything in our power to stop it.[42]

—George W. Bush

In fact, the 9/11 Commission reported, U.S. intelligence had picked up a dozen plots of a similar sort, over a period from 1994 to pre-9/11 2001, with some of them specifically mentioning the World Trade Center and the White House as potential targets. In the weeks before 9/11, the CIA had learned that in Afghanistan "everyone is talking about an impending attack."[43]

—Frank Rich, columnist

[President Bush] did not recall discussing the August 6 report with the attorney general, or whether Rice had done so.[44]

—9/11 Commission report

We have found no indication of any further discussion before September 11 among the President and his top advisers of the possibility of a threat of an al Qaeda attack in the United States. DCI Tenet visited President Bush in Crawford, Texas, on August 17 and participated in PDB briefings of the President between August 31 (after the President had returned to Washington) and September 10. But Tenet does not recall any discussions with the President of the domestic threat during this period.[45]

—9/11 Commission report

The significant problems we have cannot be solved at the same level of thinking with which we created them.[46]

—Albert Einstein

What I want to say to my Democratic friends in the Congress is they need to be very cautious not to seek political advantage by making incendiary suggestions as were made by some today that the White House had advance information that would have prevented the tragic attacks of 9/11. Such commentary is thoroughly irresponsible and totally unworthy of national leaders in a time of war.[47]

—Dick Cheney

[I]nconvenient truths do not go away just because they are not seen. Indeed, when they are not responded to, their significance doesn't diminish; it grows. For example, the administration was warned on August 6, 2001, of an attack by al-Qaeda. "Bin Ladin Determined To Strike in US," said the intelligence community in a message so important that it was the headline of the president's daily briefing that day, five weeks before the attacks of September 11. Didn't he see that clear warning? Why were no questions asked, meetings called, evidence marshaled, clarifications sought?[48]

—Al Gore

The Bush administration came under pressure on Thursday to make public the full classified version of a report from the 9/11 commission that is critical of the government's failure to heed aviation threats before the attacks on the World Trade Center and the Pentagon. . . . [C]ommission members said the administration blocked their efforts to release the report. . . . In a letter on Thursday, Representative Henry A. Waxman . . . asked that the report be made public and called for a Congressional hearing into whether the administration had "misused the classification process" to withhold it.[49]

—Eric Lichtblau, journalist

Top officials of the Bush and Clinton administrations defended their efforts against terrorism Tuesday before the national commission investigating the Sept. 11, 2001, attacks after the panel reported that they had missed diplomatic and military opportunities to capture or kill Osama bin Laden. . . . President Bush, responding directly for the first time to the accusations, told reporters he had acted against terrorism as soon as he had sufficient information.[50]

—George Edmonson, journalist

After five years of skirting even the most inarguable fact that he was president on 9/11, [President Bush] must bear some responsibility for his and our un-readiness. Mr. Bush has now moved on, unmistakably and without conscience or shame, towards rewriting history, and attempting to make the responsibility entirely Mr. Clinton's. . . . To enforce the lies of the present, it is necessary to erase the truths of the past.[51]

—Keith Olbermann, political commentator

Who controls the past controls the future; who controls the present controls the past.[52]

—George Orwell

—6—

Iraq: Stacking the Deck

Of course the people don't want war. . . . But after all it is the leaders
of the country who determine the policy, and it is always a simple matter
to drag the people along, whether it is a democracy, or a fascist dictatorship,
or a parliament, or a communist dictatorship. . . . Voice or no voice, the people
can always be brought to the bidding of the leaders. That is easy. All you have
to do is to tell them they are being attacked, and denounce the pacifists for
lack of patriotism and exposing the country to danger.[1]
—Hermann Göring, Nazi Party leader

In the fall of 2002, Bush and his White House were engaging in a carefully orchestrated campaign to shape and manipulate sources of public approval to our advantage. We'd done much the same on other issues—tax cuts and education—to great success. But war with Iraq was different. Beyond the irreversible human costs and the substantial financial price, the decision to go to war and the way we went about selling it would ultimately lead to increased polarization and intensified partisan warfare. Our lack of candor and honesty in making the case for war would later provoke a partisan response from our opponents that, in its own way, further distorted and obscured a more nuanced reality. Another cycle of deception would cloud the public's ability to see larger, underlying important truths that are critical to understand in order to avoid the same problems in the future.[2]

—Scott McClellan, former Bush press secretary

A PRE-DETERMINED WAR

My father had all this political capital built up when he drove the Iraqis out of Kuwait and he wasted it. If I have a chance to invade, if I had that much capital, I'm not going to waste it.[3]

—George W. Bush

"He was thinking about invading Iraq in 1999," said author and journalist Mickey Herskowitz. "It was on his mind." . . . Herskowitz said that Bush expressed frustration at a lifetime as an underachiever in the shadow of an accomplished father. In aggressive military action, he saw the opportunity to emerge from his father's shadow.[4]

—Russ Baker, journalist

Well before Bush 43 took office, they had become fixated on Iraq, though for reasons having much to do with their ideas about realigning the states in the Middle East and little or nothing to do with the stateless terrorism of Al Qaeda. Mr. Bush had specifically disdained such interventionism when running against Al Gore, but he embraced the cause once in office. While others might have had cavils—American military commanders testified before Congress about their already overtaxed troops and equipment in March 2002—the path was clear for a war in Iraq to serve as the political Viagra Mr. Rove needed for the election year.[5]

—Frank Rich, columnist

Rove was the first administration official to publicly make the case for using the war as a partisan issue, a marked shift in tone from Bush's repeated emphasis on unity and bipartisanship in confronting and defeating radical Islamic terrorism.[6]

—Scott McClellan, former Bush press secretary

The first sign of the Bush administration's desire to attack Iraq comes days *before* Bush's 2001 inauguration. Dick Cheney asks outgoing Defense Secretary Bill Cohen to brief the president "about Iraq and different options."[7]

—Bob Woodward, journalist

Iraq was part of the reason the White House had paid so little attention to al-Qaeda terrorist threats in the northern spring and summer of 2001, [Sen. Max] Cleland believed. Bush was targeting a different enemy, the one in Baghdad that his father had failed to overthrow.[8]

—Phillip Shenon, journalist

They were focused on Iraq, they were planning a war on Iraq, they were not paying attention to the business at hand.[9]

—Sen. Max Cleland

The policy was set. The war in Iraq was coming. And they were looking for intelligence to fit into the policy, to justify the policy.[10]

—Tyler Drumheller, CIA

The conclusion that I ultimately came to was that this was a matter of, as I've called it, faith-based intelligence. Instead of our leadership forming conclusions based on a careful reading of the intelligence we provided them, they already had their conclusion to start out with, and they were cherry-picking the information that we provided to use whatever pieces of it that fit their overall interpretation. Worse than that, they were dropping qualifiers and distorting some of the information that we provided to make it seem more alarmist and more dangerous than the information that we were giving them.[11]

—Greg Theilmann, State Department intelligence

In April 2002—nearly a year *before* the invasion of Iraq—CIA case officers stationed all over Europe were ordered to attend a special conference in Rome, during which officials from CIA's Iraq Operations Group casually told the assembled CIA officers that Iraq had been on the Bush agenda from the very beginning.[12]

—James Risen, journalist

From the very beginning, there was a conviction that Saddam Hussein was a bad person and that he needed to go.[13]

—Paul O'Neill, former Secretary of the Treasury

In response to a Bush directive, General Tommy Franks, commander of the U.S. Central Command, was already drawing up invasion plans. And Cheney was asking questions at the CIA that indicated he expected the United States to invade Iraq.[14]

—Michael Isikoff and David Corn, journalists

[N]umerous key Bush officials . . . were advocating an invasion of Iraq in order to depose Saddam for *years prior to 9/11*, and they simply seized on the terrorist attack as the principal justification for a war they had long desired.[15]

—Glenn Greenwald, lawyer/journalist

But for others in the Administration, getting rid of Saddam Hussein and his regime had been a major priority since the end of the first Gulf War. Several of the people who signed [a] 1998 open letter to Clinton urging American support for Iraqi insurgents had taken positions of authority in the Bush Administration, including Defense Secretary Donald Rumsfeld; his deputy, Paul Wolfowitz; and Douglas Feith, an undersecretary of defense policy.[16]

—Seymour Hersh, journalist

There was probably an unbroken line at least from September 11, 2001, *and probably from Bush's inauguration*, to the day the bombs started to fall on Baghdad.[17]

—Tyler Drumheller, CIA

[F]rom the first weeks of the administration they were talking about Iraq. I just found it a little disgusting that they were talking about it while the bodies were still burning in the Pentagon and at the World Trade Center.[18]

—Richard Clarke, former White House counterterrorism expert

[A]t the first NSC meeting of his presidency, Bush had said his focus would be in Iraq. . . . "Sometimes a show of force by one side can really clarify things."[19]

—Ron Suskind, journalist

He turned to Rice. "So, Condi, what are we going to talk about today? What's on the agenda?" "How Iraq is destabilizing the region, Mr. President," Rice said, in what several observers understood was a scripted exchange.[20]

—Richard Clarke, former White House counterterrorism expert

"Stability" wasn't their *goal* it was their *target*. They saw it as synonymous with stagnation. They wanted radical change in the Mideast. They were determined to drain the swamp—that is, to alter the political climate of the region so that it would no longer be so hospitable to the terrorists inhabiting it.[21]

—Thomas Ricks, journalist

The opening premise, that Saddam's regime was destabilizing the region, and the vivid possibility that he owned weapons of mass destruction—a grainy picture, perhaps misleading, but visceral—pushed analysis toward logistics: the need for better intelligence, for ways to tighten the net around the regime, for use of the U.S. Military to support Iraqi insurgents in a coup.[22]

—Ron Suskind, journalist

Getting Hussein was now the administration's focus, that much was already clear.[23]

—Paul O'Neill, former Secretary of the Treasury

Actual plans, to O'Neill's astonishment, were already being discussed to take over Iraq and occupy it—complete with disposition of oil fields, peacekeeping forces, and war crimes tribunals—carrying forward an unspoken doctrine of preemptive war.[24]

—Ron Suskind, journalist

The administration of the second George Bush did begin with Iraq on its agenda.[25]

—Richard Clarke, former White House counterterrorism expert

The idea of going after Iraq was U.S. policy. It was going to happen one way or the other.[26]

—Tyler Drumheller, CIA

[I]n the summer *before* [emphasis added] 9/11, the word came down from the top brass: we're ramping up on Iraq.[27]

—Michael Isikoff and David Corn, journalists

Bush had indicated in a major campaign speech delivered at the Citadel military academy in 1999 [that] he wished to create a more mobile and lethal force that wouldn't take the six months to assemble that his father's gulf war had required. It was an early sign, missed by most, that Bush already had Saddam Hussein on his mind.[28]

—Jacob Heilbrunn, writer

[Scooter] Libby worked with Cheney when he was Secretary of Defense under Bush I, and while at the Defense Department he assisted his former Yale professor Paul Wolfowitz in drafting a defense policy guidance paper calling for unilaterally preemptive wars and the invasion of Iraq—a decade *before* [emphasis added] the 9/11 terror attacks.[29]

—John Dean, former White House counsel

For a quarter-century, [Libby] has been affiliated in and out of government with Dick Cheney, Paul Wolfowitz and Donald Rumsfeld, forming the nucleus of a neoconservative fraternity that wanted to project unchallengeable American power across the globe. The group aspired, even *before* its return to power with the second President Bush, to liberate Iraq from Saddam Hussein and turn it into a democratic bastion that might stabilize the Middle East and safeguard oil supplies and routes.[30]

—Max Frankel, editor

The philosophy or the theory behind this change that this liberation would cause a rising up and a drive for democracy in the Middle East—it didn't square with the way the culture or the way the thinking and the situation that we had seen in my time.[31]

—Gen. Anthony Zinni

Zinni's concern deepened at a Senate hearing in February, just six weeks before the war began. As he awaited his turn to testify, he listened to Pentagon and State Department officials talk vaguely about the "uncertainties" of a postwar Iraq. He began to think they were doing the wrong thing the wrong way. "I was listening to the panel, and I realized, 'These guys don't have a clue.'"[32]

—Thomas Ricks, journalist

With Bush and his Cabinet members obviously focused on (or perhaps obsessed with) Saddam and Iraq, everyone in the intelligence community, from Tenet on down, realized it was crucial to do whatever they could—probe every corner, chase any lead—to penetrate Saddam's Iraq.[33]

—Michael Isikoff and David Corn, journalists

Why didn't anybody say anything before the war [about how weak the intelligence was]? I did. And I can tell you it was hard, because nobody wanted to hear it, and they made it very clear that they didn't want to hear it.[34]

—Tyler Drumheller, CIA

The line between the Bush national security team's preexisting desire to see Saddam gone and a new emphasis on acting against real and growing threats before they are imminent was quickly disappearing.[35]

—Scott McClellan, former Bush press secretary

Preparations for war with Iraq are not yet publicly acknowledged, but earlier in the spring, as Condoleezza Rice discusses diplomatic initiatives involving Iraq with several senators, Bush pokes his head into the room and says, "Fuck Saddam. We're taking him out."[36]

—Cullen Murphy and Todd Purdum, journalists

I'm going to kick his sorry motherfucking ass all over the Mideast.[37]

—George W. Bush

9/11 OPENS THE DOOR

[T]hey certainly thought they needed a triggering event to get a lot of their policies that they had been developing for years, the neo-conservatives saw this as an opportunity. It was already in the drawers. They just opened them and used 9/11 to push everything through. And it became a very willing public, a very willing Congress. And they were ready.[38]

—John Dean, former White House counsel

I expected to go back to a round of meetings [after September 11] examining what the next attacks could be, what our vulnerabilities were, what we could do about them in the short term. Instead, I walked into a series of discussions about Iraq. At first I was incredulous that we were talking about something other than getting Al Qaeda. Then I realized with almost a sharp physical pain that Rumsfeld and Wolfowitz were going to try to take advantage of this national tragedy to promote their agenda about Iraq. Since the beginning of the administration, indeed *well before*, they had been pressing for a war with Iraq.[39]

—Richard Clarke, former White House counterterrorism expert

Hours after the Sept. 11 attacks, Donald Rumsfeld asks Pentagon colleagues about the possibility of striking Saddam Hussein. An aide records in his notes: "hit S.H. @ same time—not only UBL [Usama Bin Laden]."[40]

—Bob Woodward, journalist

[Pentagon adviser Richard Perle] said to me, "Iraq has to pay a price for what happened yesterday, they bear responsibility." It's September the 12th. I've got the manifest with me that tells me al Qaeda did this. Nothing in my head that says there is any Iraqi involvement in this in any way, shape or form and I remember thinking to myself, as I'm about to go brief the president, "What the hell is he talking about?"[41]

—George Tenet

There was never any rigorous talk about this sweeping idea that seemed to be driving all the specific actions, [Paul] O'Neill said, echoing the comments of several other participants in the NSC discussions. From the start, we were building the case against Hussein and looking at how we could take him out and change Iraq into a new country. And, if we did that, it would solve everything. It was all about finding *a way to do it*. That was the tone of it. The President saying, "Fine. Go find me a way to do this."[42]

—Ron Suskind, journalist

On the morning of the 12th DOD's focus was already beginning to shift from al Qaeda. CIA was explicit now that al Qaeda was guilty of the attacks, but Paul Wolfowitz, Rumsfeld's deputy, was not persuaded. It was too sophisticated and complicated an operation, they said, for a terrorist group to have pulled off by itself, without a state sponsor—Iraq must have been helping them.[43]

—Richard Clarke, former White House counterterrorism expert

Bush's top terrorism official, Richard Clarke, disclosed that on the *day after* 9/11, Rumsfeld was expressly urging a military attack on Iraq. On the same day, Bush himself instructed Clarke to search for links between Iraq and Al Qaeda: "Iraq! Saddam! Find out if there's a connection," Clarke quotes Bush as ordering.[44]

—Glenn Greenwald, lawyer/journalist

On September 12th, I left the Video Conferencing Center and there, wandering alone around the situation room, was the President. He looked like he wanted something to do. He grabbed a few of us and closed the door to the conference room. "Look," he told us, "I know you have a lot to do and all . . . but I want you, as soon as you can, to go back over everything, everything. See if Saddam did this. See if he's linked in any way." I was once again taken aback, incredulous, and it showed. "But, Mr. President, Al Qaeda did this." "I know, I know, but—see if Saddam was involved. Just look. I want to know any shred. . . ." "Absolutely, we will look-again." I was trying to be more respectful, more responsive. "But you know, we have looked several times for state sponsorship of Al Qaeda and not found any real linkages to Iraq. Iran plays a little, as does Pakistan, and Saudi Arabia, Yemen." "Look into Iraq, Saddam," the president said testily and left us.[45]

—Richard Clarke, former White House counterterrorism expert

[At the post-9/11 War Cabinet meeting, after some discussion of Afghanistan, deputy defense secretary Paul Wolfowitz] turned the focus to Iraq. Afghanistan could develop into a mess, with U.S. troops mired in the country's remote mountains, seeking elusive al-Qaeda cells. Iraq, on the other hand, was a corrupt, anti-American regime waiting to be toppled. Though intelligence coming from inside Iraq continued to be thin, the Defense and State Departments, responding to the president's intense interest in Saddam Hussein, had produced dozens of reports since January on what might be done to oust Saddam and the Baathist regime.[46]

—Ron Suskind, journalist

[Y]ou have this know-it-all [Wolfowitz] who won't believe the intelligence community, and won't believe that nonstate actors can do this much damage. . . . There are two types of villains in Washington, hacks and fools. He isn't a hack. He's deeply misguided, he's impervious to evidence—and he's a serious, thoughtful guy.[47]

—anonymous source

[Bob Woodward] wrote that Rumsfeld's influential deputy, Paul Wolfowitz, wanted to target Iraq right after 9/11—not because of any certainty of a connection between Saddam and Al Qaeda, but because "war against Iraq may be easier than against Afghanistan."[48]

—Frank Rich, columnist

By the afternoon on Wednesday, Secretary Rumsfeld was talking about broadening the objectives of our response and "getting Iraq." Having been attacked by al-Qaeda, for us now to go bombing Iraq in response would be like our invading Mexico after the Japanese attacked us at Pearl Harbor.[49]

—Richard Clarke, former White House counterterrorism expert

I thought what Wolfowitz was asserting about Iraq was a reach, and I think others in the room did, too. It was like changing the subject—Iraq is not where bin Laden is and not where there's trouble. I was mystified. It's like a bookbinder accidentally dropping a chapter from one book into the middle of another one. The chapter is coherent, in its way, but it doesn't seem to fit in this book.[50]

—Paul O'Neill, former Secretary of the Treasury

After 9/11, Army war games involving Iraq began in earnest.[51]

—James Fallows, journalist

[W]ithin hours after the attack of September 11, 2001, Secretary Rumsfeld was busy attempting to find a way to link Saddam Hussein with the attack.[52]

—Al Gore

A military planner inside the Pentagon later told me that on September 13 his group was asked to draw up scenarios for an assault on Iraq, not just Afghanistan.[53]

—James Fallows, journalist

On Sept. 14, 2001, in a widely hailed appearance amid the still-smoking rubble of ground zero in Lower Manhattan, President Bush told rescue workers that "the people who knocked these buildings down will hear all of us soon." He was answered with chants of, "U.S.A.! U.S.A.!" But the administration's eye was already on Iraq. That's the war the president and his cronies wanted. It didn't matter that Saddam Hussein and Iraq had had nothing to do with Sept. 11. Iraq is where the bulk of our combat forces and most of the money and other resources would be committed. . . . From the very beginning, the so-called war on terror was viewed by the Bush crowd as a magical smoke screen, a political gift from the gods that could be endlessly manipulated to justify all kinds of policies and behavior—including the senseless war in Iraq—that otherwise would never have been tolerated by the American people. . . . The invasion of Iraq was not about terror. It was about oil and schoolboy fantasies of empire and whatever weird oedipal dynamics were at work in the Bush family.[54]

—Bob Herbert, columnist

A few days later, similar findings were also included in a much-hurried National Intelligence Estimate on Iraq's weapons of mass destruction—an analysis that hadn't been done in years, as the intelligence community had deemed it unnecessary and the White House hadn't requested it.[55]

—Charles Lewis and Mark Reading-Smith, Center for Public Integrity

To [Gen. Greg] Newbold and many others, Iraq seemed irrelevant to the problems America faced, and besides, things there appeared largely under control; Saddam Hussein had been more or less handcuffed through sanctions and other diplomatic measures. Yet here was a sign, one of several, that Saddam, and not Osama bin Laden or Mullah Omar, was most on the Bush administration's mind.[56]

—David Margolick, journalist

Of far greater concern to [Gen. Newbold] was the headlong rush to war in Iraq. It was apparent early on—from two or three days after 9/11, when, with the smoke from the smoldering Pentagon still in the air, Newbold told Douglas Feith, the undersecretary of defense for policy, of plans to go into Afghanistan. "Why are you going into Afghanistan?" he says Feith replied. "We ought to be going after Iraq." . . . It simply isn't possible now, says Newbold, to fathom how "extraordinarily inappropriate" Feith's comments sounded at the time. Then, at a meeting a few months later, as the Americans chased the leadership of al-Qaeda, he says, he heard Wolfowitz say essentially the same thing. In each instance, Newbold's reaction was the same: "Who cares about Iraq? We have this three-penny dictator, this bantam rooster of no consequence. Besides, they're quiet now anyway—who cares?"[57]

—David Margolick, journalist

The White House has always seemed less compelled to capture Osama than to use him as a pretext for invading Iraq and as a political selling point.[58]

—Maureen Dowd, columnist

"It was like they were hoping we'd find something buried in the files or come back with a different answer," Michael Sulick, deputy chief of the CIA's Directorate of Operations, later said. There was no "obvious pressure" by Cheney and Libby to change the answers, Sulick recalled. But the barrage of questions and the frequent visits by the vice president had created an environment that was subtly, but unmistakably, influencing the agency's work. The CIA's analysts, Sulick believed, had become "overly eager to please."[59]

—Michael Isikoff and David Corn, journalists

"It became a personality issue," a Pentagon consultant said of the Bush Administration's handling of intelligence. "My fact is better than your fact. The whole thing is a failure of process. Nobody goes to primary sources."[60]

—Seymour Hersh, journalist

Four days after the attacks, the president and his national security team met at Camp David to discuss the response to 9/11. The briefing material that Rumsfeld and Wolfowitz brought offered three targets in the war on terrorism: al Qaeda, Afghanistan's Taliban and Iraq. But only Wolfowitz pressed the case that day for attacking Iraq. Wolfowitz's advocacy of attacking Iraq in response to 9/11 stemmed from the same views that later led him to underestimate the strength of the Iraqi insurgency, said a person who reviewed the Pentagon briefing materials.[61]

—Thomas Ricks, journalist

It is one thing to show a man that he is in an error, and another to put him in possession of the truth.[62]

—John Locke

Ten days after the September 11, 2001, terrorist attacks on the World Trade Center and the Pentagon, President Bush was told in a highly classified briefing that the U.S. intelligence community had no evidence linking the Iraqi regime of Saddam Hussein to the attacks and that there was scant credible evidence that Iraq had any significant collaborative ties with Al Qaeda, according to government records and current and former officials with firsthand knowledge of the matter. The information was provided to Bush on September 21, 2001 during the "President's Daily Brief," a 30- to 45-minute early-morning national security briefing.[63]

—Murray Waas, journalist

■ ■ ■

The vice president's limousine sped through downtown Washington and headed over the Potomac River on its way to Langley, Virginia. It was days after Bush's outburst, and Dick Cheney was making another of his visits to CIA headquarters. These trips—unknown to the public at this point—had become the talk of the intelligence community. Cheney would arrive at agency headquarters and park himself in Director George Tenet's seventh-floor conference room. Then officers and analysts would be summoned

to brief him—on Iraq and other matters—and often encounter a withering interrogation. How do we know this? What more do you have on that? What have you done to
follow up?[64]

—Michael Isikoff and David Corn, journalists

The analysts at the CIA were beaten down defending their assessments. I've never seen
a government like this.[65]

—CIA official

Cheney was a steamroller. He pressured for the invasion of Iraq. . . . All of Cheney's
evaluations never got really tested by other people. This idea of whispering in the ear, I
think, in any large institution is a disaster.[66]

—Bob Woodward, journalist

During these sessions, Cheney demanded answers on Iraq. Cheney had long-standing
and firm views on Saddam Hussein that went back to when he had served as secretary of
defense during the first Persian Gulf War.[67]

—Michael Isikoff and David Corn, journalists

The problem for the hard-liners was that the CIA was the keeper of the vast majority
of classified intelligence on al Qaeda, and the agency's analysts had seen no evidence of
Iraqi involvement in 9/11 and had no conclusive proof of a terrorist alliance between
Saddam Hussein and Osama bin Laden. Those answers did not satisfy Wolfowitz, or his
equally certain lieutenant, Undersecretary of Defense for Policy Doug Feith.[68]

—James Risen, journalist

Vice President Cheney and his most senior aide made multiple trips to the CIA over
the past year to question analysts studying Iraq's weapons programs and alleged links
to al Qaeda, creating an environment in which some analysts felt they were being pressured to make their assessments fit with the Bush administration's policy objectives,
according to senior intelligence officials. With Cheney taking the lead in the administration last August in advocating military action against Iraq by claiming it had weapons of
mass destruction, the visits by the vice president and his chief of staff, I. Lewis "Scooter"
Libby, "sent signals, intended or otherwise, that a certain output was desired from here,"
one senior agency official said yesterday.[69]

—Walter Pincus and Dana Priest, journalists

According to a former high-level CIA official, however, Cheney was dissatisfied with the
response, and asked the agency to review the matter once again. It was the beginning of
what turned out to be a year-long tug-of-war between the CIA and the Vice President's
office. . . . Senior CIA analysts dealing with Iraq were constantly being urged by the
Vice-President's office to provide worst-case assessments on Iraqi weapons issues. "They

got pounded on, day after day," one senior Bush Administration official told me, and received no consistent backup from Tenet and his senior staff. "Pretty soon you say 'Fuck it.'" And they began to provide the intelligence that was wanted.[70]

—Seymour Hersh, journalist

Cheney was not posing the sort of questions a policy maker would need answered in order to determine whether Iraq posed a threat to the United States. He was not seeking information on *whether* Saddam was dangerous because he possessed weapons of mass destruction. He was not soliciting material that would help him decide if an invasion of Iraq was absolutely necessary. His queries were all pegged to the assumption that Iraq would be invaded.[71]

—Michael Isikoff and David Corn, journalists

Something had gone wrong in the analysis, that in some cases we were looking for what we needed to see—what we, and everyone else, knew the White House wanted us to see—and not always what was really there.[72]

—Jon Moseman, chief of staff to George Tenet

Men to a great extent believe what they want to.[73]

—Oliver Wendell Holmes Jr., U.S. Supreme Court

[T]he initial impulse for war may have had little to do with Iraq itself. . . . [A]dministration officials seem to have viewed Iraq as a kind of abstract proving ground for their pet theories about warfare, terrorism or democratization. They saw the Iraq they wanted to see.[74]

—Jacob Heilbrunn, writer

[S]ome CIA officers later griped that Tenet had gotten too close to the White House, that he had acted as if he were still a congressional staffer overly concerned with pleasing his employer—in this case, the president.[75]

—Michael Isikoff and David Corn, journalists

George Tenet came out of politics, not intelligence. His whole modus operandi was to please the Principal. We got stuck with all sorts of things. This is really the legacy of a Director who never said no to anybody.[76]

—Tyler Drumheller, CIA

[T]he intelligence used by the White House to make its case for war was stretched beyond recognition, distorted, and misrepresented. And in every case, when the evidence was questioned, there was a determined disinterest in learning the truth. On the contrary, there was an inflexible insistence on carrying out preconceived policies regardless of the evidence. First the verdict, then the trial.[77]

—Al Gore

Truth is the American bottom line. Truth above all is fundamental to who we are. It is no accident that among the first words of the first declaration of our national existence it is proclaimed: "We hold these truths to be self-evident. . . ."[78]

—Sen. John Kerry

■ ■ ■

[By January 2002] with victory in Afghanistan, the administration focus was returning to Iraq—with Rumsfeld and Wolfowitz pointing to the ease with which the Taliban had fallen of how doable Iraq would be.[79]

—Ron Suskind, journalist

In his first State of the Union address, on January 29, 2002, President Bush said that Iraq, Iran, and North Korea were an "axis of evil" that threatened world peace.[80]

—James Fallows, journalist

The enemy of the moment always represented absolute evil, and it followed that any past or future agreement with him was impossible.[81]

—George Orwell

By portraying the invasion of Iraq as the central front in an epic struggle between good and evil, President Bush sought to cloak his policy of unprovoked war in the garb of religious faith.[82]

—Al Gore

By seeking weapons of mass destruction, these regimes pose a grave and growing danger. They could provide these arms to terrorists, giving them the means to match their hatred. They could attack our allies or attempt to blackmail the United States.[83]

—George W. Bush

Error is none the better for being common, nor truth the worse for having lain neglected.[84]

—John Locke

"Saddam is evil" is not enough. A number of people are evil, and some are even our friends. "Saddam has weapons of mass destruction." A number of countries do. What the people need to know is hard data to demonstrate conclusively that Saddam has weapons of mass destruction and which he is readying to use on the people of the U.S. or the people of the West.[85]

—Peggy Noonan, columnist

By the time of this speech efforts were afoot not simply to remove Saddam Hussein but also to imagine what Iraq would be like when he was gone. In late October of 2001, while the U.S. military was conducting its rout of the Taliban from Afghanistan, the State Department had quietly begun its planning for the aftermath of a "transition" in Iraq.[86]

—James Fallows, journalist

Already by February, the talk was mostly about logistics. Not the why, but the how and how quickly. Rumsfeld, [Paul] O'Neill recalled, was focused on how an incident might cause escalated tensions—like the shooting down of an American plane in the regular engagements between U.S. fighters and Iraqi antiaircraft batteries—and what U.S. responses to such an occurrence might be. Wolfowitz was pushing for the arming of Iraqi opposition groups and sending in U.S. troops to support and defend their insurgency. He had written in Foreign Affairs magazine in 1999 that "the United States should be prepared to commit ground forces to protect a sanctuary in southern Iraq where the opposition could safely mobilize."[87]

—Ron Suskind, journalist

Bush and his aides were looking for intelligence not to guide their policy on Iraq but to market it. The intelligence would be the basis not for launching a war but for selling it.[88]

—Michael Isikoff and David Corn, journalists

The problem was that many of the important issues, like terrorism, like Iraq, were laced with important subtlety and nuance. These issues need analysis and Bush and his inner circle had no real interest in complicated analyses; on the issues that they cared about, they already knew the answers, it was received wisdom.[89]

—Richard Clarke, former White House counterterrorism expert

In November 2002, CIA station chiefs from all over the Middle East gathered in London for a secret meeting at the United States Embassy. They had been summoned by senior CIA officials from headquarters to a conference inside the CIA station spaces in Grosvenor Square. This was to be a come-to-Jesus meeting, one in which officials from headquarters would make it clear that it was time for skeptics among them to drop their reluctance to engage on Iraq. War was just a few months away. Of course, the official position of the Bush administration was that it was still open to all diplomatic options and that war with Iraq was not inevitable.[90]

—James Risen, journalist

The campaign to sell the war didn't begin in earnest until the fall of 2002. But, as I would later come to learn, President Bush had decided to confront the Iraqi regime several months earlier.[91]

—Scott McClellan, former Bush press secretary

CONFLATING 9/11 WITH IRAQ

[T]he Bush administration had repeatedly tied the Iraq war to September 11—insinuating in some people's minds a link between Iraq and the attacks themselves. . . . [A]t different junctures a majority of Americans believed that Saddam Hussein was involved in 9/11.[92]

—Thomas Kean and Lee Hamilton, 9/11 Commission cochairs

The nonexistent al Qaeda–Saddam tie-in was as much a selling point for the war as the nonexistent WMD The salesmanship was so merciless that half the country was brainwashed into believing that the 9/11 hijackers had been Iraqis.[93]

—Frank Rich, columnist

The Administration's manipulation and distortion of the intelligence about Iraq's ties to Al Qaeda and its national security threat to the United States was anything but a secret in Washington.[94]

—Seymour Hersh, journalist

The war was sold by a brilliant and fear-fueled White House propaganda campaign designed to stampede a nation still shellshocked by 9/11.[95]

—Frank Rich, columnist

The Iraqi regime possesses biological and chemical weapons, is rebuilding the facilities to make more and, according to the British government, could launch a biological or chemical attack in as little as 45 minutes after the order is given.[96]

—George W. Bush

In September 2002, Bush tells the press that Iraq can launch a biological or chemical attack within 45 minutes—an assertion that the CIA finds completely phony. Director George Tenet refers to it as the "they-can-attack-in-45-minutes shit."[97]

—Bob Woodward, journalist

Bush and his aides, [CIA Middle East officer Paul] Pillar argued, had engaged in the selective use of intelligence to create the "impression of an alliance" between Saddam and bin Laden. There was, he said, a steady flow of "rhetorical coupling" in which Bush administration officials repeatedly mentioned Iraq and 9/11 in the same breath.[98]

—Michael Isikoff and David Corn, journalists

There was almost a concern we'd find something that would slow up the war.[99]

—Tyler Drumheller, CIA

The administration used intelligence not to inform decision-making, but to justify a decision already made.[100]

—Paul Pillar, CIA

They wanted to begin with new paradigms (which just happened to reflect their policy preferences and inclinations) and then work backward to see if there might be evidence to support these theses. This was the opposite of how intelligence analysis traditionally operated: start with the available evidence (as fragmentary and contradictory as it might be) and build upward.[101]

—Michael Isikoff and David Corn, journalists

This was not an unfortunate misreading of the available evidence, causing a mistaken linkage between al Qaeda and Iraq. No, this was something else: a willful choice to make a specific linkage, whether evidence existed to support it or not. When he was preparing to invade Iraq, President Bush repeatedly gave the clear impression that Iraq was an ally and partner to the terrorist group that attacked us, al-Qaeda. In fact, not long after the attacks of 9/11, President Bush made a decision to start mentioning Osama bin Laden and Saddam Hussein in the same breath, in a cynical mantra designed to fuse them together as one in the public's mind. He repeatedly used this device in a highly disciplined manner to create a false impression in the minds of the American people that Saddam Hussein was responsible for 9/11.[102]

—Al Gore

What global terrorist networks do you believe that Iraq has relationships with this? Is al Qaeda one of those terrorist networks?

—unidentified reporter

Sure. We're not on the ground down there, but are there al Qaeda in Iraq? Yes.[103]

—Donald Rumsfeld

In fact, an assessment issued that same month by the Defense Intelligence Agency (and confirmed weeks later by CIA Director Tenet) found an absence of "compelling evidence demonstrating direct cooperation between the government of Iraq and Al Qaeda." What's more, an earlier DIA assessment said that "the nature of the regime's relationship with Al Qaeda is unclear."[104]

—Charles Lewis and Mark Reading-Smith, Center for Public Integrity

"It is hard for people outside the agency to understand how little we were thinking about Iraq," recalled one top intelligence official. The CIA's lack of focus on Iraq—and in particular, the agency's failure to see Saddam Hussein as an imminent threat to the United States—infuriated the administration's hard-liners.[105]

—James Risen, journalist

You know, one of the hardest parts of my job is to connect Iraq to the war on terror.[106]

—George W. Bush

His habit . . . is to simply assert, assert, assert until the message sinks in. It's as if war supporters believe that if they repeat the Saddam-Al Qaeda connection enough, people will eventually believe it.[107]

—Jonathan Alter, journalist

See, in my line of work you got to keep repeating things over and over and over again for the truth to sink in, to kind of catapult the propaganda.[108]

—George W. Bush

He repeats old arguments because he believes they are right, because he has no choice— in for a penny, in for a pound—and because his people believe in the dogma of the magic of repetition: Say it, say it, to break through the clutter.[109]

—Peggy Noonan, columnist

Repetition does not transform a lie into a truth.[110]

—Franklin D. Roosevelt

Whatever the Party holds to be truth *is* truth. It is impossible to see reality except by looking through the eyes of the Party.[111]

—George Orwell

Hitler wrote that "all effective propaganda must be limited to a very few points and must harp on these in slogans until the last member of the public understands what you want him to understand."[112]

—Naomi Wolf, writer

[Bush] believed he could sell anything if he repeated the pitch often enough (and often verbatim). Like other entitled boomers utterly blind to their own faults, he narcissistically assumed things to be so (and has intentions pure) because he said they were.[113]

—Frank Rich, columnist

You can't distinguish between al-Qaeda and Saddam when you talk about the war on terror.[114]

—George W. Bush

The DIA [Defense Intelligence Agency], however, had concluded otherwise. The Administration omitted in its public statements the DIA's pre-war conclusion about the likelihood of links between Saddam Hussein and al-Qaeda.[115]

—Sen. Carl Levin

This is not a partisan issue, folks. This is an issue that is important for America. This is an American issue, a uniquely American issue. And it's—as I reminded the members, that—I say uniquely American issue because I truly believe that now that the war has changed, now that we're a battlefield, [Saddam Hussein] poses a much graver threat than anybody could have possibly imagined. Other countries, of course, bear the same risk.

But there's no doubt his hatred is mainly directed at us. There's no doubt he can't stand us. After all, this is a guy that tried to kill my dad at one time.[116]

—George W. Bush

Revenge, at first though sweet, Bitter ere long back on itself recoils.[117]

—John Milton

It is always better to have no ideas than false ones; to believe nothing, than to believe what is wrong.[118]

—Thomas Jefferson

You cannot lead America to a positive tomorrow with revenge on one's mind. Revenge is so incredibly negative.[119]

—George W. Bush

An exhaustive review of more than 600,000 Iraqi documents that were captured after the 2003 U.S. invasion has found no evidence that Saddam Hussein's regime had any operational links with Osama bin Laden's al-Qaida terrorist network. . . . The new study of the Iraqi regime's archives found no documents indicating a "direct operational link" between Hussein's Iraq and al-Qaida before the invasion, according to a U.S. official familiar with the report.[120]

—Warren Strobel, journalist

[T]he vice president doesn't let facts get in the way of any argument he makes on Iraq. . . . [Y]ou have the vice president and a small band of fellow Kool-Aid drinkers who refuse to accept the reality that there never was state sponsorship by Saddam Hussein of al Qaeda and Osama bin Laden.[121]

—Roger Cressey, National Security Council

For the last three years, there have been no inspectors in Iraq, and he has aggressively pursued the development of additional weapons of mass destruction.[122]

—Dick Cheney

The myth that Iraq and al Qaeda were working together was not the result of an innocent and ignorant mistake by the White House. The president and vice president ignored clear warnings, well before the war began—from the Pentagon's Defense Intelligence Agency and from the CIA, in classified reports given directly to the White House—that the claim was false. Well before the war, intelligence officials in Europe had also made clear there was no link. "We have found no evidence of any links between Iraq and al-Qaeda," one top European terrorism investigator said in 2002. "If there were such links, we would have found them, but we have found no serious connections whatsoever."[123]

—Al Gore

■ ■ ■

June 1, 2002: In a graduation speech at West Point, Bush advances a new strategic doctrine of pre-emption, stating that the United States reserves the right to use force to deal
with threats before they "fully materialize."[124]

—Cullen Murphy and Todd Purdum, journalists

We must take the battle to the enemy, disrupt his plans, and confront the worst threats
before they emerge. If we wait for threats to fully materialize, we will have waited too
long.[125]

—George W. Bush

A key feature of the Cheney doctrine was to quietly liberate action from such accepted
standards of proof, and it was effective. Suspicion, both inside America and abroad,
became the threshold for action.[126]

—Ron Suskind, journalist

[I]t was now a guiding principle of the U.S. government that suspicion was an adequate
threshold for preventative action.[127]

—Ron Suskind, journalist

That was all Wolfowitz and his allies inside Feith's shop needed. If it was possible, it was
believable.[128]

—Michael Isikoff and David Corn, journalists

Cheney came up with the doctrine, but George W. Bush intuitively understood how
to carry it forward. A sudden blow for no reason is better than one for a good reason.
Makes your opponent second-guess themselves.[129]

—Ron Suskind, journalist

The President, in unfurling his June 2002 doctrine of preemption at West Point, was
disingenuous in suggesting that proof of an emerging threat would be needed to trigger action. No one in the inner circle believed that. . . . Where once a discernible act of
aggression against America or its national interest was the threshold for a U.S. military
response, now even proof of a threat is too constraining. America was, in sum, ready to
act, with hard evidence or not, to thwart any possible challenge.[130]

—Ron Suskind, journalist

Essentially, the "war on terror" was being guided by little more than "the principle of
actionable suspicion," as one former intelligence chief called it. "It was all happening in
the shadows, so there was no debate about it. We were operating, frantically, in a largely
evidence-free environment. But the whole concept was that not having hard evidence
shouldn't hold you back. It was about action. Continuous action."[131]

—Ron Suskind, journalist

[The Cheney Doctrine] is, in essence, prevention based on suspicion.[132]

—Ron Suskind, journalist

[I]t appears that Cheney has been susceptible to "cherry-picking," embracing those snippets of intelligence that support his dark prognosis while discarding others that don't. He is widely regarded in the intelligence community as an outlier, as a man who always goes for the worst-case scenario and sometimes overlooks less alarming or at least ambiguous signs.[133]

—Mark Hosenball, Michael Isikoff, and Evan Thomas, journalists

The problem of having to rely so heavily on thin, often immaterial, facts is that the insubstantial takes on inappropriate weight. If the president suspects something—and pines, understandably, for it to be verified—that hope itself creates an effect on decision making.[134]

—Ron Suskind, journalist

No error is more certain than the one proceeding from a hasty and superficial view of the subject.[135]

—James Madison

In the end, there are no fingerprints. No accountability.[136]

—Ron Suskind, journalist

There was no deliberation. The Cheney Doctrine had quietly prevailed. *It was not about analysis. It was about reaction.*[137]

—Ron Suskind, journalist

It was pretty clear that Rumsfeld and Cheney are ready to go to war. They have already made the decision to go to war and to them that is the only option.[138]

—Sen. Max Cleland

[E]ven in the high-stakes areas of foreign policy, the basics of analytical due diligence had, in fact, been ignored, or tapped only when a "product" was needed to support policies the White House had already settled on.[139]

—Ron Suskind, journalist

[The president] didn't ask Colin Powell, didn't ask George Tenet, the CIA Director. And I asked him, I said, "How did you not ask these key people?" And he literally said, "I know what they felt. I know what they thought."[140]

—Bob Woodward, journalist

[The White House had used] the pressure of the election to get this thing done before the election. The intensity, the manipulation, the tone of the speeches, the urgency. They were maximizing the sense Americans had that we could be attacked tomorrow. There was no question that this was being manipulated.[141]

—Sen. Chuck Hagel

I told the Chancellor that I have no war plans on my desk, which is the truth, and that we've got to use all means at our disposal to deal with Saddam Hussein.[142]

—George W. Bush

But Bush, Cheney, and a handful of other senior officials already believed they had enough information to know what to do about Iraq. . . . They were drop-dead sure of their presumptions: Iraq was a danger, Saddam had to go, and war was the only option that would achieve this policy goal. They did not need intelligence to reach these conclusions—or to test them.[143]

—Michael Isikoff and David Corn, journalists

Much of what the CIA produced turned out to be embarrassingly flawed. But it was only window dressing for decision makers who did not need intelligence to know that they knew the truth.[144]

—Michael Isikoff and David Corn, journalists

■ ■ ■

Fundamentally we have no idea what is needed unless and until we get there on the ground.[145]

—Paul Wolfowitz, former Deputy Defense Secretary

It's too soon to say with precision how much this war will cost.[146]

—Ari Fleischer, former Bush press secretary

If you don't know if it's going to last six days, six weeks or six months, how in the world can you come up with a cost estimate?[147]

—Donald Rumsfeld

This delicate moment—when we are assembling a coalition, when we are mobilizing people inside Iraq and throughout the region to help us in the event of war, and when we are still trying, through the United Nations and by other means, to achieve a peaceful solution without war—is not a good time to publish highly suspect numerical estimates and have them drive our declaratory policy.[148]

—Paul Wolfowitz, former Deputy Defense Secretary

The Bush administration has tried its best to conceal the horrendous costs of the war. It has bypassed the normal budgetary process, financing the war almost entirely through "emergency" appropriations that get far less scrutiny.[149]

—Bob Herbert, columnist

In September, Lawrence Lindsay, then the chief White House economic adviser, broke discipline. . . . Lindsay was widely criticized in "background" comments from Administration officials, and by the end of the year he had been forced to resign. His comment "made it clear Larry just didn't get it," an unnamed Administration official told the *Washington Post* when Lindsay left. Lindsay's example could hardly have encouraged others in the Administration to be forthcoming with financial projections. Indeed, no one who remained in the Administration offered a plausible cost estimate until months after the war began.[150]

—James Fallows, journalist

There's a lot of money to pay for this. It doesn't have to be U.S. taxpayer money. We are dealing with a country that can really finance its own reconstruction, and relatively soon.[151]

—Paul Wolfowitz, former Deputy Defense Secretary

There had still been few or no estimates of the war's cost from the Administration—only contentions that projections like Lawrence Lindsay's were too high. When pressed on this point, Administration officials repeatedly said that with so many uncertainties, they could not possibly estimate the cost.[152]

—James Fallows, journalist

I am reluctant to try to predict anything about what the cost of a possible conflict in Iraq would be or what the possible cost of reconstructing and stabilizing that country afterwards might be. But some of the higher-end predictions that we have been hearing recently, such as the notion that it will take several hundred thousand U.S. troops to provide stability in post-Saddam Iraq, are wildly off the mark.[153]

—Paul Wolfowitz, former Deputy Defense Secretary

In the immediate run-up to the war the Administration still insisted that the costs were unforeseeable. . . . Wolfowitz's stonewalling that day was in keeping with the policy of all senior Administration officials. Until many months after combat had begun, they refused to hazard even the vaguest approximation of what financial costs it might involve. . . . In short, anyone who actually wanted to make an estimate had plenty of information on hand.[154]

—James Fallows, journalist

I am reasonably certain that they will greet us as liberators and that will help us to keep requirements down.[155]

—Paul Wolfowitz, former Deputy Defense Secretary

[T]he Bush White House appeared to believe its own rhetoric: that there would be no need for a large and costly occupation force after the war, that Iraqi oil revenues would finance reconstruction, that Iraqis would be ever grateful to the Americans.[156]

—Michael Isikoff and David Corn, journalists

Paul Wolfowitz's whole reason for living was to start the war. They didn't have to listen to us. Somewhere along the line they had decided they were smarter than the rest of us.[157]

—military analyst

Message discipline sometimes meant avoiding forthrightness—for example, evasively dismissing questions about the risks of war as "speculation," since the decision to go to war supposedly had not yet been made.[158]

—Scott McClellan, former Bush press secretary

The president and his lieutenants insisted that no decisions about whether to invade Iraq had been made.[159]

—James Risen, journalist

The dangerous thing isn't when statesmen cannot live up to their principles. It is when they can.[160]

—A. J. P. Taylor, historian

The president took the country to war on his gut, exploited our fears and played the patriotism card to advance his political agenda.[161]

—Maureen Dowd, columnist

No passion so effectually robs the mind of all its powers of acting and reasoning as fear.[162]

—Edmund Burke

Guard against the impostures of pretended patriotism.[163]

—George Washington

We got mired in Iraq in the first place partly because Dick Cheney and Rummy thought that, post-Vietnam and post-Clinton, America was seen as soft. One shock-and-awe session, one tyrant stomped on, they reckoned, and the Arab world would no longer see Americans as wimps. That reasoning turned out to be dangerous, flying in the face of warnings from our own intelligence experts.[164]

—Maureen Dowd, columnist

In February of '02, I had a visit at Central Command, in Tampa, and the purpose was to get a briefing on the status of the war in Afghanistan. At the end of the briefing, the commanding officer, Tommy Franks, asked me to go into his office for a private meeting, and he told me that we were no longer fighting a war in Afghanistan and, among other things, that some of the key personnel, particularly some special-operations units and some equipment, specifically the Predator unmanned drone, were being withdrawn in order to get ready for a war in Iraq. That was my first indication that war in Iraq was as serious a possibility as it was, and that it was in competition with Afghanistan for matériel. We didn't have the resources to do both successfully and simultaneously.[165]

—Sen. Bob Graham

By early March, 2002, a former White House official told me, it was understood by many in the White House that the President had already decided, in his own mind, to go to war. In late summer, the White House sharply escalated the nuclear rhetoric. There were at least two immediate targets: the midterm congressional elections and the pending vote on a congressional resolution authorizing the President to take any action he deemed necessary in Iraq, to protect America's national security.[166]

—Seymour Hersh, journalist

Thanks to the administration's deliberate post-9/11 decision to make the enemy who attacked us interchangeable with the secular fascists of Iraq who did not, the original war on terrorism has been diluted in its execution and robbed of its support from the American public.[167]

—Frank Rich, columnist

The military and diplomatic effort in Afghanistan was handicapped from the start because the Administration had other concerns, and it ended badly even though it started well. . . . Throughout the fall and winter, as U.S. troops were deployed in Afghanistan, Bush asked for and received increasingly detailed briefings from General Tommy Franks about the forces that might later be necessary in Iraq. According to many people who observed the process, the stated and unstated need to be ready for Saddam Hussein put a serious crimp in the U.S. effort against bin Laden and the Taliban.[168]

—James Fallows, journalist

By invading Iraq, the President of the United States has greatly undermined the war on terrorism.[169]

—Richard Clarke, former White House counterterrorism expert

For far too long President Bush's disastrous war of choice in Iraq has leached resources and top-level attention from the war of necessity in Afghanistan.[170]

—New York Times editorial

[A] fundamentally flawed plan was executed for an invented war, while pursuing the real enemy, al-Qaeda, became a secondary effort.[171]

—Gen. Greg Newbold

Iraq, of course, was what we were ginning up for, and the effects on Afghanistan were more important, if subtler, than has generally been discussed.[172]

—James Fallows, journalist

They were especially worried about undercutting the counteroffensive against al Qaeda: "All of us understood the fight was against the terrorists, and we were willing to do anything in that regard—so, 'Why are we diverting assets and attention?'"[173]

—Thomas Ricks, journalist

Based on everything I heard at the time, I believe I can make a good guess that the plan for Afghanistan was affected by a predisposition to go into Iraq. The result of that is that they didn't have enough people to go in and stabilize the country, nor enough people to make sure these guys didn't get out.[174]

—Richard Clarke, former White House counterterrorism expert

[Brent] Scowcroft, national security advisor to the first President Bush, staked out the realist position on CBS's "Face The Nation," where he warned that a U.S. invasion of Iraq "could turn the whole region into a cauldron, and thus destroy the war on terrorism."[175]

—Thomas Ricks, journalist

The United States could certainly defeat the Iraqi military and destroy Saddam's regime. But it would not be a cakewalk. On the contrary, it undoubtedly would be very expensive—with serious consequences for the U.S. and global economy—and could as well be bloody. . . . [A] military campaign very likely would have to be followed by a large-scale, long-term military occupation.[176]

—Brent Scowcroft, former national security adviser

As the pressure mounted within the Bush administration to topple Saddam Hussein, some senior CIA officials went to George Tenet to explicitly voice their concerns that war with Iraq would hurt the ongoing battle against terrorism, former officials say.[177]

—James Risen, journalist

A man who participated in high-level planning for both Afghanistan and Iraq . . . told me, "There was absolutely no debate in the normal sense. There are only six or eight of them who make the decisions, and they only talk to each other. And if you disagree with them in public, they'll come after you, the way they did with [Gen. Eric] Shinseki."[178]

—James Fallows, journalist

Two senior military officers are known to have challenged Defense Secretary Donald Rumsfeld on the planning of the Iraq war. Army General Eric Shinseki publicly dissented and found himself marginalized. Marine Lieut. General Greg Newbold, the Pentagon's top operations officer, voiced his objections internally and then retired, in part out of opposition to the war.[179]

—*Time* magazine

They only need the military advice when it satisfies their agenda.[180]

—Gen. John Riggs

[Rumsfeld] promoted sycophants like Richard Myers and Peter Pace, while slapping down truth-tellers like Eric Shinseki. . . . Anyone who challenged the administration was painted as traitorous, so why not respected military leaders?[181]

—Maureen Dowd, columnist

Dissenters are not always right, but it is always a warning sign when they are accused of unpatriotic sentiments by politicians seeking a safe harbor from debate, from accountability, or from the simple truth.[182]

—Sen. John Kerry

I can give you many more priorities [than Iraq]. . . . It's pretty interesting that all the generals see it the same way, and all the others who have never fired a shot are so hot to see it go another way.[183]

—Gen. Anthony Zinni

▮ ▮ ▮

It was in Cincinnati on Oct. 7, 2002, that Mr. Bush gave the fateful address that sped Congressional ratification of the war just days later. The speech was a miasma of self-delusion, half-truths and hype.[184]

—Frank Rich, columnist

We know that Iraq and al Qaeda have had high-level contacts that go back a decade. . . . If the Iraqi regime is able to produce, buy, or steal an amount of highly enriched uranium a little larger than a single softball, it could have a nuclear weapon in less than a year. . . . America must not ignore the threat gathering against us. Facing clear evidence of peril, we cannot wait for the final proof—the smoking gun—that could come in the form of a mushroom cloud.[185]

—George W. Bush

Our own National Intelligence Estimate of Oct. 1 quoted State Department findings that claims of Iraqi pursuit of uranium in Africa were "highly dubious." It was on these false premises—that Iraq was both a collaborator on 9/11 and about to inflict mushroom clouds on America—that honorable and brave young Americans were sent off to fight.[186]

—Frank Rich, columnist

Mr. Bush gave a major address in Cincinnati intermingling the usual mushroom clouds with information from that discredited, "intentionally misleading" Qaeda informant.[187]

—Frank Rich, columnist

We've learned that Iraq has trained Al Qaeda members in bomb-making and poisons and deadly gases.[188]

—George W. Bush

Mr. Bush told of "high-level" Iraq-Qaeda contacts "that go back a decade" in the same notorious October 2002 speech that gave us Saddam's imminent mushroom clouds.

So effective was this propaganda that by 2003 some 44 percent of Americans believed (incorrectly) that the 9/11 hijackers had been Iraqis; only 3 percent had seen an Iraq link right after 9/11.[189]

—Frank Rich, columnist

I remember Karl Rove was out there talking at some events about how we'd use 9/11, run on 9/11 in the midterms, and that it was important to do so.[190]

—Scott McClellan, former Bush press secretary

For Mr. Rove and Mr. Bush to get what they wanted most, slam-dunk midterm election victories, and for Mr. Libby and Mr. Cheney to get what they wanted most, a war in Iraq for reasons predating 9/11, their real whys for going to war had to be replaced by fictional, more salable ones. We wouldn't be invading Iraq to further Rovian domestic politics or neocon ideology; we'd be doing so instead because there was a direct connection between Saddam and Al Qaeda and because Saddam was on the verge of attacking America with nuclear weapons. The facts and intelligence had to be fixed to create these whys; any contradictory evidence had to be dismissed or suppressed.[191]

—Frank Rich, columnist

Libby was most aggressive on intelligence related to Saddam and al-Qaeda, according to [a] CIA veteran: "He wouldn't let go of the al-Qaeda-Saddam connection."[192]

—Michael Isikoff and David Corn, journalists

I never thought Saddam was crazy. He was never going to give these guys weapons— because al-Qaeda would have been just as likely to use them against him as they would against the United States. They hated Saddam.[193]

—Michael Scheurer, CIA

The way we went to war in Iraq illustrates this larger problem. Normally, we Americans lay the facts on the table, talk through the choices before us and make a decision. But that didn't really happen with this war—not the way it should have.[194]

—Al Gore

We'd short-circuited debate over the necessity for war in Iraq and chose instead to turn it into the subject of a massive marketing blitz.[195]

—Scott McClellan, former Bush press secretary

Secrecy and wishful thinking, a Pentagon official told me in the spring of 2004, were defining characteristics of Rumsfeld's Pentagon. "They always want to delay the release of bad news—in the hope that something good will break," he said.[196]

—Seymour Hersh, journalist

∎∎∎

Cheney has repeatedly suggested that Baghdad has ties to Al Qaeda. He has pointedly refused to rule out suggestions that Iraq was somehow to blame for the 9/11 attacks and may even have played a role in the terrorist bombing of the World Trade Center in 1993. The CIA and FBI, as well as a congressional investigation into the 9/11 attacks, have dismissed this conspiracy theory. Still, as recently as Sept. 14, Cheney continued to leave the door open to Iraqi complicity. He brought up a report—widely discredited by U.S. intelligence officials—that 9/11 hijacker Muhammad Atta had met with an Iraqi intelligence officer in Prague in April 2001. And he described Iraq as "the geographic base of the terrorists who have had us under assault for many years, but most especially on 9/11." A few days later, a somewhat sheepish President Bush publicly corrected the vice president. There was no evidence, Bush admitted, to suggest that the Iraqis were behind 9/11.[197]

—Mark Hosenball, Michael Isikoff, and Evan Thomas, journalists

[Cheney] continued, "new information has come to light" revealing the lead 9/11 hijacker, Mohamed Atta, "did apparently travel to Prague on a number of occasions. And on at least one occasion, we have reporting that places him in Prague with a senior Iraqi intelligence official a few months before the attack on the World Trade Center." Was there a direct link between Saddam and Al Qaeda? Tim Russert asked after the vice president ran through a list of other possible links between the two "going back many years." Cheney replied, "I'll leave it right where it sat. I don't want to go beyond that. I've tried to be cautious and restrained in my comments, and I hope that everybody will recognize that." Few did.[198]

—Frank Rich, columnist

It's been pretty well confirmed that [9/11 hijacker Mohamed Atta] did go to Prague and he did meet with a senior official of the Iraqi intelligence service in Czechoslovakia last April, several months before the attack.[199]

—Dick Cheney

When the Atta-Saddam link was disproved later, Gloria Borger, interviewing the vice president on CNBC, confronted him about his earlier claim, and Mr. Cheney told her three times that he had never said it had been "pretty well confirmed." When a man thinks he can get away with denying his own words even though there are millions of witnesses and a video record, he clearly believes he can get away with murder.[200]

—Frank Rich, columnist

The Czech president, Vaclav Havel, has quietly told the White House he has concluded that there is no evidence to confirm earlier reports that Mohamed Atta, the leader in the

Sept. 11 attacks, met with an Iraqi intelligence officer in Prague just months before the attacks on New York and Washington, according to Czech officials.[201]

—James Risen, journalist

Czech officials had no evidence that Atta was even in their country in April 2001, when the meeting purportedly took place, and American records put him in Virginia Beach, Virginia, then. Yet not only did this refutation of the Atta-Saddam link gain no traction with the public; it also failed to deter Cheney from continuing to make the claim, as he would do repeatedly until 2004, the year when the 9/11 commission would also conclude that the Prague meeting never took place.[202]

—Frank Rich, columnist

Feith's exploitation of the Atta-Prague allegation was a case of true believers twisting skimpy intelligence reports to create illusions of proof.[203]

—Michael Isikoff and David Corn, journalists

When the administration is told specifically and repeatedly by the most authoritative sources that there is no linkage, but then in spite of the best evidence continues to make bold and confident assertions to the American people that leave the impression with 70 percent of the country that Saddam Hussein was linked to al-Qaeda and was primarily responsible for the 9/11 attack, this can only be labeled deception.[204]

—Al Gore

The CIA and the FBI had already concluded that the meeting had probably never taken place. Yet that hadn't stopped Feith's briefers from presenting the Atta charge to Libby and Hadley as if it had been fully confirmed.[205]

—Michael Isikoff and David Corn, journalists

Were there contacts between al Qaeda in Iraq? Yes, in the 1990s in Sudan. But that did not translate into state sponsorship in 2003. In effect, what the vice president has done, he's taken 2 and 2 and come up with 2,000. And we've seen that all throughout the Iraq endeavor.[206]

—Roger Cressey, National Security Council

As the rest of the world knows, the White House connived 24/7 to pound in the suggestion that Saddam ordered the attacks on 9/11. . . . To achieve this feat, Dick Cheney spent two years publicly hyping a "pretty well confirmed" (translation: unconfirmed) pre-9/11 meeting in Prague between Mohamed Atta and a Saddam intelligence officer, continuing to do so long after this specious theory had been discredited. Mr. Bush's strategy was to histrionically stir 9/11 and Iraq into the same sentence whenever possible, before the invasion and after. . . . The new propaganda strategy will be right out of Lewis Carroll: If we leave the country that had nothing to do with 9/11, then 9/11 will happen again.[207]

—Frank Rich, columnist

Not a single one of the thousands of documents found after the fall of the Taliban in Afghanistan substantiated an Iraq Qaeda alliance.[208]

—Frank Rich, columnist

■ ■ ■

The four horsemen of the apocalypse—Cheney, Rumsfeld, Powell and Rice—were dispatched en masse to the Washington talk shows, where they eagerly pointed to a front-page New York Times article amplifying subsequently debunked administration claims that Saddam had sought to buy aluminum tubes meant for nuclear weapons.[209]

—Frank Rich, columnist

On September 8, 2002 . . . Cheney was again on *Meet the Press*, this time to offer one-stop shopping for both his Iraq themes—the pre-9/11 connection between Saddam Hussein and Al Qaeda and the zeal of Saddam to acquire not just chemical and biological weapons of mass destruction but in particular the scariest of them all, nuclear weapons. "I'm not here to make a specific allegation that Iraq was somehow responsible for 9/11," Cheney said. "I can't say that." Then he made unspecific allegations suggesting exactly that.[210]

—Frank Rich, columnist

We don't want the smoking gun to be a mushroom cloud.[211]

—Condoleezza Rice

Just as Rice was making the public case against Iraq, the Defense Intelligence Agency issued a classified report entitled "Iraq's Reemerging Nuclear Weapons Program," which concluded that Baghdad was on its way to building the bomb. Vice President Cheney, sounding impatient with any further debate, went on a Sunday talk show to add that "this problem [Iraq] has to be dealt with one way or another."[212]

—James Risen, journalist

The PR campaign was highly orchestrated—numerous administration spokespersons fanned out to give statements to the national media that a "mushroom cloud" might threaten American cities unless we invaded Iraq.[213]

—Al Gore

The White House, meanwhile, had been escalating its rhetoric. In a television interview on September 8th, Condoleezza Rice, addressing questions about the strength of the

Administration's case against Iraq, said, "We don't want the smoking gun to be a mushroom cloud"—a formulation that was taken up by the hawks in the Administration. And, in a speech on October 7th, President Bush said, "Facing clear evidence of peril, we cannot wait for the final proof—the smoking gun—that could come in the form of a mushroom cloud."[214]

—Seymour Hersh, journalist

More than a decade after Saddam Hussein agreed to give up weapons of mass destruction, Iraq has stepped up its quest for nuclear weapons and has embarked on a worldwide hunt for materials to make an atomic bomb, Bush administration officials said today.[215]

—Michael Gordon and Judith Miller, journalists

Judy Miller herself was one of two reporters responsible for a notoriously credulous front-page Times story about aluminum tubes that enabled the administration's propaganda campaign to trump up Saddam's WMD arsenal.[216]

—Frank Rich, columnist

To ratchet up the pressure, the Bush administration leaked information to the American press. The *New York Times* published a story on September 8—the same day Rice issued her mushroom cloud warning—making public the evidence that Iraq had acquired aluminum tubes to rebuild its nuclear weapons program.[217]

—James Risen, journalist

Dick Cheney hammered home his warnings that Saddam Hussein had, beyond all doubt, acquired weapons of mass destruction. In September, Donald Rumsfeld said at a news conference that the link between Saddam Hussein and al-Qaeda was "not debatable."[218]

—James Fallows, journalist

Colin Powell's former top aide, Laurence Wilkinson [sic] rather bluntly puts it: In 2002 Cheney must have believed that Iraq was a spawning ground for terrorists, "otherwise I have to declare him a moron, an idiot or a nefarious bastard."[219]

—John Dean, former White House counsel

Boxed in by international sanctions, weapons inspectors, US fighter jets patrolling two huge no-fly zones and powerful rivals on all his borders, Hussein in 2003 was decidedly not a threat to America. But the Bush White House wanted a war with Iraq, and it pulled out all the stops—references to "a mushroom cloud" and calling Hussein an "ally" of Al Qaeda—to convince the rest of us it was necessary. The White House believed the ends (occupying Iraq) justified the means (exaggerating the threat). We know now those ends have proved disastrous.[220]

—Robert Scheer, journalist

President Bush and his aides used Saddam's alleged relationship with al-Qaeda, along with Iraq's supposed weapons of mass destruction, as arguments for invading Iraq after the Sept. 11, 2001, terrorist attacks. Then-Defense Secretary Donald Rumsfeld claimed in September 2002 that the United States had "bulletproof" evidence of cooperation between the radical Islamist terror group and Saddam's secular dictatorship.[221]

—Warren Strobel, journalist

■ ■ ■

A classified State Department report expresses doubt that installing a new regime in Iraq will foster the spread of democracy in the Middle East, a claim President Bush has made in trying to build support for a war, according to intelligence officials familiar with the document.[222]

—Greg Miller, journalist

In one of the great deceptive maneuvers in U.S. history, the military-industrial complex (with George W. Bush and Dick Cheney as chairman and CEO, respectively) took its eye off the real enemy in Afghanistan and launched the pointless but far more remunerative war in Iraq.[223]

—Bob Herbert, columnist

In the weeks before the United States-led invasion of Iraq, as the United States and Britain pressed for a second United Nations resolution condemning Iraq, President Bush's public ultimatum to Saddam Hussein was blunt: Disarm or face war. But behind closed doors, the president was certain that war was inevitable. During a private two-hour meeting in the Oval Office on Jan. 31, 2003, he made clear to Prime Minister Tony Blair of Britain that he was determined to invade Iraq without the second resolution, or even if international arms inspectors failed to find unconventional weapons.[224]

—Don Van Natta Jr., journalist

January 31, 2003: Bush meets at the White House with Tony Blair. A secret account of the meeting, written by Sir David Manning, Blair's chief foreign-policy adviser and later ambassador to Washington, will become public three years later. The administration's public stance is that it hopes to avoid war with Iraq. In the meeting, however, Bush and Blair agree on a start date for the war, irrespective of the outcome of UN inspections: March 10. Bush proposes that a pretext for war might be provided if an aircraft were painted with U.N. colors and sent in low over Iraq, in the hope that it would draw fire.[225]

—Cullen Murphy and Todd Purdum, journalists

Why would the U.S. president and the British prime minister spend any time concocting ways of provoking a material breach if they knew they could prove Saddam had weapons of mass destruction?[226]

—Philippe Sands, law professor

Bush also mentioned assassinating Saddam.[227]

—Michael Isikoff and David Corn, journalists

The start date for the military campaign was now penciled in for 10 March," Mr. Manning wrote, paraphrasing the president. "This was when the bombing would begin.[228]

—Don Van Natta Jr., journalist

The Downing Street Memos reveal that the purpose of authorizing UN weapons inspectors to go to Iraq was never actually to assess the threat and destroy any weapons found. Instead, the purpose was to "wrongfoot" Saddam by getting him to reject the inspectors, thus giving the American and British governments a pretext for war.[229]

—David Michael Green, political science professor

It would make a big difference politically and legally if Saddam refused to allow in the UN inspectors. If the political context were right, people would support regime change.[230]

—Tony Blair

Although the United States and Britain aggressively sought a second United Nations resolution against Iraq—which they failed to obtain—the president said repeatedly that he did not believe he needed it for an invasion. The memo indicates the two leaders envisioned a quick victory and a transition to a new Iraqi government that would be complicated, but manageable. Mr. Bush predicted that it was "unlikely there would be internecine warfare between the different religious and ethnic groups." Mr. Blair agreed with that assessment.[231]

—Don Van Natta Jr., journalist

According to the internal top secret documents later leaked as the Downing Street Memos, we know that the administration itself realized that "the case was thin" for war against Iraq, because "Saddam was not threatening his neighbours, and his WMD capability was less than that of Libya, North Korea or Iran."[232]

—David Michael Green, political science professor

The memo also shows that the president and the prime minister acknowledged that no unconventional weapons had been found inside Iraq. Faced with the possibility of not finding any before the planned invasion, Mr. Bush talked about several ways to provoke a confrontation.[233]

—Don Van Natta Jr., journalist

To make the case for war, administration officials tended to look at the worst-case scenarios for weapons of mass destruction, dismissing contrary evidence, asserting that Saddam Hussein possessed chemical and biological munitions and was on the road to getting nuclear weapons, and emphasizing the frightening possibility of his sharing them with terrorists to use against the United States. On September 7, Bush, speaking at Camp David with Prime Minister Tony Blair at his side, flatly asserted that Saddam Hussein possessed weapons of mass destruction.[234]

—Thomas Ricks, journalist

On the day before Cheney and company talked about Saddam's aluminum tubes on the Sunday chat shows, for instance, the president had been caught retailing a fiction. Appearing at Camp David with the British prime minister, Tony Blair, he told the press that "when the inspectors first went into Iraq" and were denied access, the International Atomic Energy Agency of the UN had concluded "that they were six months away" from producing a weapon. "I don't know what more evidence we need," Bush said. NBC News, which took the trouble of actually contacting the IAEA to check this out, discovered that Bush was citing a report issued in 1998 about Iraq before the 1991 Gulf War. Since then, UN weapons inspectors had destroyed Iraq's nuclear weapons sites. Both and IAEA spokesman and unnamed American officials told NBC that "there is no conclusive proof that Iraq has restarted its nuclear weapons program."[235]

—Frank Rich, columnist

Nevertheless, the administration made an internal decision that the war would be marketed around the supposed WMD threat, despite knowing it was false. The allusions to mushroom clouds, centrifuge tubes and all the rest were gross exaggerations and outright lies, and were known to be at the time by the people making them. As the Downing Street Memos reveal, a decision for war had already been made, and the public case for it was fabricated afterwards.[236]

—David Michael Green, political science professor

In retrospect, this nearly three-year-old memo explained much that had happened thereafter, starting with the White House insistence on overruling Hans Blix and all America's allies (except England) by refusing to allow the UN weapons inspectors to finish their job in Iraq.[237]

—Frank Rich, columnist

To this day Bush claims that Saddam kicked out the inspectors. That had been true five years previously, but not before the war. Hans Blix, the head of the 2002–03 weapons inspection team reported that they were getting good cooperation from the Iraqis, despite the fact that—as revealed by one of the former team members—the US had inserted American spies into prior international weapons inspection teams in Iraq.[238]

—David Michael Green, political science professor

Hans Blix, the head of the UN weapons inspection team in Iraq, told the Security Council that Iraq's destruction of 34 Al-Samoud 2 missiles was a "substantial measure of disarmament," and that Iraq was now providing information on its biological and chemical weapons. He also said that a series of searches had found "no evidence" of the mobile biological production facilities in Iraq that had been so highly touted by Powell in his presentation to the UN.[239]

—Frank Rich, columnist

Bush wanted to remove Saddam, through military action, justified by the conjunction of terrorism and WMD. But the intelligence and facts were being fixed around the policy.[240]

—Sir Richard Dearlove, British intelligence

The facts and intelligence didn't fit the policy, and so, as the Downing Street memo confirmed, they would have to be fixed (and contradictory evidence suppressed) to build a fictional narrative that would speed the march to war.[241]

—Frank Rich, columnist

One of the reasons I left was my sense that they were using the intelligence from the CIA and other agencies only when it fit their agenda. They didn't like the intelligence they were getting, and so they brought in people to write the stuff. They were so crazed and so far out and so difficult to reason with—to the point of being bizarre. Dogmatic, as if they were on a mission from God. If it doesn't fit their theory, they don't want to accept it.[242]

—intelligence official

[The White House Iraq Group's] mission was to market a war in Iraq, but the official Bush story line had it that no decision had yet been made on the war in August 2002. Dates bracketing the formation of WHIG say otherwise. July 23, 2002—a week or two before WHIG first convened in earnest—was the date of the meeting described in the Downing Street memo, during which the head of British intelligence told his peers that the Bush administration was ensuring that "the intelligence and facts" about Iraq's WMDs "were being fixed around the policy" of going to war.[243]

—Frank Rich, columnist

We know now that Rumsfeld's assistant, Douglas Feith, established a separate and parallel "intelligence" operation inside the Pentagon that was used to present flawed informa-

tion directly to the president without the knowledge of the CIA and the other professional centers of intelligence gathering and analysis in the U.S. government.[244]

—Al Gore

WHIG was to cook up the sexiest recipe for promoting the war, facts be damned.
So it did, by hyping the scariest possible scenario: nuclear apocalypse. . . . [I]t was
WHIG (equipped with the slick phrase-making of the White House speechwriter
Michael Gerson) that gave the administration its Orwellian bumper sticker, the con-
stantly reiterated warning that Saddam's "smoking gun" could be "a mushroom cloud."
. . . [T]he nuclear card, the most persistent and gripping weapon in the prewar propa-
ganda.[245]

—Frank Rich, columnist

WHIG was prepping the public for an invasion of Iraq—by footnoting a fraud.[246]

—Michael Isikoff and David Corn, journalists

One of WHIG's goals, successfully realized, was to turn up the heat on Congress so it
would rush to pass a resolution authorizing war in the politically advantageous month
just before the midterm election.[247]

—Frank Rich, columnist

Mr. Feith's Policy Counterterrorism Evaluation Group. . . . That was the secret intelligence unit established at the Pentagon to "prove" Iraq-Qaeda connections, which Vice
President Dick Cheney then would trumpet in arenas like "Meet the Press."[248]

—Frank Rich, columnist

The false statements dramatically increased in August 2002, with congressional consideration of a war resolution, then escalated through the mid-term elections and spiked
even higher from January 2003 to the eve of the invasion.[249]

—Charles Lewis and Mark Reading-Smith, Center for Public Integrity

Military force is my last option, but it may be my only choice.[250]

—George W. Bush

[I]t's clearer than ever that Mr. Bush, who still claims that war with Iraq was a last resort,
was actually spoiling for a fight.[251]

—Paul Krugman, columnist

Contradictory intelligence was largely ignored or simply disregarded. Evidence based
on high confidence from the intelligence community was lumped together with intelligence of lesser confidence. A nuclear threat was added to the biological and chemical
threats to create a greater sense of gravity and urgency. Support for terrorism was given
greater weight by playing up a dubious al Qaeda connection to Iraq. When it was all

packaged together, the case constituted a "grave and gathering danger" that needed to be dealt with urgently.[252]

—Scott McClellan, former Bush press secretary

The reason I keep insisting that there was a relationship between Iraq and Saddam and al Qaeda, because there was a relationship between Iraq and al Qaeda.[253]

—George W. Bush

[H]e continued to provide no evidence whatsoever.[254]

—Al Gore

The Sept. 11 commission reported yesterday that it has found no "collaborative relationship" between Iraq and al Qaeda, challenging one of the Bush administration's main justifications for the war in Iraq.[255]

—Walter Pincus and Dana Milbank, journalists

The White House had an overwhelming political interest in sustaining the belief in the minds of the American people that Hussein was in partnership with bin Laden. They dared not admit the truth out of fear that they would look like complete fools for launching our country into a reckless and unnecessary war against a nation that posed no immediate threat to us whatsoever.[256]

—Al Gore

I doubt that anyone ever had the chance to make the case to [Bush] that attacking Iraq would actually make America less secure and strengthen the broader radical Islamic terrorist movement. Certainly he did not hear that from the small circle of advisors who alone are the people whose views he respects and trusts.[257]

—Richard Clarke, former White House counterterrorism expert

[A]ny campaign against Iraq, whatever the strategy, cost and risks, is certain to divert us for some indefinite period from our war on terrorism.[258]

—Brent Scowcroft, former national security adviser

I retired from the military four months before the invasion, in part because of my opposition to those who had used 9/11's tragedy to hijack our security policy. . . . A few of the most senior officers actually supported the logic for war. Others were simply intimidated, while still others must have believed that the principle of obedience does not allow for respectful dissent.[259]

—Gen. Greg Newbold

[U]nder Bush, the army and the CIA have failed to put up much of a bureaucratic fight, despite deep anger and frustration within their ranks over the administration's conduct of national security policy. The docility of the American officer corps is particularly striking. One senior administration source notes that during his visits to Iraq, he invariably heard American commanders complain about such problems as the lack of sufficient troops. But during meetings and videoconferences with Bush and Rumsfeld in which this source participated, those same senior military commanders would not voice their complaints. Their silence in the face of authority allowed the White House to state publicly that U.S. commanders in the field were satisfied with the resources at their disposal and that they had never requested additional troops for Iraq.[260]

—James Risen, journalist

When something important is going on, silence is a lie.[261]

—Abe Rosenthal, editor

Our lives begin to end the day we become silent about things that matter.[262]

—Martin Luther King Jr.

America has always been stronger when we have not only proclaimed free speech, but listened to it. Yes, in every war, there have been those who demand suppression and silencing. And although no one is being jailed today for speaking out against the war in Iraq, the spirit of intolerance for dissent has risen steadily, and the habit of labeling dissenters as unpatriotic has become the common currency of the politicians currently running our country.[263]

—Sen. John Kerry

The Pentagon provided "inappropriate" analysis for its reports of a strong link between Saddam Hussein and Al Qaeda, a finding that was cited by the White House as a rationale for invading Iraq, a report by the Pentagon inspector general says. The declassified report said Defense Department officials "undercut" the intelligence community. . . . Mr. Levin, in a statement Thursday, said the analysis from Mr. Feith's office "was not supported by available intelligence and was contrary to the consensus view of the intelligence community," yet was "used by the administration to support its public arguments in its case for war." . . . Mr. Levin also pointed out, "The report specifically states that 'the CIA and DIA disavowed any "mature, symbiotic" relationship between Iraq and Al Qaeda.'"[264]

—*New York Times* editorial

[D]uring the strange "phony war" stage of Iraq discussions, most people in Washington assumed that war was coming, but there was little open discussion of exactly why it was necessary and what consequences it would bring. The pro-war group avoided questions about what would happen after a victory, because to consider postwar complications was to weaken the case for a pre-emptive strike.[265]

—James Fallows, journalist

[A] report by the Pentagon inspector general has finally confirmed that Defense Secretary Donald Rumsfeld's do-it-yourself intelligence office cooked up a link between Iraq and Al Qaeda to help justify an unjustifiable war. The report said the team headed by Douglas Feith, under secretary of defense for policy, developed "alternative" assessments of intelligence on Iraq that contradicted the intelligence community and drew conclusions "that were not supported by the available intelligence."[266]

—*New York Times* editorial

Had Bush, Cheney, and their administration been honest, they would have explained what they did, and did not, know. The reason they did not is obvious. They wanted war and felt that without their distortions, they would be unable to muster public and congressional support.[267]

—John Dean, former White House counsel

■ ■ ■

We will, in fact, be greeted as liberators.[268]

—Dick Cheney

Only an historical illiterate would have assumed that the divided Iraqis were bound to thank their invading liberators and coalesce in democratic government.[269]

—*Economist* editorial

I never saw any intelligence that led me to the conclusion that the people in D.C. were making. I never saw intelligence that we would be met with cheering crowds and bands and people throwing flowers at us. I never saw any intelligence that would allow me to conclude it would be a cakewalk.[270]

—Col. Kevin Benson

If you didn't accept the party line that this was going to be a cakewalk, rose petals, you were dismissed out of hand by the administration. So, they were fixed well before they decided to invade, in the face of some very fine advice by very fine leaders who had been working in this region for a long time.[271]

—Maj. Gen. Paul Eaton

We now know from the CIA that a comprehensive and authoritative analysis of the likely consequences of the invasion—prepared long beforehand—accurately predicted the chaos, popular resentment, and growing likelihood of civil war and that this analysis was presented to the president.[272]

—Al Gore

But, hey, how could the Bushies have known that occupying a Middle East country— and flipping the balance of power from one sect to another—without enough troops to secure it could go wrong? Who on earth could predict the inevitable?[273]

—Maureen Dowd, columnist

[The war] could last, you know, six days, six weeks. I doubt six months.[274]

—Donald Rumsfeld

The Fourth Geneva Convention, which was signed in 1949 and is mainly a commonsense list of duties—from protecting hospitals to minimizing postwar reprisals—that a victorious army must carry out. "But we were corrected when we raised this point," [International Rescue Committee vice president] Sandra Mitchell says. "The American troops would be 'liberators' rather than 'occupiers,' so the obligations did not apply. Our point was not to pass judgment on the military action but to describe the responsibilities."[275]

—James Fallows, journalist

WMD

President Bush . . . made 232 false statements about weapons of mass destruction in Iraq and another 28 false statements about Iraq's links to Al Qaeda.[276]

—Charles Lewis and Mark Reading-Smith, Center for Public Integrity

In the fall of 2001, the Bureau of Intelligence and Research undertook a major review of Iraq's progress in developing WMDs. The review was presented to Secretary of State Powell in December 2001; according to Greg Theilmann, who was one of the analysts who worked on the study, "It basically said that there is no persuasive evidence that the Iraqi nuclear program is being reconstituted." This was not entirely welcome news. Members of the Administration were already beginning to articulate what would become its most compelling argument for going to war with Iraq: the possibility that, with enough time, Saddam Hussein would be capable of attacking the United States with a nuclear weapon.[277]

—Seymour Hersh, journalist

[Treasury Secretary Paul] O'Neill was incensed. How could the White House political staff "decide to do things like this and not even consult with people in the government who know what's true or not? Who the hell is in charge here?" he ranted. "This is complete bullshit!" That night, Bush stood before the nation, described the State of the Union in the most important speech a president gives, in any given year, and said something that knowledgeable people in the U.S. government knew to be false.[278]

—Ron Suskind, journalist

The British government has learned that Saddam Hussein recently sought significant quantities of uranium from Africa.[279]

—George W. Bush

Two weeks earlier, an analyst with the State Department's Bureau of Intelligence and Research sent an email to colleagues in the intelligence community laying out why he believed the uranium-purchase agreement "probably is a hoax."[280]

—Charles Lewis and Mark Reading-Smith, Center for Public Integrity

If there was a serious internal debate within the administration over what to do about Iraq, that debate is over. The speech was just short of a declaration of war.[281]

—Charles Krauthammer, columnist

In retrospect, the speech is even more stunning than it appeared to be then, because it has become clear with the passage of time that it constructed a case that was largely false.[282]

—Thomas Ricks, journalist

[A] Defense Intelligence Agency report on chemical weapons, widely distributed to administration policymakers around the time of the president's speech, stated there was "no reliable information on whether Iraq is producing or stockpiling chemical weapons or whether Iraq has or will establish its chemical agent production facilities."[283]

—Dana Priest and Walter Pincus, journalists

It's becoming increasingly clear that Mr. Bush knew that the case he was presenting for war—a case that depended crucially on visions of mushroom clouds—rested on suspect evidence. For example, in the 2003 State of the Union address Mr. Bush cited Iraq's purchase of aluminum tubes as clear evidence that Saddam was trying to acquire a nuclear arsenal.[284]

—Paul Krugman, columnist

Our intelligence sources tell us that [Saddam] has attempted to purchase high-strength aluminum tubes suitable for nuclear weapons production.[285]

—George W. Bush

They knew the story was a flat-out lie. . . . They were unpersuasive about aluminum tubes and added this to make their case more persuasive.[286]

—former ambassador

The Niger uranium matter was not uppermost in the minds of the CIA analysts. Some of them had to deal with the issue in any case, largely because Cheney, his aide Libby and some aides at the National Security Council had repeatedly demanded more information and more analysis.[287]

—Peter Eisner, journalist

■ ■ ■

Not only do they have a robust set of programs to develop their own weapons of mass destruction; this is a place that's used it. . . . And we know he drove the inspectors out three years ago, and we know he has been actively and aggressively doing everything he can to enhance his capabilities. He has in the past had some dealings with terrorists, clearly. Abu Nidal for a long time operated out of Baghdad.[288]

—Dick Cheney

[A] senior official said the Bush administration was completing classified and unclassified versions of a report on Iraq for Congress, allies and other countries—a report that contains no new evidence of major advances on weapons of mass destruction, or of Iraqi support for Osama bin Laden's al-Qaeda terrorist network. That contrasts sharply with Cheney's warnings that Hussein soon will have a nuclear bomb, could move on his neighbors, or could supply weapons of mass destruction to terrorists.[289]

—Jonathan Landay, journalist

This is a man of great evil. . . . And he is actively pursuing nuclear weapons at this time, and we think that's cause for concern for us and for everybody in the region.[290]

—Dick Cheney

Senior U.S. officials with access to top-secret intelligence on Iraq say they have detected no alarming increase in the threat Saddam Hussein poses to American security and Middle East stability. And some top officials—notably Vice President Cheney and Defense Secretary Donald H. Rumsfeld—argue that that is the point: American intelligence can't be counted on to spot Iraqi nuclear, biological or chemical weapons breakthroughs in time to defend against them. Therefore, they say, the United States has no choice but to remove Hussein before he can use such weapons or pass them to terrorists.[291]

—Jonathan Landay, journalist

Many of us are convinced that Saddam Hussein will acquire nuclear weapons fairly soon. . . . Simply stated, there is no doubt that Saddam Hussein now has weapons of mass destruction. There is no doubt that he is amassing them to use against our friends, against our allies, and against us.[292]

—Dick Cheney

Actually, there was plenty of doubt—at the time—about that second point. According to the Senate report, there was no evidence that Mr. Hussein intended to use weapons of mass destruction against anyone, and the intelligence community never said there was.[293]

—*New York Times* editorial

Jami Miscik, deputy director in charge of the Directorate of Intelligence, recalled listening to the Vice President's speech. . . . "He said that Saddam was building his nuclear program. Our reaction was, 'Where is he getting that stuff from? Does he have a source of information that we don't know about?'" . . . Though the CIA had been directed in a presidential order in February to start focusing on Iraq, the staff had discovered no hard evidence of weapons of mass destruction.[294]

—Ron Suskind, journalist

Anthony Zinni, recently retired from the Marine Corps, sat behind Cheney on the stage that day as the speech was delivered. . . . He had been a Bush-Cheney supporter in the 2000 campaign. But as he listened to the vice president in Nashville he nearly fell off of his chair: "In my time at Centcom, I watched the intelligence and never—not once—did it say, '[Saddam Hussein] has WMD.'"[295]

—Thomas Ricks, journalist

I think the WMD problem—we'd always had a suspicion of WMD programs, but never any hard evidence. And, as time went on, it seemed less and less likely there was an existing program. I mean the vice president's term was he was "amassing" weapons of mass destruction. Clearly, there was no evidence of even an existing program, let alone amassing of weapons of mass destruction.[296]

—Gen. Anthony Zinni

Zinni's conclusion as he slowly walked off the stage that day was that the Bush administration was determined to go to war. A moment later, he had another, equally chilling thought: "These guys don't understand what they are getting into."[297]

—Thomas Ricks, journalist

Despite the Bush administration's claims about Iraq's weapons of mass destruction, U.S. intelligence agencies have been unable to give Congress or the Pentagon specific information about the amounts of banned weapons or where they are hidden, according to administration officials and members of Congress. Senior intelligence analysts say they feel caught between the demands from White House, Pentagon and other government policymakers for intelligence that would make the administration's case "and what they say is a lack of hard facts," one official said. "They have only circumstantial evidence . . . nothing that proves this amount or that," said an individual who has regularly been briefed by the CIA. . . . "They see a particular truck associated with chemical weapons activities keep reappearing, and they estimate chemical activities are there, but that and most intelligence would not pass the courtroom evidence test. For policymakers, who are out on a limb, that is not enough," one official said, adding that he questioned whether the administration is shaping intelligence for political purposes.[298]

—Walter Pincus, journalist

Cheney's speech had a powerful effect elsewhere in the government. His hardline no debate stance was adopted by others in the administration. "We know they have weapons of mass destruction," Rumsfeld would assert a month later at a Pentagon briefing. "We know they have active programs. There isn't any debate about it." Cheney's certitude also dampened skepticism in the intelligence community. "When the vice president stood up and said 'We are sure'—well, who are we to argue?" said the senior military intelligence official. . . . In fact, Cheney played that insider's card himself, dismissively telling Tim Russert in an appearance on *Meet the Press* on September 8, 2002, that those who doubted his assertions about the threat presented by Iraq haven't "seen all the intelligence that we have seen." Outside the government, Cheney's certainty framed the debate in a way that powerfully helped the administration. He had put the opposition on the defensive, effectively saying, If you think I'm wrong, prove it.[299]

—Thomas Ricks, journalist

There is no new intelligence that indicates the Iraqis have made significant advances in these programs, said a U.S. intelligence official who argues that Cheney's and Rumsfeld's focus on Iraq despite such evidence is hurting, not helping, the war on terrorism. . . . "Do I have a smoking gun? No," said another U.S. official. "Can I tell you we've been looking like crazy? Yes."[300]

—Jonathan Landay, journalist

In early October 2002, a set of documents suddenly appeared that promised to provide solid evidence that Iraq was attempting to reconstitute its nuclear program. . . . They were also just what the Administration hawks had been waiting for.[301]

—Seymour Hersh, journalist

Everybody knew at every step of the way that they were false—until they got to the Pentagon, where they were believed. . . . It's not a question as to whether they were marginal. They can't be "sort of" bad, or "sort of" ambiguous. They knew it was a fraud—it was useless. Everybody bit their tongue and said, "Wouldn't it be great if the Secretary of State said this?" The Secretary of State never saw the documents.[302]

—intelligence official

Where are the mobile vans that are nothing more than biological weapons laboratories on wheels? Why is Iraq still trying to procure uranium and the special equipment needed to transform it into material for nuclear weapons?[303]

—Colin Powell

[Iraq's UN weapons] declaration fails to account for or explain Iraq's efforts to get uranium from abroad, its manufacture of specific fuel for ballistic missiles it claims not to have, and the gaps previously identified by the United Nations in Iraq's accounting for more than two tons of the raw materials needed to produce thousands of gallons of anthrax and other biological weapons.[304]

—Condoleezza Rice

What we're giving you are facts and conclusions based on solid intelligence. I will cite some examples, and these are from human sources.[305]

—Colin Powell

As it turned out, however, two of the main human sources to which Powell referred had provided false information. One was an Iraqi con artist, code-named "Curveball," whom American intelligence officials were dubious about and in fact had never even spoken to. The other was an Al Qaeda detainee, Ibn al-Sheikh al-Libi, who had reportedly been sent to Eqypt by the CIA and tortured and who later recanted the information he had provided. Libi told the CIA in January 2004 that he had "decided he would fabricate any information interrogators wanted in order to gain better treatment and avoid being handed over to [a foreign government]."[306]

—Charles Lewis and Mark Reading-Smith, Center for Public Integrity

Mr. Powell later conceded that the United Nations speech was full of falsehoods and distorted intelligence and was a "blot" on his record.[307]

—John Broder, journalist

Once Bush's mind was made up that Saddam was building biological and nuclear weapons, it closed to alternative explanations. He thought picking through evidence was beneath him.[308]

—Jacob Weisberg, journalist

We now know of at least a half-dozen instances before the start of the Iraq war when various intelligence agencies and others signaled that evidence of Iraq's purchase of uranium in Africa might be dubious or fabricated. . . . The culmination of these warnings arrived in January 2003, the same month as the president's State of the Union address, when the White House received a memo from the National Intelligence Council, the coordinating body for all American spy agencies, stating unequivocally that the claim was baseless. Nonetheless President Bush brandished that fearful "uranium from Africa" in his speech to Congress as he hustled the country into war in Iraq.[309]

—Frank Rich, columnist

After three months of intrusive inspections, we have to date found no evidence or plausible indication of the revival of a nuclear weapons programme in Iraq.[310]

—Mohamed ElBaredei, International Atomic Energy Agency

More intriguingly, ElBaradei announced the documents purportedly proving that Iraqi officials had sought uranium in Africa were "not authentic." The bogus letters between Iraqi agents and Niger officials were so crude that they didn't even have accurate names or titles for the correspondents. Equally inauthentic, ElBaradei said, was the persistent administration claim over the past six months that Iraq had tried to purchase aluminum tubes for use in centrifuges for enrichment of that nonexistent uranium. The IAEA investigators had found detailed records going back 14 years, including invoices and blueprints, that showed that Iraq was trying to secure aluminum tubes for conventional rockets, not a nuclear program.[311]

—Frank Rich, columnist

On March 7, 2003, the head of the United Nations' nuclear watchdog agency announced that the Niger uranium documents were forgeries. The Bush administration went to war in Iraq 12 days later, without acknowledging that one of its main arguments for going to war was false.[312]

—*60 Minutes*

A former high-level intelligence official told me that American Special Forces units had been sent into Iraq in mid-March of 2003, before the start of the air and ground war, to investigate sites suspected of being missile or chemical- and biological-weapon storage depots. "They came up with nothing," the official said. "Never found a single Scud."[313]

—Seymour Hersh, journalist

Dozens of interviews with current and former intelligence officials and policymakers in the United States, Britain, France and Italy show that the Bush administration disregarded key information available at the time showing that the Iraq-Niger claim was highly questionable.[314]

—Peter Eisner, journalist

A key piece of evidence linking Iraq to a nuclear weapons program appears to have been fabricated, the United Nations' chief nuclear inspector said yesterday in a report that called into question U.S. and British claims about Iraq's secret nuclear ambitions. Documents that purportedly showed Iraqi officials shopping for uranium in Africa two years ago were deemed "not authentic" after careful scrutiny by U.N. and independent experts, Mohamed ElBaradei, director general of the International Atomic Energy Agency (IAEA), told the U.N. Security Council.[315]

—Joby Warrick, journalist

On 7th March, less than two weeks before the war against Iraq began, Mohamed ElBaradei, the director general of the International Atomic Energy Agency, in Vienna, told the UN Security Council that the documents involving the Niger-Iraq uranium sale were fakes.[316]

—Seymour Hersh, journalist

The IAEA has concluded, with the concurrence of outside experts, that these documents are in fact not authentic.[317]

—Mohamed ElBaradei, International Atomic Energy Agency

I think Mr. ElBaradei, frankly is wrong. And I think if you look at the track record of the International Atomic Energy Agency on this kind of issue, especially where Iraq's concerned, they have consistently underestimated or missed what it was Saddam Hussein was doing. I don't have any reason to believe they're any more valid this time than they've been in the past.[318]

—Dick Cheney

These documents are so bad that I cannot imagine that they came from a serious intelligence agency. It depresses me, given the low quality of the documents, that it was not stopped. At the level it reached, I would have expected more checking.[319]

—IAEA official

In February 2002, the CIA received the verbatim text of one of the documents, filled with errors easily identifiable through a simple Internet search, the interviews show. Many low- and mid-level intelligence officials were already skeptical that Iraq was in pursuit of nuclear weapons. The interviews also showed that France, berated by the Bush administration for opposing the Iraq war, honored a U.S. intelligence request to investigate the uranium claim. It determined that its former colony had not sold uranium to Iraq.[320]

—Peter Eisner, journalist

They've taken the intelligence on weapons and expanded it beyond what was justified.[321]

—Sen. Bob Kerrey

To me there is no benign interpretation of this. At the highest level it was known the documents were forgeries. Stephen Hadley knew it. Condi Rice knew it. Everyone at the highest level knew.[322]

—Melvin Goodman, government analyst

There is a possibility that the fabrication of these documents may be part of a larger deception campaign aimed at manipulating public opinion and foreign policy regarding Iraq.[323]

—Sen. Jay Rockefeller

He told us that they had no active weapons of mass destruction program.

—Tyler Drumheller, CIA

So in the fall of 2002, before going to war, we had it on good authority from a source within Saddam's inner circle that he didn't have an active program for weapons of mass destruction?

—Ed Bradley, journalist

Yes.

—Tyler Drumheller, CIA

It directly contradicts, though, what the president and his staff were telling us.

—Ed Bradley, journalist

The group that was dealing with preparation for the Iraq war came back and said they're no longer interested. And we said, "Well, what about the intel?" And they said, "Well, this isn't about intel anymore. This is about regime change." . . . They certainly took information that came from single sources on uranium, on the yellowcake story and on several other stories with no corroboration at all and so you can't say you only listen to one source, because on many issues they only listened to one source.

—Tyler Drumheller, CIA

So you're saying that if there was a single source and that information from that source backed up the case they were trying to build, then that single source was ok, but if it didn't, then the single source was not OK, because he couldn't be corroborated?

—Ed Bradley, journalist

Unfortunately, that's what it looks like.[324]

—Tyler Drumheller, CIA

When intelligence collided with their beliefs, they blew it off.[325]

—Michael Isikoff and David Corn, journalists

The White House will ruthlessly undermine any reality-based information that contradicts its propaganda, much as it dismissed the accurate WMD findings of the United Nations weapon experts Hans Blix and Mohammed ElBaradei before the war.[326]

—Frank Rich, columnist

The White House Iraq Group [WHIG], formed in August 2002 to foster "public education" about Iraq's "grave and gathering danger" to the United States, repeatedly pitched the uranium story. The alleged procurement was a minor issue for most U.S. analysts—the hard part for Iraq would be enriching uranium, not obtaining the ore, and Niger's controlled market made it an unlikely seller—but the Niger story proved irresistible to speechwriters. Most nuclear arguments were highly technical, but the public could easily grasp the link between uranium and a bomb.[327]

—Barton Gellman and Dana Linzer, journalists

As the controversy over Iraq intelligence has expanded with the failure so far of U.S. teams in Iraq to uncover proscribed weapons, intelligence officials have accused senior administration policymakers of pressuring the CIA or exaggerating intelligence information to make the case for war. The story involving the CIA's uranium-purchase probe, however, suggests that the agency also was shaping intelligence on Iraq to meet the administration's policy goals.[328]

—Walter Pincus, journalist

To get ahead, analysts learned, they had to master the trick of writing quick, short reports that would grab the attention of top policy makers. CIA analysis had become the classified equivalent of television reporters, rather than college professors. The result was that fewer analysts were taking the time to go back and challenge basic assumptions.[329]

—James Risen, journalist

For more than two years it has been widely reported that the U.S. invaded Iraq because of intelligence failures. But in fact it is far more likely that the Iraq war started because of an extraordinary intelligence success—specifically, an astoundingly effective campaign of disinformation, or black propaganda, which led the White House, the Pentagon, Britain's MI6 intelligence service, and thousands of outlets in the American media to promote the falsehood that Saddam Hussein's nuclear-weapons program posed a grave risk to the United States.[330]

—Craig Unger, journalist

A key component of President Bush's claim in his State of the Union address last January that Iraq had an active nuclear weapons program—its alleged attempt to buy uranium in Niger—was disputed by a CIA-directed mission to the central African nation in early 2002, according to senior administration officials and a former government official. But the CIA did not pass on the detailed results of its investigation to the White House or other government agencies, the officials said. The CIA's failure to share what it knew, which has not been disclosed previously, was one of a number of steps in the Bush administration that helped keep the uranium story alive until the eve of the war in Iraq, when the United Nations' chief nuclear inspector told the Security Council that the claim was based on fabricated evidence. A senior intelligence official said the CIA's action was the result of "extremely sloppy" handling of a central piece of evidence in the administration's case against then-Iraqi President Saddam Hussein. But, the official added, "It is only one fact and not the reason we went to war. There was a lot more."[331]

—Walter Pincus, journalist

The CIA, facing criticism for its failure to pass on a key piece of information that put in doubt Iraq's purported attempts to buy uranium from Niger, said yesterday it sent a cable to the White House and other government agencies in March 2002 that said the claim had been denied by officials from the central African country.[332]

—Walter Pincus, journalist

[There were] at least 14 instances prior to the 2003 State of the Union in which analysts at the CIA, the State Department, or other government agencies who had examined the Niger documents or reports about them raised serious doubts about their legitimacy— only to be rebuffed by Bush-administration officials who wanted to use the material.[333]

—Craig Unger, journalist

They were just relentless. You would take it out [of speeches and reports] and they would stick it back in. That was their favorite bureaucratic technique—ruthless relentlessness.[334]

—Lawrence Wilkerson, chief of staff to Colin Powell

The accounts put forth by Wilkerson and his colleagues strongly suggest that the CIA is under siege not because it was wrong but because it was right. Agency analysts were not serving the White House's agenda.[335]

—Craig Unger, journalist

There was, within the administration, another office parsing through intelligence on the Iraqi and terror threat. . . . The OSP [Office of Special Plans] gathered up bits and pieces of intelligence that pointed to Saddam's WMD programs and his ties to terror groups.[336]

—Mark Hosenball, Michael Isikoff, and Evan Thomas, journalists

The rising influence of the Office of Special Plans in the year before the war was accompanied by a decline in the influence of the CIA and the DIA.[337]

—Seymour Hersh, journalist

[Tenet] knew the underlying philosophy at work: that evidence, loosely defined, was summoned at the convenience of action.[338]

—Ron Suskind, journalist

■ ■ ■

[N]ew information indicates a pattern in which President Bush, Vice President Cheney and their subordinates—in public and behind the scenes—made allegations depicting Iraq's nuclear weapons program as more active, more certain and more imminent in its threat than the data they had would support. On occasion administration advocates withheld evidence that did not conform to their views. The White House seldom corrected misstatements or acknowledged loss of confidence in information upon which it had previously relied.[339]

—Barton Gellman and Walter Pincus, journalists

One of the President's core arguments for going to war against Iraq was that Saddam

Hussein was seeking to build nuclear weapons. We now know that one of the pillars of this argument was illegitimate.[340]

—Rep. Henry Waxman

On Sunday, Condoleezza Rice admitted that President Bush had used a forged document in his State of the Union speech to prove Iraq represented a nuclear threat.[341]

—Robert Scheer, journalist

For more than five years, I have been seeking answers to basic questions about why the President made a false assertion about such a fundamental matter. As the President's National Security Advisor at the time, Condoleezza Rice asserted publicly that she knew nothing about any doubts the CIA had raised about this claim prior to the 2003 State of the Union address. And former White House Counsel Alberto Gonzales asserted to the Senate—on her behalf—that the CIA approved the use of the claim in several presidential speeches. The Committee has obtained evidence that just the opposite is true.[342]

—Rep. Henry Waxman

We did not know at the time—maybe someone knew down in the bowels of the agency—but no one in our circles knew that there were doubts and suspicions that this might be a forgery. Of course it was information that was mistaken.[343]

—Condoleezza Rice

New evidence collected by a Congressional oversight committee contradicts assertions by White House officials that the CIA concurred with President Bush's claim in the 2003 State of the Union that Iraq had sought uranium from Africa.[344]

—congressional committee report

The information the Oversight Committee has received casts serious doubt on the veracity of the representations that Mr. Gonzales made on behalf of Dr. Rice. Contrary to Mr. Gonzales's assertions, the Committee has received evidence that the CIA objected to the uranium claim in both speeches, resulting in its deletion from the President's remarks. In the case of the September 26, 2002, speech, the former Deputy Director of Intelligence at the CIA told the Committee that she personally warned Dr. Rice not to use the uranium claim.[345]

—Rep. Henry Waxman

All of this contradicts what White House Counsel Gonzales told Waxman's committee in a letter on January 6, 2004— that the CIA "orally cleared" the uranium claim "for use by the President" in both September 2002 speeches.[346]

—congressional committee report

Officials who were directly involved at both the National Security Council and the CIA have reported to the Committee that the CIA rejected the use of the uranium claim in all three of the President's speeches before the State of the Union address in which its use was considered. One of these officials also told the Committee that she spoke with Dr. Rice personally about this issue and that Dr. Rice was fully aware of the CIA's warnings to stop using the claim. In fact, there is now evidence that at least four top officials at the National Security Council—Dr. Rice; Stephen Hadley, Deputy National Security Advisor; Robert Joseph, Senior Director for Proliferation Strategy, Counterproliferation, and Homeland Defense; and John Gibson, Director of Foreign Policy Speechwriting—had been warned by the CIA to stop using the uranium claim.[347]

—Rep. Henry Waxman

[T]he heart of Bush's second State of the Union address was his case for going to war against Saddam Hussein. Regrettably, it proved a moment of high deception, an endeavor to mislead Congress and the American people. Using declarative, unequivocal, and unqualified statements, Bush presented what appeared to be hard facts, the sort of information to which the commander in chief of a national security apparatus spending $400-plus billion annually was uniquely privy. But so egregious were Bush's misrepresentations that one can only conclude they were a calculated and deliberate effort to mislead Congress.[348]

—John Dean, former White House counsel

After reading Bush's proposed Iraq resolution, Senator Chuck Hagel, a Nebraska Republican, thought, "My god, this crowd down at the White House is rolling right over the top of us—and we're letting them do it."[349]

—Michael Isikoff and David Corn, journalists

This evidence would appear to raise serious questions about the veracity of the assertions that Mr. Gonzales made to Congress on behalf of Dr. Rice about a key part of the President's case for going to war in Iraq.[350]

—Rep. Henry Waxman

■ ■ ■

These are not weapons for the purpose of defending Iraq. These are offensive weapons for the purpose of inflicting death on a massive scale, developed so that Saddam can hold the threat over the head of anyone he chooses in his own region or beyond.[351]

—Dick Cheney

Mr. Libby and Mr. Cheney were in the boiler room of the disinformation factory. The vice president's repetitive hyping of Saddam's nuclear ambitions in the summer and fall of 2002 as well as his persistence in advertising bogus Saddam–al Qaeda ties were fed by the rogue intelligence operation set up in his own office.[352]

—Frank Rich, columnist

Today Saddam Hussein has the scientists and infrastructure for a nuclear weapons program, and has illicitly sought to purchase the equipment needed to enrich uranium for a nuclear weapon. Should his regime acquire fissile material, it would be able to build a nuclear weapon within a year.[353]

—George W. Bush

Abuse of words has been the great instrument of sophistry and chicanery, of party, faction, and division of society.[354]

—John Adams

In August 2002 the tone of the Bush administration's rhetoric changed sharply. That was the month, said Greg Thielmann, then director of proliferation issues in the State Department's intelligence bureau, when "the administration just started speaking about Iraq in much shriller tones." It no longer was just a concern that needed watching; it became "an imminent security threat that has to be dealt with right away." It also was the time the administration's public statements about Iraq's weapons grew more distant from the intelligence on which they were supposedly based, said Thielmann, who a month later retired from his job at the State Department, not in protest but privately disturbed by what he later called the administration's "sustained campaign of misrepresenting the intelligence on Iraq."[355]

—Thomas Ricks, journalist

What we know now from various sources is that he has continued to improve, if you can put it in those terms, the capabilities of his chemical and biological agents, and he continues to pursue a nuclear weapon.[356]

—Dick Cheney

[E]very time we offered another thing that Saddam might possibly have in his arsenal, you could feel the gratitude from the top.[357]

—CIA official

[T]here is scant evidence to tie Saddam to terrorist organizations, and even less to the Sept. 11 attacks. Indeed Saddam's goals have little in common with the terrorists who threaten us, and there is little incentive for him to make common cause with them. . . . There is little evidence to indicate that the United States itself is an object of his aggression.[358]

—Brent Scowcroft, former national security adviser

Despite the Bush administration's claims about Iraq's weapons of mass destruction, U.S. intelligence agencies have been unable to give Congress or the Pentagon specific information about the amounts of banned weapons or where they are hidden, according to administration officials and members of Congress. Senior intelligence analysts say they feel caught between the demands from White House, Pentagon and other government policy makers for intelligence that would make the administration's case "and what they say is a lack of hard facts," one official said.[359]

—Walter Pincus, journalist

David Kay, who resigned last week as the chief U.S. weapons inspector in Iraq, now says he didn't find stockpiles of WMD—or evidence of a nuclear program well under way in Saddam Hussein's Iraq—and he blames it on a greatly flawed intelligence system and analysis.[360]

—DailyKos.com

[O]n every prewar claim—a revivied nuclear program, WMD-carrying unmanned drones, stockpiles of chemical and biological weapons—Kay had uncovered nothing.[361]

—Michael Isikoff and David Corn, journalists

In October, 2004, Charles Duelfer, who succeeded Kay as head of the ISG, produced the group's final findings. There was no such arsenal, the weapons inspector concluded in a one-thousand-page report. Saddam had indeed eliminated his weapons in the early 1990's, but had tried to preserve the intellectual and physical ability to restart the weapons programs at some point. Duelfer also said that he had found no evidence of an effort to buy uranium from other countries.[362]

—Thomas Ricks, journalist

After Kay was done with [a] round of [Senate] hearings, Tenet and [deputy director John] McLaughlin told him that they received calls from White House officials asking why Kay had started out by saying weapons had yet to be found. Couldn't that, they asked, have been buried?[363]

—Michael Isikoff and David Corn, journalists

Florida senator Bill Nelson later reported that at another classified briefing, about seventy-five senators were told that not only did Saddam have biological and chemical weapons, he had the ability to use them against the East Coast of the United States via unmanned drone aircraft. It was a frightening prospect for legislators whose offices had been closed down with less than half a thimble of anthrax spores. It was also totally false.[364]

—John Dean, former White House counsel

Karl Rove, President Bush's chief political adviser, cautioned other White House aides in the summer of 2003 that Bush's 2004 reelection prospects would be severely damaged if it was publicly disclosed that he had been personally warned that a key rationale for going to war had been challenged within the administration.[365]

—Murray Waas, journalist

[Security adviser Stephen] Hadley was particularly concerned that the public might learn of a classified one-page summary of a National Intelligence Estimate, specifically written for Bush in October 2002. The summary said that although "most agencies judge" that the aluminum tubes were "related to a uranium enrichment effort," the State Department's Bureau of Intelligence and Research and the Energy Department's intelligence branch "believe that the tubes more likely are intended for conventional weapons."[366]

—Murray Waas, journalist

[T]he uranium claim would become a crucial justification for the invasion of Iraq that began less than two months later. When occupying troops found no nuclear program, the 16 words and how they came to be in the speech became a focus for critics in Washington and foreign capitals to press the case that the White House manipulated facts to take the United States to war.[367]

—Peter Eisner, journalist

Facts are stubborn things; and whatever may be our wishes, our inclination, or the dictates of our passions, they cannot alter the state of facts or evidence.[368]

—John Adams

Whether Saddam had reconstituted his bombs or was still trying to acquire them didn't much matter by this point. The vice president smothered such distinctions with a verbal blanket of doom, inviting Americans to imagine how much worse 9/11 would have been if Al Qaeda had "had a nuclear weapon and detonated it in the middle of one of our cities."[369]

—Frank Rich, columnist

[T]he intelligence about a uranium purchase, based on suspect and even forged information, acquired nine lives in Washington.[370]

—Max Frankel, editor

October's classified, ninety-page National Intelligence Estimate did not mention the yellowcake among its key findings, and carried caveats from the State Department that cast doubt on the assertion.[371]

—Ron Suskind, journalist

It turned out that much of the information about Mr. Hussein's search for uranium was questionable at best, and that it became the subject of dispute almost as soon as it was included in the 2002 National Intelligence Estimate on Iraq.[372]

—David E. Sanger and David Johnston, journalists

Beginning in mid-2002 and continuing for the rest of the year, the president devoted himself almost exclusively to insisting that Saddam Hussein's Iraq constituted a grave threat to the United States and must be confronted. Standing on his broad-based support, he campaigned to persuade Americans of the wisdom and necessity of invading Iraq, notwithstanding that Iraq had not attacked, had not threatened to attack, and lacked the capability to attack the United States.[373]

—Glenn Greenwald, lawyer/journalist

It was becoming clear that the WMD issue had been largely a propaganda vehicle used by the administration to sell the war to the press.[374]

—Marie Brenner, journalist

The [2002 National Intelligence Estimate] appeared more certain on all fronts than previous intelligence assessments, but the finding on the nuclear program was especially surprising, because it was a shift from a series of previous conclusions by the intelligence community. In fact, the estimate amounted to a serious misrepresentation of views in the intelligence community, maximizing alarming findings while minimizing internal doubts about them. *It effectively presented opinion as fact.*[375]

—Thomas Ricks, journalist

I remember thinking, "Boy, there's nothing here. If anybody takes the time to actually read this, they can't believe there actually are major WMD programs."[376]

—Peter Zimmerman, senate scientific adviser

Zimmerman, the Senate staffer, urged his colleagues with security clearances to go read the NIE, telling them the dissents were "pretty shocking." But it was too late.[377]

—Michael Isikoff and David Corn, journalists

Over a year later, when the Senate Intelligence Committee reviewed the NIE in light of evidence that became available after the war, it came to the conclusion that the collective wisdom of the U.S. intelligence community, as represented in the estimate, had been stunningly wrong. . . . Moreover, the efforts and exaggerations weren't random, but all pushed in the same direction, toward making the argument that Iraq presented a growing threat. As a political document that made the case for war the NIE of October 2002 succeeded brilliantly. As a professional intelligence product it was shameful.[378]

—Thomas Ricks, journalist

One intelligence analyst subsequently told Senate investigators that when the NIE was being assembled, "the going-in assumption was we were going to war, so this NIE was to be written with that in mind. . . . This is about going to war and giving the combatant commander an estimate on which he can properly organize."[379]

—Michael Isikoff and David Corn, journalists

In the end, the actual wording of the NIE probably didn't matter. By the time it was written, the Bush White House had already made extensive use of the faulty intelligence that had been packaged in the estimate. Bush, Cheney, Rumsfeld, Rice, Wolfowitz, and other administration officials had ignored the disputes (where they existed) and hardly questioned the limited (and flawed) intelligence that had been produced. Bush hadn't asked for the NIE, nor—as the White House would later acknowledge—did he even read it.[380]

—Michael Isikoff and David Corn, journalists

There was not a goddamn thing I or any staffer could do to stop this. We had an election coming up. The Democrats were afraid of being seen as soft on Saddam or on terrorism. The whole notion was, "Let's get the war out of the way as fast as possible and turn back to the domestic agenda"[381]

—Peter Zimmerman, senate scientific adviser

[T]he administration was looking for evidence to support conclusions it already had reached.[382]

—Thomas Ricks, journalist

They were convinced that Saddam was developing nuclear weapons, that he was reconstituting his program, and I'm afraid that's where they started.[383]

—Greg Theilmann, State Department intelligence

[T]hey cherry-picked obscure, unconfirmed information to reinforce their own political philosophies and ideologies.[384]

—Gen. Gregory Newbold

There's so much intelligence out there that it's easy to pick and choose your case. It opens things up to cherry-picking.[385]

—former Cheney aide

But we do know, with absolute certainty, that he is using his procurement system to acquire the equipment he needs in order to enrich uranium to build a nuclear weapon. . . . And increasingly, we believe that the United States may well become the target of those activities.[386]

—Dick Cheney

Mr. Cheney and Mr. Libby built their "case" by often making an end run around the CIA, State Department intelligence and the Defense Intelligence Agency. Their ally in cherry-picking intelligence was a similar cadre of neocon zealots led by Douglas Feith at the Pentagon.[387]

—Frank Rich, columnist

"[Feith and Cheney] would take individual factoids, build them into long lists, and then think because of the length of the list, it was credible," [according to a senior military intelligence official]. When the lists were rejected by intelligence professionals, they would be leaked to friendly journalists.[388]

—Thomas Ricks, journalist

[There was] a feedback loop exploited by the White House. A leak of secret intelligence produced a dramatic front-page headline that senior administration officials then used to corroborate their most alarming claim.[389]

—Michael Isikoff and David Corn, journalists

I had come to question whether the White House was telling the truth—or even had an interest in knowing the truth.[390]

—Sen. Bob Graham

By the time the public really focused on it, the decision to go to war had been made.[391]

—Thomas Ricks, journalist

In the months before the invasion of Iraq, [Gen. Norman] Schwarzkopf was worried. In January 2003 he made it clear in a lengthy interview that he hadn't seen enough evidence to persuade him that his old comrades from twelve years earlier—Cheney, Powell, and Wolfowitz—were correct in moving toward a new war. He thought UN inspections were still the proper course to follow. He also worried about the cockiness of the U.S. war plan, and even more about the potential human and financial costs of occupying Iraq.[392]

—Thomas Ricks, journalist

The most remarkable thing was the talk that we had with the vice president before we were taken to Mr. Bush. To our surprise, we had no idea we would be taken to Mr. Cheney first, but we were, and we sat down, and I thought it was more a sort of a courtesy call before we went on to President Bush. Much of it was a fairly neutral discussion, but at one point he suddenly said that you must realize that we will not hesitate to discredit you in favor of disarmament. It was a little cryptic. That was how I remembered it, and I think that's also how Mohamed [ElBaradei, the head of the International Atomic Energy Agency, who was present], remembered it. I was a little perplexed, because it was a total threat, after all, to talk about the discrediting of us. Later, when I reflected it, I think what he wanted to say was that if you guys don't come to the right conclusion, then we will take care of the disarmament.[393]

—Hans Blix, UN weapons inspector

[I]n pursuit of what they call a "moral" foreign policy, they stretched and obscured the truth. First, they hyped CIA intelligence to fit their contention that Saddam and Al

Qaeda were linked. Then they sent Colin Powell out with hyped evidence about Iraq's weapons of mass destruction. Then, when they were drawing up the battle plan, they soft-pedaled CIA and Pentagon intelligence warnings that U.S. troops would face significant resistance from Saddam's guerrilla fighters.[394]

—Maureen Dowd, columnist

Intelligence gathered by this and other governments leaves no doubt that the Iraq regime continues to possess and conceal some of the most lethal weapons ever devised.[395]

—George W. Bush

It is now beyond dispute that Iraq *did not* possess any weapons of mass destruction or have meaningful ties to Al Qaeda. This was the conclusion of numerous bipartisan government investigations, including those by the Senate Select Committee on Intelligence (2004 and 2006), the 9/11 Commission, and the multinational Iraq Survey Group, whose "Duelfer Report" established that Saddam Hussein had terminated Iraq's nuclear program in 1991 and made little effort to restart it.[396]

—Charles Lewis and Mark Reading-Smith, Center for Public Integrity

There was just a predisposition to assume that Saddam had WMD.[397]

—Charles Duelfer, weapons inspector

Duelfer's report noted that at the time of the invasion Saddam had no "plan for the revival of WMD."[398]

—Michael Isikoff and David Corn, journalists

∎ ∎ ∎

In a long-delayed report, the Senate Intelligence Committee on Thursday rebuked President Bush and Vice President Dick Cheney for making prewar claims—particularly that Iraq had close ties to Al Qaeda—that were not supported by available intelligence.[399]

—Greg Miller, journalist

[T]his is a big report. What it says is statements by the president were not substantiated by intelligence. And then it says statements by the president were contradicted by available intelligence. In other words, they made things up.[400]

—Richard Clarke, former White House counterterrorism expert

In order to make this case, more pessimistic views repeatedly had to be rejected and ignored, even if they came from area experts.[401]

—Thomas Ricks, journalist

In making the case for war, the administration repeatedly presented intelligence as fact when in reality it was unsubstantiated, contradicted or even non-existent.[402]

—Sen. Jay Rockefeller

The report shows clearly that President Bush should have known that important claims he made about Iraq did not conform with intelligence reports. In other cases, he could have learned the truth if he had asked better questions or encouraged more honest answers.[403]

—*New York Times* editorial

There was no doubt. Information from intelligence analysts or other experts in or out of government that contradicted or undermined the operating assumptions of the get-Saddam crowd was ignored or belittled.[404]

—Michael Isikoff and David Corn, journalists

There is no question we all relied on flawed intelligence. . . . But there is a fundamental difference between relying on incorrect intelligence and deliberately painting a picture to the American people that you know is not fully accurate. . . . [O]ur committee has concluded that the administration made significant claims that were not supported by the intelligence.[405]

—Sen. Jay Rockefeller

Overall, the report makes it clear that top officials, especially Mr. Bush, Mr. Cheney and Defense Secretary Donald Rumsfeld, knew they were not giving a full and honest account of their justifications for going to war.[406]

—*New York Times* editorial

President Bush, Vice President Dick Cheney and other top officials promoted the invasion of Iraq with public statements that weren't supported by intelligence or that concealed differences among intelligence agencies, the Senate Intelligence Committee said Thursday in a report that was delayed by bitter partisan infighting.[407]

—Jonathan Landay, journalist

Now we have the evidence, we have the proof, four years too late, that those statements were flat-out wrong. And these weren't close calls. They made things up.[408]

—Richard Clarke, former White House counterterrorism expert

The report documents how time and again Mr. Bush and his team took vague and dubious intelligence reports on Iraq's weapons programs and made them sound like hard and incontrovertible fact.[409]

—*New York Times* editorial

In making the case for war, the administration repeatedly presented intelligence as fact when, in reality, it was unsubstantiated, contradicted or even nonexistent. . . . Sadly, the Bush administration led the nation into war under false pretenses.[410]

—Sen. Jay Rockefeller

This syndrome begins at the top, with the president, who has cut and run from reality in Iraq.[411]

—Frank Rich, columnist

Bush and Cheney took this nation to war on *their* hunches, *their* unreliable beliefs, *their* unsubstantiated intelligence—and used deception with Congress both before and after launching the war.[412]

—John Dean, former White House counsel

I believe they ignored data because of their unjustified tendency to assume that they already knew everything they needed to know and thus had no need to react with alarm to the warnings of experts and government professionals. Their behavior, in my opinion, was reckless, but the explanation for it lies in hubris, not in some bizarre conspiracy theory.[413]

—Al Gore

In short, the Bush administration led the nation to war on the basis of erroneous information that it methodically propagated and that culminated in military action against Iraq on March 19, 2003. Not surprisingly, the officials with the most opportunities to make speeches, grant media interviews, and otherwise frame the public debate also made the most false statements, according to this first-ever analysis of the entire body of prewar rhetoric.[414]

—Charles Lewis and Mark Reading-Smith, Center for Public Integrity

Based on all the information we have today, I believe we were right to take action, and America is safer today with Saddam Hussein in prison. He retained the knowledge, the materials, the means, and the intent to produce weapons of mass destruction.[415]

—George W. Bush

That is, Saddam had had everything but the weapons and the actual programs to make them.[416]

—Michael Isikoff and David Corn, journalists

Each generation should be made to bear the burden of its own wars, instead of carrying them on, at the expense of other generations.[417]

—James Madison

[S]ecrecy, censorship, and massive systematic deception is the principal explanation for how America embraced this catastrophe.[418]

—Al Gore

It is too true, however disgraceful it may be to human nature, that nations in general will make war whenever they have a prospect of getting anything by it; nay, that absolute monarchs will often make war when their nations are to get nothing by it, but for purposes and objects merely personal, such as a thirst for military glory, revenge for personal affronts, ambition, or private compacts to aggrandize or support their particular families, or partisans. These, and a variety of other motives, which affect only the mind of the Sovereign, often lead him to engage in wars not sanctified by justice, or the voice and interests of his people.[419]

—John Jay

This administration's arrogant control of information and the massive deception perpetrated on the American people in order to gain approval for a dishonest policy led to the worst strategic mistake in the history of the United States.[420]

—Al Gore

[Bush] ambiguously stated his intentions, rooted in a policy that had been determined months earlier.[421]

—Scott McClellan, former Bush press secretary

It is error alone which needs the support of government. Truth can stand by itself.[422]

—Thomas Jefferson

UNRELIABLE SOURCES

The case regarding Saddam's chemical weapons capability . . . was based on the rantings of a single source, code-named "Curveball," whose handlers in the German intelligence service had repeatedly warned the administration that he was a drunk and a liar.[423]

—David Michael Green, political science professor

The German intelligence officials responsible for one of the most important informants on Saddam Hussein's suspected weapons of mass destruction say that the Bush administration and the CIA repeatedly exaggerated his claims during the run-up to the war in Iraq. Five senior officials from Germany's Federal Intelligence Service, or BND, said in interviews with The Times that they warned U.S. intelligence authorities that the source, an Iraqi defector code-named Curveball, never claimed to produce germ weapons and never saw anyone else do so.[424]

—Bob Drogin and John Goetz, journalists

Five top German intelligence officers say that the Bush administration and the CIA repeatedly ignored warnings about the veracity of the information that an Iraqi informant named "Curveball" was giving about Saddam Hussein's weapons of mass destruction.[425]

—Tom Regan, journalist

As we turned to the trailers, it was probably—I guess the single biggest shock I had during the entire inspection process, because I'd been powerfully moved by Powell's statement to the Council. Well, when we started tearing it apart, we discovered it was not based on several sources. It was based on one source, and it was an individual [code-named Curveball] held by German intelligence. They had denied the U.S. the right to directly interview him. And they only passed summaries—and really not very good ones—of their interrogations with him. The Germans had refused to pass us his name even. As you delved into his character and his claims, none of them bore any truth. The case just fell apart.[426]

—David Kay, weapons inspector

According to the Germans, President Bush mischaracterized Curveball's information when he warned before the war that Iraq had at least seven mobile factories brewing biological poisons. Then-Secretary of State Colin L. Powell also misstated Curveball's accounts in his prewar presentation to the United Nations on Feb. 5, 2003, the Germans said. Curveball's German handlers for the last six years said his information was often vague, mostly secondhand and impossible to confirm.[427]

—Bob Drogin and John Goetz, journalists

The Germans had warned that Curveball might be making up all or most of his story—and he was. He had never worked in the biological program; he'd been a taxi driver before heading to Germany to seek asylum. There were no mobile labs. The Bush administration had believed what it wanted to believe.[428]

—Christopher Dickey, journalist

[A]s I worked closely with President Bush, I would come to believe that sometimes he convinces himself to believe what suits his needs at the moment.[429]

—Scott McClellan, former Bush press secretary

I was astonished that the Americans used Curveball, really astonished. This was our stuff. But they presented it not in the way we knew it. They presented it as a fact, and not as the way an intelligence assessment is—*could* be, but could also be a big lie. We don't know.[430]

—Joschka Fischer, former German foreign minister

Once again, the intelligence was wrong, but the administration seized on it to ballyhoo its arguments. Had the White House bothered to ask, it would have learned that the CIA had never talked to "Curveball" before Powell's speech. When the agency did seek to interview the source, whose reports were provided by the German intelligence service, it was told, "You don't want to see him because he's crazy." Yet "Curveball" was the principal source that the administration relied on in claiming to the world that Iraq had biological weapons.[431]

—Tom Regan, journalist

At the Central Intelligence Agency, officials embraced Curveball's account even though they could not confirm it or interview him until a year after the invasion. They ignored multiple warnings about his reliability before the war, punished in-house critics who provided proof that he had lied and refused to admit error until May 2004, 14 months after the invasion.[432]

—Bob Drogin and John Goetz, journalists

■ ■ ■

Before the war, Ahmad Chalabi told Washington hawks exactly what they wanted to hear about Saddam Hussein's weapons of mass destruction and the warm welcome American troops could expect from liberated Iraqis.[433]

—*New York Times* editorial

Chalabi and the neoconservatives in the Pentagon were united by a shared vision of a radically reshaped Middle East and a belief that the overthrow of Saddam Hussein was the essential first step in the realization of that vision. . . . Chalabi provided the Office of Special Plans with information from defectors ostensibly from Saddam Hussein's weapons programs—defectors who claimed to be able to establish that the Iraqi dictator was actively developing weapons of mass destruction. Through such efforts, Chalabi grew even closer to those planning the war and what would follow. To the war planners, the Iraqi National Congress became not simply an Iraqi exile group of which Chalabi was a leader, but a kind of government-in-waiting with Chalabi at its head.[434]

—David Reiff, journalist

The Pentagon is paying $340,000 a month to the Iraqi political organization led by Ahmad Chalabi, a member of the interim Iraqi government who has close ties to the Bush administration, for "intelligence collection" about Iraq, according to Defense Department officials.[435]

—Douglas Jehl, journalist

As the longtime head of the Iraqi National Congress [I.N.C.], a prominent exile group that funneled information about Saddam Hussein's suspected weapons programs to the United States, Mr. Chalabi was a Bush administration favorite to lead Iraq, especially among top Pentagon officials who planned the invasion to oust Mr. Hussein. . . . Critics of the war still maintain that Mr. Chalabi purposely fed false information about Iraqi weapons programs to officials in the Defense Department and Mr. Cheney's office in order to goad the administration into a war that would place him in power in Baghdad.[436]

—Steven Weisman, journalist

The INC was not alone in misrepresenting and manipulating intelligence. The White House was also twisting facts and ignoring unwanted evidence as it strove to convince Americans of the pending nuclear threat from Saddam Hussein.[437]

—Seymour Hersh, journalist

[Chalabi] tirelessly connived and schemed on behalf of two dreams: for American military might to drive Saddam Hussein from power and to install himself in the dictator's place. His Washington allies needed little motivation to oust Hussein; Dick Cheney, Paul Wolfowitz and many others already regarded him as Public Enemy No. 1. But they welcomed Chalabi's ammunition, his "information," in the fight against war skeptics.[438]

—Leslie Gelb, journalist

By all appearances, Ahmad Chalabi reached the pinnacle of influence in Washington . . . when he took a seat of honor right behind Laura Bush at the president's State of the Union address. To all the world, he looked like the Iraqi exile who had returned home victorious, a favorite of the Pentagon who might run the country once the American occupation ended. . . . The intelligence about unconventional weapons that his Iraqi National Congress helped feed to senior Bush administration officials and data-starved intelligence analysts—evidence that created the urgency behind the march toward war—was already crumbling. Intelligence officials now argue some of it was fabricated.[439]

—David E. Sanger, journalist

A COVER-UP THAT FAILED

Was the difference between Mr. Bush's public portrayal of the Iraqi threat and the actual intelligence he saw large enough to validate claims that he deliberately misled the nation into war? Karl Rove apparently thought so.[440]

—Paul Krugman, columnist

Rove expressed his concerns shortly after an informal review of classified government records by then-Deputy National Security Adviser Stephen J. Hadley determined that Bush had been specifically advised that claims he later made in his 2003 State of the Union address—that Iraq was procuring high-strength aluminum tubes to build a nuclear weapon—might not be true, according to government records and interviews.[441]

—Murray Waas, journalist

[One] narrative to be unearthed in the scandal's early timeline is the motive for this reck-less vindictiveness against anyone questioning the war. . . . It was against this backdrop of mounting desperation on July 6 that Mr. Wilson went public with his incriminating claim that the most potent argument for the war in the first place, the administration's repeated intimations of nuclear Armageddon, involved twisted intelligence.[442]

—Frank Rich, columnist

Did senior Bush officials blow the cover of a U.S. intelligence officer working covertly in a field of vital importance to national security—and break the law—in order to strike at a Bush administration critic and intimidate others?[443]

—David Corn, journalist

Consider the now-disproved claims by President Bush and Colin Powell that Iraq tried to buy uranium from Niger so it could build nuclear weapons. As Seymour Hersh noted in *The New Yorker*, the claims were based on documents that had been forged so ama-teurishly that they should never have been taken seriously. I'm told by a person involved in the Niger caper that more than a year ago the vice president's office asked for an investigation of the uranium deal, so a former U.S. ambassador to Africa was dispatched to Niger. In February 2002, according to someone present at the meetings, that envoy reported to the CIA and State Department that the information was unequivocally wrong and that the documents had been forged.[444]

—Nicholas Kristoff, columnist

Through inquiries at the State Department, the vice president's office quickly learned the identity of Kristoff's unnamed source. It was former ambassador Joseph Wilson who'd been sent to Niger to investigate the uranium allegation in January 2002. Under the cloak of anonymity, the vice president and trusted aide Scooter Libby soon began an effort to discredit Wilson with selected journalists. Unknown to anyone else in the com-partmentalized, internally secretive White House—including the White House chief of staff, the national security adviser, and the CIA director—the president declassified key portions from the October 2002 NIE for the vice president and Libby to use in this effort.[445]

—Scott McClellan, former Bush press secretary

There are too many leaks of classified information in Washington. There's leaks at the executive branch; there's leaks in the legislative branch. There's just too many leaks. And if there is a leak out of my administration, I want to know who it is. And if the person has violated law, the person will be taken care of.[446]

—George W. Bush

Yeah, I did.[447]

—George W. Bush (confirming he had authorized
a leak of part of the NIE)

W. defended his authorization of a leak to rebut Joseph Wilson's contention that the administration had hyped up a story about Niger selling Saddam uranium. "I wanted people to see the truth," the president said. Of course, sometimes in order to help people see the truth, you've got to tell them a big fat lie.[448]

—Maureen Dowd, columnist

When Rice was publicly rejecting the notion of selective declassification on July 11, 2003, Scooter Libby had already leaked it to Judith Miller [of the *New York Times*] on July 8—at the vice president's direction with authority from the president.[449]

—Scott McClellan, former Bush press secretary

[A] part of the October 2002 National Intelligence Estimate that Libby did *not* leak to Miller told of the State Department's caveat that "claims of Iraqi pursuit of natural uranium in Africa," by then made public by the British, were "highly dubious," echoing a CIA assessment that "the evidence is weak" and "the Africa story is overblown." The NIE also said that the State Department accepted "the judgment of technical experts at the U.S. Department of Energy" that the aluminum tubes . . . were "poorly suited for use in gas centrifuges to be used for uranium enrichment" and were more likely to be used for the conventional weaponry of artillery rockets.[450]

—Frank Rich, columnist

But it was a separate DIA report about the claims that would lead Cheney to demand further investigation. In response, the CIA dispatched Wilson to Niger.[451]

—Peter Eisner, journalist

What Mr. Wilson found, and subsequent investigations confirmed, was that there was one trip in 1999—not "recently," but four years before Mr. Bush's statement—by an Iraqi official to Niger and that during that trip, uranium was never discussed.[452]

—*New York Times* editorial

I gave them months to correct the record, but they kept on lying.[453]

—Joseph Wilson, former ambassador

It was not until Mr. Wilson's public recounting of his African mission more than five months after the State of the Union that George Tenet at long last released a hasty statement (on a Friday evening, just after the Wilson Op-Ed piece) conceding that "these 16 words should never have been included in the text written for the president."[454]

—Frank Rich, columnist

If, however, the information was ignored because it did not fit certain preconceptions about Iraq, then a legitimate argument can be made that we went to war under false pretenses. . . . America's foreign policy depends on the sanctity of its information.[455]

—Joseph Wilson, former ambassador

But red-hot uranium was sexy, and it was Mr. Wilson's flat refutation of it that drove administration officials to seek their revenge: they told the columnist Robert Novak that Mr. Wilson had secured his (nonpaying) African mission through the nepotistic intervention of his wife, a covert CIA officer whom they outed by name. The pettiness of this retribution shows just how successfully Mr. Wilson hit the administration's jugular: his revelation threatened the legitimacy of the war on which both the president's reputation and re-election campaign had been staked.[456]

—Frank Rich, columnist

Administration officials had anonymously leaked her identity to reporters in order to punish (at worst) or discredit (at best) her husband, former ambassador Joseph Wilson, who was publicly alleging that the administration had misled the country into war in Iraq.[457]

—Scott McClellan, former Bush press secretary

To defend itself against the accusations of deliberate dishonesty leveled by Joe Wilson, Vice President Cheney and his staff were leading a White House effort to discredit Joe Wilson himself.[458]

—Scott McClellan, former Bush press secretary

The CIA's decision to send retired diplomat Joseph C. Wilson to Africa in February 2002 to investigate possible Iraqi purchases of uranium was made routinely at a low level without Director George Tenet's knowledge. . . . Wilson never worked for the CIA, but his wife, Valerie Plame, is an agency operative on weapons of mass destruction. Two senior administration officials told me that Wilson's wife suggested sending him to Niger to investigate the Italian report. The CIA says its counterproliferation officials selected Wilson and asked his wife to contact him. "I will not answer any question about my wife," Wilson told me.[459]

—Robert Novak, columnist

Yesterday, a senior administration official said that before Novak's column ran, two top White House officials called at least six Washington journalists and disclosed the identity and occupation of Wilson's wife. Wilson had just revealed that the CIA had sent him to Niger last year to look into the uranium claim and that he had found no evidence to back up the charge. Wilson's account touched off a political fracas over Bush's use of intelligence as he made the case for attacking Iraq.[460]

—Mike Allen and Dana Priest, journalists

Did the Bush administration manipulate intelligence about Saddam Hussein's weapons programs to justify an invasion of Iraq? Based on my experience with the administration in the months leading up to the war, I have little choice but to conclude that some of the intelligence related to Iraq's nuclear weapons program was twisted to exaggerate the Iraqi threat.[461]

—Joseph Wilson, former ambassador

[T]he White House went berserk when Mr. Wilson published his Op-Ed article in The Times in July 2003 about what he didn't find in Africa. Top officials gossiped incessantly about both Wilsons to anyone who would listen, Mr. Cheney and Mr. Libby conferred about them several times a day, and finally Mr. Libby, known as an exceptionally discreet White House courtier, became so sloppy that his alleged lying landed him with five felony counts. The explanation for the hysteria has long been obvious. The White House was terrified about being found guilty of a far greater crime than outing a CIA officer: lying to the nation to hype its case for war. When Mr. Wilson, an obscure retired diplomat, touched that raw nerve, all the president's men panicked because they knew Mr. Wilson's modest finding in Africa was the tip of a far larger iceberg. They knew that there was still far more damning evidence of the administration's WMD lies lurking in the bowels of the bureaucracy.[462]

—Frank Rich, columnist

At CIA Director George J. Tenet's request, the Justice Department is looking into an allegation that administration officials leaked the name of an undercover CIA officer to a journalist, government sources said yesterday. The operative's identity was published in July after her husband, former U.S. ambassador Joseph C. Wilson IV, publicly challenged President Bush's claim that Iraq had tried to buy "yellowcake" uranium ore from Africa for possible use in nuclear weapons. Bush later backed away from the claim.[463]

—Mike Allen and Dana Priest, journalists

Most troublesome to those leading the damage-control effort was documentary evidence—albeit in highly classified government records that they might be able to keep secret—that the president had been advised that many in the intelligence community believed that the tubes were meant for conventional weapons.[464]

—Murray Waas, journalist

The point of mentioning Wilson's wife, of course, was to dispel once and for all the notion that Vice President Cheney had somehow arranged Wilson's trip to Niger. The fact that Wilson's wife was involved also carried with it a whiff of nepotism, a vague sense that perhaps there was something improper in the assignment—as if Wilson had been sent by his wife "on a junket," to quote the words scrawled in the margin of his own copy of Wilson's op-ed column by none other than Vice President Cheney himself.[465]

—Scott McClellan, former Bush press secretary

Wilson's spotlight turned the spotlight squarely on the charge being leveled by . . . critics that the Bush administration had knowingly misled the public.[466]

—Scott McClellan, former Bush press secretary

At the same time they were admitting the words should not have been in the State of the Union address, they were, we now know, sending Libby out to selectively leak only those pieces that continued to support this allegation that was baseless. In other words, they were furthering the disinformation campaign.[467]

—Joseph Wilson, former ambassador

Patrick Fitzgerald, prosecutor in the Libby case, wrote in the court papers that there was an effort by "multiple" White House officials to "discredit, punish or seek revenge against" a critic of the Iraq war—a reference to Wilson.[468]

—CNN report

From the early days of the CIA leak investigation in 2003, the Bush White House has insisted there was no effort to discredit Joseph C. Wilson IV, the man who emerged as the most damaging critic of the administration's case that Saddam Hussein was seeking to build nuclear weapons. But now White House officials, and specifically President Bush and Vice President Dick Cheney, have been pitched back into the center of the nearly three-year controversy, this time because of a prosecutor's court filing in the case that asserts there was "a strong desire by many, including multiple people in the White House," to undermine Mr. Wilson.[469]

—David E. Sanger and David Johnston, journalists

Mr. Fitzgerald's filing talks not of an effort to level with Americans but of "a plan to discredit, punish or seek revenge against Mr. Wilson." It concludes, "It is hard to conceive of what evidence there could be that would disprove the existence of White House efforts to 'punish Wilson.'" Mr. Fitzgerald suggested that the White House effort was a "plan" to undermine Mr. Wilson. "Disclosing the belief that Mr. Wilson's wife sent him on the Niger trip was one way for defendant to contradict the assertion that the vice president had done so, while at the same time undercutting Mr. Wilson's credibility if Mr. Wilson were perceived to have received the assignment on account of nepotism," Mr. Fitzgerald's filing said.[470]

—David E. Sanger and David Johnston, journalists

During 2003 and 2004, the White House chose not to be open and forthright on the Plame scandal but rather to buy time and sometimes even stonewall, using the ongoing investigation as an excuse for silence. The goal was to prevent political embarrassment that might hurt the president and weaken his bid for reelection in November 2004.[471]

—Scott McClellan, former Bush press secretary

In our current imperial presidency, as in its antecedent, what may look like a narrow case involving a second banana with a child's name contains the DNA of the White House, and that DNA offers a road map to the duplicitous culture of the whole. The coming prosecution of Lewis (Scooter) Libby in the Wilson affair is hardly the end of the story. That "Cheney's Cheney," as Mr. Libby is known, would allegedly go to such lengths to obscure his role in punishing a man who challenged the administration's WMD propaganda is just one very big window into the genesis of the smoke screen (or, more accurately, mushroom cloud) that the White House used to sell the war in Iraq.[472]

—Frank Rich, columnist

Questioning the selective use of intelligence to justify the war in Iraq is neither idle sniping nor "revisionist history," as Mr. Bush has suggested.[473]

—Joseph Wilson, former ambassador

The evidence in the trial shows Vice President Dick Cheney and Mr. Libby, his former chief of staff, countermanding and even occasionally misleading colleagues at the highest levels of Mr. Bush's inner circle as the two pursued their own goal of clearing the vice president's name in connection with flawed intelligence used in the case for war. . . . Unbeknownst to their colleagues, according to testimony, the two carried out a covert public relations campaign to defend not only the case for war but also Mr. Cheney's connection to the flawed intelligence.[474]

—Jim Rutenberg, journalist

One of the most senior officials in the White House, Lewis Libby, the chief of staff for Vice President Dick Cheney, was caught lying to the FBI He appears to have been trying to cover up a smear campaign that was orchestrated by his boss against the first person to unmask one of the many untruths that President Bush used to justify invading Iraq. . . . [I]t is some of the clearest evidence yet that this administration did not get duped by faulty intelligence; at the very least, it cherry-picked and hyped intelligence to justify the war.[475]

—*New York Times* editorial

Vice President Dick Cheney's former chief of staff, I. Lewis (Scooter) Libby, testified to a federal grand jury that he had been "authorized" by Cheney and other White House "superiors" in the summer of 2003 to disclose classified information to journalists to defend the Bush administration's use of prewar intelligence in making the case to go to war with Iraq, according to attorneys familiar with the matter, and to court records.[476]

—Murray Waas, journalist

The first step towards vice is to shroud innocent actions in mystery, and whoever likes to conceal something sooner or later has reason to conceal it.[477]

—Jean-Jacques Rousseau

What we are learning from Mr. Libby's trial is just what a herculean effort it took to execute this two-pronged cover-up after Mr. Wilson's article appeared.[478]

—Frank Rich, columnist

President Bush told the special prosecutor in the CIA leak case that he directed Vice President Dick Cheney to personally lead an effort to counter allegations made by former Ambassador Joseph C. Wilson IV that his administration had misrepresented intelligence information to make the case to go to war with Iraq, according to people familiar with the president's interview. Bush also told federal prosecutors during his June 24, 2004, interview in the Oval Office that he had directed Cheney, as part of that broader effort, to disclose highly classified intelligence information that would not only defend his administration but also discredit Wilson, the sources said.[479]

—Murray Waas, journalist

Why was the White House so nervous in the summer of 2003 about the CIA's reporting on alleged Iraqi attempts to buy uranium from Niger to build a nuclear bomb? That's the big question that runs through the many little details that have emerged in the perjury trial of Vice President Cheney's former top aide, Lewis "Scooter" Libby. The trial record suggests a simple answer: The White House was worried that the CIA would reveal that it had been pressured in 2002 and early 2003 to support administration claims about Iraqi weapons of mass destruction, and that in the Niger case, the CIA had tried hard to resist this pressure. The machinations of Cheney, Libby and others were an attempt to weave an alternative narrative that blamed the CIA. . . . This trial is about a cover-up that failed.[480]

—David Ignatius, journalist

It is not merely that speeches, statistics, and records of every kind must be constantly brought up to date in order to show that the predictions of the Party were in all cases right. It is also that no change of doctrine or in political alignment can ever be admitted.[481]

—George Orwell

Vice President Dick Cheney bitterly complains that national security leaks are endangering America. Unless, of course, he's doing the leaking, tapping Scooter Libby to reveal national security information to punish a political critic.[482]

—Maureen Dowd, columnist

The trial and conviction of Scooter Libby opened the window wide on the twisted values and priorities of the hawkish operation in the vice president's office.[483]

—Bob Herbert, columnist

■ ■ ■

President Bush, fielding questions yesterday after visiting wounded soldiers at Walter Reed, declared that "the jury verdict should stand"—and then, in answer to the same question, said he was open to vacating the verdict by granting Libby a full pardon.[484]

—Dana Milbank, journalist

President Bush wiped away the [thirty-month] prison sentence of former White House aide I. Lewis "Scooter" Libby on Monday, calling it an "excessive" punishment for a "first-time offender with years of exceptional public service."[485]

—David Savage and Richard Schmitt, journalists

The deeper offense is that the president has used his pardon power to shortcircuit the investigation of a crime to which he himself was quite likely a party, and to which, his vice president, who controls him, certainly was.[486]

—Dan Froomkin, journalist

[T]he real effect of Bush's actions is to prevent Libby from revealing the truth about Bush's—and vice president Cheney's—own actions in the leak. By commuting Libby's sentence, Bush protected himself and his vice president from potential criminal exposure for their actions in the CIA Leak. As such, Libby's commutation is nothing short of another obstruction of justice."[487]

—Marcy Wheeler, journalist

It's appropriate. The president who led the nation into a disastrous war in Iraq by peddling false statements and misrepresentations has come to the rescue of a White House aide convicted of lying by commuting his sentence.[488]

—David Corn, journalist

Presidents have the power to grant clemency and pardons. But in this case, Mr. Bush did not sound like a leader making tough decisions about justice. He sounded like a man worried about what a former loyalist might say when actually staring into a prison cell.[489]

—*New York Times* editorial

Whether it's ignoring climate change to boost oil profits or feeding no-bid contracts to Halliburton, President Bush watches out for his pals—often at the expense of the American people. So it should have been no surprise Monday when the president commuted the sentence of Lewis "Scooter" Libby, saving him from 2 1/2 years in prison.

And yet, somehow it was. The contempt for the rule of law was so blatant, even for this administration.[490]

—*San Jose Mercury News* editorial

It really comes down to the administration misrepresenting the facts on an issue that was a fundamental justification for going to war. It begs the question, what else are they lying about?[491]

—Joseph Wilson, former ambassador

An administration lies to take its country to war, and then lies about critics of that lie, and then lies to prosecutors about its lies about critics of that lie. It should come as no surprise that the president's protection of those lies would be defended today with a fourth tier of lies.[492]

—Keith Olbermann, political commentator

How easy it is to abuse truth and language, when men, by habitual wickedness, have learned to set justice at defiance.[493]

—Thomas Paine

We know in America the difference between right and wrong, even if this administration doesn't. . . . [W]e have a system of justice that has been usurped in what I think is an arbitrary and capricious act by a chief executive who is corrupt to the core and an administration that has demonstrated that it has absolutely no regard for those values.[494]

—Joseph Wilson, former ambassador

The Plame matter . . . would come to represent the disturbing and intrigue-ridden story of how the Bush administration—full of we-know-best, gung ho officials keen for a war that they assumed would go well—presented a case for war that turned out to be, in virtually every aspect, fraudulent.[495]

—Michael Isikoff and David Corn, journalists

[I]t certainly smacks of a concerted effort to defraud the government of the United States by senior U.S. administration officials. If that is not a high crime and a misdemeanor, then I don't know what is.[496]

—Joseph Wilson, former ambassador

UNWAVERING PLANS

I have no plans to attack on my desk.[497]

—George W. Bush

The president's statement was true only in the most literal but trivial sense. Bush had ordered the development of a new CENTCOM war plan, repeatedly met with [Gen. Tommy] Franks to hear its details, offered his own views on the schedule for deploying troops and on the military's effort to couch the invasion as liberation.[498]

—Michael Gordon and Bernard E. Trainor, military analysts

The White House kept saying that no decision has been made about Iraq, but only the blind or the deaf could fail to see that a decision had long ago been made.[499]

—Frank Rich, columnist

Who overcomes by force, hath overcome but half his foe.[500]

—John Milton

Force does not constitute right.[501]

—Jean-Jacques Rousseau

Ari Fleischer responded by saying that the debate was already going on and the president was "listening to all sides," even though it was evident from the get-go that Bush would do pretty much whatever he always intended after a few weeks of ostentatious "listening."[502]

—Frank Rich, columnist

[A]s the Bush administration prosecuted its military campaign in Afghanistan, the prospect of striking Saddam remained a top-drawer item of consideration. On November 21—nine days after the fall of Kabul had sent thousands of Taliban and al-Qaeda fighters and supporters fleeing south—Bush took aside Rumsfeld . . . and asked him to draw up a fresh war plan for Iraq and to keep it a secret.[503]

—Michael Isikoff and David Corn, journalists

I hope this Iraq situation will be resolved peacefully. One of my New Year's resolutions is to work to deal with these situations in a way so that they're resolved peacefully.[504]

—George W. Bush

As he spoke, every operating branch of the government was preparing for war.[505]

—James Fallows, journalist

In the end, what was unique about George W. Bush's reaction to terrorism was his selection as an object lesson for potential state sponsors of terrorism, not a country that had been engaging in anti–U.S. terrorism but one that had not been, Iraq. It is hard to imagine another President making that choice.[506]

—Richard Clarke, former White House counterterrorism expert

They're going to war and there's not a damn piece of evidence to substantiate it.[507]

—Peter Zimmerman, senate scientific adviser

A bad cause seldom fails to betray itself.[508]

—James Madison

A bad cause will ever be supported by bad means and bad men.[509]

—Thomas Paine

I really think I'm going to have to do this.[510]

—George W. Bush (telling Colin Powell he had
made up his mind on war, January 13, 2003)

Two days before the invasion of Iraq in March 2003, Bush had the audacity to say, "Should Saddam choose confrontation, the American people can know that every measure has been taken to avoid war." . . . The insiders' memoirs of both Richard Clarke and Paul O'Neill showed that every measure had been taken to *embrace* war with Iraq, not avoid it.[511]

—Frank Rich, columnist

In many cases, policies weren't debated at all. There never was a formal meeting of all the president's senior advisors to debate and decide whether to invade Iraq, according to a senior administration source.[512]

—James Risen, journalist

As the Bush administration prepares to attack Iraq this week, it is doing so on the basis of a number of allegations against Iraqi President Saddam Hussein that have been challenged—and in some cases disproved—by the United Nations, European governments and even U.S. intelligence reports. For months, President Bush and his top lieutenants have produced a long list of Iraqi offenses, culminating Sunday with Vice President Cheney's assertion that Iraq has "reconstituted nuclear weapons."[513]

—Walter Pincus and Dana Milbank, journalists

Did anyone at the White House, did anyone in the defense department, ever ask you whether we should go to war in Iraq?

—Scott Pelley, journalist

The discussions that are ongoing in 2002 in the spring and summer of 2002 are "How you might do this?" Not "whether you should do this."[514]

—George Tenet

In addition to portraying a terrorist nexus between Iraq and al-Qaeda that did not exist, the Democrats said, the Bush administration "also kept from the American people . . . the sobering intelligence assessments it received at the time"—that an Iraq war could allow al-Qaeda "to establish the presence in Iraq and opportunity to strike at Americans it did not have prior to the invasion."[515]

—Walter Pincus and Karen DeYoung, journalists

The invasion of Iraq was illegal from the start. Not only was Congress lied to in order to secure its support for the invasion of Iraq, but the war lacked the support of the United Nations Security Council and thus was an aggressive war initiated on the false pretenses of weapons of mass destruction. There were no weapons of mass destruction in Iraq. Nor has any assertion of a relationship between Iraq and al Qaeda proven to be true. In the end, democracy has not come to Iraq. Its government is still being forced to bend to the will of the U.S. administration.[516]

—Walter Cronkite and David Krieger, journalists

[T]he Administration will be condemned for what it did with what was known.[517]

—James Fallows, journalist

—7—

Post-Invasion Iraq:
The House of Cards Collapses

The first casualty when war comes is the truth.[1]
—Sen. Hiram Johnson

B y the time American troops were ready to invade Iraq in March 2003, it was
too late for anyone to consider the truth. The Iraqi regime desperately sent out
a series of back-channel messages to try to tell the Americans that there were no
illicit weapons, but no one was willing to listen.[2]

—James Risen, journalist

Absolutely, we're winning. Al Qaeda is on the run.[3]

—George W. Bush

No, sir.[4]

—Defense Secretary designate Robert Gates
(in response to being asked if the U.S. was winning the war)

Of all the enemies of public liberty, war is perhaps the most to be dreaded, because it
comprises and develops the germ of every other.[5]

—James Madison

[T]he biggest intelligence mistake under the Bush presidency . . . was their ignorance
about the internal dynamics of Iraq. You know, they elected to move Saddam out without any firm understanding of what was going to follow him. And that was the costli-
est mistake. It costs us, over four years, billions and billions of dollars, thousands and
thousands of lives.[6]

—Charles Duelfer, Iraq Survey Group

That there should be a political controversy over whether there is a civil war in Iraq is a tribute to the Bush administration's Orwellian attention to political rhetoric. By the most widely accepted social science measure, Iraq is incontestably in a civil war.[7]

—Juan Cole, journalist

In our society, those who have the best knowledge of what is happening are also those who are furthest from seeing the world as it is.[8]

—George Orwell

[I]n Washington, ignorance does not disqualify someone from responsibility.[9]

—Charles Duelfer, Iraq Survey Group

I just want you to know that, when we talk about war, we're really talking about peace.[10]

—George W. Bush

You cannot simultaneously prevent and prepare for war.[11]

—Albert Einstein

A conscientious man would be cautious how he dealt in blood.[12]

—Edmund Burke

■ ■ ■

As war loomed, Iraq made broad overtures to the United States to prevent an invasion, offering to allow full, on-the-ground, American weapons inspections, anti-terrorism cooperation, oil concessions, and even backing for the U. S. position in an Israeli/Palestinian peace plan. The only thing Saddam balked at was regime change, but even then he offered to hold elections within two years' time. The Americans were also informed by the Iraqis at the time that there were no existing WMD. The Iraqi representatives "could not understand why the Americans were focused on Iraq rather than on countries, like Iran, that have long supported terrorists." The Bush administration rejected their offer, despite that it met every demand that Bush was publicly making.[13]

—David Michael Green, political science proferssor

The executive has no right, in any case, to decide the question, whether there is or is not cause for declaring war.[14]

—James Madison

Every measure has been taken to avoid war, and every measure will be taken to win it.[15]

—George W. Bush

We were told by the president that war was his last choice. But it is now clear that it was always his first preference. His former Secretary of the Treasury, Paul O'Neill, confirmed that Iraq was "topic A" at the very first meeting of the Bush National Security Council just ten days after the inauguration: "It was about finding a way to do it."[16]

—Al Gore

At the time of the invasion in 2003, the weapons inspectors were nearly done with their work, and only asked for a month or two more to finish. The Bush administration claimed that the threat of Saddam and his WMD was too grave and too urgent to wait. Bush's claim that Saddam kicked out the inspectors is not only false, but masks the actual truth, which is that the administration told the inspectors to leave because of the looming attack, before they could finish their work and by so doing remove the rationale for that attack.[17]

—David Michael Green, political science proferssor

"I don't think it is reasonable to close the door on [weapons] inspections after three and a half months," when Iraq's government is providing more cooperation than it has in more than a decade.[18]

—Hans Blix, U.N. weapons inspector

[E]rror is not a fault of our knowledge, but a mistake of our judgment, giving assent to that which is not true.[19]

—John Locke

Our nation enters this conflict reluctantly.[20]

—George W. Bush (declaring war on Iraq, March 19, 2003)

Rarely do we find men who willingly engage in hard, solid thinking. There is an almost universal quest for easy answers and half-baked solutions. Nothing pains some people more than having to think.[21]

—Martin Luther King Jr.

There is no strategy or mechanism for putting the pieces together. We're in danger of failing. . . . My contemporaries, our feelings and sensitivities were forged on the battlefields of Vietnam, where we heard the garbage and the lies, and we saw the sacrifice. I ask you, is it happening again?[22]

—Gen. Anthony Zinni

The first few days or weeks after the fighting, in this view, were crucial in setting long-term expectations. Civilians would see that they could expect a rapid return to order, and would behave accordingly—or they would see the opposite. This was the "shock and awe" that really mattered, in the Army's view: the ability to make clear who was in charge.[23]

—James Fallows, journalist

Rumsfeld and his associates, [Gen. John] Riggs says, "were almost psychopathic in their quest to be right."[24]

—David Margolick, journalist

We did not prepare ourselves for this intervention. We threw away decades worth of planning and understanding of the situation. We discounted those that warned that the assumptions were too optimistic, and we had the results we have now.[25]

—Gen. Anthony Zinni

Is it curious to you that given how much control U.S. and coalition forces now have in the country, they haven't found any weapons of mass destruction?

—George Stephanopoulos, ABC News

Not at all. . . . We know where they are. They're in the area around Tikrit and Baghdad and east, west, south and north somewhat.[26]

—Donald Rumsfeld

Sometimes I overstate for emphasis.[27]

—Donald Rumsfeld

I have begun to question our motivations. . . . I am asking, not only as a subordinate to a superior seeking justification for our course of action, but as a U.S. citizen holding my elected officials responsible for my country's leadership: Where are the weapons of mass destruction?[28]

—Lt. Cmdr. Richard Riggs

Our strategy is this: We will fight them over there so we do not have to face them in the United States of America.[29]

—George W. Bush

Allow the president to invade a neighboring nation, whenever he shall deem it necessary to repel an invasion, and you allow him to do so whenever he may choose to say he deems it necessary for such a purpose—and you allow him to make war at pleasure.[30]

—Abraham Lincoln

■ ■ ■

At every level of the chain of command, the uniformed commanders don't hesitate to ask for what they need. The problem is, the strategy from the very beginning never anticipated or resourced the transition from war fighting, to peace enforcement, to building the peace. So we lost a narrow window of opportunity. We never regained the initiative.[31]

—Gen. John Batiste

Although we've mouthed the words about this being a long war and a long struggle, the very forces that it places the greatest demand upon, our ground forces, our soldiers and Marines, we've seen no increase, no change, no adaptability on the battlefield. We're still confused about the enemy. We're stifled by the IED attacks and the problems we face. And these adjustments, over four years, have not been made. We have to ask ourselves why.[32]

—Gen. Anthony Zinni

[W]e went into this war with absolutely the wrong plan. We didn't plan for it, and we're suffering today. . . . It's all about leadership that this country desperately needs at this juncture.[33]

—Gen. John Batiste

Here is the hardest question: How could the Administration have thought that it was safe to proceed in blithe indifference to the warnings of nearly everyone with operational experience in modern military occupations? Saying that the Administration considered this a truly urgent "war of necessity" doesn't explain the indifference. Even if it feared that Iraq might give terrorists fearsome weapons at any moment, it could still have thought more carefully about the day after the war. World War II was a war of absolute necessity, and the United States still found time for detailed occupation planning.[34]

—James Fallows, journalist

They believed their own propaganda.[35]

—an anonymous senior planner

President Bush has a history of blowing off military advice from people who disagree with him, from General Batiste to General Eaton, going all the way back to Colin Powell. He doesn't listen to people who disagree with him.[36]

—Paul Reikoff, Iraq war veteran

[W]hen the president doesn't like what he hears from his generals, he kicks them out.[37]

—Richard Wolffe, journalist

W's mind is . . . closed to anybody except yes-men who tell him his policies and wars are slam-dunks.[38]

—Maureen Dowd, columnist

Before the Iraq invasion, it was about fixing the intelligence around the policy. Now it's about appointing yes men and enforcing loyalty. The Bush warriors didn't want good intelligence in the first place because it would have told them they were wrong about Saddam's ties to Al Qaeda and WMD And now they're still more concerned with turf battles than with truth-tellers and finding someone—anyone—who can tell us where Osama is. (Osama who?).[39]

—Maureen Dowd, columnist

What we are living with now is the consequences of successive policy failures. Some of the missteps include: the distortion of intelligence in the buildup to the war, Mc-Namara-like micromanagement that kept our forces from having enough resources to do the job, the failure to retain and reconstitute the Iraqi military in time to help quell civil disorder, the initial denial that an insurgency was the heart of the opposition to occupation, alienation of allies who could have helped in a more robust way to rebuild Iraq, and the continuing failure of the other agencies of our government to commit assets to the same degree as the Defense Department.[40]

—Gen. Greg Newbold

Ethnic, tribal, and religious schisms could produce civil war or fracture the state after Saddam is deposed.[41]

—Conrad C. Crane and W. Andrew Terrill, Strategic Studies Institute

I don't think anybody anticipated the level of violence that we've encountered.[42]

—Dick Cheney

More than a year earlier, long before combat began, the explicit recommendations and implicit lessons of the Future of Iraq project had given the U.S. government a very good idea of what political conflicts it could expect in Iraq.[43]

—James Fallows, journalist

By ignoring predictions of an insurgency and refusing to do homework before charging into Iraq on trumped-up pretenses, W. left our troops undermanned, inadequately armored and psychologically unprepared.[44]

—Maureen Dowd, columnist

You go to war with the army you have, not the army you might want.[45]

—Donald Rumsfeld

When Rumsfeld responded to his questioner in Kuwait that the only reason the troops still lacked armor was "a matter of production and capability," it was exposed instantly as a lie. The manufacturers that supplied the armor told the press that they had been telling the Pentagon for months that they could increase production, in the case of one company, ArmorWorks of Arizona, by as much as 100 percent.[46]

—Frank Rich, columnist

The troops were not trained for a counterinsurgency, because Bush hawks ignored the intelligence reports that predicted an insurgency and civil war. These kids were turned into sitting ducks because the neocon con to sell the war needed a gauzy prediction of Iraqi gratitude and a quick exit. . . . The virtuecrats of the right thought they would demonstrate American virtue to the world as they imposed American democracy. But now, with murder charges expected against some marines, and a cover-up investigation under way, the values president is running a war that requires a refresher course on values. A bitter irony.[47]

—Maureen Dowd, columnist

Rosy American claims of dramatically falling murder rates are being challenged by the Baghdad morgue.[48]

—Frank Rich, columnist

The Baghdad morgue has reported that at least 1,535 Iraqis died violently in the capital in August, a 17 percent drop from July but still much higher than virtually all other months. American military officials have disputed the morgue's numbers, saying military data shows that the "murder" rate dropped by 52 percent from July to August. But officials have acknowledged that that metric does not include deaths from bombings and rocket or mortar attacks.[49]

—Edward Wong, journalist

On June 16 [2004], the independent 9/11 Commission found "no collaborative relationship" between Iraq and al-Qaeda. . . . The intelligences agencies, the committee said, had reached conclusions that were either "overstated" or "not supported by the underlying intelligence." The day after the 9/11 Commission report came out, Bush insisted, "There was a relationship between Iraq and al-Qaeda." That same day, Cheney, in an interview, again stressed that the Atta-in-Prague report might be credible—even though the CIA, FBI, and the 9/11 Commission had found there was nothing to support it.[50]

—Michael Isikoff and David Corn, journalists

The more I saw, the more I thought that this was the product of the neocons who didn't understand the region and were going to create havoc there. These were dilettantes from Washington think tanks who never had an idea that worked on the ground.[51]

—Gen. Anthony Zinni

My sincere view is that the commitment of our forces to this fight was done with a casualness and swagger that are the special province of those who have never had to execute these missions—or bury the results.[52]

—Gen. Greg Newbold

I hate war as only a soldier who has lived it can, only as one who has seen its brutality, its futility, its stupidity.[53]

—Dwight Eisenhower

The White House insisted that President Bush had consulted intensively with his generals and adapted to changing circumstances. But no amount of smoke could obscure the truth: Mr. Bush has no strategy to end his disastrous war and no strategy for containing the chaos he unleashed. . . . Mr. Bush's claim that things were going so well in Iraq that he could "accept" his generals' recommendation for a "drawdown" of forces was a carnival barker's come-on.[54]

—John Broder, journalist

In a sweeping indictment of the four-year effort in Iraq, the former top commander of American forces there called the Bush administration's handling of the war "incompetent" and said the result was "a nightmare with no end in sight." Lt. Gen. Ricardo S. Sanchez, who retired in 2006 after being replaced in Iraq after the Abu Ghraib prisoner abuse scandal, blamed the Bush administration for a "catastrophically flawed, unrealistically optimistic war plan" and denounced the current addition of American forces as a "desperate" move that would not achieve long-term stability.[55]

—David Cloud, journalist

After more than four years of fighting, America continues its desperate struggle in Iraq without any concerted effort to devise a strategy that will achieve victory in that war-torn country or in the greater conflict against extremism.[56]

—Lt. Gen.Ricardo S. Sanchez

What had gone wrong? Bush, Cheney, Rumsfeld, Wolfowitz, Rice, and other administration officials had set themselves up by using the most drastic and forceful rhetoric in persuading the nation that the war was necessary. They had approached the invasion of Iraq as though it were a political campaign. They pushed aside doubt, they exaggerated, they shared information with the public selectively. Rather than argue that it was prudent to assume the worst about Saddam, they asserted they that *knew* the worst to be true.[57]

—Michael Isikoff and David Corn, journalists

[T]he War College report confirmed what the Army leadership already suspected: that its real challenges would begin when it took control of Baghdad.[58]

—James Fallows, journalist

It's hard to conceive that it would take more forces to provide stability in post-Saddam Iraq than it would take to conduct the war itself and to secure the surrender of Saddam's security forces and his army. Hard to imagine.[59]

—Paul Wolfowitz, former Deputy Defense Secretary

None of the government working groups that had seriously looked into the question had simply "imagined" that occupying Iraq would be more difficult than defeating it. They had presented years' worth of experience suggesting that this would be the central reality of the undertaking. Wolfowitz either didn't notice this evidence or chose to disbelieve it.[60]

—James Fallows, journalist

On May 29, 2003, 50 days after the fall of Baghdad, President Bush proclaimed a fresh victory for his administration in Iraq: Two small trailers captured by U.S. and Kurdish troops had turned out to be long-sought mobile "biological laboratories."[61]

—Joby Warrick, journalist

We found the weapons of mass destruction. We found biological laboratories. You remember when Colin Powell stood up in front of the world, and he said, Iraq has got laboratories, mobile labs to build biological weapons. They're illegal. They're against the United Nations resolutions, and we've so far discovered two. And we'll find more weapons as time goes on. But for those who say we haven't found the banned manufacturing devices or banned weapons, they're wrong, we found them.[62]

—George W. Bush

Unknown to the president, four days before his TV interview, the DIA had dispatched a nine-member team of civilian experts to Iraq to examine the two mobile labs that had been found. The team sent back a three-page field report the day before Bush's statement with their conclusion that the labs were not for biological weapons. Their 122-page report, finished the next month, said the labs had nothing to do with WMD.[63]

—Bob Woodward, journalist

Bush and other administration officials continued to make the claim for nearly a year, despite an unequivocal report filed from the field stating that the trailers were not, and could not be, weapons labs. Scientists and engineers on the investigating team referred to the trailers as "the biggest sand toilets in the world."[64]

—David Michael Green, political science proferssor

January 23, 2004: David Kay, the chief U.S. weapons inspector, resigns his position, affirming his belief that no WMD stockpiles will be found in Iraq; the following week he discusses his conclusions at the White House. Nine months later his successor, Charles Duelfer, will conclude officially that Iraq not only did not possess WMD but did not have an active program in place to develop them. The structural supports of Powell's UN presentation begin to crumble.[65]

—Cullen Murphy and Todd Purdum, journalists

[T]he president and his supporters were able to cloud the issue of WMDs with obfuscating assertions that no such weapons had been found "yet"—as though they existed but were hidden—or with murkier assertions that the United States *had* located something called "weapons of mass destruction related program activities." No Bush official, certainly not the president himself, acknowledged (until after the 2004 election) that Saddam simply had no WMD.[66]

—Glenn Greenwald, lawyer/journalist

But the United States government had never informed the UN weapons inspectors—a team that Bush had demanded be sent—of where to find those weapons.[67]

—David Michael Green, political science proferssor

Once we were locked into the war, and no WMD's could be found, the original plot line was dropped with an alacrity that recalled the "Never mind!" with which Gilda Radner's Emily Litella used to end her misinformed Weekend Update commentaries on "Saturday Night Live." The administration began its dog-ate-my-homework cover-up, asserting that the various warning signs about the uranium claims were lost "in the bowels" of the bureaucracy or that it was all the CIA's fault or that it didn't matter anyway, because there were new, retroactive rationales to justify the war. But the administration knows how guilty it is. That's why it has so quickly trashed any insider who contradicts its story line about how we got to Iraq, starting with the former Secretary of the Treasury Paul O'Neill and the former counterterrorism czar Richard Clarke.[68]

—Frank Rich, columnist

[L]listen, we thought there was going to be stockpiles of weapons. I thought so; the Congress thought so; the UN thought so. I'll tell you what we do know. Saddam Hussein had the capacity to make weapons. See, he had the ability to make them. He had the intent. We knew he hated America. We knew he was paying families of suiciders. We knew he tortured his own people, and we knew he had the capability of making weapons. That we do know. They haven't found the stockpiles, but we do know he could make them. And so he was a dangerous man. He was a dangerous man. The world is better off without Saddam Hussein in power. America is safer.[69]

—George W. Bush

But UN inspectors hadn't said there were weapons stockpiles before the war. In fact, during their pre-invasion inspections, they found no evidence of stockpiles. And Bush didn't note that many of the members of Congress who had thought there were WMD stockpiles had been led to that view by briefings given by his administration.[70]

—Michael Isikoff and David Corn, journalists

■ ■ ■

[I]n recent weeks, we've witnessed the troubling behavior of a president who isn't merely in a state of denial but is completely untethered from reality. It's not that he can't handle the truth about Iraq. He doesn't know what the truth is.[71]

—Frank Rich, columnist

In light of not finding the weapons of mass destruction, do you believe the war in Iraq is a war of choice or a war of necessity?

—Tim Russert, journalist

I think that's an interesting question. Please elaborate on that a little bit. A war of choice or a war of necessity? It's a war of necessity. We—in my judgment, we had no choice when we look at the intelligence I looked at that says the man was a threat. And you know, we'll find out about the weapons of mass destruction that we all thought were there. That's part of the Iraqi Survey Group and the group I put together to look at.[72]

—George W. Bush

I remember talking to the president about this question following the interview. He seemed puzzled and asked me what Russert was getting at with the question. This, in turn, puzzled me. Surely this distinction between a necessary, unavoidable war and a war that the United States could have avoided but chose to wage was an obvious one that Bush must have thought about in the months before the invasion. Evidently, it wasn't obvious to the president, nor did his national security team make sure it was. . . . It strikes me today as an indication of his lack of inquisitiveness and his detrimental resistance to reflection.[73]

—Scott McClellan, former Bush press secretary

The mark of a truly civilized man is confidence in the strength and security derived from the inquiring mind.[74]

—Felix Frankfurter, U.S. Supreme Court

When I asked President Bush about these rather consequential decisions, he said to me, "You know, I don't really remember. You should talk to Hadley"—his national security advisor. I thought this was very telling, in terms of how detached he was."[75]

—Robert Draper, Bush biographer

The clearest indication of the depth of President Bush's understanding and of his own motivations came in Diane Sawyer's interview with Bush on ABC Television. Sawyer asked Bush about the "hard fact that there were weapons of mass destruction, as opposed to the possibility that [Saddam] might move to acquire those weapons." The President's considered response was, "What's the difference?" Then he added, "The possibility that he could acquire weapons. If he were to acquire weapons, he would be the danger." Sawyer pressed on. . . . The President replied . . . Sawyer asked again. . . . Finally in exasperation, the President said, "I'm telling you that I made the right decision for America because Saddam Hussein used weapons of mass destruction and invaded Kuwait." And so Bush invaded Iraq in 2003 because Saddam had used weapons of mass destruction in the 1980s and invaded Kuwait in 1990.[76]

—Richard Clarke, former White House counterterrorism expert

[An] aide to both Bushes who described the current president's lack of curiosity said that it extends to the most important single act of his presidency, the decision to go to war in Iraq. "I don't think we will ever, ever really have George Bush level and say he did this," the aide says. "I think he has drunk his own Kool-Aid and that's all there is to it."[77]

—Todd Purdum, journalist

■ ■ ■

The level of activity that we see today from a military standpoint, I think, will clearly decline. I think they're in the last throes, if you will, of the insurgency.[78]

—Dick Cheney

As if to confirm we're in the last throes, President Bush threw any remaining caution to the winds during his news conference in the Rose Garden that same morning. Almost everything he said was patently misleading or an outright lie, a sure sign of a leader so entombed in his bunker (he couldn't even emerge for the Washington Nationals' ceremonial first pitch last week) that he feels he has nothing left to lose. . . . Mr. Bush or anyone else who sees progress in the surge is correct only in the most literal and temporary sense. Yes, an influx of American troops is depressing some Baghdad violence. But any falloff in the capital is being offset by increased violence in the rest of the country.[79]

—Frank Rich, columnist

Let me just first tell you that I've never been more convinced that the decisions I made are the right decisions.[80]

—George W. Bush

Certitude is not the test of certainty. We have been cock-sure of many things that were not so.[81]

—Oliver Wendell Holmes Jr., U.S. Supreme Court

Leaders in the White House and especially the Department of Defense were extraordinarily ignorant about Iraq.[82]

—Charles Duelfer, Iraq Study Group

President Bush is still trying to twist reality to claim that his failed effort is worth sticking with.[83]

—*New York Times* editorial

We will stay the course until the job is done, Steve. And the temptation is to try to get the President or somebody to put a timetable on the definition of getting the job done. We're just going to stay the course.[84]

—George W. Bush

[W]e must stay the course, because the end result is in our nation's interest. . . . And my message today to those in Iraq is: We'll stay the course. My message to the troops is: We'll stay the course and complete the job.[85]

—George W. Bush

And that's why we're going to stay the course in Iraq. And that's why when we say something in Iraq, we're going to do it.[86]

—George W. Bush

We will stay the course, we will complete the job in Iraq.[87]

—George W. Bush

We will stay the course, we will help this young Iraqi democracy succeed.[88]

—George W. Bush

Insanity is doing the same thing over and over again and expecting different results.[89]

—anonymous

[W]hat you have here is, you have a president who wants to leave office without having to make the tough decision on withdrawing troops from Iraq. Leave it to his successor. It's a profoundly irresponsible position, but that's the one he's taking.[90]

—Jonathan Alter, journalist

When people in power get away with telling bigger and bigger lies, they naturally think they can keep getting away with it. And for a long time, Mr. Bush and his cronies did. Not anymore. . . . To get the country to redirect its finite resources to wage war against Saddam Hussein rather than keep its focus on the war against radical Islamic terrorists, the White House had to cook up not only the fiction that Iraq was about to attack us, but also the fiction that Iraq had already attacked us, on 9/11.[91]

—Frank Rich, columnist

[N]ewly declassified information indicates the Bush Administration's use of pre-war intelligence was misleading. Specifically, newly declassified information from the Defense Intelligence Agency (DIA) from February 2002 shows that, at the same time the Administration was making its case for attacking Iraq, the DIA did not trust or believe the source of the Administration's repeated assertions that Iraq had provided al-Qaeda with chemical and biological weapons training. Additional newly declassified information from the DIA also undermines the Administration's broader claim that there were strong links between Saddam Hussein and al-Qaeda.[92]

—Sen. Carl Levin

The report also made the point that an Iraq–al Qaeda collaboration was absurd on its face: "Saddam's regime is intensely secular and is wary of Islamic revolutionary movements." But just like any other evidence that disputed the administration's fictional story lines, this intelligence was promptly disregarded.[93]

—Frank Rich, columnist

This president has his fictitious Iraqi WMD and his lies, disguised as subtle hints, linking Saddam Hussein to 9/11, and his reason of the week for keeping us there, when all of the evidence has, for at least three years, told us we needed to get as many of our kids out as quickly as we could. . . . "We'll succeed unless we quit." No, sir, we will succeed against terrorism for our country's needs towards binding up the nation's wounds when you quit, quit the monumental lie that is our presence in Iraq.[94]

—Keith Olbermann, political commentator

Our troops in Iraq are performing brilliantly. Along with Iraqi forces, they have captured or killed an average of more than 1,500 enemy fighters per month since January. . . . The success of a free Iraq is critical to the security of the United States.[95]

—George W. Bush

Mr. Bush's claims last night about how well the war is going are believable only if you use Pentagon numbers so obviously cooked that they call to mind the way Americans were duped into first supporting this war.[96]

—*New York Times* editorial

Why the hell would the Department of Defense be the organization in our government that deals with the reconstruction of Iraq? Doesn't make sense.[97]

—Gen. Anthony Zinni

An unpublished 513-page federal history of the American-led reconstruction of Iraq depicts an effort crippled before the invasion by Pentagon planners who were hostile to the idea of rebuilding a foreign country, and then molded into a $100 billion failure by bureaucratic turf wars, spiraling violence and ignorance of the basic elements of Iraqi society and infrastructure.[98]

—James Glanz and Christian Miller, journalists

We've been waiting for well over two years for the Senate Intelligence Committee to finally hold the Bush administration accountable for the fairy tales it told about Saddam Hussein's weapons. Republican leaders keep saying it is a waste of time to find out whether President Bush and other top officials deliberately misled the world. But Defense Secretary Donald Rumsfeld's bizarre responses the other day to questions about that very issue were a timely reminder of why this investigation needs to be completed promptly, thoroughly and fairly.[99]

—*New York Times* editorial

It is bad enough that Mr. Rumsfeld and others did not tell Americans the full truth—to take the best-case situation—before the war. But they are still doing it. Just look at the profoundly twisted version of events that the defense secretary offered last week at a public event in Atlanta. Ray McGovern, an analyst for 27 years at the Central Intelligence Agency, stood in the audience and asked why Mr. Rumsfeld lied about weapons of mass destruction in Iraq. The secretary shot back, "I did not lie." Then, even though no one asked about them, he said Colin Powell and Mr. Bush offered "their honest opinion" based on "weeks and weeks" of time with the CIA.[100]

—*New York Times* editorial

I'm not in the intelligence business. . . . It appears that there were not weapons of mass destruction there.[101]

—Donald Rumsfeld

[In the Battle of Tal Afar,] "the assault was primarily led by Iraqi security forces—11 Iraqi battalions backed by 5 coalition battalions providing support."[102]

—George W. Bush

With the greatest respect to the president, that's completely wrong and is extraordinarily misleading. . . . I was in that battle from the very beginning to the very end. I was with Iraqi units, right there on the front line, as they were battling with al Qaeda. They were not leading. They were being led by the U.S. Green Beret special forces with them, Green Berets who were following an American plan of attack, who were advancing with these Iraqi units as and when they were told to do so by the American battle planners. The Iraqis led nothing.[103]

— Michael Ware, journalist

[O]rdinary life is beginning to return [to Baghdad].[104]

—George W. Bush

[T]he president must have a very different definition of what normal means, because there's nothing about life in Baghdad that I would consider normal. And I lived there for four-and-a-half years.[105]

— Bobby Ghosh, journalist

MISSION ACCOMPLISHED

The end of major combat in Iraq marks a "turning of the tide" in the global fight against terrorism, President Bush said yesterday in a dramatically staged address from the flight deck of an aircraft carrier returning from the Persian Gulf.[106]

—Anne Kornblut, journalist

Bush did nothing to dispel the illusion that he had piloted the plane to the deck; in fact, he was a passenger in a pilot's costume. . . . A banner over his shoulder reading "Mission Accomplished" (which, contrary to Bush's later claim, had been purchased and placed there by his staff, not the ship's crew).[107]

—John Dean, former White House counsel

We found out in dribs and drabs that virtually everything about that day was bogus. . . . The landing was bogus. The Navy turned around the carrier Abraham Lincoln beforehand, ensuring we would not have noticed exotic San Diego in the background.

The plane was bogus. It turned out the ship was close enough to shore for the president to have used a safer and cheaper helicopter instead. The ship was bogus. It should have been docked, but was kept at sea for hours, extending the sailors' ten month tour so that the president could get a nap on board. The explanations for the banner were the height of bogusness. The White House actually blaming it on the sailors. The tactic of hiding behind the military, a sign of bogus things yet to bogus come.[108]

—Keith Olbermann, political commentator

[M]ajor combat operations in Iraq have ended. In the battle of Iraq, the United States and our allies have prevailed.[109]

—George W. Bush

Media strategists noted afterward that [the Bush team] had choreographed every aspect of the event, even down to the members of the Lincoln crew arrayed in coordinated shirt colors over Mr. Bush's right shoulder and the "Mission Accomplished" banner placed to perfectly capture the president and the celebratory two words in a single shot. The speech was specifically timed for what image makers call "magic hour light" which cast a golden glow on Mr. Bush.[110]

—Elizabeth Bumiller, journalist

This is the administration that . . . wrapped a "Mission Accomplished" banner around a carrier held offshore for an extra day to showcase a strutting president in a flight suit.[111]

—*Chatanooga Times Free Press* editorial

In this battle, we have fought for the cause of liberty and for the peace of the world. Our nation and our coalition are proud of this accomplishment.[112]

—George W. Bush

In both image and word that day, what Bush did was tear down the goalposts at halftime in the game.[113]

—Thomas Ricks, journalist

It was just another of the broken promises and false claims of success that we've heard from Mr. Bush for years, from shock and awe, to bouquets of roses, to mission accomplished.[114]

—*New York Times* editorial

The battle of Iraq is one victory in a war on terror that began on September the 11th, 2001 and still goes on. . . . The liberation of Iraq is a crucial advance in the campaign against terror. We have removed an ally of Al Qaida and cut off a source of terrorist funding.[115]

—George W. Bush

On May 1, 2003, Mr. Bush celebrated "Mission Accomplished." On May 29, Mr. Bush announced that "we found the weapons of mass destruction." On July 2, as attacks increased on American troops, Mr. Bush dared the insurgents to "bring 'em on." But the mission was not accomplished, the weapons were not found and the enemy kept bringing 'em on.[116]

—Frank Rich, columnist

In the long and storied history of bogusness, there have been few days on which the bogus could be found in such depth and breadth, in such quantity and quality as we can find looking back on the fateful events of May 1st, 2003, a date that will live in bogusity. . . . [F]orget for a moment the mission accomplished banner, which actually was not bogus in a way, because our troops really did accomplish what they were sent to do, remove Saddam Hussein and make sure Iraq did not pose a threat. It only turned out to be bogus when Mr. Bush decided that mission was not mission accomplished enough.[117]

—Keith Olbermann, political commentator

This was a war worth fighting. It ended quickly with few civilian casualties and with little damage to Iraq's cities, towns or infrastructure. It ended without the Arab world rising up against us, as the war's critics feared, without the quagmire they predicted, without the heavy losses in house-to-house fighting they warned us to expect. . . . Iraqis are freer today and we are safer. Relax and enjoy it.[118]

—Richard Perle, neoconservative

[T]hey, in effect, helped create the very circumstances that allowed al Qaeda to establish links inside Iraq. It's just stunning.[119]

—Roger Cressey, National Security Council

The ultimate chutzpah is that Mr. Bush, the man who sold us Saddam's imminent mushroom clouds and "Mission Accomplished," is trivializing the chaos in Iraq as propaganda. The enemy's "sophisticated" strategy, he said in last weekend's radio address, is to distribute "images of violence" to television networks, Web sites and journalists to "demoralize our country." This is a morally repugnant argument.[120]

—Frank Rich, columnist

The Bush administration offered three basic rationales for the U.S. intervention in Iraq: the threat it believed was posed by Saddam's WMD; the supposed nexus it saw between

Saddam Hussein's government and transnational terrorism; and the need to liberate an oppressed people. In the spring of 2004, the first two arguments were undercut by official findings by the same government that had invaded Iraq, and the third was tarred by the revelation of the Abu Ghraib scandal.[121]

—Thomas Ricks, journalist

We have long since lost count of all the historic turning points and fast-evaporating victories hyped by this president. The toppling of Saddam's statue, "Mission Accomplished," the transfer of sovereignty and the purple fingers all blur into a hallucinatory loop of delusion. . . . And what exactly is our task? Mr. Bush's current definition— "as the Iraqis stand up, we will stand down"—could not be a better formula for quagmire. Twenty-eight months after the fall of Saddam, only "a small number" of Iraqi troops are capable of fighting without American assistance, according to the Pentagon— a figure that Joseph Biden puts at "fewer than 3,000." At this rate, our 138,000 troops will be replaced by self-sufficient locals in roughly 100 years.[122]

—Frank Rich, columnist

The bottom line is this: Congress's failure to fund our troops on the front lines will mean that some of our military families could wait longer for their loved ones to return from the front lines. And others could see their loved ones headed back to the war sooner than they need to. That is unacceptable to me, and I believe it is unacceptable to the American people.[123]

—George W. Bush

Effective immediately, active Army units now in the Central Command area of responsibility and those headed there will be deployed for not more than 15 months.[124]

—Robert Gates, Defense Secretary

All but the most blindly devoted Bush supporters can see that Bush administration officials have no clue about what to do in Iraq tomorrow, much less a month from now. . . . It's not even clear that [Bush] understands how bad the situation in Iraq is or how close he is to losing public support for the war, a support that once lost may be impossible to regain.[125]

—Robert Kagan, columnist

George Bush, Dick Cheney and Don Rumsfeld think you're stupid. Yes, they do. . . . What could possibly be more injurious and insulting to the U.S. military than to send it into combat in Iraq without enough men—to launch an invasion of a foreign country not by the Powell Doctrine of overwhelming force, but by the Rumsfeld Doctrine of just enough troops to lose? What could be a bigger insult than that? . . . This administration never had a plan for the morning after, and we've been making it up—and paying the price—ever since.[126]

—Thomas Friedman, journalist

The administration's guilt (or at least embarrassment) about its lies in fomenting the war quickly drove it to hide the human price being paid for those lies. (It also tried to hide the financial cost of the war by keeping it out of the regular defense budget, but that's another, if related, story.) The steps the White House took to keep casualties out of view were extraordinary, even as it deployed troops to decorate every presidential victory rally and gave the Pentagon free rein to exploit the sacrifices of Jessica Lynch and Pat Tillman in mendacious PR stunts.[127]

—Frank Rich, columnist

When those accounts turned out to be largely fiction, [Lynch] became a symbol of Bush administration propaganda and the press's credulity in buying it.[128]

—Frank Rich, columnist

EXPLOITING SACRIFICES

We report tonight on the death of one time NFL football player Pat Tillman. He died in Afghanistan. . . . Mr. Tillman didn't have to go in the Army. He didn't need the money. In fact, he walked away from millions when he enlisted. He didn't go for the publicity surely, in fact he shunned it when he made his decision. He went in the days after 9/11 because he believed it was his duty.[129]

—Aaron Brown, journalist

The military will say very little about the Afghan ambush that killed NFL safety Pat Tillman, and that's probably how he would have wanted it.[130]

—Lee Cowan, journalist

"Pat Tillman was an inspiration on and off the football field, as with all who have made the ultimate sacrifice in the war on terror. His family is in the thoughts and prayers of President and Mrs. Bush," Taylor Gross, a spokesman for the White House, said in a statement.[131]

—MSNBC report

When President Bush spoke at [a] dinner at week's end, he followed his jokes with a eulogy about Tillman's sacrifice. But he kept the circumstances of Tillman's death vague, no doubt because the White House did indeed get the message that the Pentagon's press release about Tillman's losing his life in battle was fiction. Yet it would be four more weeks before Pat Tillman's own family was let in on the truth.[132]

—Frank Rich, columnist

An insinuation, which a man who makes it does not believe himself, is equal to lying. It is the cowardice of lying. It unites the barest part of that vice with the meanest of all others. An open liar is a highwayman in his profession, but an insinuating liar is a thief skulking in the night.[133]

—Thomas Paine

Within hours of Pat Tillman's death, the Army went into information-lockdown mode, cutting off phone and Internet connections at a base in Afghanistan, posting guards on a wounded platoon mate, and ordering a sergeant to burn Tillman's uniform.[134]

—Scott Lindlaw, journalist

Just seven days after Pat Tillman's death, a top general warned there were strong indications that it was friendly fire and President Bush might embarrass himself if he said the NFL star-turned-soldier died in an ambush, according to a memo obtained by The Associated Press.[135]

—Associated Press report

Tillman's uniform and body armor were burned a day after he was killed, starting a string of deception (including a lame explanation that the blood-covered clothes had to be destroyed as a biohazard) and negating any chance of lessons—that's criminal.[136]

—*Arizona Republic* editorial

That Corporal Tillman was killed by friendly fire appears to have been known to his fellow soldiers within a day of the incident, if not sooner. But at some point in the first few days another story was concocted asserting that he had died from enemy fire as he heroically tried to help the unit that shot him. The truth did not emerge—and was not conveyed to his family—until more than a month had gone by and a well-publicized and widely televised memorial service had taken place.[137]

—*New York Times* editorial

"Did it seem like Pat's death was being treated differently than any other soldier's death because of his high profile?" [Katie] Couric asks. "Absolutely," one of the [Army Rangers who was with Tillman that day] replies.[138]

—*60 Minutes* excerpt

[I]mmediately after Corporal Tillman's death, at least 97 White House officials exchanged hundreds of e-mails about how the White House should respond. Yet weeks later, when the truth came out, there was nary an e-mail peep about the astonishing change. Is that because officials had lost interest?[139]

—*New York Times* editorial

The Tillman family has charged that the military and the Bush administration deliberately deceived his relatives and the nation to avoid turning public opinion against the war.[140]

—Associated Press report

[T]he Pat Tillman story turned out to be spin. Less than a month after the army released a stirring description of the circumstances of Tillman's death charging up a hill in Afghanistan, Central Command issued a perfunctory new release saying that Tillman had died instead "as a probable result of friendly fire while his unit was engaged in combat with enemy forces." As with the good-news form letters from the front, the authorship of the fictional press release about Tillman's firefight remained a mystery.[141]

—Frank Rich, columnist

The great enemy of the truth is very often not the lie: deliberate, continued, and dishonest; but the myth: persistent, persuasive, and unrealistic.[142]

—John F. Kennedy

After a yearlong probe, military investigators said Monday they found no criminal negligence in the friendly-fire death of Tillman, the former Arizona Cardinals player. But a second investigation, looking at the aftermath, revealed an attempt to cover up the circumstances of Tillman's death that went far up the chain of command. Investigators are recommending that nine officers, including four generals, be held accountable for making critical errors.[143]

—*Arizona Republic* editorial

[T]he circumstances of Tillman's April 22, 2004, death were kept from his family and the American public; the Army maintained he was cut down by enemy bullets in an ambush, even though many soldiers knew he was mistakenly killed by his own comrades.[144]

—Scott Lindlaw, journalist

The administration clearly was using this case for its own political reasons. This cover-up started within minutes of Pat's death, and it started at high levels.[145]

—Patrick Tillman, Pat's father

Kevin [Tillman], who had served in the same platoon, recoiled at the "calculated lies," including a Silver Star awarded his brother because the Army needed a hero as much as it feared a scandal. It was weeks before the Tillmans learned the truth. "We've all been betrayed," Pat's mother Mary Tillman said. "We never thought they would use him the way they did."[146]

—Nancy Gibbs, journalist

Pat Tillman's family firmly rejected the Defense Department's findings into the former NFL star's friendly-fire death in Afghanistan, calling for congressional investigations into what they see as broad malfeasance and a cover-up.[147]

—Scott Lindlaw, journalist

What the hearing underscored was the likelihood that the White House also knew very early on what the Army knew and covered up: the football star's supposed death in battle in Afghanistan, vividly described in a Pentagon press release awarding him a Silver Star, was a complete fabrication, told to the world (and Tillman's parents) even though top officers already suspected he had died by friendly fire. The White House apparently decided to join the Pentagon in maintaining that lie so that it could be milked for PR purposes on two television shows, the correspondents' dinner on May 1, 2004, and a memorial service for Tillman two days later.[148]

—Frank Rich, columnist

To see why the administration wanted to keep the myth going, just look at other events happening in the week before. . . . On April 28, 2004, CBS broadcast the first photographs from Abu Ghraib; on April 29 a poll on The Times's front page found the president's approval rating on the war was plummeting; on April 30 Ted Koppel challenged the administration's efforts to keep the war dead hidden by reading the names of the fallen on "Nightline." Tillman could be useful to help drown out all this bad news, and to an extent he was.[149]

—Frank Rich, columnist

∎ ∎

Jessica Lynch, a 19-year-old private first class missing since the ambush of an Army maintenance company 10 days ago in southern Iraq, has been rescued by Special Operations forces. She had been held in a hospital near Nasiriyah because of multiple wounds, officials said.[150]

—*Washington Post* report

A senior Administration official said today President Bush welcomed the news of the dramatic rescue of a US Army soldier held captive for 10 days in Iraq, telling Defense Secretary Donald Rumsfeld yesterday, "That's great!" Special forces rescued Private Jessica Lynch, 19, and recovered the bodies of other soldiers in a midnight raid on an Iraqi hospital. Lynch was with a maintenance convoy ambushed by Iraqi forces March 23.[151]

—White House bulletin

Jessica Lynch became an icon of the war. An all-American heroine, the story of her capture by the Iraqis and her rescue by U.S. special forces became one of the great patriotic moments of the conflict. It couldn't have happened at a more crucial moment, when the talk was of coalition forces bogged down, of a victory too slow in coming. Her rescue will go down as one of the most stunning pieces of news management yet conceived. It provides a remarkable insight into the real influence of Hollywood producers on the

Pentagon's media managers, and has produced a template from which America hopes to present its future wars.[152]

—John Kampfner, journalist

Jessica Lynch. You know the one. The sweet, American-pie 19-year-old soldier and kindergarten-teacher wanna-be whose army squad took a wrong turn in Iraq and was, apparently, ambushed. And some of her comrades were killed and she was taken prisoner, full of stab wounds and bullet holes, and she was whisked off to a ragged Iraqi hospital and held for eight days by vicious Iraqi guards and ostensibly abused, and later supposedly "rescued" in the most daring and macho made-for-TV moment of the war by elite teams of hunky U.S. Army Rangers and U.S. Navy SEALs. Wow. Except that it never really happened that way.[153]

—Malcom Morford, journalist

A continual circulation of lies among those who are not much in the way of hearing them contradicted, will in time pass for the truth; and the crime lies not in the believer but in the inventor.[154]

—Thomas Paine

It's the power of the story that always counts first, and the selling of it that comes second. Accuracy is optional.[155]

—Frank Rich, columnist

The news of her rescue, complete with the spooky green night-video footage, came at just the moment when the nation was hungry for good news out of a hard war. . . . It was all so well timed, such an emotional turning point, that questions began to rise. . . . Was it really such a daring rescue if there was no one guarding her anymore by the time the commandos whisked her out?[156]

—Nancy Gibbs, journalist

Releasing its five-minute film to the networks, the Pentagon claimed that Lynch had stab and bullet wounds, and that she had been slapped about on her hospital bed and interrogated. It was only thanks to a courageous Iraqi lawyer, Mohammed Odeh al-Rehaief, that she was saved. According to the Pentagon, Al-Rehaief risked his life to alert the Americans that Lynch was being held. Just after midnight, Army Rangers and Navy Seals stormed the Nassiriya hospital. Their "daring" assault on enemy territory was captured by the military's night-vision camera. They were said to have come under fire, but they made it to Lynch and whisked her away by helicopter. That was the message beamed back to viewers within hours of the rescue.[157]

—John Kampfner, journalist

Contentious at its inception, confusing in its execution and devastating in its effect, the invasion of Iraq reeked of impending disaster. Iraqis resisted, sandstorms slowed the advance, "smart" weapons hit markets and residences and U.S. soldiers were taken prisoner. An impending humanitarian crisis loomed, as Basra and later Baghdad were deprived of water and electricity. Then the miracle occurred. The damsel-in-distress was rescued (Pvt. Jessica Lynch). . . . It was a feel-good ending to an otherwise disturbing script.[158]

—Steve Ludwig, columnist

In all this, Jessica Lynch herself, unable to speak, was reduced to a mere Pawn, an innocent bystander in the production of her own big-budget, action-packed biopic. When she emerged a year later, ABC's Diane Sawyer asked if it bothered her that she had been showcased by the military. "Yeah, it does," she answered. "It does that they used me as a way to symbolize all this stuff. I mean, yeah, it's wrong."[159]

—Frank Rich, columnist

[T]his is how we fabricate our history. This is how we spin our patriotism, how we bake our jingoistic cake, the Lynch tale the most apt and definitive myth of the war so far. Because Jessica's story . . . does not rely on truths. We do not rely on first-hand reports. We do not rely on anything so piffling and small and dangerous as honesty. We rely, simply, on PR. We believe the TV images of the bogus "rescue" at the expense of common sense because we are a nation drunk on the idea that the U.S. can do no wrong and TV would never lie.[160]

—Malcom Morford, journalist

[F]ormer Army Pvt. Jessica Lynch testified in Washington, D.C., about the real story of her capture and rescue while serving in Iraq in 2003. She spoke before the House Government Reform Committee along with the family of fallen Army Ranger Pat Tillman. . . . At the hearing, the chairman of the House panel, Henry Waxman, accused the government of inventing "sensational details and stories" about Tillman's death and [the] Lynch rescue.[161]

—Caitlin Johnson, journalist

I'm no hero, the people who served with me who died are the real heroes. The truth of war is not always easy. The truth is always more heroic than the hype. I'm still confused as to why they chose to lie and try to make me a legend when the real heroes were my fellow soldiers that day.[162]

—Jessica Lynch

The American military has been accused of telling lies about two of its most famous soldiers. Official versions of the rescue of prisoner of war Jessica Lynch and the death of former U.S. football star Pat Tillman turned both into national heroes. But the propaganda was dismissed as "utter fiction" at a Capitol Hill hearing to expose the false battlefield stories peddled by the Pentagon.[163]

—David Gardner, journalist

INCONVENIENT TRUTHS AND "A PACK OF LIES"

[R]ecall that General Abizaid, when he first brought up the fact that we were facing an insurgency, was challenged on that notion by the former secretary of defense. . . . They would not tolerate a challenging opinion to what they thought was going to be the outcome of an invasion conducted by a small force.[164]

—Maj. Gen. Paul Eaton

Before the Iraq war Mr. Rumsfeld muzzled commanders who warned that we were going in with too few troops, and sidelined State Department experts who warned that we needed a plan for the invasion's aftermath. But when the war went wrong, he began talking about "unknown unknowns" and going to war with "the army you have," ducking responsibility for the failures of leadership that have turned the war into a stunning victory—for Iran.[165]

—Paul Krugman, columnist

The message is that there are no knowns. There are things we know that we know. There are known unknowns; that is to say there are things we now know we don't know. But there are also unknown unknowns—things we do not know we don't know. So when we do the best we can and we pull all this information together, and we then say, "Well, that's basically what we see as the situation," that is really only the known knowns and the known unknowns. And each year we discover a few more of those unknown unknowns.[166]

—Donald Rumsfeld

Failure in Iraq would be a disaster for the United States. . . . America will change our strategy to help the Iraqis carry out their campaign to put down sectarian violence and bring security to the people of Baghdad. This will require increasing American force levels. So I've committed more than 20,000 additional American troops to Iraq.[167]

—George W. Bush

President Bush told Americans last night that failure in Iraq would be a disaster. The disaster is Mr. Bush's war, and he has already failed. Last night was his chance to stop offering more fog and be honest with the nation, and he did not take it.[168]

—*New York Times* editorial

He that is the author of a war lets loose the whole contagion of hell and opens a vein
that bleeds a nation to death.[169]

—Thomas Paine

The new WHIG is a 24/7 Pentagon information "war room" conceived in the last throes
of the Rumsfeld regime and run by a former ABC News producer. White House "facts"
about the surge's triumph are turning up unsubstantiated in newspapers and on TV.
Instead of being bombarded with dire cherry-picked intelligence about WMD, this
time we're being serenaded with feel-good cherry-picked statistics offering hope. Once
again the fix is in. . . . The "decrease in violence" fable is even more insidious. Though
both General Petraeus and a White House fact sheet have recently boasted of a 75 percent decline in sectarian attack, this number turns out to be as cooked as those tallies
of Saddam's weapons sites once peddled by WHIG.[170]

—Frank Rich, columnist

The U.S. military's claim that violence has decreased sharply in Iraq in recent months
has come under scrutiny from many experts within and outside the government, who
contend that some of the underlying statistics are questionable and selectively ignore
negative trends. Reductions in violence form the centerpiece of the Bush administration's claim that its war strategy is working. . . . Others who have looked at the full range
of U.S. government statistics on violence, however, accuse the military of cherry-picking
positive indicators and caution that the numbers—most of which are classified—are
often confusing and contradictory.[1710]

—Karen DeYoung, journalist

Asked to explain what he means that the Bush administration has not told the truth
about Iraq, [Bob] Woodward says, "I think probably the prominent, most prominent
example is the level of violence." . . . Woodward says the government had kept this
trend secret for years before finally declassifying the graph just three weeks ago. And
Woodward accuses President Bush and the Pentagon of making false claims of progress
in Iraq—claims, contradicted by facts that are being kept secret. . . . "Why is that secret?
The insurgents know what they're doing. They know the level of violence and how effective they are. Who doesn't know? The American public," he adds.[172]

—60 Minutes excerpt

What's surprising is not that this White House makes stuff up, but that even after all
the journalistic embarrassments in the run-up to the war its fictions can still infiltrate
the real news.[173]

—Frank Rich, columnist

Those who are most enraged about the administration's reckless misadventures are incredulous that it repeatedly gets away with the same stunts. Last week the president was still invoking 9/11 to justify the war in Iraq, which he again conflated with the war on Islamic jihadism—the war we are now losing, by the way, in Afghanistan and Somalia.[174]

—Frank Rich, columnist

You know, right after September the 11th, I knew that some would forget the dangers we face, some would hope that the world would be what it's not: a peaceful place where people wouldn't want to do harm to those of us who love freedom. I vowed that day, after September the 11th, to do everything I could to protect the American people. And I was able to make that claim because there were people such as yourselves, who are willing to be on the front line in the war on terror.[175]

—George W. Bush

A year or so ago, it was our war, and we claimed it proudly. But gone is the hubris. Let's face it: Iraq is not going to be America's showcase in the Arab-Muslim world.[176]

—Fouad Ajami, journalist

On almost every issue involving postwar Iraq—troop strength, international support, the credibility of exiles, de-Baathification, handling Ayatollah Ali Sistani—Washington's assumptions and policies have been wrong. By now most have been reversed, often too late to have much effect. This strange combination of arrogance and incompetence has not only destroyed the hopes for a new Iraq. It has had the much broader effect of turning the United States into an international outlaw in the eyes of much of the world.[177]

—Fareed Zakaria, journalist

In reviewing progress on the three fronts of this war, even the most sanguine optimist cannot yet conclude that we are winning or that we can win without some significant changes of policy.[178]

—John Lehman, 9/11 Commission

Of the Sunday interviewers, it was George Stephanopoulos who went for the jugular by returning to that nonexistent uranium from Africa. He forced Ms. Rice to watch a clip of her appearance on his show in June 2003, when she claimed she did not know of any serious questions about the uranium evidence before the war. Then he came as close as any Sunday host ever has to calling a guest a liar.[179]

—Frank Rich, columnist

But that statement wasn't true. You and your deputy had both received memos in October 2002 from the CIA about this intelligence and they raised serious questions about it.[180]

—George Stephanopoulos, ABC News (to Secretary of State Condoleezza Rice)

Ms. Rice pleaded memory loss, but the facts remain. She received a memo raising serious questions about the uranium in October 2002, three months before the president included the infamous 16 words on the subject in his State of the Union address. Her deputy, Stephen Hadley, received two memos as well as a phone call of warning from Mr. Tenet. . . . Ms. Rice's latest canard wasn't an improvisation; it was a scripted set-up for the president's outrageous statement three days later.[181]

—Frank Rich, columnist

For America the decision we face in Iraq is not whether we ought to take sides in a civil war, it's whether we stay in the fight against the same international terrorist network that attacked us on 9/11.[182]

—George W. Bush

Such statements about the present in Iraq are no less deceptive—and no less damaging to our national interest—than the lies about uranium and Qaeda-9/11 connections told in 2002–3. This country needs facts, not fiction, to make its decisions about the endgame of the war, just as it needed (but didn't get) facts when we went to war in the first place. To settle for less is to make the same tragic error twice.[183]

—Frank Rich, columnist

▌▌▌

Saddam Hussein's regime is a grave and gathering danger.[184]

—George W. Bush

The situation in Iraq is grave and deteriorating.[185]

—Iraq Study Group Report

December 6, 2006: The independent Iraq Study Group, chaired by former secretary of state James Baker and former congressman Lee Hamilton, issues a report setting out 79 recommendations for the future conduct of the Iraq war. The report is brushed aside by the president. Lawrence Eagleburger, one of the group's members, says of Bush after the report is delivered, "I don't recall, seriously, that he asked any questions."[186]

—Cullen Murphy and Todd Purdum, journalists

Cheney was there, never said a word, not a—of course, the recommendations from his point of view were awful, but he never criticized. Bush was very gracious, said we've worked hard and did this great service for the country—and he ignored it so far as I can see. He fundamentally didn't agree with it.[187]

—Lee Hamilton, Iraq Study Group co-chair

[T]here is significant underreporting of the violence in Iraq. The standard for recording attacks acts as a filter to keep events out of reports and databases. A murder of an Iraqi is not necessarily counted as an attack. If we cannot determine the source of a sectarian attack, that assault does not make it into the database. A roadside bomb or a rocket or mortar attack that doesn't hurt U.S. personnel doesn't count. For example, on one day in July 2006 there were 93 attacks or significant acts of violence reported. Yet a careful review of the reports for that single day brought to light 1,100 acts of violence.[188]

—Iraq Study Group report

Recommendation 78: The Director of National Intelligence and the Secretary of Defense should also institute immediate changes in the collection of data about violence and the sources of violence in Iraq to provide a more accurate picture of events on the ground.[189]

—Iraq Study Group report

[T]he White House gets away with falsifying reality, sliming its opponents and sowing hyped fears of Armageddon.[190]

—Frank Rich, columnist

Good policy is difficult to make when information is systematically collected in a way that minimizes its discrepancy with policy goals.[191]

—Iraq Study Group report

We figured that maybe 5 of the 79 recommendations would ever be considered, and I think we were pretty right.[192]

—Sen. Alan Simpson, Iraq Study Group

■ ■ ■

The same folks that are bombing innocent people in Iraq were the ones who attacked us in America on September the 11th, and that's why what happens in Iraq matters to the security here at home.[193]

—George W. Bush

The president wants to play on Al Qaeda because he thinks Americans understand the threat Al Qaeda poses. But I don't think he demonstrates that fighting Al Qaeda in Iraq precludes Al Qaeda from attacking America here tomorrow. Al Qaeda, both in Iraq and globally, thrives on the American occupation.[194]

—Bruce Riedel, Mideast policy expert

Regime change in Iraq, [the Bush administration] said, would have a sweeping symbolic effect on worldwide sources of terror. That seems to have been true—but in the opposite way from what the President intended. It is hard to find a counterterrorism specialist who thinks that the Iraq War has reduced rather than increased the threat to the United States.[195]

—James Fallows, journalist

Mr. Bush and his team continue to spout disinformation and vacuous slogans about victory and, of course, more character assassination. . . . The aim of these attacks is to avoid truly engaging criticism of Mr. Bush's Iraq policy. . . . Mr. Bush denied Americans a serious debate about starting this war. It's far past time for a serious and honest debate about how to end it.[196]

—*New York Times* editorial

So you look at [the] situation today in Afghanistan or even in Iraq, and you've got people who have doubts. . . . And those doubts are encouraged, obviously, when they see the kind of debate that we've had in the United States, suggestions, for example, that we should withdraw U.S. forces from Iraq, simply feed into that whole notion, validates the strategy of the terrorists.[197]

—Dick Cheney

They promised bipartisanship and then showed that to them bipartisanship meant that their party would rule and the rest would have to follow or be branded with ever escalating hysteria as morally or intellectually confused, as appeasers. As those who, in the vice president's words, yesterday, "validate the strategy of the terrorists." They promised protection and then showed that to them protection meant going to war against a despot whose hand they had once shaken, a despot who we learn from our own Senate Intelligence Committee, hated al Qaeda as much as we did. The polite phrase for how so many of us were duped in to supporting a war on the false premise it had something to do with 9/11, is "lying by implication." The impolite phrase is "impeachable offense."[198]

—Keith Olbermann, political commentator

On the one year anniversary of President Bush's State of the Union address justifying his "New Way Forward" in Iraq, it is clear that the surge has failed to meet its objectives.[199]

—Center for American Progress

America will hold the Iraqi government to the benchmarks it has announced.[200]

—George W. Bush

Despite the fact that the Iraqi government has only met three of the 18 benchmarks laid out last year, an end to U.S. military and financial commitment is nowhere in sight.[201]

—Center for American Progress

More fiction. Prime Minister Nuri al-Maliki's own political adviser, Sadiq al-Rikabi, says it would take "a miracle" to pass the legislation America wants. Asked on Monday whether the Iraqi Parliament would stay in Baghdad this summer rather than hightail it to vacation, [White House press secretary] Tony Snow was stumped.[202]

—Frank Rich, columnist

This president is never one to let facts get in the way of a political agenda.[203]

—Frank Rich, columnist

[W]e have grown accustomed to this president's disconnect from reality and his habit of tilting at straw men, like Americans who don't care about terrorism because they question his mismanagement of the war or don't worry about what will happen after the United States withdraws, as it inevitably must.[204]

—*New York Times* editorial

■ ■ ■

Democrats on a deeply divided Senate Intelligence Committee on Friday accused the Bush administration of ignoring pre-invasion warnings from the nation's spy agencies that a war in Iraq could be followed by violence and division and that it could strengthen the hands of Al Qaeda and of Iran.[205]

—Scott Shane, journalist

The intelligence assessments, made in January 2003 and widely circulated within the Bush administration before the war, said that establishing democracy in Iraq would be "a long, difficult and probably turbulent challenge." The assessments noted that Iraqi political culture was "largely bereft of the social underpinnings" to support democratic development.[206]

—Walter Pincus and Karen DeYoung, journalists

The most chilling and prescient warning from the intelligence community prior to the war was that the American invasion would bring about instability in Iraq that would be exploited by Iran and al Qaeda terrorists.[207]

—Sen. John D. Rockefeller IV

But virtually everyone who had thought about the issue had warned about the risk of looting. U.S. soldiers could have prevented it—and would have, if so instructed.[208]

—James Fallows, journalist

Freedom's untidy, and free people are free to make mistakes and commit crimes and do bad things. They're also free to live their lives and do wonderful things, and that's what's going to happen here.[209]

—Donald Rumsfeld

Liberty cannot be purchased by a wish.[210]

—Thomas Paine

[T]he Administration will be found wanting for its carelessness. Because of warnings it chose to ignore, it squandered American prestige, fortune, and lives.[211]

—James Fallows, journalist

I strongly agree that we've got to continue to make it clear to the Iraqi government that this is—the solution to Iraq, an Iraq that can govern itself, sustain itself and defend itself, is more than a military mission. It's precisely the reason why I sent more troops into Baghdad: to be able to provide some breathing space for this democratically elected government to succeed. And it's hard work, and I understand it's hard work.[212]

—George W. Bush

Oh what a malleable war Iraq has been. First it was waged to vanquish Saddam's (nonexistent) nuclear arsenal and his (nonexistent) collaboration with Al Qaeda. Then it was going to spread (nonexistent) democracy throughout the Middle East. Now it is being rebranded as a fight against Tehran. Mr. Bush keeps saying that his saber rattling about Iran is not "a pretext for war." Maybe so, but at the very least it's a pretext for prolonging the disastrous war we already have.[213]

—Frank Rich, columnist

The capture of Saddam Hussein, the interim government, the interim constitution, the permanent government, the permanent constitution, the Iraqi vote of January 2005, of October 2005, of December 2005, the prime minister of 2004, and 2005, and 2006. And when political milestones peter out, we are told to give the military plans another chance, the new ways forward, the surge of 2005, the surge of 2006, the surge of 2007, this one expected to bring us at least into 2008. If it comes to seem as though they want this war to last forever, consider how far-reaching were their goals when national optimism permitted our leaders to voice the goals out loud.[214]

—Keith Olbermann, political commentator

[W]hen war becomes literally continuous, there is no such thing as military necessity. Technical progress can cease and the most palpable facts can be denied or disregarded.[215]

—George Orwell

A nation that continues year after year to spend more money on military defense than on programs of social uplift is approaching spiritual doom.[216]

—Martin Luther King Jr.

I think that they thought this would be a quick, easy joy ride through Iraq, get rid of this thug, Saddam Hussein, and be home by Christmas in 2003. And then like kids playing with matches, it blew up in their faces, and ever since, they've been retrofitting rationales for it.[217]

—Frank Rich, columnist

[T]he administration has constantly shifted its goals in Iraq to avoid accepting failure and blame—only to see the new goals drift beyond reach each time. Liberation of Iraqis became occupation by Americans, democracy became an unattainable centralized "national unity" government and this year's military surge has become a device for achieving political reconciliation among people who do not want to reconcile.[218]

—Jim Hoagland, journalist

The Bushies can continue to claim that the invasion of Iraq was justified because Saddam was a threat to our security. Unless, of course, he wasn't, and the Cheney cabal was simply abusing the trust of Americans to push a wild-eyed political scheme.[219]

—Maureen Dowd, columnist

In advocating and prosecuting this war, he passed on a chance to get Abu Musab al Zarqawi, to get Moqtada al Sadr, to get bin Laden. He sent in fewer troops than the generals told him to. He ordered the Iraqi army disbanded and the Iraqi government de-Baathified. He shortchanged Iraqi training.[220]

—Keith Olbermann, political commentator

This is the same administration, after all, that distorted secret and notoriously unreliable intelligence to pave the way to the Iraq war; that contemptuously disregarded the advice of generals who, before they were sacked, pleaded for a post-invasion plan to win the peace and the need for more troops to contain ancient sectarian rifts that were sure to be unleashed once Saddam Hussein's dictatorship was toppled.[221]

—*Chattanooga Times Free Press* editorial

He neglected to plan for widespread looting. He did not anticipate sectarian violence. He sent in troops without life-saving equipment. He gave jobs to foreign contractors and not Iraqis. He staffed U.S. positions there based on partisanship, not professionalism. He and his government told us America had prevailed, mission accomplished, the resistance was in its last throes. He has insisted more troops were not necessary. He has now insisted more troops are necessary. He has insisted it's up to the generals, and then removed some of the generals who said more troops would not be necessary. He has trumpeted the turning points, the fall of Baghdad, the death of Uday and Qusay, the capture of Saddam, a provisional government, a charter, a constitution, the trial of Saddam, elections, purple fingers, another government, the death of Saddam.[222]

—Keith Olbermann, political commentator

This is the administration whose leader recklessly taunted insurgents to "bring it on," who then prohibited pictures of the resulting arrivals of coffins bearing the bodies of our dead soldiers, and who exacerbated the insurgency by authorizing torture of detainees and denying the Geneva Conventions treaty.[223]

—*Chattanooga Times Free Press* editorial

He has assured us we would be greeted as liberators with flowers. As they stood up, we would stand down. We would stay the course. We were never about stay the course. We would never have to go door to door in Baghdad, and last night, that to gain Iraqi's trust, we would go door to door in Baghdad. He told us the enemy was al Qaeda, foreign fighters, terrorists, Baathists, and now Iran and Syria.[224]

—Keith Olbermann, political commentator

And it is the same administration that has dumped the entire cost of this unnecessary war on our children, running up outrageous debt to pay for the war—the national debt has soared from $5.7 trillion to $9 trillion since 2001 alone—while giving stunning tax cuts to the nation's wealthiest citizens and cutting the vital social programs on which ordinary Americans rely.[225]

—*Chattanooga Times Free Press* editorial

Now it can be told: President Bush and Vice President Dick Cheney based their [2004] re-election campaign on lies, damned lies and statistics. . . . The damned lies included Mr. Bush's declaration, in his "Mission Accomplished" speech, that "we have removed an ally of Al Qaeda."[226]

—Paul Krugman, columnist

It is an easy thing to tell a lie, but it is difficult to support the lie after it is told.[227]

—Thomas Paine

Maybe the Bush White House can't conduct a war, but no one has ever impugned its ability to lie about its conduct of a war.[228]

—Frank Rich, columnist

Let's not forget that they got us into this war on the basis of a series of lies. Lies to the U.N., lies about aluminum tubes, lies about the involvement of Iraq with 9/11.[229]

—Naomi Wolf, writer

They didn't tell the truth during the 2004 campaign, where they lied, literally, about whether or not they knew where Osama bin Laden was. They knew where he was, but for purposes of the election, they avoided responsibility for that and now they're trying to pretend that they've got them on the run. They don't have them on the run. Al Qaeda, notwithstanding the capture of a number of people, which we applaud— that's important. But what's more important is guaranteeing that you're changing the minds of people in the world who are moving away from democracy, away from aligning themselves with the United States and with our allies.[230]

—Sen. John Kerry

As he campaigned, in the summer of 2004, George Bush repeatedly reassured audiences that his policies had made America safer. "We've turned the corner," was the refrain in his stump speech. "We're moving America forward by extending freedom and peace around the world." Iraq and Afghanistan, he said, "are now governed by strong leaders. They're on the path to free elections." America, he added, would engage its enemies around the world "so we do not have to face them here at home."[231]

—Seymour Hersh, journalist

The report [from the CIA station chief in Baghdad], [an NSC staffer] recalled, said that "all the trends were in the wrong direction, and it could get far worse." . . . Days later, Bush asserted, "We've made a lot of progress on the ground."[232]

—Michael Isikoff and David Corn, journalists

We're making really good progress.[233]

—George W. Bush

We're making steady progress in implementing our five-step plan toward the goal we all want, completing the mission so that Iraq is stable and self-governing and American troops can come home with the honor they have earned.[234]

—George W. Bush

We're making really good progress [in Iraq].[235]

—George W. Bush

Iraq has made incredible political progress.[236]

—George W. Bush

Iraqis are making inspiring progress.[237]

—George W. Bush

I think if you look at what's transpired in Iraq, Chris, we have, in fact, made enormous progress.[238]

—Dick Cheney

In Mr. Bush's world, America is making real progress in Iraq. In the real world . . . the index that generals use to track developments shows an inexorable slide toward chaos. . . . In Mr. Bush's world, there are only two kinds of Americans: those who are against terrorism, and those who somehow are all right with it. . . . When the president of the United States gleefully bathes in the muck to divide Americans into those who love their country and those who don't, it is destructive to the fabric of the nation he is supposed to be leading.[239]

—*New York Times* editorial

If we don't stop extending our troops all around the world in nation-building missions, we're going to have a serious problem coming down the road.[240]

—George W. Bush

Before Mr. Bush was elected he said he was no nation builder. Nation building was wrong for America. Now he says it is vital for America. He said he would never have put U.S. troops under foreign control. Today U.S. troops observe Iraqi restrictions. He told us about WMDs, mobile labs, secret sources, aluminum tubing, yellow cake. He has told us the war is necessary because Saddam was a threat, because of 9/11, because of Osama bin Laden, al Qaeda, because of terrorism in general, to liberate Iraq, to spread freedom, to spread democracy, to keep the oil out of the hands of potentially terrorist controlled states, because this was a guy who tried to kill his dad. The war would pay for itself. It would cost 1.7 billion dollars, 100 billion, 400 billion, half a trillion dollars. And after all of that, today it is his credibility versus that of generals, diplomats, allies, Republicans, Democrats, the Iraq Study Group, past presidents, voters last November, and the majority of the American people.[241]

—Keith Olbermann, political commentator

I think that if you look at the conflict that's involved here and remember that Iraq is just part of the larger war—it is, in fact, a global war that stretches from Pakistan all the way around to North Africa. . . . And Iraq is the current central battlefield in that war, and we must win there.[242]

—Dick Cheney

This White House gang is so practiced in lying with a straight face that it never thinks twice about recycling its greatest hits. Hours after Mr. Cheney's Fox interview, President Bush was on *60 Minutes*, claiming that before the war "everybody was wrong on weapons of mass destruction" and that "the minute we found out" the WMD didn't exist he "was the first to say so."[243]

—Frank Rich, columnist

The minute we found out we—they didn't have weapons of mass destruction, I was the first to say so. . . . Everybody was wrong on weapons of mass destruction, and there was an intelligence failure, which we're trying to address. But I was as surprised as anybody he didn't have them.[244]

—George W. Bush

Americans largely believed they were misled into supporting the invasion of Iraq not by virtue of erroneous intelligence but due to *deliberate deceit*.[245]

—Glenn Greenwald, lawyer/journalist

A clear majority—55 percent—now says the administration deliberately misled the country in making its case for war with Iraq.[246]

—Richard Morin and Dan Balz, journalists

President Bush and his aides, explaining their reasons for sending more American troops to Iraq, are offering an incomplete, oversimplified and possibly untrue version of events there that raises new questions about the accuracy of the administration's statements about Iraq. . . . But the president's account understates by at least 15 months when Shiite death squads began targeting Sunni politicians and clerics. It also ignores the role that Iranian-backed Shiite groups had in death squad activities prior to the Samarra bombing.[247]

—Mark Seibel, journalist

The [National Intelligence Estimate] assessment, by American intelligence agencies, expressed deep doubts about the abilities of Iraqi politicians to hold together an increasingly balkanized country, and about whether Iraqi troops might be able to confront powerful militias over the next 18 months and assume more responsibility for security. The analysis, the first such estimate on Iraq in more than two years, described in sober language a rapidly unraveling country in which security has worsened despite four years of efforts by the administration.[248]

—Mark Mazzetti, journalist

Bottom line is that we've had enormous successes and we will continue to have enormous successes.[249]

—Dick Cheney

Even after releasing parts of an intelligence report so pessimistic that it may as well have been titled "Iraq: We're Cooked," Bush officials clung to their alternate reality, using nonsensical logic and cherry-picking whatever phrases they could find in the report that they could use to sell the Surge.[250]

—Maureen Dowd, columnist

The reality on the ground is, we've made major progress.[251]

—Dick Cheney

Pretending things are better than they are will not make them so. America has some very hard strategic choices pressing down on it in Iraq—much more complicated than whether to set an arbitrary target date for troop withdrawal.[252]

—*New York Times* editorial

Nobody has ever suggested that the attacks of September the 11th were ordered by Iraq.[253]

—George W. Bush

Not exactly. Dick Cheney and other hawks in the administration repeatedly said that there was a connection between Iraq and 9/11, citing an unconfirmed, single-source intelligence report that 9/11 ringleader Mohamad Atta met with an Iraqi intelligence official in Prague five months before the attack. Yet the FBI and the CIA (and later the 9/11 Commission) had concluded that there was no evidence to substantiate this report and that the meeting likely did not happen. True, Bush officials did not claim that Saddam had "ordered" the attack, but they did suggest that Baghdad had participated in the attack—even when there was no evidence to support that assertion.[254]

—David Corn, journalist

The neocons insist that it was the execution of the war that was wrong. Actually, it was wrong to go to war with a trumped-up casus belli and without ever debating what could happen if they took a baseball bat to a beehive. A war designed to bring moral good shouldn't start with a pack of lies.[255]

—Maureen Dowd, columnist

For years the president and his supporting cast of arrogant, bullying characters have tried to put the best face on this war. They had no idea what they were doing when they ordered the invasion of Iraq, and they still don't. Many of the troops who were assured that the Iraqis would welcome them with open arms are now dead.[256]

—Bob Herbert, columnist

You don't have to be a cynic to ask if the White House's practice of bestowing better jobs on those who bungled the war might be a form of hush money. Mr. Wolfowitz was promoted to the World Bank despite a Pentagon record that included (in part) his prewar hyping of bogus intelligence about WMD and a nonexistent 9/11-Saddam connection; his assurance to the world that Iraq's oil revenues would pay for reconstruction; and his public humiliation of Gen. Eric Shinseki after the general dared tell Congress (correctly) that several hundred thousand troops would be needed to secure Iraq after the invasion. Once the war began, Mr. Wolfowitz cited national security to bar businesses from noncoalition countries (like Germany) from competing for major contracts in Iraq.[257]

—Frank Rich, columnist

W. believes in self-determination only if he's doing the determining.[258]

—Maureen Dowd, columnist

In case after case, the president has pursued policies chosen in advance of the facts—policies designed to benefit friends and supporters.[259]

—Al Gore

Far from addressing the popular appeal of the enemy that attacked us, Bush handed that enemy precisely what it wanted and needed, proof that America was at war with Islam, that we were the new Crusaders come to occupy Muslim land. Nothing America could have done would have provided Al Qaeda and its new generation of cloned groups a better recruitment device than our unprovoked invasion of an oil-rich Arab country. Nothing else could have so well negated all our other positive acts and so closed Muslim eyes and ears to our subsequent calls for reform in their region. It was as if Osama bin Laden, hidden in some high mountain redoubt, were engaging in long-range mind control of George Bush, chanting "invade Iraq, you must invade Iraq."[260]

—Richard Clarke, former White House counterterrorism expert

I would say this is a defining moment in the history of a free Iraq. . . . This is a test and a moment for the Iraqi government, which strongly has supported Prime Minister Maliki's actions. . . . And so—the other that's interesting about this, by the way—this happens to be one of the provinces where the Iraqis are in the lead—Iraqis are in the lead, and that's what they are in this instance.[261]

—George W. Bush

It was a defining moment all right. Mr. Maliki's impulsive and ill-planned attempt to vanquish the militias in southern Iraq loyal to his Shiite rival, the cleric Moktada al-Sadr, was a failure that left Mr. Sadr more secure than before. Though some Iraqi armed forces were briefly in the lead, others mutinied. Eventually American and British forces and air power had to ride to the rescue in both Basra and Baghdad. Even then, the result was at best a standoff, with huge casualties. The battle ended only when Mr. Maliki's own political minions sought a cease-fire.[262]

—Frank Rich, columnist

Rather than seeking to work with the majority in the Islamic world to mold Muslim opinion against the radicals' values, we did exactly what Al Qaeda said we would do. We invaded and occupied an oil-rich country that posed no threat to us, while paying scant time and attention to the Israeli-Palestinian problem. We delivered to al Qaeda the greatest recruitment propaganda imaginable and made it difficult for friendly Islamic governments to be seen working closely with us.[263]

—Richard Clarke, former White House counterterrorism expert

When you boil down precisely what went wrong with the Bush Iraq policy, it's fairly simple. He waged the politics of blind faith. He used a counterfeit combination of misdirected vengeance and misguided dogma to dominate the national discussion, bypass reason, silence dissent, and intimidate those who questioned his logic both inside and outside the administration.[264]

—Al Gore

"Let me tell you my gut feeling," a senior figure at one of America's military-sponsored think tanks told me recently, after we had talked for twenty minutes about details of the campaigns in Afghanistan and Iraq. "If I can be blunt, the Administration is full of shit. In my view we are much, much worse off now than when we went into Iraq. That is not a partisan position. I voted for these guys. But I think they are incompetent, and I have had a very close perspective on what is happening. Certainly in the long run we have harmed ourselves. We are playing to the enemy's political advantage. Whatever tactical victories we may gain along the way, this will prove to be a strategic blunder."[265]

—James Fallows, journalist

■ ■ ■

The biggest regret of all the presidency has to have been the intelligence failure in Iraq. I wish the intelligence had been different, I guess.[266]

—George W. Bush

Bush had arrived in Washington vowing to inaugurate a new, post-Clinton era of "personal responsibility" in which "people are accountable for their actions." Eight years later he holds himself accountable for nothing.[267]

—Frank Rich, columnist

After everything the American public and the world have learned about how Mr. Bush and Vice President Dick Cheney manipulated Congress, public opinion and anyone else they could bully or lie to, Mr. Bush is still acting as though he decided to invade Iraq after suddenly being handed life and death information on Saddam Hussein's arsenal.[268]

—*New York Times* editorial

The Middle East in 2008 is a freer, more hopeful, and more promising place than it was in 2001.[269]

—George W. Bush

A stark assessment of terrorism trends by American intelligence agencies has found that the American invasion and occupation of Iraq has helped spawn a new generation of Islamic radicalism and that the overall terrorist threat has grown since the Sept. 11 attacks.[270]

—Mark Mazetti, journalist

Immediately after September the 11th, we gave the Taliban in Afghanistan two options: Surrender the leaders of al Qaeda—or you can share in their fate. When the regime leaders made their choice, we made ours. We removed the Taliban from power, we shut down the terrorist training camps, and we liberated more than 25 million Afghans.[271]

—George W. Bush

Al-Qaeda has regained some of its pre-Sept. 11 strength based on support from within Pakistan, leading to a 16 per cent jump in the number of attacks in Afghanistan, a U.S. government report said Wednesday. . . . The report says insurgents in Afghanistan, led by the Taliban, are being fed by a strengthened al-Qaeda.[272]

—CBS News report

The release of a new report Tuesday that says Al Qaeda has reorganized to pre-9/11 strength and is preparing for a major U.S. strike has sparked debate among government officials and observers about the Bush administration's foreign policy and counterterrorism efforts.[273]

—Tom Peter, journalist

A military intelligence report . . . concludes al Qaeda has largely restored itself to pre-9/11 strength. . . . While the military has maintained that al Qaeda is on the run in Iraq, by any number of measures the terror group and its affiliates are as strong as ever.[274]

—Jonathan Karl, journalist

I was invited to a conference in Saudi Arabia on Iraq, and a Saudi said to me, Look, Mr. Fischer, when President Bush wants to visit Baghdad, it's a state secret, and he has to enter the country in the middle of the night and through the back door. When [Iran's] President Ahmadinejad wants to visit Baghdad, it's announced two weeks beforehand or three weeks. He arrives in the brightest sunshine and travels in an open car through a cheering crowd to downtown Baghdad. Now, tell me, Mr. Fischer, who is running the country?[275]

—Joschka Fischer, former German foreign minister and vice-chancellor

Ours will be remembered as the Enron era. Enron itself is a distant memory—much like all that circa 2000 talk of a smoothly efficient CEO presidency led by a Harvard MBA and a former chief executive of Halliburton. But even as American business has since been purged by prosecutions and reforms, the mutant Enron version of the CEO culture still rules in Washington: uninhibited cronyism, cooked books, special-favors networks, the banishment of whistle-blowers and accountability. More than ideology, this ethos has sabotaged even the best of American intentions, whether in Iraq or New Orleans.[276]

—Frank Rich, columnist

One of our difficulties now is getting the rest of the world to accept our assessment of the seriousness of an issue, because they say, You screwed it up so badly with Iraq, why would we believe that you're any better today? And it's a damn hard question to answer.[277]

—Sen. Bob Graham

—8—

Torture and Rendition

We also have to work, though, sort of the dark side, if you will. We've got
to spend time in the shadows in the intelligence world. A lot of what needs to
be done here will have to be done quietly, without any discussion, using sources
and methods that are available to our intelligence agencies, if we're going to be
successful. That's the world these folks operate in, and so it's going to be vital
for us to use any means at our disposal, basically, to achieve our objectives.[1]
—Dick Cheney

Our greatest evils flow from ourselves.[2]

—Jean-Jacques Rousseau

This is a different kind of war. You're not going to see our victories. Our
victories are going to occur in dark alleys as our intelligence forces and law enforcement
forces go after this threat.[3]

—George W. Bush

The White House was fighting terror with terror.[4]

—Seymour Hersh, journalist

[T]here was "before 9/11" and "after 9/11." After 9/11, the gloves came off.[5]

—Cofer Black, CIA

[T]he Administration sought license to torture.[6]

—Frederick A. O. Schwarz Jr. and Aziz Z. Huq, lawyers

■ ■ ■

Former State Department counselor Philip D. Zelikow and retired FBI agent Ali Sou-
fan told members of the Senate Judiciary Committee about their unsuccessful attempts
to block or reverse detainee interrogation techniques that included waterboarding and
repeatedly slamming detainees into flexible walls. . . . Zelikow and his colleagues had
forcefully argued that the Bush White House should halt the practices. He said he wrote
a memo challenging the legality of the interrogation techniques. The most controversial
of those techniques—waterboarding—had ended in 2003. He said administration officials tried to destroy the memo, which is still classified, in early 2006. That experience,
Zelikow said, "told me that the lawyers involved in that opinion did not welcome peer
review and indeed would shut down challenges even inside the government. If I was
right, their whole interpretation . . . was unsound."[7]

—Carrie Johnson, journalist

We had captured these people. We had pursued interrogation in a normal way. We decided that we needed some enhanced techniques. So we went to the Justice Department.
And the controversy has arisen over the opinions written by the Justice Department.
The reason we went to the Justice Department wasn't because we felt we were going to
take some kind of free hand assault on these people or that we were in the torture business. We weren't. And specifically, what we got from the Office of Legal Counsel were
legal memos that laid out what is appropriate and what's not appropriate, in light of our
international commitments. If we had been about torture, we wouldn't have wasted our
time going to the Justice Department.[8]

—Dick Cheney

These memos are not an honest attempt to set the legal limits on interrogations, which
was the authors' statutory obligation. They were written to provide legal immunity
for acts that are clearly illegal, immoral and a violation of this country's most basic
values. . . . And it all played out with the blessing of the defense secretary, the attorney
general, the intelligence director and, most likely, President Bush and Vice President
Dick Cheney.[9]

—New York Times editorial

[W]hat we have here is a very clear conspiracy to commit a war crime. These people are
not stupid, they just had no morals. And so, what they set about to do is to usurp the
democratic leadership, rein them in, get lawyers to say it was OK. It was a broad conspiracy to commit a war crime, which remains a crime, and the people who committed
it remain criminals.[10]

—Jonathan Turley, law professor

President Bush and his aides have not only condoned torture and abuse at secret prisons, but they have conducted a systematic campaign to mislead Congress, the American people and the world about those policies.[11]

—*New York Times* editorial

How much did President Bush know specifically about the methods that were being used? We know that you—and you have said—that you approved this . . .

—Bob Schieffer, journalist

Right.

—Dick Cheney

. . . somewhere down the line. Did President Bush know everything you knew?

—Bob Schieffer, journalist

I certainly, yes, have every reason to believe he knew—he knew a great deal about the program. He basically authorized it. I mean, this was a presidential-level decision. And the decision went to the president. He signed off on it.[12]

—Dick Cheney

We really don't have much of a question about the president's role here. He's never denied that he was fully informed of these measures. He, in fact, early on in his presidency—he seemed to brag that they were using harsh and tough methods. And I don't think there's any doubt that he was aware of this.[13]

—Jonathan Turley, law professor

[M]ore than 3,000 suspected terrorists have been arrested in many countries. Many others have met a different fate. Let's put it this way: They are no longer a problem to the United States and our friends and allies.[14]

—George W. Bush

After the attacks of 9/11, Mr. Bush authorized the creation of extralegal detention camps where Central Intelligence Agency operatives were told to extract information from prisoners who were captured and held in secret. Some of their methods—simulated drownings, extreme ranges of heat and cold, prolonged stress positions and isolation—had been classified as torture for decades by civilized nations. The administration clearly knew this; the CIA modeled its techniques on the dungeons of Egypt, Saudi Arabia and the Soviet Union. The White House could never acknowledge that. So its lawyers concocted documents that redefined "torture" to neatly exclude the things American jailers were doing and hid the papers from Congress and the American people. Under Attorney General Alberto Gonzales, Mr. Bush's loyal enabler, the Justice Department even declared that those acts did not violate the lower standard of "cruel, inhuman or degrading treatment." That allowed the White House to claim that it did not condone torture, and to stampede Congress into passing laws that shielded the interrogators who abused prisoners, and the men who ordered them to do it, from any kind of legal accountability.[15]

—*New York Times* editorial

Reading through the memoranda written by Bush administration lawyers on how prisoners of the "war on terror" can be treated is a strange experience. The memos read like the advice of a mob lawyer to a mafia don on how to skirt the law and stay out of prison. Avoiding prosecution is literally a theme of the memoranda. Americans who put physical pressure on captives can escape punishment if they can show that they did not have an "intent" to cause "severe physical or mental pain or suffering." And "a defendant could negate a showing of specific intent . . . by showing that he had acted in good faith that his conduct would not amount to the acts prohibited by the statute."[16]

—Anthony Lewis, journalist

[B]y definition, if it was authorized by the president, it did not violate our obligations under the Conventions Against Torture.[17]

—Condoleezza Rice

Rice is now portraying herself as merely being a conduit for approving the CIA's interrogation regime: "I conveyed the authorization of the administration to the agency." Well, there are only two more-senior officials than Rice in this context, and that's Bush and then-Vice President Dick Cheney. If she hadn't made a decision on the part of the administration for the Abu Zubaydah interrogation plan, only one of these two men would have had the authority to do so.[18]

—Spencer Ackerman, journalist

[W]ell before the President had determined what legal approach his administration would take, Cheney delivered a hard-edged speech at the U.S. Chamber of Commerce in Washington declaring that terrorists do not "deserve to be treated as prisoners of war." Cheney evidently staked out this position on his own. . . . Of all the complicated legal arguments made by the Bush Administration in the first months after September 11, none more directly cleared the way for torture than this.[19]

—Jane Mayer, journalist

What sets us apart from our enemies in this fight . . . is how we behave. In everything we do, we must observe the standards and values that dictate that we treat noncombatants and detainees with dignity and respect. While we are warriors, we are also human beings.[20]

—Gen. David Petraeus

Justice is due, even to an enemy.[21]

—Thomas Paine

What occurred in the last eight years was an assault on who we are.[22]

—Jonathan Turley, law professor

War crimes will be prosecuted. War criminals will be punished. And it will be no defense to say, "I was just following orders."[23]

—George W. Bush

In the name of protecting national security, the executive branch sanctioned coerced confessions, extrajudicial detention, and other violations of individuals' liberties that had been prohibited since the country's founding. They turned the Justice Department's Office of Legal Counsel into a political instrument, which they used to expand their own executive power at the expense of long-standing checks and balances. When warned that these policies were unlawful and counterproductive, they ignored the experts and made decisions outside of ordinary bureaucratic channels, and often outside of the public's view.[24]

—Jane Mayer, journalist

The Bush administration's view that the president, in time of war, is unrestrained by law is on display in a series of internal Justice and Defense Department memoranda written in 2002 and 2003 and publicly revealed in 2004. In those memos, Bush administration lawyers argued that Congress is powerless to interfere with the president's authority to order torture of enemy prisoners if the president decides such action will be useful in prosecuting the war on terror.[25]

—Gene Healy and Timothy Lynch, lawyers

[A] secret statement of the President's views, which he signed on February 7, 2002, had a loophole that applied worldwide.[26]

—Seymour Hersh, journalist

I accept the legal conclusion of the Department of Justice and determine that none of the provisions of Geneva apply to our conflict with al-Qaida in Afghanistan or elsewhere throughout the world because, among other reasons, al-Qaida is not a High Contracting Party to Geneva.[27]

—George W. Bush

Thus, neither Taliban nor al-Qaeda prisoners would be treated as prisoners of war. Nor would they be accorded the baseline benefits of Common Article 3. The President's memo bore the Orwellian title "Humane Treatment of al-Qaeda and Taliban Detainees." In fact, it voided almost every existing legal guarantee of humane treatment in wartime and replaced them with a virtual invitation to engage in coercive interrogations.[28]

—Frederick A. O. Schwarz Jr. and Aziz Z. Huq, lawyers

I accept the legal conclusion of the attorney general and the Department of Justice that I have the authority under the Constitution to suspend Geneva as between the United States and Afghanistan.[29]

—George W. Bush

[T]hey're trying to change the federal law that makes it a crime in the United States to engage in torture or to violate the Geneva Convention provisions. . . . They think they're above the greatest document we ever had, the Constitution of the United States.[30]

—John Dean, former White House counsel

The Pentagon has decided to omit from new detainee policies a key tenet of the Geneva Convention that explicitly bans "humiliating and degrading treatment," according to knowledgeable military officials, a step that would mark a further, potentially permanent, shift away from strict adherence to international human rights standards.[31]

—Julian Barnes, journalist

According to the memos, prohibiting torture infringes on the president's constitutional power as commander in chief. As an August 1, 2002, memo puts it, "Congress can no more interfere with the president's conduct of the interrogation of enemy combatants than it can dictate strategic or tactical decisions on the battlefield." . . . The Constitution's text will not support anything like the doctrine of presidential absolutism the administration flirts with in the torture memos.[32]

—Gene Healy and Timothy Lynch, lawyers

According to the Bush-Cheney Doctrine, we cannot foreswear the fool's gold of information secured by torturing prisoners or creating a shadow justice system with no rules and no transparency.[33]

—Sen. John Kerry

Whoever fights monsters should see to it that in the process he does not become a monster. And when you look long into an abyss, the abyss also looks into you.[34]

—Friedrich Nietzsche

■ ■ ■

We don't torture, that's not what we're involved in.[35]

—Dick Cheney

What's your definition of the word "torture?"

—Richard Wolffe, journalist

Of what?

—George W. Bush

The word "torture." What's your definition?

—Richard Wolffe, journalist

It is—that's defined in U.S. law, and we don't torture.

—George W. Bush

Can you give me your version of it, sir?

—Richard Wolffe, journalist

Yeah. Whatever the law says.[36]

—George W. Bush

It's Orwellian in its logic. They're doing this with other areas and they're just thinking because they say it, a lot of people will, in fact, believe it. I think the overwhelming majorities now have lost all faith and trust in this administration and its ability to tell the truth.[37]

—John Dean, former White House counsel

The object of persecution, is persecution. The object of torture, is torture. The object of power . . . is power.[38]

—George Orwell

[Douglas] Feith's argument left captives in the war on terror in legal limbo. Feith nonetheless packaged his argument with Orwellian cleverness as a defense of the Geneva Conventions, arguing in a memo, which Rumsfeld shared with President Bush, that it would defile the Geneva Conventions to extend their rights to such disreputable warriors.[39]

—Jane Mayer, journalist

Torture, according to the Bush Administration, is legal because the president says it is. . . . Using faulty logic, OLC [the Justice Department's Office of Legal Counsel] lawyers undermined the spirit and purpose of antitorture laws by promulgating an absurdly narrow definition of "torture." Moreover, the executive branch kept OLC legal interpretations secret, preventing Congress from responding.[40]

—Frederick A. O. Schwarz Jr. and Aziz Z. Huq, lawyers

[E]verything we did was in consultation with professionals in our government who understand, you know, how to use techniques in a way that gets information with, you know, within the law, necessary to protect the American people.[41]

—George W. Bush

In legal opinions on torture, the OLC pressed a theory of unlimited presidential power that gave presidents authority to set aside permanently *any* law of the United States, including laws against torture, in the name of national security. Claims to such royal presidential powers are, in effect, wholesale rejections of America's system of checks and balances.[42]

—Frederick A. O. Schwarz Jr. and Aziz Z. Huq, lawyers

If the OLC says a previously outlawed practice, such as waterboarding, is legal, it is nearly impossible to prosecute U.S. officials who followed that advice on good faith.[43]

—Jane Mayer, journalist

On the question of so-called torture, we don't do torture. We never have. It's not something that this administration subscribes to. Again, we proceeded very cautiously. We checked. We had the Justice Department issue the requisite opinions in order to know where the bright lines were that you could not cross.

—Dick Cheney

Did you authorize the tactics that were used against Khalid Sheikh Mohammed?

—Jonathan Karl, journalist

I was aware of the program, certainly, and involved in helping get the process cleared, as the agency in effect came in and wanted to know what they could and couldn't do. And they talked to me, as well as others, to explain what they wanted to do. And I supported it.[44]

—Dick Cheney

So, you have the vice president sitting there, saying, "Yes, we talked about it, they came to me, I supported it and I helped to put it through." The only problem is what he is describing is, most certainly and unambiguously, a war crime.[45]

—Jonathan Turley, law professor

The OLC, with its tremendous authority to issue "golden shields" to the executive branch against prosecution, was designed to exercise independent judgment. But according to another former administration official, a conservative lawyer who was troubled by the leverage over the office that was exerted by the White House, "They didn't care if the opinions would stand scrutiny. They just wanted to check a box saying, 'OLC says it's legal.' They wanted lawyers who would tell them that whatever they wanted to do was okay."[46]

—Jane Mayer, journalist

Unthinking respect for authority is the greatest enemy of truth.[47]

—Albert Einstein

The Justice Department delivered a classified opinion on Aug. 1, 2002, stating that the U.S. law against torture "prohibits only the worst forms of cruel, inhuman or degrading treatment" and therefore permits many others. Distributed under the signature of Assistant Attorney General Jay S. Bybee, the opinion also narrowed the definition of "torture" to mean only suffering "equivalent in intensity" to the pain of "organ failure . . . or even death." That same day, Aug. 1, 2002, [John] Yoo signed off on a second secret opinion, the contents of which have never been made public. According to a source with direct knowledge, that opinion approved as lawful a long list of interrogation techniques proposed by the CIA—including waterboarding, a form of near-drowning that the U.S. government has prosecuted as a war crime since at least 1901. The opinion drew the line against one request: threatening to bury a prisoner alive.[48]

—Mark Silva, journalist

If all else failed, Yoo and Bybee advised, the President could argue that torture was legal because he authorized it. The commander in chief, according to the OLC, had inherent powers to order any interrogation technique he chose. Under this interpretation, U.S. laws and treaties banning torture—despite having been signed into law by earlier presidents—were deemed unconstitutional and therefore null. By this logic, the President was literally above the law.[49]

—Jane Mayer, journalist

To pave the way for the military commissions, Yoo wrote an opinion on Nov. 6, 2001, declaring that Bush did not need approval from Congress or federal courts. Yoo said in an interview that he saw no need to inform the State Department, which hosts the archives of the Geneva Conventions and the government's leading experts on the law of war.[50]

—Barton Gellman and Jo Becker, journalists

As Yoo explained it, Congress doesn't have the power to "tie the president's hands in regard to torture as an interrogation technique." He continued, "It's the core of the commander in chief function. They can't prevent the president from ordering torture."[51]

—Jane Mayer, journalist

[I]n the view of Bush's lawyers, all such statutes, including those prohibiting torture, secret detention, and warrantless surveillance, could now be set aside.[52]

—Jane Mayer, journalist

[Cheney counsel David] Addington, under Gonzales's name, appealed to the president by quoting Bush's own declaration that "the war against terrorism is a new kind of war." Addington described the Geneva Conventions as "quaint," casting [Colin] Powell as a defender of "obsolete" rules devised for another time. If Bush followed Powell's lead, Addington suggested, U.S. forces would be obliged to provide athletic gear and commissary privileges to captured terrorists.[53]

—Barton Gellman and Jo Becker, journalists

Once in U.S. custody, the President's lawyers said, these suspects could be held incommunicado, hidden from their families and international monitors such as the Red Cross, and subjected to unending abuse, so long as it didn't meet the lawyers' own definition of torture. And they could be held for the duration of the war against terrorism, a struggle in which victory had never been clearly defined.[54]

—Jane Mayer, journalist

We don't torture people. Let me say that again to you, we don't torture people. OK?[55]

—George Tenet, former CIA director

We used [waterboarding] against these three detainees because of the circumstances at the time. There was the belief that additional catastrophic attacks against the homeland were inevitable. And we had limited knowledge about al-Qaida and its workings. Those two realities have changed.[56]

—Michael Hayden, former CIA director

Human Rights Watch, which has been calling on the government to outlaw waterboarding as a form of illegal torture, called Hayden's testimony "an explicit admission of criminal activity." Joanne Mariner, the group's counterterrorism director, said Hayden's testimony "gives the lie" to the administration's claims that the CIA has not used torture. "Waterboarding is torture, and torture is a crime," she said.[57]

—Lara Jakes Jordan, journalist

The United Nations' torture investigator criticized the White House Wednesday for defending the use of waterboarding and urged the U.S. to give up its defense of "unjustifiable" interrogation methods. . . . The White House on Wednesday defended the use of waterboarding, saying it is legal—not torture as critics argue—and has saved American lives.[58]

—Bradley Klapper, journalist

It's torture; it's illegal.[59]

—*Los Angeles Times* editorial

There is bitter irony in the fact that more than fifty years [after the Geneva Conventions were ratified], the man who was later to become attorney general, Alberto Gonzales, consigned these hard-won prescriptions to history's dustbin as "quaint" and "obsolete." Gonzales apparently did not know that many of these rules were originally proposed by America to protect American soldiers.[60]

—Frederick A. O. Schwarz Jr. and Aziz Z. Huq, lawyers

The same grotesque misunderstanding of what is really involved in torture was responsible for the tone in the memo from Alberto Gonzales, who wrote on January 25, 2002, that the attack of 9/11 "renders obsolete Geneva's strict limitations on questioning of enemy prisoners and renders quaint some of its provisions."[61]

—Al Gore

When the Justice Department publicly declared torture "abhorrent" in a legal opinion in December 2004, the Bush administration appeared to have abandoned its assertion of nearly unlimited presidential authority to order brutal interrogations. But soon after Alberto R. Gonzales's arrival as attorney general in February 2005, the Justice Department issued another opinion, this one in secret. It was a very different document, according to officials briefed on it, an expansive endorsement of the harshest interrogation techniques ever used by the Central Intelligence Agency.[62]

—Scott Shane, David Johnston, and James Risen, journalists

Asked about [torture] assertions, Mark Mansfield, a CIA spokesman, said, "the United States does not conduct or condone torture." He said a small number of "hardened terrorists" had required what he called "special methods of questioning" in what he called a lawful and carefully run program.[63]

—William Glaberson, journalist

The United States does not torture. It's against our laws, and it's against our values.[64]

—George W. Bush

▮ ▮ ▮

The Justice Department on Thursday made public detailed memos describing brutal interrogation techniques used by the Central Intelligence Agency. . . . In dozens of pages of dispassionate legal prose, the methods approved by the Bush administration for extracting information from senior operatives of Al Qaeda are spelled out in careful detail—like keeping detainees awake for up to 11 straight days, placing them in a dark, cramped box or putting insects into the box to exploit their fears.[65]

—Mark Mazzetti and Scott Shane, journalists

The documents lay out in clinical, painstaking detail a series of practices intended to get prisoners to share intelligence about past wrongdoing and future attacks. The legalistic analysis under anti-torture laws and the Geneva Conventions is at odds with the severity of the strategies, which include 11-day limits on sleep deprivation as well as waterboarding and nude shackling.[66]

—Carrie Johnson and Julie Tate, journalists

To read the four newly released memos on prisoner interrogation written by George W. Bush's Justice Department is to take a journey into depravity.[67]

—*New York Times* editorial

These memos are so embarrassing. . . . They're embarrassing morally, they're embarrassing legally. The lawyers are going to have a lot of fun pulling this stuff apart and showing the flaws in it. This was not good law. It will never be good moral judgment.[68]

—John Dean, former White House counsel

Step by step, experts considered the legality of slapping prisoners' faces and abdomens, dousing them with water, and confining them in small boxes, with the last strategy limited to two hours. The techniques were designed to inspire "dread," according to a footnote. Some of the practices were used against more than a dozen detainees whom authorities considered to be of particularly high intelligence value after the Sept. 11, 2001, terrorist strikes.[69]

—Carrie Johnson and Julie Tate, journalists

In one of the more nauseating passages, Jay Bybee, then an assistant attorney general and now a federal judge, wrote admiringly about a contraption for waterboarding that would lurch a prisoner upright if he stopped breathing while water was poured over his face. He praised the Central Intelligence Agency for having doctors ready to perform an emergency tracheotomy if necessary.[70]

—*New York Times* editorial

[I]t's not Bybee's perverted lawyering and pornographic amorality that make his memo worthy of special attention. It merits a closer look because it actually does add something new—and, even after all we've heard, something shocking—to the five-year-old torture narrative. When placed in full context, it's the kind of smoking gun that might free us from the myths and denial that prevent us from reckoning with this ugly chapter in our history.[71]

—Frank Rich, columnist

Through these memos, Justice Department lawyers authorized interrogators to use the most barbaric interrogation methods, including methods that the U.S. once prosecuted as war crimes. The memos are based on legal reasoning that is spurious on its face, and in the end these aren't legal memos at all—they are simply political documents that were meant to provide window dressing for war crimes.[72]

—Jameel Jaffer, lawyer

The United States itself treated waterboarding as torture when the Japanese used it against our troops in World War II. Yet through pages and pages of dense legal reasoning, the Office of Legal Counsel lawyers somehow reach the conclusion that these tactics, even when employed in combination and over a 30-day period, are not torture, and not even cruel, inhuman, or degrading.[73]

—David Cole, journalist

Together, the four memos give an extraordinarily detailed account of the CIA's methods and the Justice Department's long struggle, in the face of graphic descriptions of brutal tactics, to square them with international and domestic law. Passages describing forced nudity, the slamming of detainees into walls, prolonged sleep deprivation and the dousing of detainees with water as cold as 41 degrees alternate with elaborate legal arguments concerning the international Convention Against Torture.[74]

—Mark Mazzetti and Scott Shane, journalists

[T]orture was a premeditated policy approved at our government's highest levels.[75]

—Frank Rich, columnist

The healthy man does not torture others—generally it is the tortured who turn into torturers.[76]

—Carl Jung, psychologist

The memos include what in effect are lengthy excerpts from the agency's interrogation manual, laying out with precision how each method was to be used. Waterboarding, for example, involved strapping a prisoner to a gurney inclined at an angle of "10 to 15 degrees" and pouring water over a cloth covering his nose and mouth "from a height of approximately 6 to 18 inches" for no more than 40 seconds at a time. But a footnote to a 2005 memo made it clear that the rules were not always followed. Waterboarding was used "with far greater frequency than initially indicated" and with "large volumes of water" rather than the small quantities in the rules, one memo says, citing a 2004 report by the CIA's inspector general.[77]

—Mark Mazzetti and Scott Shane, journalists

CIA interrogators used waterboarding, the near-drowning technique that top Obama administration officials have described as illegal torture, 266 times on two key prisoners from Al Qaeda, far more than had been previously reported. The CIA officers used waterboarding at least 83 times in August 2002 against Abu Zubaydah, according to a 2005 Justice Department legal memorandum. . . . The 2005 memo also says that the CIA used waterboarding 183 times in March 2003 against Khalid Shaikh Mohammed, the self-described planner of the Sept. 11, 2001, terrorist attacks.[78]

—Scott Shane, journalist

■ ■ ■

[T]he key thing being sent down in terms of the request by the policymakers, by the White House, is find a link between Saddam and al Qaeda so that we essentially can link Saddam to the 9/11 attacks and then march into Iraq with the anger of 9/11 behind us.

That was the goal and that was being passed down as the directive. . . . [A]s frustration built inside of the White House—that there was no link that was established—because the CIA told the White House from the very start there is no Saddam/al Qaeda link. "We checked it out. We did every which way. Sorry." The White House simply wouldn't take no for an answer and it went with another method. Torture was the method.[79]

—Ron Suskind, journalist

While we were [at Guantanamo] a large part of the time we were focused on trying to establish a link between al Qaida and Iraq and we were not successful in establishing a link between al Qaida and Iraq. The more frustrated people got in not being able to establish that link . . . there was more and more pressure to resort to measures that might produce more immediate results.[80]

—Maj. Charles Burney

Consider: If you have a much-hyped threat that you've used to lead the nation to war—and if case after case against the "dangerous terrorists" falls apart—don't you need false confessions? If you torture prisoners, you will certainly obtain an endless stream of false confessions. In this sense, Guantanamo is an efficient machine for producing a high-value political product: false confessions by brown people with Muslim names.[81]

—Naomi Wolf, writer

It was directed by the president and the vice president. They were involved day to day. The president was getting briefings. The vice president—what techniques are we using; he was asking, "Are they working, what is the yield?" This came from the very top.[82]

—Ron Suskind, journalist

In other words, the ticking time bomb was not another potential Qaeda attack on America but the Bush administration's ticking timetable for selling a war in Iraq; it wanted to pressure Congress to pass a war resolution before the 2002 midterm elections. Bybee's memo was written the week after the then-secret (and subsequently leaked) "Downing Street memo," in which the head of British intelligence informed Tony Blair that the Bush White House was so determined to go to war in Iraq that "the intelligence and facts were being fixed around the policy." A month after Bybee's memo, on Sept. 8, 2002, Cheney would make his infamous appearance on "Meet the Press," hyping both Saddam's WMDs and the "number of contacts over the years" between Al Qaeda and Iraq. If only 9/11 could somehow be pinned on Iraq, the case for war would be a slamdunk.[83]

—Frank Rich, columnist

My problem is it comes back to this concept where we'll say, it's OK to torture, because we got the answer that we wanted. But see, that in itself tells us the broader question, and the biggest concern of all, is what we want is a particular answer. If I hook you up to something, if I use water, if I use electricity, if I use all sorts of various techniques, quote unquote, that means I get what I want. [But] we don't want just the things that we want. We want the truth. It's about the effectiveness of it and that's the fundamental question, let alone the moral question.[84]

—Jack Rice, CIA

The treatment of the detainees in Guantanamo Bay is proper, it's humane, it's appropriate. And it is fully consistent with the international conventions.[85]

—Donald Rumsfeld

No written guidelines on what constituted "humane treatment" existed. Even the White House could not define it.[86]

—Frederick A. O. Schwarz Jr. and Aziz Z. Huq, lawyers

On Dec. 2, 2002, Mr. Rumsfeld authorized the interrogators at Guantánamo to use a range of abusive techniques that were already widespread in Afghanistan, enshrining them as official policy.[87]

—New York Times editorial

In many newspapers around the globe "Guantanamo" is much more than the name of a beautiful harbor on Cuba's southern coast. It has become shorthand for a whole litany of American excesses in George W. Bush's "global war on terror," the most visible example of how the United States blithely ignores the values of due process and rule of law that it so aggressively preaches, if necessary at the point of a gun. . . . The point is that when our government mocks transparency and tries to conduct this war of ideas in the shadows, away from prying eyes, we defeat ourselves.[88]

—Eugene Robinson, columnist

They're very well-treated down there. They are living in the tropics. They are well-fed. They've got everything they could possibly want. There isn't any other nation in the world that would treat people who were determined to kill Americans the way we are treating these people.[89]

—Dick Cheney

By the fall of 2002, the U.S. military in Guantanamo was subjecting prisoners to treatment that would have been unimaginable, and prosecutable, before September 11.[90]

—Jane Mayer, journalist

You are welcome to go there yourself. Maybe you have. And take a look at the conditions. I urge members of our press corps to go down to Guantanamo and see how they are treated, and to see—and to look at the facts.[91]

—George W. Bush

Yes, the 520 or so prisoners still at Guantanamo have been given hearings before military panels. But that's where the lack of transparency comes in, because a secret military hearing is the same as no hearing at all. The U.S. Supreme Court has made clear that the Guantanamo prisoners have at least some right to appeal their detention in the federal courts. But rather than abide by the court's rulings, the administration has stalled and obfuscated. That's the contempt for due process.[92]

—Eugene Robinson, columnist

I got the sense that America had lost its moral bearings. [The military tribunals] bore no resemblance to what you or I would call a trial. There was no jury, no presumption of innocence, and no right to counsel.[93]

—Joe Margulies, lawyer

Yoo's March 2003 opinion . . . declared that federal laws prohibiting assault, maiming, and other crimes did not apply to the military interrogators in Guantanamo. The sum effect of the pages and pages of arguments was that Guantanamo was, for all intents and purposes, a law-free zone.[94]

—Jane Mayer, journalist

Many detainees locked up at Guantanamo were innocent men swept up by U.S. forces unable to distinguish enemies from noncombatants.[95]

—Andrew Selsky, journalist

There are still innocent people there. Some have been there six or seven years.[96]

—Lawrence Wilkerson, chief of staff to Colin Powell

Many of the aggressive interrogation techniques [were] a direct result of the pressure we felt from Washington to obtain intelligence and the lack of policy guidance being issued from Washington.[97]

—Dave Becker, Guantanamo Bay interrogator

This is not about an impetus to foil an upcoming potential al Qaeda attacks. The impetus here is largely political-diplomatic. The White House had a political-diplomatic problem. It wanted it solved in the run-up to the war. And mind you, and I think the data will show this—after the invasion, when it becomes clear in the summer, just a few months after in 2003, that there are no WMD in Iraq. That's the summer of Joe Wilson and Valerie Plame—my goodness, there are no WMD. Now, the White House is being hit with a charge that they took us to war under false pretenses. That's when the frustration is acute. My question, the question for investigators now, is: How many of these interrogations were driven specifically by a desire to come up with the Saddam/al Qaeda link? It's essentially rivers coming together. This gets to the key issue, certainly in criminal cases: intent. What was driving action? What were they looking for? What was the real impetus?[98]

—Ron Suskind, journalist

[T]hey were desperate to find a link between Al Qaeda and Iraq.[99]

—Sen. Carl Levin

[W]e must acknowledge that our government methodically authorized torture and lied about it. But we also must contemplate the possibility that it did so not just out of a sincere, if criminally misguided, desire to "protect" us but also to promote an unnecessary and catastrophic war. Instead of saving us from "another 9/11," torture was a tool in the campaign to falsify and exploit 9/11 so that fearful Americans would be bamboozled into a mission that had nothing to do with Al Qaeda. The lying about Iraq remains the original sin from which flows much of the Bush White House's illegality.[100]

—Frank Rich, columnist

The unintended consequence of a U.S. policy that provides for the torture of prisoners is that it could be used by our adversaries as justification for the torture of captured U.S. personnel.[101]

—government memo

The International Committee of the Red Cross concluded in a secret report that the Bush administration's so-called enhanced interrogation methods, used on "high-value" terrorism suspects, plainly constituted torture. . . . The Red Cross . . . is a stunning account of how the Bush administration spat on our laws, traditions and ideals.[102]

—Eugene Robinson, columnist

Those who can make you believe absurdities can make you commit atrocities.[103]

—Voltaire

Even as the executive branch sought to extend the geographic scope of the "war" in a way that augmented its own power, it also was systematically paring away, through secret legal opinions, the legal protections that applied specifically in wartime. Rather than follow the Geneva rules, which would have required a hearing to determine any captive's status even in wartime, the Justice Department argued that an "enemy combatant" deserved *no* independent judicial review of the basis of their detention.[104]

—Frederick A. O. Schwarz Jr. and Aziz Z. Huq, lawyers

[There is] evidence of a "common plan to violate the Geneva Conventions" by President Bush, his White House counsel Alberto Gonzales, and others.[105]

—John Dean, former White House counsel

Crime is contagious. If the government becomes a lawbreaker, it breeds contempt for the law; it invites every man to become a law unto himself. . . . [T]o declare that the government may commit crimes in order to secure the conviction of a private criminal —would bring terrible retribution.[106]

—Louis D. Brandeis, U.S. Supreme Court

This is a monument to executive supremacy and the imperial presidency.[107]

—Eugene Fidell, law professor

Ever since Americans learned that American soldiers and intelligence agents were torturing prisoners, there has been a disturbing question: How high up did the decision go to ignore United States law, international treaties, the Geneva Conventions and basic morality? The answer, we have learned recently, is that—with President Bush's clear knowledge and support—some of the very highest officials in the land not only approved the abuse of prisoners, but participated in the detailed planning of harsh interrogations and helped to create a legal structure to shield from justice those who followed the orders.[108]

—*New York Times* editorial

This isn't something that's done willy-nilly. It's not something that an agency officer just wakes up in the morning and decides he's going to carry out an enhanced technique on a prisoner. This was a policy decision made at the White House with the National Security Council and the Justice Department.[109]

—John Kiriakou, CIA

Cruelty disfigures our national character. It is incompatible with our constitutional order, with our laws, and with our most prized values. . . . Where cruelty exists, law does not.[110]

—Alberto Mora, lawyer

We used to wonder where war lived, what it was that made us so vile. And now we realize that we know where it lives, that is inside ourselves.[111]

—Albert Camus

[E]ven as we were tracking down a heinous enemy, Osama bin Laden, who operated out of a cave, our government started moving our own legal system into a cave of sorts. Bush issued an executive order to set up military tribunals in which neither the verdicts, evidence, nor punishments ever had to be revealed to the public.[112]

—Frank Rich, columnist

The top Bush administration official in charge of deciding whether to bring Guantánamo Bay detainees to trial has concluded that the U.S. military tortured a Saudi national who allegedly planned to participate in the Sept. 11, 2001, attacks, interrogating him with techniques that included sustained isolation, sleep deprivation, nudity and prolonged exposure to cold, leaving him in a "life-threatening condition."[113]

—Bob Woodward, journalist

We tortured [Mohammed al-] Qahtani. His treatment met the legal definition of torture. . . . The techniques they used were all authorized, but the manner in which they applied them was overly aggressive and too persistent. . . . You think of torture, you think of some horrendous physical act done to an individual. This was not any one particular act; this was just a combination of things that had a medical impact on him, that hurt his health. It was abusive and uncalled for. And coercive. Clearly coercive. . . . [T]here still has to be a line that we should not cross. And unfortunately what this has done, I think, has tainted everything going forward.[114]

—Susan Crawford, judge

As Judge Crawford's pointed out, in that same article, this taint—and she is well aware—has grown to the point that it has contaminated everything Guantanamo and everything military commissions. The use of torture jeopardizes your ability to prosecute someone. It jeopardizes—and the reason it does is not some higher that if we do this then they are absolved. The reason it does is it produces unreliable information. It's a taint that taints everything.[115]

—Lt. Cmdr. Charles Swift (Ret.)

In some cases, we determine that individuals we have captured pose a significant threat, or may have intelligence that we and our allies need to have to prevent new attacks. Many are al Qaeda operatives or Taliban fighters trying to conceal their identities, and they withhold information that could save American lives. In these cases, it has been necessary to move these individuals to an environment where they can be held secretly, questioned by experts, and—when appropriate—prosecuted for terrorist acts.[116]

—George W. Bush

They'll never charge anyone. There's no incentive to. The way they've set things up, they can hold and interrogate them forever.[117]

—Stephen Kenny, lawyer

Everything this administration did was—had a legal basis to it, otherwise we would not have done it.[118]

—George W. Bush

A report released Thursday by leaders of the Senate Armed Services Committee said top Bush administration officials, including Donald H. Rumsfeld, the former defense secretary, bore major responsibility for the abuses committed by American troops in interrogations at Abu Ghraib in Iraq; Guantánamo Bay, Cuba; and other military detention centers.[119]

—Scott Shane and Mark Mazzetti, journalists

The report shows how actions by these men "led directly" to what happened at Abu Ghraib, in Afghanistan, in Guantánamo Bay, Cuba, and in secret CIA prisons.[120]

—*New York Times* editorial

A bipartisan panel of senators has concluded that former defense secretary Donald H. Rumsfeld and other top Bush administration officials bear direct responsibility for the harsh treatment of detainees at Guantánamo Bay, and that their decisions led to more serious abuses in Iraq and elsewhere.[121]

—Joby Warrick and Karen DeYoung, journalists

It said these top officials, charged with defending the Constitution and America's standing in the world, methodically introduced interrogation practices based on illegal tortures devised by Chinese agents during the Korean War. Until the Bush administration, their only use in the United States was to train soldiers to resist what might be done to them if they were captured by a lawless enemy.[122]

—*New York Times* editorial

[It] most certainly is a crime to participate, to create, to—in many ways—monitor a torture program. And, indeed, it's one of the crimes that defines a nation committed to the rule of law.[123]

—Jonathan Turley, law professor

The report is the most direct refutation to date of the administration's rationale for using aggressive interrogation tactics—that inflicting humiliation and pain on detainees was legal and effective, and helped protect the country. The 25-member panel, without one dissent among the 12 Republican members, declared the opposite to be true. The administration's policies and the resulting controversies, the panel concluded, "damaged our ability to collect accurate intelligence that could save lives, strengthened the hand of our enemies, and compromised our moral authority."[124]

—Joby Warrick and Karen DeYoung, journalists

Torture and abuse are against my moral fabric. The cliché still bears repeating: Such outrages are inconsistent with American principles. And then there's the pragmatic side: Torture and abuse cost American lives. I learned in Iraq that the No. 1 reason foreign fighters flocked there to fight were the abuses carried out at Abu Ghraib and Guantanamo. Our policy of torture was directly and swiftly recruiting fighters for al-Qaeda in Iraq. . . . How anyone can say that torture keeps Americans safe is beyond me—unless you don't count American soldiers as Americans.[125]

—Matthew Alexander, interrogator

Some may argue that we would be more effective if we sanctioned torture or other expedient methods to obtain information from the enemy. They would be wrong. Beyond the basic fact that such actions are illegal, history shows that they also are frequently neither useful nor necessary.[126]

—Gen. David H. Petraeus

[T]he administration has been so busy loop-holing the Constitution and our treaties that they haven't realized a lot of techniques that work. Torture has been shown not to work because people give misleading information. . . . So, what this is really about, it's not about security and national security, what all this torture stuff is about and all these secret opinions about something much more basic, that's . . . incompetence.[127]

—Neal Katyal, lawyer

[T]he president had an illegal, unconstitutional structure for detaining people that he was destroying, in a sense, the reputation of our country and hurting the values of our country in other lands where we need people's support. And, finally, he admits what all of us have known under the ground for a long time, that we have these secret prisons which the United States doesn't condone.[128]

—Sen. John Kerry

It is better . . . to correct error while new and before it becomes inveterate by habit and custom.[129]

—Thomas Jefferson

Rumsfeld issued an oral order that would have momentous consequences for the way the world viewed American power abroad. He wanted Major General Geoffrey Miller, the commander in Guantanamo, to "Gitmoize" Iraq, as Army Reserve Brigadier General Janis Karpinski, who oversaw the detention facilities there, later described it.[130]

—Jane Mayer, journalist

ABU GHRAIB

All of the Army's problems in Iraq in 2003—poor planning, clumsy leadership, strategic confusion, counterproductive tactics, undermanning, being overly reactive—came together in the treatment of prisoners, a wide-ranging scandal that eventually was summarized in the phrase "Abu Ghraib," after the big prison west of Baghdad where many prisoners wound up, and where some were tortured.[131]

—Thomas Ricks, journalist

The U.S. military yesterday charged six American soldiers with indecency and assaulting Iraqi prisoners at the Abu Ghraib prison, the former Iraqi torture center now used as an allied military detention facility.[132]

—Carol Rosenberg, journalist

The roots of the Abu Ghraib prison scandal lie not in the criminal inclinations of a few Army reservists but in the reliance of George Bush and Donald Rumsfeld on secret operations and the use of coercion—and eye-for-an-eye retribution—in fighting terrorism.[133]

—Seymour Hersh, journalist

What happened in Abu Ghraib prison was, at best, a fundamental breakdown in the chain of command under Mr. Rumsfeld's authority, or, at worst, part of a deliberate policy somewhere in the military-intelligence command of sexually humiliating prisoners to soften them up for interrogation, a policy that ran amok.[134]

—Thomas Friedman, journalist

In Saddam Hussein's Iraq, the Abu Ghraib prison in Baghdad was widely feared as a place into which men disappeared, never to be heard from again. In U.S.-occupied Iraq, the same prison, which now contains Iraqi prisoners of war, has become notorious again.[135]

—*Washington Post* editorial

President Bush on Friday strongly condemned the alleged mistreatment of Iraqi prisoners by U.S. soldiers even as graphic pictures of abuses aired around the world, angering Arabs and threatening to further undermine the occupation of Iraq. The images, first broadcast Wednesday on the CBS program "60 Minutes II," show male and female American troops, smiling, posing, laughing or giving the thumbs-up sign in front of naked Iraqi men held at the notorious Abu Ghraib prison, the center for torture during the Saddam Hussein regime.[136]

—Esther Schrader and Patrick J. McDonnell, journalists

You can't imagine what it's like to go to a closed room where you have a classified briefing, and stand shoulder to shoulder with your colleagues in the Senate, and see hundreds and hundreds of slides like those, most of which have never been publicly disclosed. I had a sick feeling when I left. It was then that I began to have suspicions that something significant was happening at the highest levels of the government when it came to torture policy.[137]

—Sen. Richard Durbin

The senior American commander in Iraq has ordered the first punishments in the abuse of prisoners by American soldiers there, issuing severe reprimands to six who served in supervisory positions at Abu Ghraib prison and a milder "letter of admonishment" to a seventh.[138]

—Thom Shanker and Dexter Filkins, journalists

Do you really think a group of kids from rural Virginia decided to do this on their own? Decided that the best way to embarrass Arabs and make them talk was to have them walk around nude? The notion that Arabs are particularly vulnerable to sexual humiliation had become a talking point among pro-war Washington conservatives in the months before the March 2003 invasion of Iraq.[139]

—Seymour Hersh, journalist

The abuses at Abu Ghraib, GTMO and elsewhere cannot be chalked up to the actions of a few bad apples. Attempts by senior officials to pass the buck to low ranking soldiers while avoiding any responsibility for abuses are unconscionable. The message from top officials was clear; it was acceptable to use degrading and abusive techniques against detainees. Our investigation is an effort to set the record straight on this chapter in our history that has so damaged both America's standing and our security. America needs to own up to its mistakes so that we can rebuild some of the good will that we have lost.[140]

—Sen. Carl Levin

Accurately or not, Bush Administration officials later described the abuses at Abu Ghraib and Guantanamo as the unauthorized actions of a few ill-trained personnel. By contrast, CIA officials have never denied that the treatment of the high-value detainees was expressly approved by President Bush.[141]

—Jane Mayer, journalist

I think it's absolutely clear that this kind of behavior is absolutely not the norm for American men and women in uniform. . . . That's why it's such a disservice to everyone else, that a few bad apples can create some large problems for everybody.[142]

—Paul Wolfowitz, former Deputy Defense Secretary

Claims, such as the one made by former Deputy Secretary of Defense Paul Wolfowitz that detainee abuses could be chalked up to the unauthorized acts of a "few bad apples," were simply false. The truth is that, early on, it was senior civilian leaders who set the tone. Vice President Dick Cheney suggested that the United States turn to the "dark side" in our response to 9/11, White House Counsel Alberto Gonzales called parts of the Geneva Conventions "quaint," and President Bush determined that provisions of the Geneva Conventions did not apply to certain detainees. Other senior officials followed the President and Vice President's lead, authorizing policies that included harsh and abusive interrogation techniques.[143]

—Sen. Carl Levin

The abuse of prisoners at Abu Ghraib flowed directly from the abuse of truth that characterized the administration's march to war and the abuse of trust that was placed in President Bush by the American people in the aftermath of September 11.[144]

—Al Gore

As former soldiers, we knew that you don't have this kind of pervasive attitude out there unless you've condoned it. And whether you did it explicitly or not is irrelevant. If you did it at all, indirectly, implicitly, tacitly—you pick the word—you're in trouble because that slippery slope is truly slippery, and it will take years to reverse the situation, and we'll probably have to grow a new military.[145]

—Lawrence Wilkerson, chief of staff to Colin Powell

At Abu Ghraib, a few sadistic prison guards abused inmates in violation of American law, military regulation and simple decency. For the harm they did to Iraqi prisoners and to America's cause, they deserved and received Army justice. And it takes a deeply unfair cast of mind to equate the disgraces of Abu Ghraib with the lawful, skillful, and entirely honorable work of CIA personnel trained to deal with a few malevolent men. Those personnel were carefully chosen from within the CIA and were especially prepared to apply techniques within the boundaries of their training and the limits of the law. Torture was never permitted. And the methods were given careful legal review before they were approved. Interrogators had authoritative guidance on the line between toughness and torture, and they knew to stay on the right side of it.[146]

—Dick Cheney

Cheney's involvement in trying to conceal the import of Abu Ghraib was not unusual; it was a sign of the teamwork at the top.[147]

—Seymour Hersh, journalist

The CIA waterboarders get Cheney's praise, but the grunts at Abu Ghraib and their superior officers get punishment and jail. That does not seem to be a consistent approach when the explanation is identical.[148]

—Gen. Janis Karpinski, former commander of U.S. prisons in Iraq

In top-secret meetings about enhanced interrogations, I made my own beliefs clear. I was and remain a strong proponent of our enhanced interrogation program. The interrogations were used on hardened terrorists after other efforts failed. They were legal, essential, justified, successful, and the right thing to do. The intelligence officers who questioned the terrorists can be proud of their work, proud of the results, because they prevented the violent death of thousands, perhaps hundreds of thousands of people.[149]

—Dick Cheney

This is one of the most shameful aspects of these memos. And a knowledge that people at the highest levels of our government had about these memos, actually sat together and wrote them and rewrote them and crafted them to meet the requirements of these techniques that they wanted to use. They were well aware—these people, Rumsfeld,

Sanchez, all of them were well aware of these policies and these memorandums while these soldiers were being accused five years ago.[150]

—Gen. Janis Karpinski, former commander of U.S. prisons in Iraq

The senior leadership in the White House has been aware since January of the mess at Abu Ghraib, and, more importantly, of the fact that photographs and videotapes existed, and might someday reach the public.[151]

—Seymour Hersh, journalist

[T]here's no question that in 2003, what was happening in Abu Ghraib and other division and brigade detention centers all over Iraq amounted to torture, and it put the whole mission at risk. It created more of an insurgency, certainly more than there needed to be.[152]

—Maj. Gen. John Batiste, U.S. Army (Ret.)

General Antonio Taguba was assigned to investigate further. By statute, he could only probe those lower than himself in rank, guaranteeing that those above him in the chain of command would escape blame.[153]

—Jane Mayer, journalist

U.S. officials said the review, by Maj. Gen. Antonio M. Taguba, found that prisoners at Abu Ghraib were regularly subjected to cruel and harsh punishments. . . . Taguba found a pattern of "sadistic, blatant, and wanton criminal abuses" at the prison.[154]

—Sewell Chan and Michael Amon, journalists

The abuses included threats of rape and the pouring of cold water and liquid from chemical lights on detainees, said the internal report by Maj. Gen. Antonio Taguba. According to the report, detainees were beaten with a broom handle, and one was sodomized with "a chemical light and perhaps a broomstick."[155]

—*San Francisco Chronicle* report

The Taguba report found evidence that MPs were aggressively encouraged to set the stage for questioning of prisoners—a fact, Taguba wrote, that contributed to the abuse. At Abu Ghraib, "interrogators actively requested that MP guards set physical and mental conditions for favorable interrogation of witnesses," Taguba wrote.[156]

—Patrick McDonnell, journalist

On the afternoon of May 6, 2004, Army Major General Antonio M. Taguba was summoned to meet, for the first time, with Secretary of Defense Donald Rumsfeld in his Pentagon conference room. . . . In the meeting, the officials professed ignorance about Abu Ghraib. "Could you tell us what happened?" Wolfowitz asked. Someone else asked, "Is it abuse or torture?" At that point, Taguba recalled, "I described a naked detainee lying on the wet floor, handcuffed, with an interrogator shoving things up his rectum, and said, "That's not abuse. That's torture." There was quiet." At best, Taguba said, "Rumsfeld was in denial."[157]

—Seymour Hersh, journalist

They always shoot the messenger. To be accused of being overzealous and disloyal—that cuts deep into me. I was being ostracized for doing what I was asked to do. . . . There was no doubt in my mind that this stuff—the explicit images—was gravitating upward. It was standard operating procedure to assume that this had to go higher. The President had to be aware of this.[158]

—Gen. Antonio Taguba

BLACK SITES

Within days of 9/11, President Bush signed a secret executive order authorizing a new policy of "extraordinary rendition." A "rendition" involves the transfer of an individual to another country without any judicial proceedings. Post-9/11, the phrase "extraordinary rendition" was coined to distinguish a new practice: the transfer of people suspected of having a connection to terrorism to a country that uses torture to extract information. A suspect is picked up, often outside the United Stated, and—without any judicial process—disappears into a global network of detention facilities run by the United States or other nations. Most of these nations, such as Syria, Egypt, or Jordan, are routinely condemned in the State Department's human rights reports as persistent torturers.[159]

—Frederick A. O. Schwarz Jr. and Aziz Z. Huq, lawyers

A few days after terrorists toppled the World Trade Center in 2001, Vice President Dick Cheney said the U.S. would have to "work . . . the dark side" in order to destroy Osama bin Laden's network. Just what the dark side could mean became clearer last month when George Bush suddenly announced that 14 suspected al-Qaeda terrorists had been shipped from mysterious overseas locations to the U.S. detention center at Guantánamo Bay, Cuba. It was the first White House confirmation of a secret CIA-operated network of overseas prisons, places where unorthodox methods of interrogation were not unknown.[160]

—Michael Duffy, journalist

Were it not for this program, our intelligence community believes that al Qaeda and its allies would have succeeded in launching another attack against the American homeland. By giving us information about terrorist plans we could not get anywhere else, this program has saved innocent lives.[161]

—George W. Bush

The interrogation methods were authorized beginning in 2002, and some were used as late as 2005 in the CIA's secret overseas prisons.[162]

—Mark Mazzetti and Scott Shane, journalists

The establishment of a series of secret prisons around the world and the widespread use of harsh interrogation tactics against prisoners in American custody has been part of a broader and disquieting pattern by the Bush administration. The White House has interpreted the constitutional powers of the president to fight terrorism in such an expansive way that long-standing rules governing the military and intelligence communities have been skirted or ignored, and secret intelligence activities inside the United States have been approved that may be violating the civil liberties of American citizens.[163]

—James Risen, journalist

The irony of the United States rewarding striving democracies, with histories as police states, for their help in secretly interrogating prisoners outside the protection of the law evidently was not dwelled upon. "We told them we'd help them join NATO if they helped us torture people," a cynical former CIA officer said.[164]

—Jane Mayer, journalist

Condoleezza Rice, John D. Ashcroft and other top Bush administration officials approved as early as the summer of 2002 the CIA's use at secret prisons of harsh interrogation methods, including waterboarding. . . . Rice gave a key early green light when, as President George W. Bush's national security adviser, she met on July 17, 2002, with the CIA's then-director, George J. Tenet, and "advised that the CIA could proceed with its proposed interrogation of Abu Zubaida," subject to approval by the Justice Department, according to the timeline.[165]

—R. Jeffrey Smith and Peter Finn, journalists

President Bush, defending a clandestine U.S. prison system abroad for terrorism suspects, said Monday that his administration would continue to aggressively battle terrorism in sometimes unconventional but always lawful ways. Brushing aside international criticism of the CIA-run prisons set up in eight countries, Bush said that the nation is at war with an enemy "that lurks and plots and plans and wants to hurt America again. And so, you bet, we'll aggressively pursue them, but we'll do so under the law." Bush, who spoke to reporters during a brief visit to the capital of Panama, also asserted, "We do not torture."[166]

—Michael Fletcher, journalist

On September 6, 2006 . . . Bush admitted for the first time that America had been holding secret prisoners for years, without charges and outside the reach of authorities, and subjecting them to "an alternative set of procedures." He announced that he had emptied the black sites and transferred these suspects to Guantanamo Bay.[167]

—Jane Mayer, journalist

In addition to the terrorists held at Guantanamo, a small number of suspected terrorist leaders and operatives captured during the war have been held and questioned outside the United States, in a separate program operated by the Central Intelligence Agency.[168]

—George W. Bush

Suspected Qaeda prisoners were taken to secret sites, or to Guantánamo, or grabbed by "rendition" teams who took them to countries where interrogators had long experience with torture, or simply held incommunicado in American military prisons. Still another measure: dispensing with warrants when tapping into phone conversations between the United States and suspected terrorists or their contacts in the rest of the world.[169]

—Christopher Dickey, journalist

Extraordinary rendition . . . became national policy via secretive executive lawmaking that circumvented Congress and repudiated the proper role of the federal courts. And the underlying legal justifications for extraordinary rendition . . . rely on monarchical prerogatives that are completely incompatible with a Constitution of separate branches, sharing power.[170]

—Frederick A. O. Schwarz Jr. and Aziz Z. Huq, lawyers

Pressed about the Convention Against Torture, a treaty that President Reagan had signed and that the Senate ratified in 1984, Gonzales revealed for the first time that the administration legal team had secretly concluded that the treaty had force only on domestic soil, where the U.S. Constitution applies. Thus, for noncitizens held overseas, no rules applies.[171]

—Charlie Savage, journalist

Mr. Gonzales . . . tortured the law to justify torture.[172]

—*New York Times* editorial

We don't kick the (expletive) out of them. We send them to other countries so they can kick the (expletive) out of them.[173]

—anonymous U.S. official

The abuse and torture of prisoners continued at prisons run by the CIA and specialists from the torture-resistance program remained involved in the military detention system until 2004.[174]

—*New York Times* editorial

Once upon a time, it was the United States that urged all nations to obey the letter and the spirit of international treaties and protect human rights and liberties. American leaders denounced secret prisons where people were held without charges, tortured and killed. And the people in much of the world, if not their governments, respected the United States for its values. The Bush administration has dishonored that history and squandered that respect.[175]

—*New York Times* editorial

Just as habeas corpus, or some equivalent procedure, is the cornerstone of virtually every democracy, so is a secret prison system without habeas corpus the cornerstone of every dictatorship. You cannot push an open society into submission without a secret prison or, more effective still, a system of secret prisons.[176]

—Naomi Wolf, writer

The complex bureaucratic network of extraordinary rendition, disappearances, and black sites is grounded in a set of secret presidential laws and classified Justice Department legal opinions that undercut the rules enacted by Congress, enforced by the courts, and known to the people. Both this system of secret laws and the ultimate legal justifications for unchecked executive power to transfer suspects to torture are inconsistent with a government of checks and balances.[177]

—Frederick A. O. Schwarz Jr. and Aziz Z. Huq, lawyers

CIA Director Michael Hayden said Thursday that the agency destroyed videotapes of interrogations they performed in 2002 of two top terrorism suspects out of fear the tapes would be leaked and make public the identities of the interrogators.[178]

—Alan Gomez, journalist

The Central Intelligence Agency in 2005 destroyed at least two videotapes documenting the interrogation of two Qaeda operatives in the agency's custody, a step it took in the midst of Congressional and legal scrutiny about its secret detention program, according to current and former government officials. The videotapes showed agency operatives in 2002 subjecting terrorism suspects—including Abu Zubaydah, the first detainee in CIA custody—to severe interrogation techniques. The tapes were destroyed in part because officers were concerned that video showing harsh interrogation methods could expose agency officials to legal risks, several officials said.[179]

— Mark Mazzetti, journalist

[F]or the last six years, this administration has been assaulting the Constitution. I mean, you go back whether it was secret prisons, rendition, Abu Ghraib, Guantanamo, habeas corpus, water-boarding, walking away from the Geneva conventions, the list just goes on. The destruction of these tapes at the CIA. I mean, how many more items, how many more pieces of evidence do you know that this administration just has a disregard for?[180]

—Sen. Christopher Dodd

This doesn't look like a war on terrorism, but a war on our own values.[181]

—Nicholas D. Kristof, columnist

The rest of the world is completely convinced that we are busy torturing people. Whether that is true or not, the fact we keep refusing to provide these protections in our formal directives puts a lot of fuel on the fire.[182]

—Oona Hathaway, law professor

Maher Arar, a Syrian-born Canadian, was stopped at Kennedy Airport in 2002 while returning from a family vacation. After being held in solitary confinement in a Brooklyn detention center and interrogated without proper access to a lawyer, he was spirited off to Syria. He was tortured there for months before officials decided that their suspicions that he was a member of Al Qaeda were mistaken and let him go. Mr. Arar was a victim of extraordinary rendition, America's notorious program of outsourcing interrogations to governments known to use torture.[183]

—*New York Times* editorial

The CIA has been hiding and interrogating some of its most important al Qaeda captives at a Soviet-era compound in Eastern Europe, according to U.S. and foreign officials familiar with the arrangement. The secret facility is part of a covert prison system set up by the CIA nearly four years ago that at various times has included sites in eight countries, including Thailand, Afghanistan and several democracies in Eastern Europe, as well as a small center at the Guantanamo Bay prison in Cuba, according to current and former intelligence officials and diplomats from three continents. . . . The existence and locations of the facilities—referred to as "black sites" in classified White House, CIA, Justice Department and congressional documents—are known to only a handful of officials in the United States and, usually, only to the president and a few top intelligence officers in each host country. . . . The black-site program was approved by a small circle of White House and Justice Department lawyers and officials, according to several former and current U.S. government and intelligence officials.[184]

—Dana Priest, journalist

In the name of fighting terrorism—and with a clear goal of avoiding accountability—the Bush administration has imposed a level of secrecy on its operations that has no place in a democracy. . . . In recent years, a number of important lawsuits have raised credible allegations of government abuses including torture, kidnapping, rendition and domestic eavesdropping. All too often, judges have blocked these suits without examining how and why going forward would compromise the nation's security.[185]

—*New York Times* editorial

Just before Bush signed [Sen. John] McCain's Detainee Treatment Act into law, on December 30, 2005, Addington unsheathed the red pen he kept in his pocket and eviscerated the compromise language that had been worked out between Congress and the White House. In its place, he wrote a presidential "signing statement" suggesting that Bush would only enforce the new law "in a manner consistent with" his constitutional role as commander in chief. It was one of hundreds of similar notes he had insinuated into the legislative record, reserving the President's right to ignore Congress.[186]

—Jane Mayer, journalist

What torture produces in practice is misinformation, as its victims, desperate to end the pain, tell interrogators whatever they want to hear. . . . The central drive of the Bush administration—more fundamental than any particular policy—has been the effort to eliminate all limits on the president's power. Torture, I believe, appeals to the president and the vice president precisely because it's a violation of both law and tradition. By making an illegal and immoral practice a key element of U.S. policy, they're asserting their right to do whatever they claim is necessary.[187]

—Paul Krugman, columnist

There is an important and deadly serious lesson here, for American politicians as well as military commanders: The rule of law matters, even where America's worst enemies are concerned. Although it has become fashionable, in certain Washington circles, to play down the importance of "outdated" forms of international law such as the Geneva Convention on prisoners of war, this incident demonstrates just how important it is to teach the rules of the Geneva Convention to soldiers at all levels and to apply them as strictly as possible.[188]

—*Washington Post* editorial

We wanted this to be about change. We wanted it to have the President saying he was committed to closing Guantanamo. But instead of turning the page, they laminated it.[189]

—Rep. Henry Waxman

The president or vice president, repeatedly expressed a desire, or need, to a senior official. It's clear that neither elected official wants to know too much about the *hows*. They just want it done, accomplished, to do something—as the president often said to top aides—"you didn't know you were capable of." With such prodding, the United States would slip into the darkness of ethical abysses.[190]

—Ron Suskind, journalist

I have heard nothing to suggest that information obtained from enhanced interrogation techniques has prevented an imminent terrorist attack. And I have heard nothing that makes me think the information obtained from these techniques could not have been obtained through traditional interrogation methods used by military law enforcement interrogators. On the other hand, I do know that coercive interrogations can lead detainees to provide false information in order to make the interrogation stop.[191]

—Sen. Jay Rockefeller

In looking back, one of the most remarkable features of this struggle is that almost from the start, and at almost every turn along the way, the Bush Administration was warned that the short-term benefits of its extralegal approach to fighting terrorism would have tragically destructive long-term consequences both for the rule of law and America's interests in the world. These warnings came not just from political opponents, but also from experienced allies, including the British Intelligence Service, the experts in the traditionally conservative military and the FBI, and perhaps most surprisingly, from a series of loyal Republican lawyers inside the administration itself. The number of patriotic critics inside the administration and out who threw themselves into trying to head off what they saw as a terrible departure from America's ideals, often at an enormous price to their own careers, is both humbling and reassuring.[192]

—Jane Mayer, journalist

How far you can go without destroying from within what you are trying to defend from without?[193]

—Dwight Eisenhower

AFTERWORD

In his writings, the brilliant social observer Malcolm Gladwell suggests various pathways of insight and understanding into our world. In *Blink*, Gladwell examines rapid cognition—the thinking and judgments we each form instantly when presented with situations, facts or other stimuli. Those initial or early conclusions, he writes, are powerful and often correct. In *The Tipping Point*, Gladwell examines how ideas, messages, and products are dispersed. The progression from abstract, little-known idea or product to widespread acceptance is sometimes serendipitous and often fascinating.

I mention these in relation to the genesis of this book. What was the catalyst in accumulating and analyzing volumes of material? In attempting to trace those paths as they were experienced, some patterns emerged, particularly through the prisms of Gladwell's perspectives. The "Blink moment" is relatively easy. George W. Bush entered the national stage during the campaign for the 2000 election. His character, intellect, and ability to lead were on display. 'Nuf said. Bush, perhaps unwittingly, became the national spokesman for an anti-intellectualism movement.

The "Tipping Point?" Allowing Dick Cheney's search for a running mate to self-select? "My Pet Goat?" When it somehow became necessary to invade Iraq because of what people in Afghanistan had done? "Mission Accomplished?" Abu Ghraib? Torture? The mismanagement of Iraq? For many, it was the "incompetence and blindness"[1] exhibited in the response to Hurricane Katrina including "Brownie, you're doin' a heckuva job." As columnist Maureen Dowd wrote, "The bumbling Bush team that ignored the warning 'Bin Laden Determined to Attack Inside the United States' also ignored one that went something like: 'Katrina Determined to Attack New Orleans.'"[2]

In 2006, Paul Krugman wrote, "Since 2000, we've seen what happens when people who aren't interested in the facts, who believe what they want to believe, sit in the White House. Osama bin Laden is still at large, Iraq is a mess, New Orleans is a wreck. And, of course, we've done nothing about global warming."[3]

In this corner, while all of these contributed, the tipping point was none of these. Instead, it was a domestic issue: the appointment of a federal judge. Exercising their advise-and-consent role, Senate Democrats had opposed Bush's nomination of Charles Pickering to a federal appeals court. Pickering's decades-long record as a Mississippi lawyer and federal judge portrayed him as insensitive to civil rights issues. To circumvent the opposition, in early 2005 Bush "proudly" exploited a loophole that allows the president to make appointments during congressional recesses. More abuse of power. Another example of failure to recognize separation of powers. And he repeated the practice five weeks later to install another controversial judge in an appeals court seat.

But the domestic abuses of power did not end (or begin) there. In addition to fighting the war on terrorism, the Bush administration was also engaged in a war on science. Under the Bush administration, the Environmental Protection Agency was anything but a protector of the environment—another Orwellian testament to the administration's newspeak proclivity. Even after the U.S. Supreme Court ruled that the Clean Air Act requires the EPA to regulate greenhouse gases emitted by cars and trucks if agency scientists determine that the pollutants are a danger to the public, the EPA refused. A memorandum issued by then-EPA head Stephen Johnson stated that carbon dioxide is not a pollutant to be regulated when approving power plants. He cited "sound policy considerations"—yet another example of the administration creating realities by claiming "things are as we say they are." Here, Johnson had, in effect, overruled the Supreme Court, proving the point made by Sen. Barbara Boxer that administration officials were "environmental outlaws."[4]

Johnson was among many global warming deniers in the Bush administration. Another was Phillip Cooney, the chief of staff for the White House Council on Environmental Quality. His job was to advise the president on the environmental implications of decisions that the president makes. He apparently also viewed himself as an editor charged with examining scientific documents issued by various federal agencies, then removing statements damaging to the oil and coal industries. It is reported that he suppressed or altered several major studies on global warming. It seems one goal was to protect the interests of clients he had in his previous job—chief lobbyist for the American Petroleum Institute. As one critic said, "The corporations don't have to lobby the government any more. They are the government."[5]

According to NASA's top climate expert, Dr. James Hansen, editing like Cooney's amounted to censorship and muddied the public debate over a pressing environmental issue. Nearly half of 279 global scientists said in a survey that at some point they had been told to delete any reference to "global warming" or "climate change" from a report.[6]

Moreover, the Bush administration tried to silence the scientists themselves. In the wake of Hurricane Katrina, for example, the administration refused to allow a top federal scientist whose research links increased hurricane intensity to global warming to speak to the press. It sent out a gag order to stop government polar scientists, demanding that anyone attending international scientific conventions agree not to speak to reporters. "Interference with communication of science to the public has been greater during the current administration than at any time in my career," Hansen testified before Congress in 2007, and also suggested that NASA's press office had become an "office of propaganda."[7] All this was part of a campaign to sow doubts about climate change. "In many ways, the administration's refusal to budge on global warming mirrors its intransigence on Iraq."[8] According to former Treasury Secretary Paul O'Neill, the administration "cherry-picked" the science on climate change to justify taking no action, "just like it cherry-picked the intelligence on weapons of mass destruction" to justify the invasion of Iraq.[9]

The Bush administration's protection of "dirty" energy interests soon became routine and anything but surprising—but no less damaging. Early in Bush's presidency, his policy specifically called for no sacrifice when it came to energy consumption. "The president believes," his press secretary said, "that it should be the goal of policymakers to protect the American way of life. The American way of life is a blessed one."[10] Still, Bush pledged an allegiance to conservation: "We must and we will conserve more in the United States."[11] But over the next four years, Bush slashed funding for federal efficiency programs by nearly one-third.[12]

Moreover, there was Dick Cheney's energy task force formed in the president's second week. In typical Cheney-esque fashion, the industry-infused group met behind closed doors, used confidential memos, and received and issued secret recommendations. "There was no pretense of openness or democratic process."[13]

At the 2008 G8 Summit, Bush surprised world leaders with a joke about his poor record on the environment as he exited. He ended a private meeting with the words: "Goodbye from the world's biggest polluter."[14] Many in attendance did not get the joke—one that it seems, was on us.

While information should be free, at the same time it remains a precious commodity. It is the lifeblood of a democracy, whether it is one that is well established or one just beginning to experiment with democratic principles and practices. The people require accurate data to determine their futures. A government that distorts, controls or censors information—including by lying—disrespects its citizens and degrades the democratic process. It is no coincidence that between 2001 and 2009 when government lying reached new levels, the U.S. democracy was as broken as it has ever been. Its citizens—not to mention branches of the government itself—had been removed from the process. An executive branch with an ever-expanding lust for power saw to that.

As then-candidate Barack Obama said in his August 2008 acceptance speech for his party's nomination, we are a better country than this. "Enough." While the Bush administration is over, the consequences will be enduring. The hope here is this volume contributes to an ability to recognize the signals of any future leaders with despotic tendencies, particularly those with the Orwellian propensity of creating alternate realities by manipulating information. The signs were there between 2000 and 2008, though many—some in a post-9/11 fog of "patriotism" that included mistaking dissent for disloyalty and an unwillingness to speak truth to power—refused to see them. Like those who ultimately exposed these signals, we simply need to be ready and willing to recognize them. In that way—and to once again borrow from Gladwell, this time from his third book—George W. Bush and presidencies like his will become outliers.

SELECTED BIBLIOGRAPHY

9/11 Commission Report. New York: W. W. Norton, 2004.

Baker, James A. III, Lee H. Hamilton, et al. *The Iraq Study Group Report: The Way Forward: A New Approach*. New York: Vintage Books, 2006.

Clarke, Richard A. *Against All Enemies: Inside America's War on Terror*. New York: Free Press, 2004.

Countdown, MSNBC.

Dean, John W. *Worse Than Watergate: The Secret Presidency of George W. Bush*. New York: Warner Books, 2004.

Dickey, Christopher. "The Constitution in Peril," *Newsweek*, October 8, 2007, 62.

Drumheller, Tyler. *On the Brink: An Insider's Account of How the White House Compromised American Intelligence*. New York: Carroll & Graf Publishers, 2006.

Duelfer, Charles. *Hide and Seek: The Search for Truth in Iraq*. New York: Public Affairs, 2009.

Duffy, Michael. "The Cheney Branch of Government," *Time*, June 22, 2007.

Fallows, James. *Blind Into Baghdad: America's War In Iraq*. New York, Vintage Books, 2006.

Gelman, Barton. *Angler: The Cheney Vice Presidency*. New York: Penguin Group, 2009.

Gordon, Michael R., and Gen. Bernard E. Trainor. *Cobra II: The Inside Story of the Invasion and Occupation of Iraq*. New York: Pantheon Books, 2006.

Gore, Al. *The Assault on Reason*. New York: The Penguin Press, 2007.

Green, David Michael. "What Every American Should Know About Iraq," June 15, 2007, http://www.commondreams.org/archive/2007/06/15/1896/.

Greenwald, Glenn. *A Tragic Legacy: How a Good vs. Evil Mentality Destroyed the Bush Presidency*. New York: Crown Publishers, 2007.

Hamdan v. Rumsfeld, 548 U.S. 557 (2006).

Hamdi v. Rumsfeld, 542 U.S. 507 (2004).

Healy, Gene, and Timothy Lynch. "Power Surge: The Constitutional Record of George W. Bush," Cato Institute report, 2006.

Hersh, Seymour M. *Chain of Command: The Road From 9/11 to Abu Ghraib*. New York: Harper Collins, 2004.

Isikoff, Michael, and David Corn. *Hubris: The Inside Story of Spin, Scandal, and the Selling of the Iraq War*. New York: Crown Publishers, 2006.

Krugman, Paul. "Sweet Little Lies," *New York Times*, April 9, 2007.

Lewis, Anthony. "The Imperial Presidency," *New York Times*, November 4, 2007.

Madison, James, Alexander Hamilton, and John Jay. *The Federalist Papers*. Clinton Rossiter, ed. New York: Penguin, 1961.

Mayer, Jane. *The Dark Side: The Inside Story of How the War on Terror Turned Into a War on American Ideals*. New York: Doubleday, 2008.

———. "The Hidden Power," *The New Yorker*, July 3, 2006, http://www.newyorker.com/archive/2006/07/03/060703fa_fact1.

McClellan, Scott. *What Happened: Inside the Bush White House and Washington's Culture of Deception*. New York: Public Affairs, 2008.

Murphy, Cullen, and Todd S. Purdum. "Farewell to All That: An Oral History of the Bush White House," *Vanity Fair*, February 2009.

Newbold, Lt. Gen. (Ret.) Greg. "Why Iraq Was a Mistake," *Time*, April 9, 2006.

Orwell, George. *1984*. New York: Penguin, 1949.

Rich, Frank. *The Greatest Story Ever Sold: The Decline and Fall of Truth From 9/11 to Katrina*. New York: Penguin Press, 2006.

Ricks, Thomas E. *Fiasco: The American Military Adventure in Iraq*. New York: Penguin Press, 2006.

Risen, James. *State of War: The Secret History of the CIA and the Bush Administration*. New York: Free Press, 2006.

Savage, Charlie. *Takeover: The Return of the Imperial Presidency and the Subversion of American Democracy*. New York: Little Brown and Co., 2007.

Schlesinger, Arthur M., Jr. *The Imperial Presidency*. Boston: Houghton Mifflin Co., 1973.

Schwarz, Frederick A. O. Jr., and Aziz Z. Huq. *Unchecked and Unbalanced: Presidential Power in a Time of Terror*. New York: New Press, 2007.

Shane, Scott, and Eric Lichtblau. "Cheney Pushed U.S. to Widen Eavesdropping," *New York Times*, May 14, 2006.

Shenon, Phillip. *The Commission: The Uncensored History of the 9/11 Investigation*. New York: Twelve, 2008.

Suskind, Ron. *The One Percent Doctrine: Deep Inside America's Pursuit of Its Enemies Since 9/11*. New York: Simon & Schuster, 2006.

———. *The Price of Loyalty: George W. Bush, the White House, and the Education of Paul O'Neill*. New York: Simon & Schuster, 2004.

———. "Faith, Certainty and the Presidency of George W. Bush," *New York Times Magazine*, October 17, 2004, http://www.nytimes.com/2004/10/17/magazine/17BUSH.htm.

Tumulty, Karen. "Inside Bush's Secret Spy Net," *Time*, May 22, 2006.

Turley, Jonathan. "The Bush J.D. Curse," *USA Today*, August 29, 2007.

Wilentz, Sean. "The Worst President in History?" *Rolling Stone*, April 21, 2006.

Wilson, Joseph C. IV. "What I Didn't Find in Africa," *New York Times*, July 6, 2003.

Wolf, Naomi. *The End of America: Letter of Warning to a Young Patriot*. White River Junction, VT: Chelsea Green Publishing, 2007.

Woodward, Bob. *The War Within: A Secret White House History 2006–2008*, New York: Simon & Schuster, 2008.

———. *State of Denial: Bush at War, Part II*, New York: Simon & Schuster, 2006.

———. *Plan of Attack*, New York: Simon & Schuster, 2004.

NOTES

Introduction

1. Carl Ford Jr., State Deptartment chief intelligence officer, quoted in Michael Isikoff and David Corn, *Hubris: The Inside Story of Spin, Scandal, and the Selling of the Iraq War* (New York: Crown Publishers, 2006), 229.
2. Alexander Meiklejohn, *Political Freedom: The Constitutional Powers of the People* (New York: Harper, 1960), 27.
3. Ron Suskind, *The One Percent Doctrine: Deep Inside America's Pursuit of Its Enemies Since 9/11* (New York: Simon & Schuster, 2006), 5.
4. Merriam-Webster Online, 1: "truth that comes from the gut, not books" (Stephen Colbert, Comedy Central's "The Colbert Report," October 2005); 2: "the quality of preferring concepts or facts one wishes to be true, rather than concepts or facts known to be true" (American Dialect Society, January 2006), http://www.merriam-webster.com/info/06words.htm.
5. Charles Lewis and Mark Reading-Smith, "False Pretenses," The Center for Public Integrity, http://www.publicintegrity.org/WarCard/.
6. Suskind, *One Percent Doctrine*, 296–297.

Part I: The Imperial Presidency

1. Scott Horton, "George W. Bush's Disposable Constitution," *Harper's*, March 3, 2009, http://harpers.org/archive/2009/03/hbc-90004488. Horton is a legal expert in international human rights.
2. Arthur M. Schlesinger Jr., *The Imperial Presidency* (Boston: Houghton Mifflin Co., 1973), ix.
3. Ibid.
4. Ibid. x–xi.
5. John W. Dean, *Worse Than Watergate: The Secret Presidency of George W. Bush* (New York: Warner Books, 2004), 219.
6. Ibid., 21.
7. It should be noted that George W. Bush was not the first president to invoke the signing statement. However, he used it more than all previous presidents combined, and usually in a different manner. See, e.g., Dean, *Worse Than Watergate*.
8. The theory relies on Article II of the U.S. Constitution "The executive power shall be vested in a President of the United States of America." The Bush White House argued that the president had "inherent and limitless powers in his role as commander in chief, above the system of checks and balances." See Steve Clemons, "Democratic Imperative: Bush's 'Unitary Executive' Notion Must be Obliterated," http://www.thewashingtonnote.com/archives/001262.php.
9. As is the case in virtually any cultural environment, the disapproval of dissent and the mar-

ginalization of those who did express dissent tended to suppress any subsequent expression of disagreement. This phenomenon is commonly referred to as the chilling effect.

Chapter 1: Presidential Power

1. Al Gore, *The Assault on Reason* (New York: Penguin, 2007), 71.
2. "Politics, Pure and Cynical," editorial, *New York Times*, March 14, 2007.
3. Bruce Fein, on *Countdown*, MSNBC, September 24, 2007.
4. Paul Krugman, "Forgive and Forget?" *New York Times*, January 16, 2009.
5. Lawrence Wilkerson, quoted in Cullen Murphy and Todd S. Purdum, "Farewell to All That: An Oral History of the Bush White House," *Vanity Fair*, February 2009, 100. Wilkerson was a top aide and later chief of staff to Secretary of State Colin Powell. Emphasis in original.
6. Jack Goldsmith, quoted in Murphy and Purdum, ibid., 156. Goldsmith was legal adviser at the Department of Defense and later head of the Justice Department's Office of Legal Counsel.
7. George Orwell, *1984* (New York: Penguin, 1949), 263.
8. Phillip Cooper, quoted in Charlie Savage, "Bush Challenges Hundreds of Laws: President Cites Powers of His Office," *Boston Globe*, April 30, 2006. Cooper is a professor at Portland State University who has studied the administration's approach to executive power.
9. Scott McClellan, *What Happened: Inside the Bush White House and Washington's Culture of Deception* (New York: Public Affairs, 2008), 247. McClellan was Bush press secretary, 2003–2006.
10. Lawrence Wilkerson, quoted in Murphy and Purdum, "Farewell to All That," 90.
11. Philip Cooper, quoted in Carl Hulse, "FBI Raid Divides G.O.P. Lawmakers and White House," *New York Times*, May 24, 2006.
12. Christopher Dickey, "The Constitution in Peril," *Newsweek*, October 8, 2007.
13. James Madison, *The Federalist Papers*, No. 51, ed. Clinton Rossiter (New York: Penguin, 1961), 322.
14. Frederick A. O. Schwarz Jr. and Aziz Z. Huq, *Unchecked and Unbalanced: Presidential Power in a Time of Terror* (New York: New Press, 2007,) 186.
15. George W. Bush, "Why You Should Vote for Me," *USA Today*, November 7, 2000.
16. Bush, presidential oath, January 20, 2001; Bush, presidential oath, January 20, 2005.
17. Gene Healy and Timothy Lynch, "Power Surge: The Constitutional Record of George W. Bush," Cato Institute report, 2006, http://www.cato.org/pubs/wtpapers/powersurge_healy_lynch.pdf, 23.
18. Jonathan Turley, on *Countdown*, MSNBC, January 4, 2007. Turley is a constitutional law professor at George Washington University.
19. Healy and Lynch, "Power Surge," 2.
20. Thomas Hobbes, *A Dialogue Between a Philosopher and a Student of the Common Laws of England*, ed. Joseph Cropsey (Chicago: University of Chicago Press, 1971), 55.
21. John W. Dean, *Conservatives Without Conscience* (New York: Viking, 2006), xiii.
22. Thomas Hobbes, *Leviathan* (London: George Routledge and Sons, 1886), 65.
23. Gore, *Assault on Reason*, 160.
24. John Adams, in *Papers of John Adams*, ed. Robert Joseph Taylor (Cambridge: Harvard University Press, 1977), 255.
25. Healy and Lynch, "Power Surge," 1.
26. John Locke, *Two Treatises of Government*, (London: R. Butler, et al., 1821), 119.
27. James Madison, in *Letters and Other Writings of James Madison* (Philadelphia: J. B. Lippincott & Co. 1865), 4:51.
28. John Adams, in *Wit and Wisdom of American Presidents*, ed. Joslyn T. Pine (N. Chelmsford, MA: Courier Dover, 2000), 4.
29. Youngstown Sheet & Tube Co. v. Youngstown, 343 U.S. 579, 640 (1952).
30. John Milton, *The Tenure of Kings and Magistrates*, ed. William Talbot Allison (New York: H. Holt and Company, 1911), 3.
31. Bush, May 21, 1999, quoted in Wayne Slater, "Regulators Rebuff Bush Over Web Site That Pokes Fun at Him," *Dallas Morning News*, April 21, 2000.
32. Milton, "The Tenure of Kings and Magistrates," 754.
33. Bush, in remarks during a signing ceremony for a defense spending bill, August 5, 2004, http://www.thesmokinggun.com/archive/0805042bush1.html.

34. Benjamin Franklin, *Poor Richard's Almanack* (Waterloo, IA: U.S.C. Publishing Co. 1914), 62.
35. Bush, *U.S. News & World Report*, April 3, 2000, 20.
36. Albert Einstein, in *Bite-Size Einstein*, eds. Jerry Mayer and John P. Holms (New York: St. Martin's, 1996), 38.
37. Bush, on *60 Minutes*, CBS, November 17, 2002, http://www.cbsnews.com/stories/2002/11/17/60minutes/main529657.shtml.
38. Jack Goldsmith, quoted in Anthony Lewis, "The Imperial Presidency," *New York Times*, November 4, 2007.
39. Franklin, *Poor Richard's Almanack*, 16.
40. Martin Luther King Jr., *Strength to Love* (Philadelphia: Fortress Press, 1981), 43.
41. John Milton, "Samson Agonistes," in *The Complete Poetical Works of John Milton*, ed. William Vaughn Moody (Boston: Houghton, Mifflin and Co., 1899), 294.
42. Youngstown Sheet & Tube Co. v. Sawyer, 343 U.S. 579, 641 (1952).
43. Jane Mayer, "The Hidden Power," *New Yorker*, July 3, 2006, http://www.newyorker.com/archive/2006/07/03/060703fa_fact1.
44. Hobbes, *Leviathan*, 52.
45. Sean Wilentz, "The Worst President in History?" *Rolling Stone*, April 21, 2006, http://www.truth-out.org/article/sean-wilentz-the-worst-president-history. Wiltenz is a history professor at Princeton University.
46. Abraham Lincoln, "The Great Principle of Equality" (speech, Kalamazoo, MI, August 27, 1856). From a collection, *Lincoln on Democracy*, ed. Mario Matthew Cuomo, Harold Holzer, and G. S. Boritt, (New York: Fordham University Press, 2004), 84.
47. Bruce Fein, quoted in Mayer, "The Hidden Power." Fein is a constitutional law expert and served as associate deputy attorney general in the Reagan Justice Department. Emphasis in original.
48. Frank Rich, "The Wiretappers That Couldn't Shoot Straight," *New York Times*, January 8, 2006.
49. Learned Hand, *The Spirit of Liberty* (Chicago: University of Chicago Press, 1977), 189–191.
50. John Dean, on *Countdown*, MSNBC, October 10, 2007.
51. Schlesinger, *Imperial Presidency*, 2.
52. John Nichols, on *Bill Moyers Journal*, PBS, July 13, 2007.
53. James Madison, in *Letters and Other Writings of James Madison* (Philadephia: J. B. Lippincott & Co. 1867), 1:425.
54. Bruce Fein, on *Bill Moyers Journal*, PBS, July 13, 2007.
55. John Milton, "Areopagitica," in *Primer of Intellectual Freedom*, ed. Howard Jones (Cambridge: Harvard University Press, 1949), 169.
56. Patrick Henry, "Speech at the Virginia House of Delegates," in John Bartlett, *Familiar Quotations* (Boston: Little Brown and Co., 1937), 270.
57. Jonathan Turley, on *Countdown*, MSNBC, January 4, 2007.
58. Benjamin Franklin, in *The Papers of Benjamin Franklin*, ed. Leonard W. Labaree (New Haven: Yale University Press, 1963), 6:242.
59. Ishmael Reed, "The Patriot Act of the 18th Century," June 27, 2004, *Time*, http://www.time.com/time/magazine/article/0,9171,994570,00.html.
60. Mayer, "The Hidden Power."
61. Schwarz and Huq, *Unchecked and Unbalanced*, 187.
62. Mayer, "The Hidden Power."
63. Hugo L. Black, "Justice Black, 85 Tomorrow, Has No Plans to Leave Court," *New York Times*, February 26, 1971.
64. James Madison, *The Federalist Papers*, No. 45, ed. Clinton Rossiter (New York: Penguin, 1961), 292.
65. Thomas Jefferson, "Notes on the State of Virginia," quoted in James Madison, *The Federalist Papers*, No. 48, ed. Clinton Rossiter (New York: Penguin, 1961), 310–311. Emphasis in original.
66. Healy and Lynch, "Power Surge," 9.
67. Bob Herbert, "The Real Patriots," *New York Times*, February 19, 2007.
68. John Dean, on *Countdown*, MSNBC, May 12, 2006.
69. Dean, *Conservatives Without Conscience*, 161.
70. Ron Suskind, *One Percent Doctrine: Deep Inside America's Pursuit of Its Enemies Since 9/11* (New York: Simon & Schuster, 2006), 17.

71. Dean, *Conservatives Without Conscience*, 182.
72. Schwarz and Huq, *Unchecked and Unbalanced*, 1.
73. John Dean, on *Countdown*, MSNBC, October 10, 2007.
74. Dean, *Worse Than Watergate*, 182.
75. Gore, *Assault on Reason*, 65.
76. Barton Gelman, *Angler: The Cheney Vice Presidency* (New York: Penguin Group, 2008), 82.
77. Dean, *Conservatives Without Conscience*, 158.
78. Dick Cheney, quoted in James Taranto, "A Strong Executive," *Wall Street Journal*, January 28, 2006.
79. Krugman, "Forgive and Forget?"
80. Maureen Dowd, "Vice Axes That 70's Show," *New York Times*, December 28, 2005.
81. Cheney, quoted in Maureen Dowd, ibid.
82. Wilentz, "The Worst President in History?"
83. Schwarz and Huq, *Unchecked and Unbalanced*, 2.
84. Wilentz, "The Worst President in History?"
85. James Madison, in *Selected Writings of James Madison*, ed. Ralph Louis Ketcham (Indianapolis: Hackett Publishing, 2006), 161.
86. William O. Douglas, in Ernest Lindley, "Of Civil Liberties," *Washington Post,* January 5, 1948.
87. Naomi Wolf, *The End of America: Letter of Warning to a Young Patriot* (White River Junction: VT: Chelsea Green Publishing, 2007), 129.
88. Bush, quoted in "Transition of Power," CNN, December 18, 2000, http://transcripts.cnn.com/TRANSCRIPTS/0012/18/nd.01.html.
89. Orwell, *1984*, 263.
90. See "President Issues Military Order," White House news release, November 13, 2001, http://www.fas.org/irp/offdocs/eo/mo-111301.htm.
91. Wolf, *End of America*, 59.
92. Isabel Hilton, "The 800lb Gorilla in American Foreign Policy," *The Guardian*, July 28, 2004, http://www.guardian.co.uk/world/2004/jul/28/usa.comment.
93. Hamdan v. Rumsfeld, 548 U.S. 557, 636 (2006).
94. James Madison, *Notes of Debates in the Federal Convention of 1787*, ed. Adrienne Koch (Athens: Ohio University Press 1966), 272.
95. Alexander Hamilton, "The Farmer Refuted," in *The Works of Alexander Hamilton*, 2nd ed. (New York: G. P. Putnam's Sons, 1904), 119.
96. John Adams, in *The Writings of Thomas Jefferson,* ed. Albert Ellery Bergh (Washington, DC: Thomas Jefferson Memorial Association of the United States, 1905), 13:426–427.
97. William O. Douglas, *We The Judges* (New York: Doubleday, 1956), 256.
98. Youngstown Sheet & Tube Co. v. Sawyer, 343 U.S. 579, 594 (1952).
99. John Adams, in Alan Axelrod, *Revolutionary Management: John Adams on Leadership* (Guilford, CT: Lyons Press, 2008), 125.
100. Albert Einstein, quoted in Jonathan M. Hyman and Lela P. Love, "If Portia Were a Mediator: An Inquiry Into Justice in Mediation," *Clinical Law Review* (2002), 9:157.
101. James Madison, *The Federalist Papers*, No. 63, ed. Clinton Rossiter (New York: Penguin, 1961), 387.
102. Thomas Paine, "Common Sense," in *The Political Writings of Thomas Paine* (Granville, NJ: George H. Evans, 1839), 1:3.
103. Schlesinger, *Imperial Presidency*, 10.
104. Dwight D. Eisenhower, "Farewell Address," January 17, 1961, http://coursesa.matrix.msu.edu/~hst306/documents/indust.html.
105. Schlesinger, *Imperial Presidency*, 5.
106. Thomas Paine, *The Works of Thomas Paine* (Philadelphia: E. Haskell, 1854), 3:132.
107. Schwarz and Huq, *Unchecked and Unbalanced*, 7.
108. Lawrence Wilkerson, quoted in Jane Mayer, "The Memo," *New Yorker*, February 27, 2006, http://www.newyorker.com/archive/2006/02/27/060227fa_fact.
109. Bruce Fein, quoted in Mayer, ibid.
110. Mark Hosenball, Michael Isikoff, and Evan Thomas, "Cheney's Long Path to War," *Newsweek*, November 17, 2003, 34.

111. Thomas Hobbes, quoted in *The English Philosophers From Bacon to Mill*, ed. Edwin A. Burtt (New York: The Modern Library, 1939), 163.
112. Dean, *Worse Than Watergate*, 94. Emphasis in original.
113. Frank Rich, *The Greatest Story Ever Sold: The Decline and Fall of Truth From 9/11 to Katrina* (New York: Penguin, 2006), 2.
114. Dean, *Conservatives Without Conscience*, 169.
115. Schwarz and Huq, *Unchecked and Unbalanced*, 204.
116. Bruce Bartlett, quoted in Dana Milbank and Jonathan Weisman, "Conservatives Restive About Bush Policies," *Washington Post*, May 10, 2004, A1. Bartlett is a conservative economist with the National Center for Policy Analysis.
117. Jonathan Turley, on *Countdown*, MSNBC, May 10, 2006.
118. Charlie Savage, *Takeover: The Return of the Imperial Presidency and the Subversion of American Democracy* (New York: Little Brown and Co., 2007), 237.
119. "Don't Veto, Don't Obey," editorial, *New York Times*, June 22, 2007.
120. Michael Isikoff, "Extraordinary Measures," Newsweek.com, March 2, 2009, http://www.newsweek.com/2009/03/02/extraordinary-measures.html.
121. "The Tortured Memos," editorial, *New York Times*, March 4, 2009.
122. John C. Yoo and Robert J. Delahunty, "Memorandum for Alberto R. Gonzales, Counsel to the President," U.S. Department of Justice, Office of Legal Counsel, October 23, 2001, http://www.usdoj.gov/opa/documents/memomilitaryforcecombatus10232001.pdf.
123. Kate Martin, quoted in Isikoff, "Extraordinary Measures." Martin is the director for the Center for National Security Studies, a Washington think tank.
124. Yoo and Delahunty, "Memorandum for Alberto R. Gonzales."
125. Neil A. Lewis, "Memos Reveal Scope of the Power Bush Sought," *New York Times*, March 3, 2009.
126. Jane Mayer, *The Dark Side: The Inside Story of How the War on Terror Turned Into a War on American Ideals* (New York: Doubleday, 2008), 50–51.
127. Isikoff, "Extraordinary Measures."
128. Neil A. Lewis, "Memos Reveal Scope of the Power Bush Sought," *New York Times*, March 3, 2009.
129. "The Tortured Memos."
130. Sen. Sheldon Whitehouse, on *Countdown*, MSNBC, March 4, 2009.
131. Jonathan Turley, on *Countdown*, MSNBC, March 3, 2009.
132. Isikoff, "Extraordinary Measures."
133. Scott Horton, on *Countdown*, MSNBC, March 5, 2009.
134. Jonathan Turley, on *Countdown*, MSNBC, March 3, 2009.
135. "The Tortured Memos."
136. Jonathan Turley, on *Countdown*, MSNBC, March 3, 2009.
137. James Madison, *The Federalist Papers*, No. 47, ed. Clinton Rossiter (New York: Penguin, 1961), 301.
138. Schwarz and Huq, *Unchecked and Unbalanced*, 2. Emphasis in original.
139. John Nichols, on *Bill Moyers Journal*, PBS, July 13, 2007.
140. Schwarz and Huq, *Unchecked and Unbalanced*, 1.
141. Myers v. United States, 272 U.S. 52, 293 (1926).
142. Jonathan Turley, on *Countdown*, MSNBC, February 19, 2009.
143. James Madison, *The Republic of Letters: The Correspondence Between Thomas Jefferson and James Madison, 1776–1826* (New York: W. W. Norton & Co., 1995), 376.
144. Schlesinger, *The Imperial Presidency* (2004 Introduction), xxiv.
145. John Adams, in *The Revolutionary Writings of John Adams*, ed. C. Bradley Thompson (Indianapolis: Liberty Fund, 2000), 291–292.
146. John Dean, on *Countdown*, MSNBC, April 6, 2006.
147. Paul Krugman, "Limiting the Damage," *New York Times*, November 6, 2006.
148. Bush, "President Bush Holds Press Conference," White House news release, March 13, 2002, http://georgewbush-whitehouse.archives.gov/news/releases/2002/03/20020313-8.html.
149. Youngstown Sheet & Tube Co. v. Sawyer, 343 U.S. 579, 587–588 (1952).
150. Michael Duffy, "The Cheney Branch of Government," *Time*, June 22, 2007.
151. Cheney, quoted in Dean, *Worse Than Watergate*, 182.
152. John Nichols, on *Bill Moyers Journal*, PBS, July 13, 2007.

153. Sen. John Kerry, "The War In Iraq" (speech, Boston, April 22, 2006), http://blog.thedemo-craticdaily.com/?p=2723.
154. McClellan, *What Happened*, 311.
155. John Nichols, on *Bill Moyers Journal*, PBS, July 13, 2007.
156. Dean, *Worse Than Watergate*, 83.
157. Rep. Robert Wexler, "Wexler Lays Out Case for Impeachment in Special Judiciary," Capitol Hill press release, July 25, 2008. Wexler is chairman of the Subcommittee on Europe and a senior member of the House Foreign Affairs Committee and the House Judiciary Committee.
158. Bruce Fein, on *Bill Moyers Journal*, PBS, July 13, 2007.
159. "Dick Cheney Rules," editorial, *New York Times*, June 3, 2007.
160. William O. Douglas, *We The Judges*, 256.
161. Jack Rakove, quoted in David E. Sanger, "There's a Small Matter of Checks and Balances," *New York Times*, January 27, 2002. Rakove is a Stanford University history professor.
162. Gore, *Assault on Reason*, 140.
163. Schwarz and Huq, *Unchecked and Unbalanced*, 8.
164. Dean, *Worse Than Watergate*, 96.
165. Al Gore, "Remarks to Moveon.org" (speech, New York University, August 7, 2003), http://www.scoop.co.nz/stories/WO0308/S00109.htm.
166. "Dick Cheney Rules."
167. Naomi Wolf, on *Hardball*, MSNBC, August 17, 2007.
168. Youngstown Sheet & Tube Co. v. Sawyer, 343 U.S. 579, 643–644 (1952).
169. James Madison, *The Federalist Papers*, No. 48, ed. Clinton Rossiter (New York: Penguin, 1961), 309–310.
170. Youngstown Sheet & Tube Co. v. Sawyer, 343 U.S. 579, 644 (1952).
171. Schwarz and Huq, *Unchecked and Unbalanced*, 161.
172. English jurist who lived 1723–1760. His works are still considered authoritative regarding pre-Revolutionary War common law.
173. Schlesinger, *Imperial Presidency*, 3.
174. Schwarz and Huq, *Unchecked and Unbalanced*, 178.
175. Alexander Hamilton, *The Federalist Papers*, No. 75, ed. Clinton Rossiter (New York: Penguin, 1961), 451.
176. Schwarz and Huq, *Unchecked and Unbalanced*, 178–179.
177. Alexander Hamilton, *The Federalist Papers*, No. 69, ed. Clinton Rossiter (New York: Penguin, 1961), 417–418. Emphasis in original.
178. Schlesinger, *Imperial Presidency*, 4–5.
179. Adam Cohen, "Congress, the Constitution and War: The Limits on Presidential Power," *New York Times*, January 29, 2007.
180. Youngstown Sheet & Tube Co. v. Sawyer, 343 U.S. 579, 630 (1952).
181. James Madison, in *The Writings of James Madison*, ed. Gaillard Hunt (New York: G. P. Putnam's Sons, 1906), 6:311–312.
182. Adam Cohen, "Congress, the Constitution and War: The Limits on Presidential Power," *New York Times*, January 29, 2007.
183. Youngstown Sheet & Tube Co. v. Sawyer, 343 U.S. 579, 642 (1952).
184. David Michael Green, "What Every American Should Know About Iraq," June 15, 2007, http://www.commondreams.org/archive/2007/06/15/1896/.
185. James Madison, *The Federalist Papers*, No. 51, ed. Clinton Rossiter (New York: Penguin, 1961), 322.
186. Schwarz and Huq, *Unchecked and Unbalanced*, 2.
187. George Washington, in *The Writings of George Washington,* ed. Jared Sparks (New York: Harper & Brothers, 1847), 376.
188. Schwarz and Huq, *Unchecked and Unbalanced*, 173.
189. Wolf, *The End of America*, 26.
190. James Madison, *The Federalist Papers*, No. 51, ed. Clinton Rossiter (New York: Penguin, 1961), 322.
191. John Locke, "The Second Treatise of Government," in Two Treatises of Government, ed. Peter Laslett (Cambridge: Cambridge University Press, 1988), 149.

192. James Madison, *The Federalist Papers*, No. 48, ed. Clinton Rossiter (New York: Penguin, 1961), 308.
193. Youngstown Sheet & Tube Co. v. Sawyer, 343 U.S. 579, 655 (1952).
194. Healy and Lynch, "Power Surge," 10.
195. Francis Biddle, "The Power of Democracy: It Can Meet All Conditions," in Patrick Washburn, *A Question of Sedition: The Federal Government's Investigation of the Black Press During World War II* (New York: Oxford University Press, 1986), 51. Biddle was U.S. Attorney General, 1941–1945.
196. Montesquieu, in *The Great Legal Philosophers*, ed. Clarence Morris (Philadelphia: University of Pennsylvania Press, 1991), 169.
197. Jonathan Turley, on *Countdown*, MSNBC, January 4, 2007.
198. Wexler, "Wexler Lays Out Case for Impeachment in Special Judiciary."

Chapter 2: The Rule of Law

1. Thomas Paine, "Common Sense," in *Common Sense and Other Political Writings*, ed. Nelson F. Adkins (New York: Liberal Arts, 1953), 32.
2. "The Torture Sessions," editorial, *New York Times*, April 20, 2008.
3. Jonathan Turley, on *Countdown*, MSNBC, May 11, 2006. Turley is a constitutional law professor at George Washington University.
4. William Jennings Bryan, "Bryan's Ten Rules for the New Voter," *Baltimore Sun*, April 25, 1915.
5. Patrick Fitzgerald, quoted in Scott Shane and Neil A. Lewis, "Bush Commutes Libby Sentence, Saying 30 Months 'Is Excessive,'" *New York Times*, July 3, 2007. Fitzgerald is U.S. Attorney for the Northern District of Illinois and served as special counsel in the "Valerie Plame Affair" which led to the prosecution of Cheney chief of staff "Scooter" Libby.
6. Rep. Jane Harman, quoted in Karen Tumulty, "Inside Bush's Secret Spy Net," *Time*, May 22, 2006, 35.
7. Dwight D. Eisenhower, "United States Law Day Address," *Time*, May 5, 1958, 11.
8. Frederick A. O. Schwarz Jr. and Aziz Z. Huq, *Unchecked and Unbalanced: Presidential Power in a Time of Terror* (2007), 1.
9. Jane Mayer, "The Hidden Power," *New Yorker*, July 3, 2006, http://www.newyorker.com/archive/2006/07/03/060703fa_fact1.
10. Dan Eggen and Dafna Linzer, "Judge Rules Against Wiretaps: NSA Program Called Unconstitutional," *Washington Post*, August 18, 2006.
11. ACLU v. National Security Agency, 438 F. Supp. 2d 754, 781 (2006).
12. "Ruling for the Law," *New York Times*, editorial, August 18, 2006.
13. ACLU v. National Security Agency, 438 F. Supp. 2d 754, 771 (2006).
14. Jonathan Mahler, "A Check Against Fear," *New York Times*, June 30, 2006.
15. Abraham Lincoln and Stephen Arnold Douglas, *The Political Debates Between Abraham Lincoln and Stephen A. Douglas in the Senatorial Campaign of 1858 in Illinois: Together with Certain Preceding Speeches of Each at Chicago, Springfield, Etc.*, ed. George Haven Putnam (New York: G. P. Putnam's Sons, 1912), 83.
16. Alexander Hamilton, *The Federalist Papers*, No 22, ed. Clinton Rossiter (New York: Penguin, 1961), 150.
17. Gene Healy and Timothy Lynch, "Power Surge: The Constitutional Record of George W. Bush," Cato Institute report, 2006, http://www.cato.org/pubs/wtpapers/powersurge_healy_lynch.pdf, 23.
18. Mark Mazzetti and David Johnston, "Bush Weighed Using Military in Arrests," *New York Times*, July 25, 2009.
19. Eugene Robinson, "An Easy Call: Lying," *Washington Post*, May 12, 2006.
20. Keith Olbermann, commentary on *Countdown*, MSNBC, July 3, 2007.
21. Thomas Jefferson, in *The Writings of Thomas Jefferson* (Washington: Jefferson Memorial Association, 1907), 237.
22. Healy and Lynch, "Power Surge," 12.
23. George W. Bush, "Remarks at the National Governors' Association Conference," February 26, 2001, http://www.presidency.ucsb.edu/ws/index.php?pid=45884.
24. Healy and Lynch, "Power Surge," 17.
25. Ibid., 19.

26. Joint Anti-Fascist Refugee Committee v. McGrath, 341 U.S. 123, 177, 179 (1951).
27. "Stampeding Congress, Again," editorial, *New York Times*, August 3, 2007.
28. Jack Goldsmith, *The Terror Presidency: Law and Judgment Inside the Bush Administration* (New York: W. W. Norton & Company, 2007), 181. Goldsmith is former Assistant Attorney General, Office of Legal Counsel.
29. Bruce Fein, on *Bill Moyers Journal*, PBS, July 13, 2007. Fein is a constitutional law expert and served as associate deputy attorney general in the Reagan Justice Department.
30. Katrina VanDen Heuvel, on *Scarborough Country*, MSNBC, March 20, 2007.
31. "A Sudden Taste for the Law," editorial, *New York Times*, May 24, 2006.
32. Jonathan Turley, "Gonzales Is Tough on Crime? Hardly," *USA Today*, August 15, 2007.
33. "Alberto Gonzales, The Sequel," editorial, *New York Times*, January 28, 2009.
34. Thomas Paine, *The Age of Reason*, ed. Moncure Danile Conway (New York: G. P. Putnam's Sons, 1896), 22.
35. "Degrading America's Image," editorial, *New York Times*, June 6, 2006.
36. Jonathan Turley, on *Countdown*, MSNBC, May 10, 2006.
37. Justice William J. Brennan Jr., "The Quest to Develop a Jurisprudence of Civil Liberties in Times of Security Crises," *Israel Yearbook on Human Rights* (1988), 18:11.
38. James Madison, in The Complete Madison: His Basic Writings, ed. Saul K. Padover (New York: Harper, 1953), 258.
39. Thomas L. Friedman, "Iraq II or a Nuclear Iran," *New York Times*, April 19, 2006.
40. Bob Herbert, "Mr. Vice President, It's Time to Go," *New York Times*, February 16, 2006.
41. John Locke, "Of the State of Nature," in *Introduction to Contemporary Civilization in the West* (New York: Columbia University Press, 1960), 1026.
42. John Adams, *Familiar Letters of John Adams and His Wife Abigail Adams*, ed. Charles Francis Adams (New York: Hurd and Houghton, 1876), 76.
43. Jonathan Turley, on *Countdown*, MSNBC, May 10, 2006.
44. Bill Mahrer, on *Real Time*, HBO, March 16, 2007.
45. "Spies, Lies and FISA," editorial, *New York Times*, October 14, 2007.
46. "Another Rebuke on Guantánamo," editorial, *New York Times*, June 25, 2008.
47. "The Fine Print," editorial, *New York Times*, January 30, 2008.
48. Naomi Wolf, *The End of America: Letter of Warning to a Young Patriot* (White River Junction: VT: Chelsea Green Publishing, 2007), 144.
49. Schwarz and Huq, *Unchecked and Unbalanced*, 92.
50. "Read the Fine Print," editorial, *New York Times*, July 25, 2006.
51. Charlie Savage, "Bush Challenges Hundreds of Laws: President Cites Powers of His Office," *Boston Globe*, April 30, 2006.
52. John Locke, in William Blackstone, *Commentaries on the Laws of England* (Philadelphia: Geo. T. Bisell Co., 1922), 3, n.3.
53. Frank Rich, "Why Libby's Pardon Is a Slam Dunk," *New York Times*, March 11, 2007.
54. Sen. Robert C. Byrd, quoted in Carl Hulse, "Lawmakers to Investigate Bush on Laws and Intent," *New York Times*, June 20, 2007.
55. Savage, "Bush Challenges Hundreds of Laws."
56. Al Gore, *The Assault on Reason* (New York: Penguin, 2007), 226.
57. Savage, "Bush Challenges Hundreds of Laws."
58. Bruce Fein, quoted in Mayer," The Hidden Power."
59. Charlie Savage, *Takeover: The Return of the Imperial Presidency and the Subversion of American Democracy* (New York: Little Brown and Co., 2007), 231.
60. John W. Dean, *Conservatives Without Conscience* (New York: Viking, 2006), 161.
61. David Golove, quoted in Savage, "Bush Challenges Hundreds of Laws." Golove is a New York University law professor who specializes in executive-power issues.
62. Savage, *Takeover*, 224–225.
63. Ibid., 229.
64. Eric Lichtblau, "White House Denies Switch in Mail Policy," *New York Times*, January 5, 2007.
65. "President asserts power to edit privacy reports," Associated Press, October 5, 2006, http://www.msnbc.msn.com/id/15145197/.
66. Bruce Fein, quoted in Savage, "Bush Challenges Hundreds of Laws."
67. Savage, *Takeover*, 238.

68. Ibid., 241. Emphasis in original.
69. "The ABA Task Force on Presidential Signing Statements," quoted in Savage, *Takeover*, 245.
70. "President asserts power to edit privacy reports."
71. "The Imperial Presidency 2.0," editorial, *New York Times*, January 7, 2007.
72. Jonathan Turley, on *Countdown*, MSNBC, June 19, 2007.
73. Robert Pear, "Legal Group Faults Bush for Ignoring Parts of Bills," *New York Times*, July 24, 2006.
74. James Madison, in *Letters and other Writings of James Madison*, ed. Henry B. Humphrey (Philadelphia: J. B. Lippincott, 1865), 277.
75. "Read the Fine Print," editorial, *New York Times*, July 25, 2006.
76. Lou Dobbs, "Why Is the President Ignoring Our Laws?" CNN.com, July 26, 2006, http://www.cnn.com/2006/US/07/25/dobbs.july26/index.html.
77. Jonathan Turley, on *Countdown*, MSNBC, January 4, 2007.
78. "The Fine Print," editorial, *New York Times*, January 30, 2008.
79. Jonathan Turley, on *Countdown*, MSNBC, May 11, 2006.
80. Schwarz and Huq, *Unchecked and Unbalanced*, 144.
81. Martin Luther King Jr., "Letter from a Birmingham Jail," reprinted in S. Jonathan Bass, Blessed are the Peacemakers: Martin Luther King Jr., Eight White Religious Leaders, and "The Letter from Birmingham Jail" (Baton Rouge: Louisiana State University Press 2001), 238–239.
82. "O'Connor Decries Republican Attacks on Courts," NPR, March 10, 2006, http://www.npr.org/templates/story/story.php?storyId=5255712.
83. Eugene Robinson, "Closing Time at Guantanamo," *Washington Post*, June 20, 2006.
84. Stephen Henderson, "Detainees Win Access to Courts: Supreme Court Rulings Deliver a Legal Blow to the Administration's Antiterrorism Policy," *Philadelphia Inquirer*, June 29, 2004.
85. Hamdi v. Rumsfeld, 542 U.S. 507, 536 (2004).
86. Jonathan Turley, on *The Rachel Maddow Show*, MSNBC, December 4, 2008.
87. Hamdi v. Rumsfeld, 542 U.S. 507, 554–555 (2004)).
88. David Stout, "Justices, 6–3, Sidestep Ruling on Padilla Case," *New York Times*, April 3, 2006.
89. James Monroe, "First Inaugural Address," in *The Addresses and Messages of Presidents of the United States*, ed. Edwin Williams (New York: Edward Walker, 1846), 1:393.
90. Stout, "Justices, 6–3, Sidestep Ruling on Padilla Case."
91. Thomas Paine, in *The Complete Writings of Thomas Paine*, ed. Philip S. Foner (New York: Citadel Press, 1945), 2:588.
92. Stout, "Justices, 6–3, Sidestep Ruling on Padilla Case."
93. "The High Court Punts," editorial, *New York Times*, April 4, 2006.
94. Dahlia Lithwick, "The Imperial Presidency," *Washington Post*, January 14, 2007.
95. Korematsu v. United States, 323 U.S. 214, 243 (1944).
96. "The High Court Punts."
97. Stout, "Justices, 6–3, Sidestep Ruling on Padilla Case."
98. David E. Sanger and Scott Shane, "Court's Ruling Is Likely To Force Negotiations Over Presidential Power," *New York Times*, June 30, 2006.
99. "A Victory for the Rule of Law," editorial, *New York Times*, June 30, 2006.
100. Bruce Fein, quoted in Peter Baker and Michael Abramowitz, "A Governing Philosophy Rebuffed: Ruling Emphasizes Constitutional Boundaries," *Washington Post*, June 30, 2006.
101. "Dick Cheney Rules," editorial, *New York Times*, June 3, 2007.
102. Thomas Paine, "The Crisis," in *The Writings of Thomas Paine*, ed. Moncure Daniel Conway (New York: G. P. Putnam's Sons, 1894), 1:324.
103. Peter Baker and Michael Abramowitz, "A Governing Philosophy Rebuffed: Ruling Emphasizes Constitutional Boundaries," *Washington Post*, June 30, 2006.
104. Healy and Lynch, "Power Surge," 16. Emphasis in original.
105. Gore, *Assault on Reason*, 132.
106. Jonathan Turley, "The Bush J.D. Curse," *USA Today*, August 29, 2007.
107. Lithwick, "Imperial Presidency."
108. Krulewitch v. United States, 336 U.S. 440, 458 (1949).
109. David G. Savage, "The Guantanamo Decision: High Court Rejects Bush's Claim That He Alone Sets Detainee Rules," *Los Angeles Times*, June 30, 2006.
110. Gore, *Assault on Reason*, 131.

111. "The President and the Courts," editorial, *New York Times*, March 20, 2006.

112. Eugene Robinson, "Checking the Decider," *Washington Post*, June 30, 2006.

113. Hamdan v. Rumsfeld, 548 U.S. 557, 635 (2006).

114. Bill Goodman, quoted in Bob Herbert, "The Law Gets a Toehold," *New York Times*, July 13, 2006. Goodman is legal director of the Center for Constitutional Rights.

115. Hamdan v. Rumsfeld, 548 U.S. 557, 636 (2006).

116. Linda Greenhouse, "Justices, 5–4, Back Detainee Appeals for Guantanamo," *New York Times*, June 13, 2008.

117. "Justice 5, Brutality 4," editorial, *New York Times*," June 13, 2008.

118. Eugene Robinson, "A Victory for the Rule of Law," *Washington Post*, June 13, 2008.

119. Boumediene v. Bush, 128 S.Ct. 2229, 2277 (2008).

120. Robinson, "A Victory for the Rule of Law."

121. Ibid.

122. Jonathan Turley, on *Countdown,* MSNBC, June 12, 2008. Emphasis in original.

123. John Bellinger III, quoted in Cullen Murphy and Todd S. Purdum, "Farewell to All That: An Oral History of the Bush White House," *Vanity Fair*, February 2009, 100. Bellinger was legal adviser to the National Security Council, and later to the secretary of state.

124. Adam Zagorn, "Why Were These U.S. Attorneys Fired?" *Time*, March 7, 2007, http://www.time.com/time/nation/article/0,8599,1597085,00.html.

125. Thomas L. Friedman, "Failing By Example," *New York Times*," May 16, 2007.

126. Frank Rich, "The Armstrong Williams NewsHour," *New York Times*, June 26, 2005.

127. "For Attorney General," editorial, *New York Times*, January 22, 2009.

128. James Madison, *The Federalist Papers*, No. 51, ed. Clinton Rossiter (New York: Penguin, 1961), 324.

129. Katrina vanden Heuvel, on *Scarborough Country*, MSNBC, March 20, 2007.

130. Paul Krugman, "Sweet Little Lies," *New York Times*, April 9, 2007.

131. David Iglesias, quoted in Murphy and Purdum, "Farewell to All That," 157–158. Iglesias was one of eight U.S. attorneys fired by the Bush administration in 2006.

132. "The Fantasy Behind the Scandal," editorial, *New York Times*, April 15, 2007.

133. Paul Krugman, "Surging and Purging," *New York Times*, January 19, 2007.

134. Adam Cohen, "Why Have So Many U.S. Attorneys Been Fired? It Looks a Lot Like Politics," *New York Times*, February 26, 2007.

135. Jonathan Turley, on *Countdown,* MSNBC, March 12, 2007.

136. John Dean, on *Countdown,* MSNBC, March 13, 2007.

137. "The Failed Attorney General," editorial, *New York Times*, March 11, 2007.

138. David Johnston and John M. Broder, "New E-mail Gives Dismissal Detail," *New York Times*, March 20, 2007.

139. "The Failed Attorney General," editorial, *New York Times*, March 11, 2007.

140. Jonathan Turley, on *Countdown,* MSNBC, May 1, 2007.

141. Turley, "The Bush J.D. Curse."

142. Bob Herbert, "Illegal and Inept," *New York Times*, February 9, 2006.

143. "White House Shell Game," editorial, *New York Times*, August 24, 2007.

144. "A Scandal That Keeps Growing," editorial, *New York Times*, May 6, 2007.

145. "Secrets and Rights," editorial, *New York Times*, February 2, 2008.

146. "Defying the Imperial Presidency," editorial, *New York Times*, July 26, 2007.

147. "The Need to Know," editorial, *New York Times*, August 11, 2007.

148. Sen. Patrick Leahy, "New Leadership Needed At Justice Department Without Delay," Sen. Leahy press release, December 12, 2008, http://leahy.senate.gov/press/press_releases/release/?id=6c05da64-323a-4cd2-bd82-b4fc83baffc7.

149. Jamie Gorelick, "Another Blow To Justice," *Washington Post*, July 29, 2008.

150. Jonathan Turley, on *Countdown,* MSNBC, May 22, 2008.

151. Eric Lichtblau, "Report Faults Aides In Hiring at Justice Dept.," *New York Times*, July 29, 2008.

152. Ibid.

153. Randall Mikkelsen, "Justice Dept. Hiring Marred by Politics: Probe," *Washington Post*, June 24, 2008.

154. Paul Krugman, "Forgive and Forget?" *New York Times*, January 16, 2009.

155. Eric Lichtblau, "Report Cites Politics at Justice Dept.," *New York Times*, January 13, 2009.

156. Krugman, "Forgive and Forget?"
157. Jonathan Turley, on *Countdown,* MSNBC, May 2, 2007.
158. "Undermining Justice," editorial, *New York Times,* January 15, 2009.
159. Gorelick, "Another Blow To Justice."
160. "There Was Smoke—and Fire," editorial, *New York Times,* July 29, 2008.
161. Michael Mukasey, "Prepared Remarks of Attorney General Michael B. Mukasey Before the American Bar Association," August 12, 2008, http://www.justice.gov/archive/ag/speeches/2008/ag-speech-0808121.html. Mukasey was U.S. Attorney General, 2007–2009.
162. "Politics, Pure and Cynical," editorial, *New York Times,* March 14, 2007.
163. "Tap-Dancing as Fast as He Can," editorial, *New York Times,* July 20, 2006.
164. Sean Wilentz, "The Worst President in History?" *Rolling Stone,* April 21, 2006. Wiltenz is a history professor at Princeton University.
165. Peter Baker, "Bush Denies Congress Access to Aides," *Washington Post,* July 9, 2007.
166. Sen. Patrick Leahy, "Comment Of Sen. Patrick Leahy, D-Vt., Chairman, Senate Judiciary Committee, On White House Letter Regarding Executive Privilege Claim," July 9, 2007, http://www.allamericanpatriots.com/48726282_patrick_leahy_judiciary_chairmen_leahy_conyers_seek_basis_president_s_executive_privilege_c

Chapter 3: Secrecy and "Vice"
1. Jeremy Bentham, "Essay on Political Tactics," in *The Works of Jeremy Bentham* (London: Simpkin, Marshall & co., 1843), 2:315.
2. David C. Vladeck, quoted in "Secrecy in the Bush Administration," Committee on Oversight and Government Reform, September 14, 2004, http://docs.google.com/viewer?a=v&q=cache:Xqi3oNQtXm4J:www.fas.org/sgp/library/waxman.pdf+%E2%80%9CSecrecy+in+the+Bush+Administration,%E2%80%9D+Committee+on+Oversight+and+Government+Reform&hl=en&gl=us&pid=bl&srcid=ADGEEShWIOsxS67BhRd6m-S1CS61HcdqbpBkEbplKfD-J9yCILwV0HW3kQ1XeRjm6okrFh4-ta_yuGYGhU87rCSREqbXuRpMgGK4RKnnleGY-GOmVbF1IBcZvHBmdxdFcIvfvqtp4mW4Zo&sig=AHIEtbR4Lj2g7DNaqgpApumkYOBq50d5qA, 31. Vladeck is a professor in the Georgetown Law Center, specializing in government litigation.
3. "The Cult of Secrecy at the White House," editorial, *New York Times,* February 7, 2008.
4. George W. Bush, quoted in James Dao, "Bush, Wooing Pennsylvania, Attacks Gore's Character," *New York Times,* October 27, 2000.
5. Vladeck, quoted in "Secrecy in the Bush Administration," 31.
6. Thomas Paine, *The Political and Miscellaneous Works of Thomas Paine* (London: R. Carlile, 1819), 1:155
7. "Secrecy in the Bush Administration," 1.
8. Scott Shane, "Cheney Is Linked to Concealment of CIA Project," *New York Times,* July 12, 2009.
9. John W. Dean, *Worse Than Watergate: The Secret Presidency of George W. Bush* (New York: Warner Books, 2004), xiii.
10. Al Gore, *The Assault on Reason* (New York: Penguin, 2007), 17.
11. House Committee on Government Operations, Availability of Information From Federal Departments and Agencies, 86th Cong., 2d sess., 1960, House Rept. 86–2084, 36.
12. Edmund Burke, in *The Great Thoughts,* ed. George Seldes (New York: Ballantine, 1985), 59.
13. Thomas Jefferson, in *Thomas Jefferson: The Life and Selected Writings of Thomas Jefferson,* eds. Adrienne Koch & William Peden (New York: Modern Library 1993), 418.
14. James Madison, in John Hoppus, *The Crisis of Popular Education* (London: John Snow, 1847), 32.
15. Jean-Jacques Rousseau, *Emile; or, On Education* (Sioux Falls, SD: NuVision Publications, 2007), 12.
16. Woodrow Wilson, *Congressional Government: A Study in American Politics* (Mineola, NY: Dover Publications, 2006), 303.
17. Dean, *Worse Than Watergate,* 185–186.
18. Thomas Jefferson, quoted in Michael Traynor, *Citizenship in a Time of Repression,* 2005 Wisconsin Law Review 1, 34, n.119.
19. Jeremy Bentham, *The Works of Jeremy Bentham* (London: Simpkin, Marshall & Co., 1843), 6:397.

20. Dean, *Worse Than Watergate*, 201.
21. Ron Suskind, *The One Percent Doctrine: Deep Inside America's Pursuit of Its Enemies Since 9/11* (New York: Simon & Schuster, 2006), 98.
22. Patrick Henry in *The Complete Anti-Federalist*, ed. Herbert Storing (Chicago: University of Chicago Press, 1981), 5:237.
23. Tom Connors, quoted in Dean, *Worse Than Watergate*. Connors is with the Society of American Archivists.
24. "Secrecy in the Bush Administration," 81.
25. Frederick A. O. Schwarz Jr. and Aziz Z. Huq, *Unchecked and Unbalanced: Presidential Power in a Time of Terror* (New York: The New Press, 2007), 109.
26. Schaefer v. United States, 251 U.S. 466, 494 (1920).
27. Thomas Paine, in Rights of Man, Common Sense, and Other Political Writings, ed. Mark Philp (New York: Oxford University Press, 1995), 297.
28. Christopher Dickey, "The Constitution in Peril," *Newsweek*, October 8, 2007, 65.
29. James Madison, in *The Writings of James Madison, 1787–1790*, ed. Gaillard Hunt (New York: G. P. Putnam's Sons, 1904), 5:377.
30. "Secrecy in the Bush Administration," iii.
31. James Madison, in *The Writings of James Madison*, ed. Gaillard Hunt (New York: G. P. Putnam's Sons, 1910), 9:103.
32. Schwarz and Huq, *Unchecked and Unbalanced*, 105. Emphasis in original.
33. Arthur M. Schlesinger Jr., *The Imperial Presidency* (Boston: Houghton Mifflin Co., 1973), xxiv.
34. Schwarz and Huq, *Unchecked and Unbalanced*, 124.
35. Olmstead v. United States, 277 U.S. 438, 573 (1928).
36. Glenn Greenwald, *A Tragic Legacy: How a Good vs. Evil Mentality Destroyed the Bush Presidency* (New York: Crown Publishers, 2007), 230.
37. "History Deleted at the White House," editorial, *New York Times*, Jul 13, 2008.
38. Ibid.
39. Gore, *Assault on Reason*, 244.
40. Schwarz and Huq, *Unchecked and Unbalanced*, 201.
41. Dean, *Worse Than Watergate*, xvi.
42. Schwarz and Huq, *Unchecked and Unbalanced*, 7.
43. Dean, *Worse Than Watergate*, 21.
44. Gore, *Assault on Reason*, 243–244.
45. William Jennings Bryan, "Bryan's Ten Rules for the New Voter," *Baltimore Sun*, April 25, 1915.
46. Steven Garfinkel, quoted in Christopher H. Schmitt and Edward T. Pound, "Keeping Secrets: The Bush Administration Is Doing the Public's Business Out of the Public Eye," *U.S News & World Report*, December 14, 2003, http://www.usnews.com/usnews/news/articles/031222/22secrecy.htm. Garfinkle is a retired government lawyer and expert on classified information.
47. Scott McClellan, *What Happened: Inside the Bush White House and Washington's Culture of Deception* (New York: Public Affairs, 2008), 145. McClellan was Bush press secretary, 2003–2006.
48. Dean, *Worse Than Watergate*, 18.
49. Charlie Savage, *Takeover: The Return of the Imperial Presidency and the Subversion of American Democracy* (New York: Little Brown and Co., 2007), 93.
50. Schmitt and Pound, "Keeping Secrets."
51. "Dick Cheney Rules," editorial, New York Times, June 3, 2007.
52. Schmitt and Pound, "Keeping Secrets."
53. Roger Pilon, quoted in Schmitt and Pound, ibid. Pilon is vice president of legal affairs for the Cato Institute.
54. John Dean, on *Countdown*, MSNBC, April 6, 2006.
55. Thomas Jefferson, in *The Papers of Thomas Jefferson*, ed. Julian P. Boyd (Princeton: Princeton University Press, 1950), 12:478.
56. Abraham Lincoln on Preserving Liberty (speech, Edwardsville, IL, September 11, 1854), http://showcase.netins.net/web/creative/lincoln/speeches/liberty.htm.
57. "Secrecy in the Bush Administration."

58. Whitney v. California, 274 U.S. 357, 375–76 (1925).
59. "Secrecy in the Bush Administration."
60. Richard A. Clarke, *Against All Enemies: Inside America's War on Terror* (New York: Free Press, 2004), 245.
61. "Secrecy in the Bush Administration," 1.
62. "The Declaration of the Rights of Man and of the Citizen, 1789," quoted in David G. Ritchie, *Natural Rights* (New York: The Macmillan Co., 1903), 150.
63. Jeremy Bentham, *The Works of Jeremy Bentham, Part VIII*, ed. John Bowring (Edinburgh: William Tait, 1839), 423.
64. Savage, *Takeover*, 162.
65. Ibid., 163.
66. Dean, *Worse Than Watergate*, 201.
67. Savage, *Takeover*, 89.
68. Louis D. Brandeis, *Other People's Money and How the Bankers Use It* (New York: F. A. Stokes, 1914), 62.
69. Martin Luther King Jr., *Strength to Love* (Philadelphia: Fortress Press, 1981), 53.
70. George Washington, in *The Writings of George Washington*, ed. Worthington Chauncey Ford (New York: G. P. Putnam's Sons, 1891), 12:452.
71. Savage, *Takeover*, 90.
72. Ibid.
73. Rep. Rahm Emanuel, on *Countdown*, MSNBC, June 26, 2007.
74. Barton Gellman and Jo Becker, "A Different Understanding With the President," *Washington Post*, June 24, 2007.
75. "Dick Cheney Rules," editorial, *New York Times*, June 3, 2007.
76. Thomas Jefferson, in *The Writings of Thomas Jefferson*, ed. Paul L. Ford (New York: G. P. Putnam's Sons, 1899), 10:4.
77. James Madison, in *The Writings of James Madison, 1819–1836*, ed. Galliard Hunt (New York: G. P. Putnam's Sons, 1910), 9:103.
78. John Milton, "Areopagitica" in *Primer of Intellectual Freedom*, ed. Howard Jones (Cambridge: Harvard University Press, 1949), 169.
79. Savage, *Takeover*, 90.
80. S. Res. 21, 94th Cong. §1 (1975), quoted in Final Report of the Senate Select Committee to Study Governmental Operations with Respect to Intelligence Activities: Book II (1976), 139.
81. James Madison, in Hugh B. Urban, *The Secrets of the Kingdom* (Lanham, MD: Rowman & Littlefield, 2007), 201.
82. Peter Baker, "Cheney Defiant on Classified Material: Executive Order Ignored Since 2003," *Washington Post*, June 22, 2007.
83. Savage, *Takeover*, 237.
84. Sen. John Kerry, "The War In Iraq" (speech, Boston, May 19, 2008), available at http://vote-ne.org/Issue.aspx?Issue=BUSIraq&Office=USPresident&Election=VA20041102GA.——Peter Weitzel, quoted in Charlie Savage, "In War's Name, Public Loses Information," *Boston Globe*, April 24, 2005. Weitzel was with the Coalition of Journalists for Open Government.
85. American Communications Association v. Douds, 339 U.S. 382, 442 (1950).
86. "White House of Mirrors," editorial, *New York Times*, June 24, 2007.
87. McClellan, *What Happened*, 229.
88. Kathryn S. Olmsted, quoted in Adam Liptak, "Cheney's To-Do Lists, Then and Now," *New York Times*, February 11, 2007. Olmstead is a history professor at the University of California at Davis.
89. "The Fine Art of Declassification" editorial, *New York Times*, September 27, 2006.
90. Bob Herbert, "The Kafka Strategy," *New York Times*, September 18, 2006.
91. James Madison, in The Founders' Almanac, ed. Matthew Spalding (Washington: Heritage Foundation, 2002), 133.
92. Thomas Jefferson, in Thomas Jefferson Political Writings, eds. Joyce Appleby and Terence Ball (New York: Cambridge University Press, 1999), 293.
93. John Trenchard and Thomas Gordon, *Cato's Letters: Essays On Liberty, Civil and Religious and Other Important Subjects* (New York: Da Capo Press, 1971), 1:96.
94. Palko v. Connecticut, 302 U.S. 319, 327 (1937).

95. Martin Luther King Jr., *Letter from the Birmingham City Jail*, April 16, 1963, http://www.stanford.edu/group/King/frequentdocs/birmingham.pdf.

96. William O. Douglas, in The Douglas Letters, ed. Melvin Urofsky (Bethesda, MD: Adler & Adler, 1987), 162.

97. Hon. Leonie Brinkema, quoted in Phil Hirschkorn, "Judge Blasts Government Secrecy," CNN, April 7, 2006, http://www.cnn.com/2006/LAW/04/07/moussaoui/index.html.

98. Schlesinger, *Imperial Presidency*, xx–xxi.

99. "An Opportunity Lost," Coalition of Journalists for Open Government, July 3, 2008, http://www.cjog.net/documents/Part_1_2007_FOIA_Report.pdf.

100. Laurie Kellman, "Congress Eases Access to Gov't Records," *USA Today*, December 18, 2007, http://www.usatoday.com/news/topstories/2007-12-18-2764771848_x.htm.

101. "White House Shell Game," editorial, *New York Times*, August 24, 2007.

102. "Bush Sidestep Mustn't Block Free Information," editorial, *Honolulu Advertiser*, February 7, 2008.

103. Scott Shane, "Agency Is Target in Cheney Fight on Secrecy Data," *New York Times*, June 22, 2007.

104. Michael Duffy, "The Cheney Branch of Government," *Time*, June 22, 2007.

105. "The CIA Report," editorial, *New York Times*, August 23, 2007.

106. "White House Shell Game."

107. Detroit Free Press v. Ashcroft, 303 F.3d 681, 683 (3rd Cir. 2002).

108. Herbert v. Lando, 441 U.S. 153, 184–85 (1979).

109. James Madison, in David P. Currie, *The Constitution in Congress: The Federalist Period, 1789–1801* (Chicago: The University of Chicago Press, 1997), 191, n. 141.

110. Maureen Dowd, "Vice Axes That 70's Show," *New York Times*, December 28, 2005.

111. Gellman and Becker, "'A Different Understanding With the President."

112. Maureen Dowd, "A Vice President Without Borders, Bordering on Lunacy," *New York Times*, June 24, 2007.

113. Michael Traynor, "Citizenship in a Time of Repression," *Wisconsin Law Review* 1:14 (2005).

114. Learned Hand, "Telling The Bar," *Washington Post*, May 27, 1951.

115. Albert Einstein, in Walter Isaacson, *Einstein: His Life and Universe* (New York: Simon & Schuster, 2007), 22.

116. Joshua Micah Marshall, Talking Points Memo, January 17, 2006, http://www.talkingpoints-memo.com/archives/007455.php.

117. Al Gore, "Remarks to Moveon.org," New York University, August 7, 2003, http://www.scoop.co.nz/stories/WO0308/S00109.htm.

118. Dennis v. United States, 341 U.S. 494, 556 (1951).

119. Schmitt and Pound, "Keeping Secrets."

120. Suskind, *One Percent Doctrine*, 293.

121. Dean, *Worse Than Watergate*, 102.

122. Dan Eggen, "White House Blocks Release of FBI Files," *Washington Post*, July 17, 2008.

123. Henry Waxman, quoted in Eggen, ibid.

124. Bill Maher, on *Real Time*, HBO, March 16, 2007.

125. Peter Baker and Charles Babington, "Bush Addresses Uproar Over Spying," *Washington Post*, December 20, 2005.

126. Dick Cheney, on *Fox News Sunday*, FOX, December 21, 2008, http://www.foxnews.com/story/0,2933,470706,00.html.

127. Sen. Jay Rockefeller, quoted in Greg Miller and Maura Reynolds, "U.S. Spying Plan Lacked Congress' Scrutiny, Leading Democrat Says," *Los Angeles Times*, December 20, 2005. Sen. Rockefeller was the ranking Democrat on the Senate Intelligence Committee.

128. Ron Hutcheson, "Bush Asserts Right to Eavesdrop in U.S.," *San Jose Mercury News*, December 20, 2005.

129. Sen. Jay Rockefeller, letter to Vice President Dick Cheney, quoted in John Diamond, "Gonzales, General Lay Out Case for Spying," *USA Today*, December 20, 2005.

130. "A Crack in the Stone Wall" editorial, *New York Times*, November 30, 2006.

131. James Risen and Eric Lichtblau, "Bush Lets U.S. Spy on Callers Without Courts," *New York Times*, December 16, 2005.

132. Kathy Kiley and Andrea Stone, "Bush Defends NSA Data Collection Program," *USA Today*, May 11, 2006.

133. Bush, "President's Radio Address," May 13, 2006, http://www.thefreelibrary.com/Presidential+Weekly+Radio+Address/2006/May/13-p52002.
134. James Risen, *State of War: The Secret History of the CIA and the Bush Administration* (New York: Free Press, 2006), 43–44.
135. Jean-Jacques Rousseau, *The Social Contract & Discourses* (New York: E. P. Dutton & Co., 1913), 5.
136. "A Spy Program in From the Cold," editorial, *New York Times*, January 18, 2007.
137. Risen, *State of War*, 43.
138. Kerry, "The War In Iraq."
139. "NSA Domestic Surveillance Began 7 Months Before 9/11, Convicted Qwest CEO Claims," Wired.com, October 11, 2007, http://blog.wired.com/27bstroke6/2007/10/nsa-asked-for-p.html.
140. Risen, *State of War*, 42.
141. "Stampeding Congress, Again," editorial, *New York Times*, August 3, 2007.
142. Bush, quoted in Baker and Babington, "Bush Addresses Uproar Over Spying."
143. Aleksandr Solzhenitsyn, *The Gulag Archipelago, 1918–1956*, trans. H. T. Willetts and Thomas P. Whitney (Boulder: Westview Press, 1997), 47.
144. "Mr. Bush v. the Bill of Rights," editorial, *New York Times*, June 18, 2008.
145. Schwarz and Huq, *Unchecked and Unbalanced*, 135.
146. Risen and Lichtblau, "Bush Lets U.S. Spy on Callers Without Courts."
147. Ibid.
148. Risen, *State of War*, 52.
149. Ibid., 48.
150. John Dean, on *Countdown*, MSNBC, May 12, 2006.
151. Suskind, *One Percent Doctrine*, 37.
152. Gene Healy and Timothy Lynch, "Power Surge: The Constitutional Record of George W. Bush," Cato Institute report, 2006, 13, http://www.cato.org/pubs/wtpapers/powersurge_healy_lynch.pdf.
153. "Report Reveals Number of Secret FBI Subpoenas," Associated Press, April 28, 2006, http://www.godlikeproductions.com/forum1/message228618/pg1.
154. Eric Lichtblau and James Risen, "Spy Agency Mined Vast Data Trove, Officials Report," *New York Times*, December 24, 2005. Emphasis added.
155. Eugene Robinson, "An Easy Call: Lying," *Washington Post*, May 12, 2006.
156. Leslie Cauley, "NSA Has Massive Database of Americans' Phone Calls," *USA Today*, May 11, 2006.
157. Anthony D. Romero, quoted in Barton Gellman and Arshad Mohammed, "Date on Phone Calls Monitored," *Washington Post*, May 12, 2006. Romero is executive director of the American Civil Liberties Union.
158. Robinson, "An Easy Call."
159. Gellman and Mohammed, "Date on Phone Calls Monitored."
160. "An Ever-Expanding Secret," editorial, *New York Times*, May 12, 2006.
161. Eugene Robinson, "An Easy Call."
162. Risen, *State of War*, 58.
163. Cauley, "NSA Has Massive Database of Americans' Phone Calls."
164. Risen, *State of War*, 59.
165. Cauley, "NSA Has Massive Database of Americans' Phone Calls."
166. Risen, *State of War*, 47–48.
167. Ibid., 45.
168. Greenwald, *Tragic Legacy*, 94. Emphasis in original.
169. Rep. Edward Markey, quoted in Karen Tumulty, "Inside Bush's Secret Spy Net," *Time*, May 22, 2006, 34.
170. "Bush Untethered," editorial, *New York Times*, September 17, 2006.
171. Bruce Fein, on *Countdown*, MSNBC, September 24, 2007. Fein is a constitutional law expert and served as associate deputy attorney general in the Reagan Justice Department.
172. Dan Eggen, "NSA Spying Part of Broader Effort: Intelligence Chief Says Bush Authorized Secret Activities Under One Order," *Washington Post*, August 1, 2007.
173. Schwarz and Huq, *Unchecked and Unbalanced*, 136.
174. Ibid., 139.

175. Duffy, "The Cheney Branch of Government."
176. Frank Rich, "Has He Started Talking to the Walls?" *New York Times*, December 3, 2006.

Chapter 4: Creating Realities
1.   An unidentified Bush aide, quoted in Ron Suskind, "Faith, Certainty, and the Presidency of George W. Bush," *New York Times Magazine*, October 17, 2004, http://www.nytimes.com/2004/10/17/magazine/17BUSH.html. In *The Greatest Story Ever Sold*, Frank Rich suggests the aide "sounded uncannily like Karl Rove."
2.   Christopher Dickey, "The Constitution in Peril," *Newsweek*, October 8, 2007, 60.
3.   Thomas Jefferson, quoted in Charles A. Beard, *The Nation*, July 7, 1826, 8.
4.   Dickey, "The Constitution in Peril," 60.
5.   Whitney v. California, 274 U.S. 357, 375 (1927).
6.   Roth v. United States, 354 U.S. 476, 484 (1957).
7.   Dennis v. United States 341 U.S. 494, 550 (1951).
8.   New York Times v. Sullivan, 376 U.S. 254, 269 (1964), quoting Roth v. United States, 354 U.S. 476, 484 (1957).
9.   Thomas Jefferson, quoted in Thomas E. Cronin, *Direct Democracy: The Politics of Initiative, Referendum, and Recall* (Cambridge: Harvard University Press, 1989), 40.
10. West Virginia Board of Education v. Barnette, 319 U.S. 624, 642 (1943).
11. Lawrence Wilkerson, on *The Rachel Maddow Show,* MSNBC, April 24, 2009. Wilkerson was a top aide and later chief of staff to Secretary of State Colin Powell.
12. Jon Meacham, "An Opportunity for Tehran," *Newsweek*, July 20, 2009, 11.
13. Voltaire, in *Civilizations' Quotations*, ed. Richard Alan Kreiger (New York: Algora Publishing, 2002), 239.
14. Frederick Douglass, in *Life and Writings of Frederick Douglass*, ed. Philip Foner (New York: International Publishers, 1950), 1:144.
15. Howard Zinn, quoted in Sharon Basco, "Dissent In Pursuit Of Equality, Life, Liberty And Happiness," thomaspaine.com, July 3, 2002.
16. Richard N. Haass, "The Dilemma of Dissent," *Newsweek*, May 18, 2009, 34. Haass was director of policy planning for the Department of State, where he was a principal adviser to Secretary of State Colin Powell, January 2001 to June 2003.
17. Thomas Jefferson, quoted in Richard Hofstadter and Walter P. Metzger, *The Development of Academic Freedom in the United States* (New York: Columbia University Press 1955), 239.
18. Glenn Greenwald, *A Tragic Legacy: How a Good vs. Evil Mentality Destroyed the Bush Presidency* (New York: Crown Publishers, 2007), 84.
19. Gene Healy and Timothy Lynch, "Power Surge: The Constitutional Record of George W. Bush," Cato Institute report, 2006, 4, http://www.cato.org/pubs/wtpapers/powersurge_healy_lynch.pdf.
20. Scott McClellan, *What Happened: Inside the Bush White House and Washington's Culture of Deception* (New York: Public Affairs, 2008), 129. McClellan was Bush press secretary, 2003–2006.
21. Evan Thomas, "Katrina: How Bush Blew It," *Newsweek*, September 19, 2005, http://www.msnbc.msn.com/id/9287434/print/1/displaymode/1098/.
22. Sen. John Kerry, "A Right and Responsibility to Speak Out," speech in Boston, April 22, 2006, http://www.johnkerry.com/2006/4/22/a-right-and-responsibility-to-speak-out.
23. Benjamin Franklin, "An Apology for Printers," in *Writings of Benjamin Franklin*, ed. Albert Henry Smyth (New York: Macmillan Co., 1907), 2:174.
24. Roth v. United States, 354 U.S. 476, 483 (1957).
25. Jane Mayer, *The Dark Side: The Inside Story of How the War on Terror Turned Into a War on American Ideals* (New York: Doubleday, 2008), 178.
26. Jonathan Turley, on *Countdown*, MSNBC, January 4, 2007. Turley is a constitutional law professor at George Washington University.
27. Ron Suskind, *The Price of Loyalty: George W. Bush, the White House, and the Education of Paul O'Neill* (New York: Simon & Schuster, 2004), 125.
28. Schaefer v. United States, 251 U.S. 466, 494 (1920).
29. Jim Wallis, quoted in Ron Suskind, "Without A Doubt," *New York Times Magazine*, October 17, 2004. Wallis is a pastor who met with Bush.

30. West Virgiaa. Board of Education v. Barnette, 319 U.S. 624, 641 (1943).
31. John Stuart Mill, "Essay on Liberty," in *Essential Works of John Stuart Mill*, ed. Max Lerner (New York: Bantam, 1961), 266.
32. Zechariah Chafee Jr., *Free Speech in the United States*, 2nd ed. (Cambridge: Harvard University Press, 1941), xiii.
33. Thomas L. Friedman, "Saying No to Bush's Yes Men," *New York Times*, May 17, 2006.
34. Paul Krugman, "The Crony Fairy," *New York Times*, April 28, 2006.
35. Frank Rich, "Iraq Is the Ultimate Aphrodisiac," *New York Times*, April 22, 2007.
36. Rajiv Chandrasekaran, "Ties to GOP Trumped Know-How Among Staff Sent to Rebuild Iraq," *Washington Post*, September 17, 2006.
37. James Risen, *State of War: The Secret History of the CIA and the Bush Administration* (New York: Free Press, 2006) 134.
38. Dwight D. Eisenhower, quoted in D. Gibson Walton, "President's Message: Privileges and Responsibilities—Pro Bono Legal Services," *Houston Lawyer* 36:6 (1998).
39. McClellan, *What Happened*, 210.
40. Paul Krugman, "The Mensch Gap," *New York Times*, February 20, 2006.
41. Paul Krugman, "Limiting the Damage," *New York Times* November 6, 2006.
42. Al Gore, *The Assault on Reason* (New York: Penguin, 2007), 62.
43. Learned Hand, *The Spirit of Liberty*, 2nd ed. (New York: Knopf, 1953), 190.
44. John Stuart Mill, *On Liberty*, ed. Gertrude Himmelfarb (Baltimore: Penguin, 1974), 77.
45. Abrams v. United States, 250 U.S. 616, 630 (1919).
46. John Stuart Mill, "Essay On Liberty," in *On Liberty and Other Writings*, ed. Stefan Collini (New York: Cambridge University Press, 1989), 20.
47. John W. Dean, *Worse Than Watergate: The Secret Presidency of George W. Bush* (New York: Warner Books, 2004), 185.
48. John Milton, *Complete English Poems,* 4th ed., ed. Gordon Campbell (London: J. M. Dent, 1990), 610.
49. John Adams, "Dissertation on Canon and Feudal Law," in *The Portable John Adams*, ed. John Patrick Diggins (New York: Penguin Books, 2004), 219.
50. American Communications Assn. v. Douds, 339 U. S. 382, 442 (1950).
51. Thomas Jefferson, in *Pocket Patriot, Quotes from American Heroes*, ed. Kelly Nickell (Cincinnati: Writer's Digest Books: 2005), 25.
52. John Stuart Mill, quoted in John H. Garvey and Frederick F. Schauer, *The First Amendment: A Reader* (St. Paul: West Publishing Co., 1992), 68.
53. Cass R. Sunstein, *Why Societies Need Dissent* (Cambridge: Harvard University Press, 2003), 151.
54. Learned Hand, *The Bill of Rights* (Cambridge: Harvard University Press, 1958), 57.
55. Harry Kalven Jr., "New York Times Case: A Note on 'The Central Meaning of the First Amendment,'" *Supreme Court Review* 205 (1964).
56. Alexander Meiklejohn, Testimony on the Meaning of the First Amendment during the first session of the 84th Congress (1955).
57. Greenwald, *A Tragic Legacy*, 86.
58. Theodore Roosevelt, *Letters* (Cambridge: Harvard University Press, 1951), 1320.
59. Ari Fleischer, "Press Briefing by Ari Fleischer," White House news release, September 26, 2001, http://www.presidency.ucsb.edu/ws/index.php?pid=47571.
60. John Ashcroft, testimony to Senate Judiciary Committee, December 7, 2001, http://www.slate.com/?id=2059538. Ashcroft was U.S. Attorney General, 2001–2005.
61. Frank Rich, *The Greatest Story Ever Sold: The Decline and Fall of Truth From 9/11 to Katrina* (New York: Penguin, 2006), 39.
62. Schaefer v. United States, 251 U.S. 466, 495 (1920).
63. Cullen Murphy and Todd S. Purdum, "Farewell to All That: An Oral History of the Bush White House," *Vanity Fair*, February 2009, at 149.
64. McClellan, *What Happened*, 123.
65. West Virginia Board of Education v. Barnette, 319 U. S. 624, 641 (1943).
66. McClellan, *What Happened*, 122.
67. Frederick A. O. Schwarz Jr. and Aziz Z. Huq, *Unchecked and Unbalanced: Presidential Power in a Time of Terror* (New York: New Press, 2007), 7.

68. James Madison, quoted in *Romance in the Ivory Tower: The Rights and Liberty of Conscience* (Cambridge: MIT Press, 2007), 70.
69. Risen, *State of War*, 132.
70. Maureen Dowd, "Father and Son Reunion," *New York Times*, May 10, 2006.
71. Stephen Dinanand and Christina Bellantoni, "Bush Nominates Hayden As Next Director of CIA," *Washington Times*, May 9, 2006.
72. Paul Krugman, "Wrong Is Right," *New York Times*, February 19, 2007.
73. John Stuart Mill, quoted in Alan Hayworth, *Free Speech* (New York: Routledge, 2007), 78.
74. John Locke, *Essay Concerning Human Understanding* (London: Thomas Tegg, 1832), 1:xlii.
75. Paul Krugman, "Limiting the Damage," *New York Times*, November 6, 2006.
76. Barenblatt v. United States, 309 U.S. 109, 162 (1959).
77. Martin Luther King Jr., *Strength to Love* (Philadelphia: Fortress Press, 1981), 26.
78. Todd S. Purdum, "Inside Bush's Bunker," *Vanity Fair*, October 2007, 393.
79. Rich, *Greatest Story Ever Sold*, 209.
80. McClellan, *What Happened*, 240.
81. George W. Bush, quoted in Oliver Burkeman, "Bush Reveals He Is a Guardian Reader," *The Guardian*, November 18, 2006, http://www.guardian.co.uk/media/2006/nov/18/theguardian.pressandpublishing (quoting an October 2003 Fox News interview).
82. Bush, quoted in Bob Woodward, *Bush at War, Part III* (New York: Simon & Schuster, 2006), 342.
83. Bill Sammon, *Misunderestimated* (New York: Regan Books, 2004), 127–128.
84. Bush, quoted in Helen Thomas, "No Wonder Bush Doesn't Connect with the Rest of the Country," *Seattle Post-Intelligencer*, October 15, 2003.
85. Greenwald, *A Tragic Legacy*, 85.
86. Evan Thomas and Richard Wolffe, "Bush in the Bubble," *Newsweek*, December 19, 2005, http://www.newsweek.com/id/51430/page/4.
87. McClellan, *What Happened*, 253.
88. Benjamin Franklin, *Poor Richard's Almanack* (Waterloo, IA: U.S.C. Publishing Co., 1914), 16.
89. Dan Bartlett, quoted in Michael Isikoff and David Corn, *Hubris: The Inside Story of Spin, Scandal, and the Selling of the Iraq War* (New York: Crown Publishers, 2006), 296. Bartlett was White House communications director, 2002–2005.
90. Richard Clarke, quoted in Murphy and Purdum, "Farewell to All That," 90, 93. Clarke was chief White House counterterrorism adviser.
91. Suskind, "Without A Doubt."
92. Paul O'Neill, quoted in Suskind, *Price of Loyalty*, 156. O'Neill was Treasury Secretary, 2001–2002.
93. Thomas Paine, in *The Political Writings of Thomas Paine*, ed. E. H. Evans (Cambridge: Harvard University, 1839), 88.
94. Suskind, *Price of Loyalty*, 293.
95. King, *Strength to Love*, 17.
96. Gore, *Assault on Reason*, 116.
97. Ron Suskind, *One Percent Doctrine: Deep Inside America's Pursuit of Its Enemies Since 9/11* (New York: Simon & Schuster, 2006), 290.
98. Greenwald, *A Tragic Legacy*, xii.
99. Ibid., 56.
100. New York Times v. Sullivan, 376 U.S. 254, 297 (1964).
101. Garrison v. Louisiana, 379 U.S. 64, 75 (1964).
102. Greenwald, *A Tragic Legacy*, 90. Emphasis in original.
103. McClellan, *What Happened*, 242.
104. George Orwell, *1984* (New York: Penguin, 1949), 213.
105. Frank Rich, "The Wiretappers That Couldn't Shoot Straight," *New York Times*, January 8, 2006.
106. John W. Dean, *Conservatives Without Conscience* (New York: Viking, 2006), xxxvii.
107. Greenwald, *A Tragic Legacy*, 57.
108. Ibid., 100 (emphasis added).
109. Ibid., 105.
110. Schwarz and Huq, *Unchecked and Unbalanced*, 200.
111. Seymour M. Hersh, *Chain of Command: The Road From 9/11 to Abu Ghraib* (New York: Harper Collins, 2004), 252.
112. Schwarz and Huq, *Unchecked and Unbalanced*, 197.

113. Risen, *State of War*, 76.
114. Schwarz and Huq, *Unchecked and Unbalanced*, 193.
115. Ibid., 196.
116. Greenwald, *A Tragic Legacy*, 124.
117. Risen, *State of War*, 128.
118. Frank Rich, "Eight Days in July," *New York Times*, July 24, 2005.
119. Greenwald, *A Tragic Legacy*, 82.
120. Ibid., 84–85.
121. Christine Todd Whitman, quoted in Suskind, "Without A Doubt." Whitman was EPA administrator, 2001–2003.
122. Dean, *Worse Than Watergate*, 65.
123. Thomas Jefferson, in *The Writings of Thomas Jefferson, 1784–1787*, ed. Paul Leicester Ford (New York: G. P. Putnam's Sons, 1894), 4:467.
124. Healy and Lynch, "Power Surge," 6.
125. Beauharnais v. Illinois, 343 U.S. 250, 263–264 (1952).
126. United States v. Associated Press, 52 F. Supp. 362, 372 (S.D.N.Y. 1943).
127. Kenneth R. Bazinet, "W's Forums Packed With Fans: 'Ask Bush' Events Tightly Controlled," *New York Daily News*, August 15, 2004.
128. Bush, "The President's News Conference," October 28, 2003, http://www.presidency.ucsb.edu/ws/index.php?pid=63859.
129. Griswold v. Connecticut, 381 U.S. 479, 482 (1965).
130. Abraham Lincoln, in *The Collected Works of Abraham Lincoln*, ed. Roy P. Basler (Piscataway, NJ: Rutgers University Press, 1955), 3:376.
131. Thomas Paine, *The Age of Reason* (New York: Truth Seeker Co., 1898), vii.
132. Thomas Jefferson, in *The Writings of Thomas Jefferson, 1784–1787*, ed. Paul Leicester Ford (New York: G. P. Putnam's Sons, 1894), 370.
133. Zechariah Chaffee, *Free Speech in the United States* (Cambridge: Harvard University Press, 1948), 367.
134. Colleen Redman, "Rediscovering Patriotism," April 30, 2003, http://www.commondreams.org/views03/0430-10.htm.
135. West Virginia Board of Education v. Barnette, 319 U.S. 624, 639 (1943).
136. Purdum, "Inside Bush's Bunker," 391.
137. Texas v. Johnson, 491 U.S. 397, 414. (1989).
138. Abrams v. United States, 250 U.S. 616, 630 (1919).
139. John Milton, *Areopagitica* (Cambridge: Harvard University Press, 1918), 58.
140. Suskind, *One Percent Doctrine*, 295–296.
141. Krugman, "Crony Fairy."
142. Milton, *Areopagitica*, ed. J. W. Hales (London: MacMillan and Co., 1884), vii.
143. Risen, *State of War*, 65.
144. Alexander Meiklejohn, *Free Speech and Its Relation to Self-Government* (New York: Harper Brothers, 1955), 27.
145. Gore, *Assault on Reason*, 56. Emphasis in original.
146. Harry Kalven Jr., "New York Times Case: A Note on 'The Central Meaning of the First Amendment,'" *Supreme Court Review* 191, 205 (1964).
147. Communications Association v. Douds, 339 U.S. 382, 442 (1950).
148. New York Times v. Sullivan, 376 U.S. 254, 282–283 (1964).
149. Whitney v. California, 274 U.S. 357, 376 (1927).
150. Gore, *Assault on Reason*, 113–114.
151. Risen, *State of War*, 135.
152. Gen. Anthony Zinni, quoted in Gore, *Assault on Reason*, 183.
153. Gore, *Assault on Reason*, 184.
154. Thomas I. Emerson, *Toward a General Theory of the First Amendment* (New York: Random House, 1966), 7.
155. David Margolick, "The Night of the Generals," *Vanity Fair*, April 2007, 247–248.
156. Hersh, *Chain of Command*, 169.
157. James Fallows, *Blind Into Baghdad: America's War In Iraq* (New York, Vintage Books, 2006), 130.

158. Jay Garner, quoted in Murphy and Purdum, "Farewell to All That," 152. Garner was director of the Office for Reconstruction and Humanitarian Assistance in Iraq, 2003.
159. Fallows, *Blind Into Baghdad*, 227.
160. Risen, *State of War*, 129–130.
161. Ibid., 109.
162. Ibid., 110.
163. Emerson, *Toward a General Theory of the First Amendment*, 9.
164. Aamer Madhani, "Top U.S. Commander in Mideast Resigns After Questioning Policy," *Chicago Tribune*, March 11, 2008.
165. Mark Thompson, "Iran Dissent Cost Fallon His Job," *Time*, March 12, 2008, http://www.time.com/time/nation/article/0,8599,1721491,00.html.
166. Emerson, *Toward a General Theory of the First Amendment*, 12.
167. Phillip Shenon, *The Commission: The Uncensored History of the 9/11 Investigation* (New York: Twelve, 2008), 37, 38.
168. Sen. John Kerry, "A Right and Responsibility to Speak Out."
169. Thomas Jefferson, in Richard E. Labunski, *James Madison and the Struggle for the Bill of Rights* (New York: Oxford University Press, 2006), 104.
170. Naomi Wolf, *The End of America: Letter of Warning to a Young Patriot* (White River Junction: VT: Chelsea Green Publishing, 2007), 28.
171. Thomas Jefferson, *The Writings of Thomas Jefferson*, eds. Andrew A. Lipscomb and Albert Ellery Bergh (Washington, DC: Jefferson Memorial Association, 1905), 10:175.
172. United States v. Verdugo-Urquidez, 494 U.S. 259, 288 (1990).
173. Alexander Hamilton, *The Federalist Papers*, No. 22, ed. Clinton Rossiter (New York: Penguin, 1961), 152.
174. Abraham Lincoln, in *Selected Writings and Speeches of Abraham Lincoln*, ed. T. Harry Williams (Chicago: Packard and Co.), 36–37.
175. James Madison, *The Federalist Papers*, No. 49, ed. Clinton Rossiter (New York: Penguin, 1961), 313–314.
176. Time v. Firestone, 424 U.S. 448, 471 (1976).
177. Suskind, *One Percent Doctrine*, 292.
178. George Washington, "Address to Both Houses of Congress," in Thorvald Solberg, *Copyright in Congress, 1789–1904* (Buffalo: William S. Hein, 2006), 115–116.
179. Schlesinger, *Imperial Presidency*, x.
180. Whitney v. California, 274 U.S. 357, 377 (1927).
181. Dennis v. United States, 341 U.S. 494, 584 (1951).
182. New York Times v. Sullivan, 376 U.S. 254, 270 (1964).
183. Suskind, *One Percent Doctrine*, 291–292.
184. Gore, *Assault on Reason*, 58.
185. McClellan, *What Happened*, 309.
186. Wolf, *End of America*, 128.
187. Thomas Jefferson, in *The Life and Writings of Thomas Jefferson*, ed. Samuel E. Forman (Indianapolis: Bowen-Merrill, 1900), 437.
188. Bruce Bartlett, in Suskind, "Faith, Certainty and the Presidency of George W. Bush."
189. Suskind, "Faith, Certainty and the Presidency of George W. Bush."
190. Rich, *Greatest Story Ever Sold*, 13.
191. Suskind, *One Percent Doctrine*, 246.
192. Gore, *Assault on Reason*, 47.
193. Greenwald, *A Tragic Legacy*, xiii.
194. American Communications Association v. Douds, 339 U.S. 382, 438 (1950).
195. Suskind, "Faith, Certainty and the Presidency of George W. Bush."
196. Greenwald, *A Tragic Legacy*, 45–46.
197. Benjamin Franklin, in S. Austin Allibone, *A Critical Dictionary of English Literature and British and American Authors* (Philadelphia: J. B. Lippincott Company, 1899), 2:1484.
198. Greenwald, *A Tragic Legacy*, 56–57.
199. Benjamin Franklin, in *New England Courant*, July 23, 1722.
200. Greenwald, *A Tragic Legacy*, 48.
201. Paul O'Neill, quoted in Suskind, *Price of Loyalty*, 127.

202. Purdum, "Inside Bush's Bunker."
203. Paul O'Neill, quoted in Suskind, *Price of Loyalty*, 292. Emphasis in original.
204. John J. DiIulio Jr., quoted in Suskind, *Price of Loyalty*, 170. DiIulio ran Bush's faith-based initiative.
205. Bush, quoted in Gore, *Assault on Reason*, 108.
206. Keith Olbermann, on *Countdown*, MSNBC, September 25, 2006.
207. Gore, *Assault on Reason*, 60.
208. Wolf, *End of America*, 9.
209. Charlie Savage, *Takeover: The Return of the Imperial Presidency and the Subversion of American Democracy* (New York: Little Brown and Co., 2007), 106.
210. Maureen Dowd, "Live From Baghdad: More Dying," *New York Times*, May 31, 2006.
211. Thomas L. Friedman, "Don't Ask, Don't Know, Don't Help," *New York Times*, March 7, 2007.
212. Franklin, *Poor Richard's Almanack*, 1758.
213. Frank Rich, "Why Libby's Pardon Is a Slam Dunk," *New York Times*, March 11, 2007.
214. Frank Rich, "The Petraeus-Crocker Show Gets the Hook," *New York Times*, April 13, 2008.
215. Thomas Jefferson, in *The Works of Thomas Jefferson*, ed. Paul Leicester Ford (New York: G. P. Putnam's Sons, 1905). 10:418.
216. Bob Herbert, "Lift the Curtain," *New York Times,* March 8, 2007.
217. Suskind, *One Percent Doctrine*, 99.
218. Jean-Jacques. Rousseau, *Discourse On the Sciences and Arts (First Discourse)* (Hanover, NH: University Press of New England, 1992), 13.
219. Paul Krugman, "Sweet Little Lies," *New York Times*, April 9, 2007.
220. Thomas Carlyle, *The French Revolution: A History* (London: Thomas Nelson & Sons, 1902), 34.
221. Dean, *Worse Than Watergate*, 103–104.
222. Donald Rumsfeld, quoted in Eric Schmitt, "Rumsfeld Looking For Help In Finding Outlawed Arms," *New York Times*, April 18, 2003.
223. Charles Lewis and Mark Reading-Smith, "False Pretenses," The Center for Public Integrity, http://www.publicintegrity.org/WarCard/.
224. Al Gore, "Remarks to Moveon.org" (speech, New York University, August 7, 2003), http://www.scoop.co.nz/stories/WO0308/S00109.htm.
225. Thomas Jefferson, in *The Life and Writings of Thomas Jefferson*, ed. S. E. Forman (Indianapolis: The Bowen-Merrill Company, 1900), 181.
226. Wolf, *End of America*, 130–131.
227. Benjamin Franklin, *Life and Times of Benjamin Franklin*, ed. James Parton (New York: Mason Brothers, 1865), 1:232.
228. McClellan, *What Happened*, 230.
229. John Adams, quoted in *Wit and Wisdom of the American Presidents*, ed. Joslyn T. Pine (Courier Dover, 2000), 4.
230. Gore, *Assault on Reason*, 60.
231. Scott D. O'Reilly, "Bushspeak: Bush and Orwell," July 21, 2003, http://www.dissentvoice.org/Articles7/OReilly_Bushspeak.htm.
232. Orwell, *1984*, 155.
233. Naomi Wolf, on *Hardball*, MSNBC, August 17, 2007.
234. Orwell, *1984*, 214.
235. Keith Olbermann, commentary, *Countdown*, MSNBC, October 18, 2006.
236. Hersh, *Chain of Command*, 367.
237. Krugman, "Sweet Little Lies."
238. Wolf, *End of America*, 127. Emphasis in original.
239. Gore, *Assault on Reason*, 112.
240. Rich, *Greatest Story Ever Sold*, 166.
241. Ibid., 167–168.
242. David Barstow and Robin Stein, "Under Bush, a New Age of Prepackaged News," *New York Times*, March 13, 2005.
243. Frank Rich, "The Armstrong Williams NewsHour," *New York Times*, June 26, 2005.
244. Frank Rich, "The White House Stages Its 'Daily Show,'" *New York Times*, February 20, 2005.
245. Rich, *Greatest Story Ever Sold*, 171.
246. Ibid., 170.

247. Rich, "The White House Stages Its 'Daily Show.'"
248. Rich, *Greatest Story Ever Sold*, 174.
249. Thomas I. Emerson, "Toward a General Theory of the First Amendment," *Yale Law Journal*, 72:883 (1963).
250. Albert Einstein, *Out of My Later Years* (London: Thams and Hudson, 1950), 19.
251. Hersh, *Chain of Command*, 362.

Part II: The War President

1. George W. Bush, on *Meet the Press*, NBC, February 8, 2004, http://www.msnbc.msn.com/id/4179618/.
2. Jane Mayer, *The Dark Side: The Inside Story of How the War on Terror Turned Into a War on American Ideals* (New York: Doubleday, 2008), 332.
3. Charles Duelfer, on *The Rachel Maddow Show*, MSNBC, May 14, 2009. Duelfer was head of the Iraq Survey Group.
4. Rob Richer, quoted in Ron Suskind, *The Way of the World* (New York: HarperCollins, 2008), 367. Richer was the associate deputy director of operations of the CIA.
5. Ron Suskind, *The One Percent Doctrine: Deep Inside America's Pursuit of Its Enemies Since 9/11* (New York: Simon & Schuster, 2006), 26. Emphasis in original.
6. Bush, "Press Conference by the President," White House news release, July 12, 2007, http://georgewbush-whitehouse.archives.gov/news/releases/2007/07/20070712-5.html.
7. Eugene Robinson, "Bush's Cognitive Dissonance," *Washington Post*, July 20, 2007.
8. Bush, "President Bush Discusses Situation in Georgia," White House news release, August 15, 2008, http://georgewbush-whitehouse.archives.gov/news/releases/2008/08/20080815.html.
9. Richard Perle, "Turkey at the Crossroads," American Enterprise Institute for Public Policy Research, September 22, 2003, http://www.aei.org/events/contentID.20031003144313426/default.asp. Perle was chair of the Defense Policy Board Advisory Committee 2001–2003 and is a self-described neoconservative who strongly advocated regime change in Iraq.
10. Tina Susman and Caesar Ahmed, "Iraqi Protesters Burn Bush Effigy," *Los Angeles Times*, November 22, 2008.
11. "Bush 'Not Insulted' By Thrown Shoes," ABC News, December 14, 2008, http://abcnews.go.com/Politics/BushLegacy/Story?id=6460837&page=2.

Chapter 5: September 11 Run-up

1. See, e.g., "Bin Ladin Determined To Strike in US," http://www.gwu.edu/~nsarchiv/NSAEBB/NSAEBB116/pdb8-6-2001.pdf.
2. Tyler Drumheller, *On the Brink: An Insider's Account of How the White House Compromised American Intelligence* (New York: Carroll & Graf Publishers, 2006), 21. Drumheller was chief of CIA covert operations in Europe.
3. Bush, quoted in Suskind, *One Percent Doctrine*, 2.
4. Condoleezza Rice, "National Security Advisor Holds Press Briefing," White House press release, May 16, 2002, http://911research.wtc7.net/cache/wtc/info/whitehouse_20020516_13.html.
5. David Plotz, "What You Think You Know About Sept. 11 . . . But Don't," *Slate*, September 10, 2003, http://slate.msn.com/id/2088092/.
6. Ibid.
7. Dick Cheney, quoted in "In Cheney's Words: The Risk of 'the Wrong Choice." *New York Times*, Sept. 8, 2004.
8. President's Daily Brief, August 6, 2001, as read by Sen. Bob Kerrey during 9/11 Commission hearing, "Transcript of Rice's 9/11 Testimony," CNN.com, May 19, 2004, http://www.cnn.com/2004/ALLPOLITICS/04/08/rice.transcript/.
9. Bush, "President Meets with Muslim Leaders," White House news release, September 26, 2001, http://georgewbush-whitehouse.archives.gov/news/releases/2001/09/20010926-8.html.
10. FBI memo, quoted in "9-11 Commission Report," http://www.911independentcommission.org/fbi3182004.html. See also "9/11 Independent Commission," March 18, 2004, http://www.911independentcommission.org/fbi3182004.html.
11. Richard A. Clarke, *Against All Enemies: Inside America's War on Terror* (New York: Free Press, 2004), 225–226

12. Michael Elliot, "They Had a Plan," *Time*, August 4, 2002, http://www.time.com/time/covers/1101020812/story.html.
13. Condoleezza Rice, quoted in Peter Baker, "Bush and Clinton Teams Debate Pre-9/11 Efforts," *Washington Post*, September 27, 2006.
14. National Commission on Terrorist Attacks Upon the United States, http://www.9-11commission.gov/report/911Report_Ch8.htm.
15. Keith Olbermann, on *Countdown*, MSNBC, September 27, 2006.
16. Richard Clarke, memo to Condoleezza Rice, January 25, 2001, quoted in *The 9/11 Commission Report* (New York: W. W. Norton, 2004), 201. Emphasis in original.
17. Andrea Mitchell, on *Hardball*, MSNBC, October 2, 2006.
18. Michael Isikoff and David Corn, *Hubris: The Inside Story of Spin, Scandal, and the Selling of the Iraq War* (New York: Crown Publishers, 2006), 76.
19. Paul Kurtz, on *Countdown*, September 27, 2006. Kurtz was NSC director for counterterrorism, 1999–2002.
20. Elliot, "They Had a Plan."
21. Richard Clarke, quoted in Phillip Shenon, *The Commission: The Uncensored History of the 9/11 Investigation* (New York: Twelve, 2008), 283.
22. Albert Einstein, quoted in *Bite-Size Einstein*, eds. Jerry Mayer and John P. Holms (New York: St. Martin's, 1996), 38.
23. Paul Kurtz, on *Countdown*, MSNBC, September 27, 2006.
24. Shenon, *The Commission*, 296.
25. Roger Cressey, on *Countdown*, MSNBC, October 2, 2006. Cressey is a former member of the National Security Council under presidents Clinton and Bush.
26. Philip Shenon and Mark Mazzetti, "CIA Chief Warned Rice on Al Qaeda," *New York Times*, October 3, 2006.
27. Clarke, *Against All Enemies*, 235.
28. Roger Cressey, on *Countdown*, MSNBC, October 2, 2006.
29. Clarke, *Against All Enemies*, 237–238.
30. Lawrence Wilkerson, quoted in Cullen Murphy and Todd S. Purdum, "Farewell to All That: An Oral History of the Bush White House," *Vanity Fair*, February 2009, 153. Wilkerson was a top aide and later chief of staff to Secretary of State Colin Powell.
31. Shenon, *The Commission*, 198.
32. Ari Fleischer, quoted on *News Hour*, PBS, May 16, 2002, http://www.pbs.org/newshour/bb/terrorism/jan-june02/bkgdhijack_5-16.html. Fleischer was White House press secretary, 2001–2003.
33. Bob Drogin, "U.S. Had Plan for Covert Afghan Options Before 9/11," *Los Angeles Times*, May 18, 2002.
34. Dan Eggen and Walter Pincus, "Rice Defends Pre-9/11 Anti-Terrorism Efforts," *Washington Post*, April 9, 2004.
35. Shenon, *The Commission*, 238.
36. Philip Shenon, "9/11 Panel Presses Rice on Early Warnings," *New York Times*, April 9, 2004.
37. "Transcript of Rice's 9/11 Testimony," CNN.com, May 19, 2004, http://www.cnn.com/2004/ALLPOLITICS/04/08/rice.transcript/. See also Shenon, *The Commission*, 298. Ben-Veniste was a member of the 9/11 Commission.
38. Frank Rich, *The Greatest Story Ever Sold: The Decline and Fall of Truth From 9/11 to Katrina* (New York: Penguin, 2006), 47–48.
39. Shenon, *The Commission*, 237.
40. Richard Clarke, quoted in Murphy and Purdum, "Farewell to All That," 96.
41. Donald Rumsfeld, "Secretary of Defense Donald H. Rumsfeld, Interview with Rush Limbaugh (As Released by the Pentagon)," FDCH Political Transcripts, May 16, 2002.
42. Bush, on *Wolf Blitzer Reports*, CNN, April 5, 2004.
43. Rich, *The Greatest Story Ever Sold*, 66.
44. *The 9/11 Commission Report* (New York: W. W. Norton, 2004), 260.
45. Ibid., 262.
46. Albert Einstein, quoted in Marc S. Klein, "Reframing the 'Tort Reform' Debate (and Our Participation in It)," *New Jersey Lawyer*, January 1995, 39.

47. Cheney, quoted on *The News Hour with Jim Lehrer*, PBS, May 17, 2002, http://www.pbs.org/
     newshour/bb/terrorism/jan-june02/bkgddots_5-17.html.
48. Al Gore, "The Moment of Truth," *Vanity Fair*, May 2006, 171.
49. Eric Lichtblau, "Critics Want Full Report of 9/11 Panel," *New York Times*, February 11, 2005.
50. George Edmonson, "9/11 Blame Scattered: Bush, Clinton Teams Swear They Did All They
     Could," *Atlanta Journal-Constitution*, March 24, 2004.
51. Keith Olbermann, on *Countdown*, MSNBC, September 25, 2006.
52. George Orwell, *1984* (New York: Penguin, 1949), 248.

Chapter 6: Iraq: Stacking the Deck
1.   Hermann Göring, Nuremberg Trials, April 18, 1946, Holocaust Research Project, http://www.
     holocaustresearchproject.org/holoprelude/goering.html.
2.   Scott McClellan, *What Happened: Inside the Bush White House and Washington's Culture of
     Deception* (New York: Public Affairs, 2008), 125. McClellan was Bush press secretary, 2003–
     2006.
3.   George W. Bush, quoted in Kim Cobb, "Writer Says Bush Talked About War in 1999," *Hous-
     ton Chronicle*, November 1, 2004.
4.   Russ Baker, "Bush Wanted To Invade Iraq If Elected in 2000," October 27, 2004, http://russ-
     baker.com/archives/Guerrilla%20News%20Network%20-%20Bush.htm.
5.   Frank Rich, "Karl and Scooter's Excellent Adventure," *New York Times*, October 23, 2005.
6.   McClellan, *What Happened*, 132.
7.   Bob Woodward, *Plan of Attack* (New York: Simon & Schuster, 2004), 9 (emphasis added).
8.   Phillip Shenon, *The Commission: The Uncensored History of the 9/11 Investigation* (New York:
     Twelve, 2008), 129.
9.   Sen. Max Cleland, quoted in ibid., 129.
10. Tyler Drumheller, in "A Spy Speaks Out," *60 Minutes*, CBS News, April 23, 2006, http://
     www.cbsnews.com/stories/2006/04/21/60minutes/main1527749.shtml.   Drumheller was
     chief of CIA covert operations in Europe.
11. Greg Theilmann, on *Frontline*, "Truth, War & Consequences," PBS, October 9, 2003, http://
     www.pbs.org/wgbh/pages/frontline/shows/truth/interviews/thielmann.html. Theilmann was
     director of the Strategic, Proliferation and Military Affairs Office at the State Department's
     Intelligence Bureau.
12. James Risen, *State of War: The Secret History of the CIA and the Bush Administration* (New York:
     Free Press, 2006), 77 (emphasis added).
13. Paul O'Neill, on "Bush Sought 'Way' to Invade Iraq?" *60 Minutes*, CBS, January 11, 2004,
     http://www.cbsnews.com/stories/2004/01/09/60minutes/main592330.shtml.   O'Neill   was
     Treasury Secretary, 2001–2002.
14. Michael Isikoff and David Corn, *Hubris: The Inside Story of Spin, Scandal, and the Selling of the
     Iraq War* (New York: Crown, 2006), 11.
15. Glenn Greenwald, *A Tragic Legacy: How a Good vs. Evil Mentality Destroyed the Bush Presidency*
     (New York: Crown, 2007), 100. Emphasis in original.
16. Seymour M. Hersh, *Chain of Command: The Road From 9/11 to Abu Ghraib* (New York:
     Harper Collins, 2004), 167.
17. Tyler Drumheller, *On the Brink: An Insider's Account of How the White House Compromised
     American Intelligence* (New York: Carroll & Graf Publishers, 2006), 207 (emphasis added).
18. Richard Clarke, quoted in Cullen Murphy and Todd S. Purdum, "Farewell to All That: An
     Oral History of the Bush White House," *Vanity Fair*, February 2009, 96.
19. Ron Suskind, *The One Percent Doctrine: Deep Inside America's Pursuit of Its Enemies Since 9/11*
     (New York: Simon & Schuster, 2006), 233.
20. Ron Suskind, *The Price of Loyalty: George W. Bush, the White House, and the Education of Paul
     O'Neill* (New York: Simon & Schuster, 2004), 72.
21. Thomas E. Ricks, *Fiasco: The American Military Adventure in Iraq* (New York: Penguin, 2006),
     48. Emphasis in original.
22. Suskind, *Price of Loyalty*, 73–74.
23. O'Neill, quoted in ibid., 75.
24. Ibid., 129.

25. Richard A. Clarke, *Against All Enemies: Inside America's War on Terror* (New York: Free Press, 2004), 264.
26. Drumheller, "A Spy Speaks Out."
27. Isikoff and Corn, *Hubris*, 13. Emphasis added.
28. Jacob Heilbrunn, "The Rumsfeld Doctrine," (review of *Cobra II*, by Michael R. Gordon and Bernard E. Trainor), *New York Times*, April 30, 2006.
29. John W. Dean, *Conservatives Without Conscience* (New York: Viking, 2006), 79. Emphasis added.
30. Max Frankel, "The Washington Back Channel," *New York Times*, March 25, 2007 (emphasis added).
31. Gen. Anthony Zinni, on *Meet the Press*, NBC, April 15, 2007.
32. Thomas Ricks, "For Vietnam Vet Anthony Zinni, Another War on Shaky Territory," *Washington Post*, December 23, 2003.
33. Isikoff and Corn, *Hubris*, 13.
34. Tyler Drumheller, quoted in Risen, *State of War*, 119.
35. McClellan, *What Happened*, 128.
36. Murphy and Purdum, "Farewell to All That," 149.
37. Bush, quoted in Isikoff and Corn, *Hubris*, 1.
38. John Dean, on *Countdown*, MSNBC, October 10, 2007.
39. Clarke, *Against All Enemies*, 30–31 (emphasis added).
40. Woodward, *Plan of Attack*, 25.
41. George Tenet, on *60 Minutes*, CBS, April 29, 2007, http://www.cbsnews.com/stories/2007/04/25/60minutes/main2728375.shtml.
42. Suskind, *Price of Loyalty*, 86. Emphasis in original.
43. Clarke, *Against All Enemies*, 30–31.
44. Greenwald, *Tragic Legacy*, 100. Emphasis in original.
45. Clarke, *Against All Enemies*, 32.
46. Suskind, *Price of Loyalty*, 188.
47. An anonymous source, quoted in Ricks, *Fiasco*, 30–31.
48. Frank Rich, *The Greatest Story Ever Sold: The Decline and Fall of Truth From 9/11 to Katrina* (New York: Penguin, 2006), 67.
49. Clarke, *Against All Enemies*, 30–31.
50. Paul O'Neill, quoted in Suskind, *Price of Loyalty*, 188.
51. James Fallows, *Blind Into Baghdad: America's War In Iraq* (New York: Vintage, 2006), 50.
52. Al Gore, *The Assault on Reason* (New York: Penguin, 2007), 107.
53. Fallows, *Blind Into Baghdad*, 50.
54. Bob Herbert, "The Fear Factor," *New York Times*, April 17, 2006.
55. Charles Lewis and Mark Reading-Smith, "False Pretenses," The Center for Public Integrity, http://www.publicintegrity.org/WarCard/.
56. David Margolick, "The Night of the Generals," *Vanity Fair*, April 2007, 247. Newbold was the Pentagon's top operations officer.
57. Ibid., 279.
58. Maureen Dowd, "Googling Past the Graveyard," *New York Times*, January 21, 2006.
59. Isikoff and Corn, *Hubris*, 4–5.
60. Hersh, *Chain of Command*, 218.
61. Ricks, *Fiasco*, 30–31.
62. John Locke, *An Essay Concerning Human Understanding*, ed. Peter Nidditch (Oxford: Clarendon Press, 1975), 283.
63. Murray Waas, "Key Bush Intelligence Briefing Kept From Hill Panel," *The National Journal*, November 22, 2005, http://nationaljournal.com/about/njweekly/stories/2005/1122nj1.htm.
64. Isikoff and Corn, *Hubris*, 3.
65. A former CIA official, quoted in Hersh, *Chain of Command*, 224.
66. Bob Woodward, on "The Decider," MSNBC, December 29, 2008.
67. Isikoff and Corn, *Hubris*, 4.
68. Risen, *State of War*, 72.
69. Walter Pincus and Dana Priest, "Some Iraq Analysts Felt Pressure From Cheney Visits," *Washington Post*, June 5, 2003.
70. Hersh, *Chain of Command*, 227–228.

71. Isikoff and Corn, *Hubris*, 11. Emphasis in original.
72. Jon Moseman, quoted in Suskind, *One Percent Doctrine*, 242. Moseman was chief of staff to CIA director George Tenet.
73. Oliver Wendell Holmes Jr., "Natural Law," in *The Great Legal Philosophers*, ed. Clarence Morris (Philadelphia: University of Pennsylvania Press, 1991), 435.
74. Heilbrunn, "The Rumsfeld Doctrine."
75. Isikoff and Corn, *Hubris*, 31.
76. Tyler Drumheller, quoted in Jane Mayer, *The Dark Side: The Inside Story of How the War on Terror Turned Into a War on American Ideals* (New York: Doubleday, 2008), 145.
77. Gore, *Assault on Reason*, 107.
78. Sen. John Kerry, "A Right and Responsibility to Speak Out," speech in Boston, April 22, 2006, http://www.johnkerry.com/2006/4/22/a-right-and-responsibility-to-speak-out.
79. Suskind, *Price of Loyalty*, 204.
80. Fallows, *Blind Into Baghdad*, 51.
81. George Orwell, *1984* (New York: Penguin, 1949), 34.
82. Gore, *Assault on Reason*, 54.
83. Bush, "Address Before a Joint Session of the Congress on the State of the Union," January 29, 2002, http://www.presidency.ucsb.edu/ws/index.php?pid=29644.
84. John Locke, *An Essay Concerning Human Understanding* (London: Tegg, 1841), 390–391.
85. Peggy Noonan, "Time to Put the Emotions Aside," *Wall Street Journal*, September 11, 2002, http://www.opinionjournal.com/columnists/pnoonan/?id=110002249.
86. Fallows, *Blind Into Baghdad*, 51.
87. Suskind, *Price of Loyalty*, 96–97.
88. Isikoff and Corn, *Hubris*, 16.
89. Clarke, *Against All Enemies*, 243.
90. Risen, *State of War*, 79.
91. McClellan, *What Happened*, 126.
92. Thomas Kean and Lee Hamilton, *Without Precedent: The Inside Story of the 9/11 Commission* (New York: Knopf, 2006), 248. Kean and Hamilton were co-chairs of the 9/11 Commission.
93. Frank Rich, "Return to the Scene of the Crime," *New York Times*, August 27, 2006.
94. Hersh, *Chain of Command*, 363.
95. Frank Rich, "The 'Good Germans' Among Us," *New York Times*, October 14, 2007.
96. Bush, "Radio Address by the President to the Nation," White House news release, September 28, 2002, http://georgewbush-whitehouse.archives.gov/news/releases/2002/09/20020928.html.
97. Woodward, *Plan of Attack*, 190.
98. Isikoff and Corn, *Hubris*, 411.
99. Tyler Drumheller, quoted in Frank Rich, "Bush of a Thousand Days," *New York Times*, April 30, 2006.
100. Paul Pillar, quoted in Rich, *Greatest Story Ever Sold*, 188. Pillar was National Intelligence Officer for the Middle East, 2000–2005. Pillar served in the CIA for thirty years, including as National Intelligence Officer for the Middle East, 2000–2005.
101. Isikoff and Corn, *Hubris*, 108.
102. Gore, *Assault on Reason*, 108.
103. *Fox on the Record with Greta Van Sustern*, FoxNews, July 30, 2002.
104. Lewis and Reading-Smith, "False Pretenses,"
105. Risen, *State of War*, 71.
106. Bush, in an interview with Katie Couric for a CBS News special about 9/11, September 6, 2006, http://www.cbsnews.com/stories/2006/09/06/five_years/main1980074.shtml.
107. Jonathan Alter, "Totally Unconvincing," *Newsweek*, March 7, 2003, http://www.newsweek.com/id/58055.
108. Bush, quoted in Zay N. Smith, "Veterans Still Fighting the War at Home," *Chicago Sun-Times*, May 26, 2005.
109. Peggy Noonan, "To Beat a Man, You Need a Plan," *Wall Street Journal*, September 15, 2006, http://www.opinionjournal.com/columnists/pnoonan/?id=110008942.
110. Franklin D. Roosevelt, radio address to the *New York Herald Tribune* Forum, October 26, 1939, http://www.presidency.ucsb.edu/ws/?pid=15828.
111. Orwell, *1984*, 249. Emphasis in original.

112. Naomi Wolf, *The End of America: Letter of Warning to a Young Patriot* (White River Junction: VT: Chelsea Green Publishing, 2007), 126.
113. Rich, *Greatest Story Ever Sold*, 13.
114. Bush, quoted in Daniel Benjamin, "Saddam Hussein and Al Qaeda Are Not Allies," *New York Times*, September 30, 2002.
115. Sen. Carl Levin, "Levin Says Newly Declassified Information Indicates Bush Administration's Use of Pre-War Intelligence Was Misleading," U.S. Senate press release, November 6, 2005, http://levin.senate.gov/newsroom/release.cfm?id=248339.
116. Bush, White House Press release, September 26, 2002.
117. John Milton, *Paradise Lost* (London: Cassell and Company, 1894), 262.
118. Thomas Jefferson, in *Memoir, Correspondence and Miscellanies, from the Papers of Thomas Jefferson,* (Charlottesville: F. Carr & co., 1829), 2:336.
119. Dan Balz and Terry M. Neal, "Bush Calls Gore an 'Obstacle to Reform,'" *Washington Post*, March 23, 2000.
120. Warren P. Strobel, "Study: Iraq Had No Link to al-Qaida: Pentagon Finds the 'Bulletproof' Prewar Evidence Turned Out Bogus, *Houston Chronicle*, March 11, 2008.
121. Roger Cressey, on *Countdown*, MSNBC, April 6, 2007. Cressey is a former member of the National Security Council under presidents Clinton and Bush.
122. Dick Cheney, quoted in "Meet the Press Transcript for Sept. 10, 2006 (http://www.msnbc.msn.com/id/14720480/).
123. Gore, *Assault on Reason*, 109.
124. Murphy and Purdum, "Farewell to All That," 149.
125. Bush, "President Bush Delivers Graduation Speech at West Point," White House news release, June 1, 2002, *http://georgewbush-whitehouse.archives.gov/news/releases/2002/06/20020601-3.html.*
126. Suskind, *One Percent Doctrine*, 163.
127. Ibid., 171.
128. Isikoff and Corn, *Hubris*, 105.
129. Suskind, *One Percent Doctrine*, 216.
130. Ibid., 214.
131. Ibid., 166.
132. Ibid., 150.
133. Mark Hosenball, Michael Isikoff, and Evan Thomas, "Cheney's Long Path to War," *Newsweek*, November 17, 2004, http://www.newsweek.com/id/60579.
134. Suskind, *One Percent Doctrine*, 164.
135. James Madison, *Letters and Other Writings of James Madison* (Philadelphia: J. B. Lippincott & Co., 1865), 3:277.
136. Suskind, *Price of Loyalty*, 120.
137. Suskind, *One Percent Doctrine*, 79. Emphasis in original.
138. Sen. Max Cleland, quoted in Ricks, *Fiasco*, 60.
139. Suskind, *One Percent Doctrine*, 328.
140. Bob Woodward, on *The Decider*, MSNBC, December 29, 2008.
141. Sen. Chuck Hagel, quoted in Isikoff and Corn, *Hubris*, 151.
142. Bush, "President Bush Meets with German Chancellor Schroeder," White House news release, May 23, 2002, http://georgewbush-whitehouse.archives.gov/news/releases/2002/05/20020523-1.html.
143. Isikoff and Corn, *Hubris*, 15.
144. Ibid., 16.
145. *Cost of War*, CNN, March 4, 2003, http://archives.cnn.com/TRANSCRIPTS/0303/04/ltm.05.html.
146. Ibid.
147. Ibid.
148. Paul Wolfowitz, testimony to House Budget Committee, February 27, 2003, quoted in Fallows, *Blind Into Baghdad*, 82.
149. Bob Herbert, "The $2 Trillion Nightmare," *New York Times*, March 4, 2008.
150. Fallows, *Blind Into Baghdad*, 65–66.
151. Paul Wolfowitz, quoted in ibid., 84.
152. Fallows, *Blind Into Baghdad*, 81.

153. Paul Wolfowitz, quoted in ibid., 98–99.

154. Fallows, *Blind Into Baghdad*, 82–83.

155. Paul Wolfowitz, quoted in James Fallows, "Karmic Justice," *The Atlantic*, December 7, 2008, http://jamesfallows.theatlantic.com/archives/2008/12/karmic_justice_gen_eric_shinse.php.

156. Isikoff and Corn, *Hubris*, 412.

157. A military analyst, quoted in ibid., 198.

158. McClellan, *What Happened*, 146.

159. Risen, *State of War*, 87.

160. Generally attributed to historian A. J. P. Taylor. See, e.g., Heilbrunn, "The Rumsfeld Doctrine."

161. Maureen Dowd, "A Wake Up Call for Hillary," *New York Times*, March 2, 2008.

162. Edmund Burke, *Burke's Works*, ed. James Prior (London: George Bell & Sons, 1886), 1:88.

163. George Washington, in *American Patriotism*, ed. Selim H. Peabody (New York: John B. Alden, 1886), 195.

164. Maureen Dowd, "Delusion and Illusion Worthy of Dickens," *New York Times*, January 25, 2006.

165. Sen. Bob Graham, quoted in Murphy and Purdum, "Farewell to All That," 100, 148. Graham was Democratic senator from Florida and chairman of the Senate Intelligence Committee.

166. Hersh, *Chain of Command*, 229–230.

167. Frank Rich, "Too Soon? It's Too Late for 'United 93,'" *New York Times*, May 7, 2006.

168. Fallows, *Blind Into Baghdad*, 122–123.

169. Richard Clarke, quoted in Shenon, *The Commission*, 286.

170. "Where Do We Go From Here?" editorial, *New York Times*, July 7, 2008.

171. Lt. Gen. Greg Newbold (Ret.), "Why Iraq Was a Mistake," *Time*, April 9, 2006, http://www.time.com/time/magazine/article/0,9171,1181587,00.html.

172. Fallows, *Blind Into Baghdad*, 125.

173. Ricks, *Fiasco*, 40, quoting Gen. Greg Newbold.

174. Richard Clarke, quoted in Fallows, *Blind Into Baghdad*, 127.

175. Ricks, *Fiasco*, 47.

176. Brent Scowcroft, "Don't Attack Saddam," editorial, *Wall Street Journal*, August 15, 2002. Scowcroft was U.S. National Security Advisor, 1974–1977 and 1989–1993.

177. Risen, *State of War*, 76.

178. Fallows, *Blind Into Baghdad*, 130.

179. Newbold, "Why Iraq Was a Mistake." *Time* magazine, editors foreword.

180. John Riggs, in "Gen. Riggs Joins in Call for Rumsfeld to Quit," NPR, April 13, 2006, http://www.npr.org/templates/story/story.php?storyId=5340711.

181. Maureen Dowd, "The Rummy Mutiny," *New York Times*, April 15, 2006.

182. Kerry, "A Right and Responsibility to Speak Out."

183. Gen. Anthony Zinni, quoted in Isikoff and Corn, *Hubris*, 28.

184. Frank Rich, "Someone Tell the President the War Is Over," *New York Times*, August 14, 2005.

185. Bush, "President Bush Outlines Iraqi Threat," White House press release, Cincinnati, OH, October 7, 2002, http://georgewbush-whitehouse.archives.gov/news/releases/2002/10/20021007-8.html.

186. Rich, "Someone Tell the President the War Is Over."

187. Frank Rich, "'We Do Not Torture' and Other Funny Stories," *New York Times*, November 13, 2005.

188. Bush, "President Bush Outlines Iraqi Threat."

189. Frank Rich, "Where Were You That Summer of 2001?" *New York Times*, February 25, 2007.

190. Scott McClellan, quoted in Murphy and Purdum, "Farewell to All That," 97.

191. Rich, "Karl and Scooter's Excellent Adventure."

192. Isikoff and Corn, *Hubris*, 6.

193. Michael Scheuer, quoted in Isikoff and Corn, *Hubris*, 123. Scheuer was a CIA analyst who once headed the Bin Laden unit.

194. Al Gore, "Remarks to Moveon.org," New York University, August 7, 2003, http://www.scoop.co.nz/stories/WO0308/S00109.htm.

195. McClellan, *What Happened*, 249.

196. Hersh, *Chain of Command*, 285.

197. Mark Hosenball, Michael Isikoff, and Evan Thomas, "How Dick Cheney Sold the War," *Newsweek*, November 17, 2003.

198. Rich, *Greatest Story Ever Sold*, 59.

199. Cheney, on *Meet the Press,* NBC, December 9, 2001.
200. Frank Rich, "One Step Closer to the Big Enchilada," *New York Times,* October 30, 2005.
201. James Risen, "Prague Discounts An Iraqi Meeting," *New York Times,* October 21, 2002.
202. Rich, *Greatest Story Ever Sold,* 65.
203. Isikoff and Corn, *Hubris,* 103.
204. Gore, *Assault on Reason,* 110.
205. Isikoff and Corn, *Hubris,* 102.
206. Roger Cressey, on *Countdown,* MSNBC, April 6, 2007.
207. Frank Rich, "Return to the Scene of the Crime," *New York Times,* August 27, 2006.
208. Rich, *Greatest Story Ever Sold,* 216.
209. Frank Rich, "As the Iraqis Stand Down, We'll Stand Up," *New York Times,* September 9, 2007.
210. Rich, *Greatest Story Ever Sold,* 59.
211. Condolezza Rice, on *Late Edition,* CNN, September 8, 2002, http://transcripts.cnn.com/TRANSCRIPTS/0209/08/le.00.html.
212. Risen, *State of War,* 92.
213. Gore, *Assault on Reason,* 104.
214. Hersh, *Chain of Command,* 231.
215. Michael R. Gordon and Judith Miller, "Threats and Responses," *New York Times,* September 8, 2002.
216. Frank Rich, "We're Not in Watergate Anymore," *New York Times,* July 10, 2005.
217. Risen, *State of War,* 92.
218. Fallows, *Blind Into Baghdad,* 138.
219. Dean, *Conservatives Without Conscience,* 160.
220. Robert Scheer, "The Big Lie Technique," *The Nation,* November 16, 2005.
221. Strobel, "Study: Iraq Had No Link to al-Qaida."
222. Greg Miller, "Democracy Domino Theory Not Credible," *Los Angeles Times,* March 14, 2003.
223. Bob Herbert, "Ike Saw It Coming," *New York Times,* February 27, 2006.
224. Don Van Natta Jr., "Bush Was Set on Path to War, Memo by British Adviser Says," *New York Times,* March 27, 2006.
225. Murphy and Purdum, "Farewell to All That," 151.
226. Philippe Sands, quoted in Rich, *Greatest Story Ever Sold,* 190. Sands is a British professor of international law.
227. Isikoff and Corn, *Hubris,* 180.
228. Don Van Natta Jr., "Bush Was Set on Path to War."
229. David Michael Green, "What Every American Should Know About Iraq," June 15, 2007, http://www.commondreams.org/archive/2007/06/15/1896/.
230. Tony Blair, quoted in "Indignation Grows in U.S. Over British Prewar Documents," *Los Angeles Times,* May 12, 2005.
231. Van Natta Jr., "Bush Was Set on Path to War."
232. Green, "What Every American Should Know About Iraq."
233. Van Natta, "Bush Was Set on Path to War."
234. Ricks, *Fiasco,* 58.
235. Rich, *Greatest Story Ever Sold,* 65.
236. Green, "What Every American Should Know About Iraq."
237. Rich, *Greatest Story Ever Sold,* 175–176.
238. Green, "What Every American Should Know About Iraq."
239. Rich, *Greatest Story Ever Sold,* 70.
240. Sir Richard Dearlove, quoting the Downing Street Memo, in Murphy and Purdum, "Farewell to All That," 149.
241. Rich, *Greatest Story Ever Sold,* 217.
242. A former intelligence official, quoted in Hersh, *Chain of Command,* 218–219.
243. Rich, *Greatest Story Ever Sold,* 189.
244. Gore, *Assault on Reason,* 111–112.
245. Frank Rich, "Why Libby's Pardon Is a Slam Dunk," *New York Times,* March 11, 2007.
246. Isikoff and Corn, *Hubris,* 59.
247. Rich, "Karl and Scooter's Excellent Adventure."
248. Frank Rich, "All the President's Flacks," *New York Times,* December 4, 2005.

249. Lewis and Reading-Smith, "False Pretenses."
250. Bush, quoted in McClellan, *What Happened*, 140.
251. Paul Krugman, "Yes He Would," *New York Times*, April 10, 2006.
252. McClellan, *What Happened*, 144–145.
253. Bush, "President Discusses Economy, Iraq in Cabinet Meeting," White House press release, June 17, 2004, http://georgewbush-whitehouse.archives.gov/news/releases/2004/06/20040617-3.html.
254. Gore, *Assault on Reason*, 109.
255. Walter Pincus and Dana Milbank, "Al Qaeda-Hussein Link Is Dismissed," *Washington Post*, June 17, 2004.
256. Gore, *Assault on Reason*, 112.
257. Clarke, *Against All Enemies*, 244.
258. Brent Scowcroft, "Don't Attack Saddam."
259. Newbold, "Why Iraq Was a Mistake."
260. Risen, *State of War*, 4.
261. Abe Rosenthal, quoted in "Abe Rosenthal of The Times," editorial, *New York Times*, May 12, 2006.
262. Martin Luther King Jr. quoted in William Ury, *The Power of a Positive No* (New York: Random House, 2007), 14.
263. Kerry, "A Right and Responsibility to Speak Out."
264. "Hussein-Qaeda Link 'Inappropriate,' Report Says" *New York Times*, April 6, 2007.
265. Fallows, *Blind Into Baghdad*, 8.
266. "The Build-a-War Workshop," editorial, *New York Times*, February 10, 2007.
267. John W. Dean, *Worse Than Watergate: The Secret Presidency of George W. Bush* (New York: Warner Books, 2004), 140.
268. Cheney, on *Meet the Press*, NBC, March 16, 2003.
269. *The Economist*, quoted in Anthony Lewis, "The Imperial Presidency," *New York Times*, Nov. 4, 2007.
270. Col. Kevin Benson, quoted in Isikoff and Corn, *Hubris*, 197. Benson was a Third Army officer assigned by CENTCOM to draft plans for post invasion Iraq.
271. Maj. Gen. Paul Eaton (Ret.) U.S. Army, on *Hardball*, MSNBC, May 14, 2007.
272. Gore, *Assault on Reason*, 114–115.
273. Maureen Dowd, "Didn't See It Coming, Again," *New York Times*, February 1, 2006.
274. Donald Rumsfeld, Town Hall Meeting at Aviano Air Base, Italy, February 7, 2003 (quoted in, e.g., Dana Milbank, "Upbeat Tone Ended with War," *Washington Post*, March 29, 2003).
275. Fallows, *Blind Into Baghdad*, 71.
276. Lewis and Reading-Smith, "False Pretenses."
277. Hersh, *Chain of Command*, 225.
278. Suskind, *The Price of Loyalty*, 109.
279. Bush, "Address Before a Joint Session of the Congress on the State of the Union," January 28, 2003, http://www.presidency.ucsb.edu/ws/index.php?pid=29645.
280. Lewis and Reading-Smith, "False Pretenses."
281. Charles Krauthammer, "Redefining the War," *Washington Post*, February 1, 2002.
282. Ricks, *Fiasco*, 49.
283. Dana Priest and Walter Pincus, "Bush Certainty On Iraq Arms Went Beyond Analysts' Views," *Washington Post*, June 7, 2003.
284. Krugman, "Yes He Would."
285. Bush, "Address Before a Joint Session of the Congress on the State of the Union," January 28, 2003.
286. A retired ambassador, quoted in Isikoff and Corn, *Hubris*, 245.
287. Peter Eisner, "How Bogus Letter Became a Case for War," *Washington Post*, April 3, 2007.
288. Cheney, quoted in Michael R. Gordon, "Cheney Rejects Criticism By Allies Over Stand on Iraq," *New York Times*, February 16, 2002.
289. Jonathan S. Landay, "What It Can't Detect in Iraq Worries U.S.," *Philadelphia Inquirer*, September 8, 2002.
290. Cheney, quoted in "The Vice President Appears on Late Edition," White House news release, March 24, 2002, http://georgewbush-whitehouse.archives.gov/vicepresident/news-speeches/speeches/vp20020324-2.html.
291. Landay, "What It Can't Detect in Iraq Worries U.S."

292. Cheney, "Vice President Speaks at VFW 103rd National Convention," White House news release, August 26, 2002, http://georgewbush-whitehouse.archives.gov/news/releases/2002/08/20020826.html.

293. "The Truth About the War," editorial, *New York Times*, June 6, 2008.

294. Suskind, *One Percent Doctrine*, 168–169.

295. Ricks, *Fiasco*, 50.

296. Gen. Anthony Zinni, on *Meet the Press*, NBC, April 15, 2007.

297. Thomas Ricks, "For Vietnam Vet Anthony Zinni, Another War on Shaky Territory," *Washington Post*, December 23, 2003.

298. Walter Pincus, "U.S. Lacks Specifics on Banned Arms," *Washington Post*, March 16, 2003.

299. Ricks, *Fiasco*, 51.

300. Landay, "What It Can't Detect in Iraq Worries U.S."

301. Hersh, *Chain of Command*, 231, 232.

302. A former high-level intelligence official, quoted in Hersh, *Chain of Command*, 233.

303. Colin Powell, "Remarks at the World Economic Forum," Secretary of State Press Release, January 26, 2003, http://docs.google.com/viewer?a=v&q=cache:9HJ_VTuTy6QJ:merln.ndu.edu/archivepdf/nss/state/16869.pdf+Colin+Powell,+%E2%80%9CRemarks+at+the+World+Economic+Forum,%E2%80%9D&hl=en&gl=us&pid=bl&srcid=ADGEEShEALr3jmjw_SqFBgtldRaDJEnVazhqpgigLtudHv6TO8UmEhTlgHJuvz1qhahBlOy3LwfIfZgjISnx2kITgIXjUX-Zhk1EKFHIENDQrWQrx5RcjHsfFIKlYURE0TjIS3OzL4R56&sig=AHIEtbSbNUIc2tcCi-tYJQE3DafZaaBXlrg.

304. Condoleezza Rice, "Why We Know Iraq Is Lying," *New York Times*, January 23, 2003.

305. Colin Powell, "A Policy of Evasion and Deception," United Nations speech, February 5, 2003, http://www.washingtonpost.com/wp-srv/nation/transcripts/powelltext_020503.html.

306. Lewis and Reading-Smith, "False Pretenses."

307. John M. Broder, "Powell Tried to Warn Bush on Iraq, Book Says," *New York Times*, October 1, 2006.

308. Jacob Weisberg, "Fishing for a Way to Change the World," *Newsweek,* January 28, 2008, 32.

309. Frank Rich, "Why Dick Cheney Cracked Up," *New York Times*, February 4, 2007.

310. Mohamed ElBaredei, in "IAEA Sees Progress in Identifying Iraq's Nuclear Capabilities, Security Council Told," UN News Centre, March 7, 2003, http://www.un.org/apps/news/storyAr.asp?NewsID=6380&Cr=iraq&Cr1=inspect. ElBaredei was International Atomic Energy Agency Director-General.

311. Rich, *Greatest Story Ever Sold*, 70–71.

312. "A Spy Speaks Out," *60 Minutes*, CBS News, April 23, 2006, http://www.cbsnews.com/stories/2006/04/21/60minutes/main1527749.shtml.

313. Hersh, *Chain of Command*, 240.

314. Peter Eisner, "How Bogus Letter Became a Case for War," *Washington Post*, April 3, 2007.

315. Joby Warrick, "Some Evidence on Iraq Called Fake," *Washington Post*, March 8, 2003.

316. Hersh, *Chain of Command*, 205.

317. ElBaredei, in "IAEA Sees Progress in Identifying Iraq's Nuclear Capabilities, Security Council Told."

318. Cheney, on *Meet the Press*, NBC, March 16, 2003, http://www.mtholyoke.edu/acad/intrel/bush/cheneymeetthepress.htm.

319. An anonymous senior IAEA official, quoted in Hersh, *Chain of Command*, 205.

320. Peter Eisner, "How Bogus Letter Became a Case for War," *Washington Post*, April 3, 2007.

321. Bob Kerrey, quoted in Seymour M. Hersh, "Selective Intelligence," *New Yorker*, May 12, 2003, 44.

322. Melvin Goodman, quoted in Craig Unger, "The War They Wanted," *Vanity Fair*, July 2006, http://www.vanityfair.com/politics/features/2006/07/yellowcake200607. Goodman is a former CIA and State Department analyst.

323. Sen. Jay Rockefeller, quoted in Walter Pincus (with additional reporting by Bob Woodward), "U.S. Lacks Specifics on Banned Arms," *Washington Post*, March 16, 2003. Rockefeller was chairman of the Senate Select Committee on Intelligence.

324. Drumheller, in "A Spy Speaks Out."

325. Isikoff and Corn, *Hubris*, 412.

326. Rich, "As the Iraqis Stand Down."

327. Barton Gellman and Dana Linzer, "A 'Concerted Effort' to Discredit Bush Critic," *Washington Post* April 9, 2006.

328. Walter Pincus, "CIA Did Not Share Doubt on Iraq Data: Bush Used Report of Uranium Bid," *Washington Post*, June 12, 2003.

329. Risen, *State of War*, 6.

330. Unger, "The War They Wanted."

331. Pincus, "CIA Did Not Share Doubt on Iraq Data."

332. Walter Pincus, "CIA Says It Cabled Key Data to White House," *Washington Post*, June 13, 2003.

333. Unger, "The War They Wanted."

334. Lawrence Wilkerson, quoted in Unger, ibid. Wilkerson was a top aide and later chief of staff to Secretary of State Colin Powell.

335. Unger, "The War They Wanted."

336. Hosenball, Isikoff, and Thomas, "How Dick Cheney Sold the War."

337. Hersh, *Chain of Command*, 221–222.

338. Suskind, *One Percent Doctrine*, 177.

339. Barton Gellman and Walter Pincus, "Depiction of Threat Outgrew Supporting Evidence," *Washington Post*, August 10, 2003.

340. Rep. Henry A. Waxman, "Memorandum Re: The President's Claim that Iraq Sought Uranium from Niger," December 18, 2008, http://www.google.com/search?q=Rep.+Henry+A.+Waxman%2C+%E2%80%9CMemorandum+Re%3A+The+President%E2%80%99s+Claim+that+Iraq+Sought+Uranium+from+Niger%2C%E2%80%9D+December+18%2C+2008&ie=utf-8&oe=utf-8&aq=t&rls=org.mozilla:en-US:official&client=firefox-a. Waxman is chair of the House Committee on Oversight and Government Reform.

341. Robert Scheer, "Bad Iraq Data From Start to Finish," *Los Angeles Times*, June 10, 2003.

342. Waxman, "Memorandum Re: The President's Claim that Iraq Sought Uranium from Niger."

343. Condoleezza Rice, quoted in Scheer, "Bad Iraq Data From Start to Finish."

344. "House Oversight committee says new evidence contradicts White House uranium claims," OhMyGov.com, December 18, 2008, http://ohmygov.com/blogs/general_news/archive/2008/12/18/house-oversight-committee-says-new-evidence-contradicts-white-house-uranium-claims.aspx.

345. Waxman, "Memorandum Re: The President's Claim that Iraq Sought Uranium from Niger."

346. "House Oversight committee says new evidence contradicts White House uranium claims."

347. Waxman, "Memorandum Re: The President's Claim that Iraq Sought Uranium from Niger."

348. Dean, *Worse Than Watergate*, 143.

349. Isikoff and Corn, *Hubris*, 64.

350. Waxman, "Memorandum Re: The President's Claim that Iraq Sought Uranium from Niger."

351. Cheney, quoted in "In Cheney's Words: The Administration Case for Removing Saddam Hussein," *New York Times*, August 27, 2002.

352. Rich, "Karl and Scooter's Excellent Adventure."

353. Bush, "President Bush's Weekly Radio Address," Federal News Service, September 14, 2002.

354. John Adams, *The Works of John Adams* (Boston: Little, Brown and Company 1856), 377.

355. Ricks, *Fiasco*, 46.

356. Cheney, quoted on *News Hour*, PBS, August 7, 2002.

357. An anonymous senior CIA official, quoted in Suskind, *One Percent Doctrine*, 189.

358. Scowcroft, "Don't Attack Saddam."

359. Pincus, "U.S. Lacks Specifics on Banned Arms."

360. "Bush: The Orwell Presidency," Daily Kos, March 1, 2006, http://www.dailykos.com/story/2006/3/1/151651/0701/352/190838.

361. Isikoff and Corn, *Hubris*, 328.

362. Ricks, *Fiasco*, 376.

363. Isikoff and Corn, *Hubris*, 328–329.

364. Dean, *Worse Than Watergate*, 141.

365. Murray Waas, "Insulating Bush," *National Journal*, March 30, 2006, http://news.nationaljournal.com/articles/0330nj1.htm.

366. Ibid.

367. Peter Eisner, "How Bogus Letter Became a Case for War," *Washington Post*, April 3, 2007.

368. John Adams, in *The Works of John Adams, Second President of the United States*, ed. Charles Francis Adams (Boston: Little Brown, 1856), 1:113.
369. Rich, *Greatest Story Ever Sold*, 72.
370. Frankel, "Washington Back Channel."
371. Suskind, *One Percent Doctrine*, 244.
372. David E. Sanger and David Johnston, "With One Filing, Prosecutor Puts Bush in Spotlight," *New York Times*, April 11, 2006.
373. Greenwald, *Tragic Legacy*, 5.
374. Marie Brenner, "Lies and Consequences: Sixteen Words That Changed the World," *Vanity Fair*, April 2006.
375. Ricks, *Fiasco*, 52 (emphasis added).
376. Peter Zimmerman, quoted in Isikoff and Corn, *Hubris*, 134. Zimmerman was Senate Foreign Relations Committee scientific adviser.
377. Ibid.
378. Ricks, *Fiasco*, 52–53.
379. Isikoff and Corn, *Hubris*, 135.
380. Ibid., 137.
381. Peter Zimmerman, quoted in Isikoff and Corn, *Hubris*, 137–138.
382. Ricks, *Fiasco*, 54–55.
383. Greg Theilmann, quoted in Ricks, *Fiasco*, 54–55.
384. Gen. Gregory Newbold, quoted in Ricks, *Fiasco*, 55.
385. A former Cheney aide, quoted in Hersh, *Chain of Command*, 228.
386. Cheney, quoted in Robin Wright, "Threat by Iraq Grows, U.S. Says," *Los Angeles Times*, September 9, 2002.
387. Rich, "Karl and Scooter's Excellent Adventure."
388. Ricks, *Fiasco*, 54.
389. Isikoff and Corn, *Hubris*, 33.
390. Sen. Bob Graham, quoted at Isikoff and Corn, *Hubris*, 140.
391. Ricks, *Fiasco*, 58.
392. Ibid., 82.
393. Hans Blix, quoted in Murphy and Purdum, "Farewell to All That," 149–150. **Blix was** chief weapons inspector for the United Nations.
394. Maureen Dowd, "Back Off, Syria and Iran!" *New York Times*, March 30, 2003.
395. Bush, "President Says Saddam Hussein Must Leave Iraq Within 48 Hours," White House news release, March 17, 2003, http://georgewbush-whitehouse.archives.gov/news/releases/2003/03/20030317-7.html.
396. Lewis and Reading-Smith, "False Pretenses." Emphasis in original.
397. Charles Duelfer, on *The Rachel Maddow Show*, MSNBC, February 27, 2009. Duelfer led the CIA weapons inspection team in Iraq after the war began.
398. Isikoff and Corn, *Hubris*, 374.
399. Greg Miller, "Senate War Report Rebukes Bush, Cheney," *Los Angeles Times*, June 6, 2008.
400. Richard Clarke, on *Countdown*, MSNBC, June 5, 2008.
401. Ricks, *Fiasco*, 59.
402. Sen. Jay Rockefeller, quoted in Greg Miller, "Panel: Bush Exaggerated Pre-War Data," *Chicago Tribune*, June 6, 2008.
403. "The Truth About the War," editorial, *New York Times*, June 6, 2008.
404. Isikoff and Corn, *Hubris*, 18.
405. Sen. Jay Rockefeller, quoted in Jonathan S. Landay, "Intelligence Didn't Support Going to War, Panel Finds," *St. Paul Pioneer-Press*, June 6, 2008.
406. "The Truth About the War."
407. Landay, "Intelligence Didn't Support Going to War, Panel Finds."
408. Richard Clarke, on *Countdown*, MSNBC, June 5, 2008.
409. "The Truth About the War."
410. Sen. Jay Rockefeller, quoted in Miller, "Senate War Report Rebukes Bush, Cheney."
411. Frank Rich, "The Sunshine Boys Can't Save Iraq," *New York Times*, December 10, 2006.
412. Dean, *Worse Than Watergate*, 152. Emphasis in original.
413. Gore, *Assault on Reason*, 178.

414. Lewis and Reading-Smith, "False Pretenses."
415. Bush, "President Bush Discusses Iraq Report," October 7, 2004, http://www.globalsecurity. org/wmd/library/news/iraq/2004/10/iraq-041007-whitehouse01.htm.
416. Isikoff and Corn, *Hubris*, 375.
417. James Madison, "Universal Peace," in *The Writings of James Madison* (New York: G. P. Putnam's Sons, 1906), 6:90.
418. Gore, *Assault on Reason*, 103.
419. John Jay, *The Federalist Papers*, No. 4, ed. Clinton Rossiter (New York: Penguin, 1961), 46.
420. Gore, *Assault on Reason*, 119.
421. McClellan, *What Happened*, 119.
422. Thomas Jefferson, *Life, Writings, and Opinions of Thomas Jefferson*, ed. B. L. Rayner (New York: A. Francis and W. Boardman, 1832), 219.
423. Green, "What Every American Should Know About Iraq."
424. Bob Drogin and John Goetz, "The Curveball Saga: How U.S. Fell Under the Spell of 'Curveball,'" *Los Angeles Times*, November 20, 2005.
425. Tom Regan, "Germany: CIA Knew 'Curveball' Was Not Trustworthy," *Christian Science Monitor*, November 21, 2005.
426. David Kay, quoted in Murphy and Purdum, "Farewell to All That," 152–153. Kay was chief U.S. weapons inspector in Iraq.
427. Drogin and Goetz, "The Curveball Saga."
428. Christopher Dickey, "The Constitution in Peril," *Newsweek*, October 8, 2007.
429. McClellan, *What Happened*, 49.
430. Joschka Fischer, quoted in Murphy and Purdum, "Farewell to All That," 153. Fischer was German foreign minister and vice-chancellor. Emphasis in original.
431. Regan, "Germany: CIA Knew 'Curveball' Was Not Trustworthy."
432. Drogin and Goetz, "The Curveball Saga."
433. "Friends Like This," editorial, *New York Times*, May 21, 2004.
434. David Reiff, "Blueprint for a Mess," *New York Times*, November 2, 2003.
435. Douglas Jehl, "Pentagon Pays Iraq Group, Supplier of Incorrect Spy Data," *New York Times*, March 11, 2004.
436. Steven R. Weisman, "Chalabi, as Iraqi Deputy, Gets a Cautious Welcome in Washington," *New York Times*, November 9, 2005. Hersh, *Chain of Command*, 212.
437. Leslie H. Gelb, "Neoconner," *New York Times*, April 27, 2008.
438. David E. Sanger, "A Seat of Honor Lost to Open Political Warfare," *New York Times*, May 21, 2004.
439. Krugman, "Yes He Would."
440. Waas, "Insulating Bush."
441. Frank Rich, "Eight Days in July," *New York Times*, July 24, 2005.
442. David Corn, "A White House Smear," *The Nation*, July 16, 2006, http://www.commondreams.org/views03/0717-13.htm.
443. Nicholas Kristoff, "Missing In Action: Truth," *New York Times*, May 6, 2003.
444. McClellan, *What Happened*, 8.
445. Bush, "President Discusses Job Creation With Business Leaders," White House news release, September 30, 2003, http://georgewbush-whitehouse.archives.gov/news/releases/2003/09/20030930-9.html.
446. Bush, quoted in McClellan, *What Happened*, 294.
447. Maureen Dowd, "Wag the Camel," *New York Times*, April 12, 2006.
448. McClellan, *What Happened*, 295.
449. Rich, *Greatest Story Ever Sold*, 187.
450. Peter Eisner, "How Bogus Letter Became a Case for War," *Washington Post*, April 3, 2007.
451. "A Libby Verdict" editorial, *New York Times*, March 7, 2007.
452. Joseph C. Wilson IV, quoted in Hersh, *Chain of Command*, 242. Wilson was U.S. ambassador to Gabon from 1992 to 1995.
453. Frank Rich, "The Two Wars of the Worlds," *New York Times*, July 3, 2005.
454. Frank Rich, "What I Didn't Find in Africa," *New York Times*, July 6, 2003.
455. Frank Rich, "We're Not in Watergate Anymore," *New York Times*, July 10, 2005.
456. McClellan, *What Happened*, 1–2.
457. Ibid., 171.

458. Robert D. Novak, "Mission to Niger," *Washington Post*, July 14, 2003.
459. Allen and Priest, "Bush Administration Is Focus of Inquiry."
460. Wilson, "What I Didn't Find in Africa."
461. Rich, "Why Dick Cheney Cracked Up."
462. Mike Allen and Dana Priest, "Bush Administration Is Focus of Inquiry: CIA Agent's Identity Was Leaked to Media," *Washington Post*, September 28, 2003.
463. Waas, "Insulating Bush."
464. McClellan, *What Happened*, 173.
465. Ibid., 168.
466. Joseph Wilson IV, quoted in David Gelber and Joel Bach, "CIA Spy Speaks Out," Common Dreams, http://www.commondreams.org/headlines06/0424-03.htm.
467. "Bush Acknowledges Declassifying Intelligence," CNN, April 10, 2006, http://www.cnn.com/2006/POLITICS/04/10/whitehouse.leak/index.html.
468. David E. Sanger and David Johnston, "With One Filing, Prosecutor Puts Bush in Spotlight," *New York Times*, April 11, 2006.
469. Ibid.
470. McClellan, *What Happened*, 3–4.
471. Rich, "One Step Closer."
472. Wilson, "What I Didn't Find in Africa."
473. Jim Rutenberg, "Trial Spotlights Cheney's Power as an Infighter," *New York Times*, February 20, 2007.
474. "A Libby Verdict" editorial, *New York Times*, March 7, 2007.
475. Murray Waas, "Cheney 'Authorized' Libby to Leak Classified Information," *National Journal*, February 9, 2006, http://nationaljournal.com/about/njweekly/stories/2006/0209nj1.htm.
476. Jean-Jacques Rousseau, quoted in *Memorable Quotations: French Writers of the Past*, Carol A. Dingle, ed. (iUniverse, 2000), 148.
477. Rich, "Why Dick Cheney Cracked Up."
478. Murray Waas, "Bush Directed Cheney To Counter War Critic," *National Journal*, July 3, 2006, http://news.nationaljournal.com/articles/0703nj1.htm.
479. David Ignatius, "A Failed Cover-Up: What the Libby Trial is Revealing," *Washington Post*, February 2, 2007.
480. Orwell, *1984*, 213.
481. Maureen Dowd, "Smoking Dutch Cleanser," *New York Times*, February 11, 2006.
482. Bob Herbert, "Lift the Curtain" *New York Times*, March 8, 2007.
483. Dana Milbank, "Through the Looking Glass, Darkly," *Washington Post*, July 4, 2007.
484. David G. Savage and Richard B. Schmitt, "Bush Spares Libby from Prison," *Los Angeles Times*, July 3, 2007.
485. Dan Froomkin, "Obstruction of Justice, Continued," washingtonpost.com, http://www.washingtonpost.com/wp-dyn/content/blog/2007/07/03/BL2007070301366.html, July 3, 2007.
486. Marcy Wheeler, "Just Another Obstruction of Justice," *The Guardian*, July 3, 2007, http://www.guardian.co.uk/commentisfree/2007/jul/03/libbysentenceagain.
487. David Corn, "Bush Commutes Libby's Jail Sentence," *The Nation*, July 7, 2007, http://www.democraticunderground.com/discuss/duboard.php?az=view_all&address=103x292120.
488. "Soft On Crime," editorial, *New York Times*, July 3, 2007.
489. "Bush Flouts Law in Favor of Libby," editorial, *San Jose Mercury News*, July 3, 2007.
490. Joseph Wilson, quoted in Richard Leiby and Walter Pincus, "Retired Envoy: Nuclear Report Ignored," *Washington Post*, July 6, 2003.
491. Keith Olbermann, on *Countdown*, MSNBC, July 3, 2007.
492. Thomas Paine, from "The Crisis," in *The Political Works of Thomas Paine* (Chicago: Belfords, Clarke & Co., 1879), 185.
493. Joseph Wilson, on *Countdown*, MSNBC, July 2, 2007.
494. Isikoff and Corn, *Hubris*, 19.
495. Joseph Wilson, on *Countdown*, MSNBC, November 21, 2007.
496. Bush, quoted in Isikoff and Corn, *Hubris*, 2. The statement was made in April 2002.
497. Michael Gordon and Bernard E. Trainor, *Cobra II: the Inside Story of the Invasion and Occupation of Iraq* (New York: Pantheon, 2006), 51–52.
498. Rich, *Greatest Story Ever Sold*, 62.

499. John Milton, "Paradise Lost," in *The Portable Milton*, ed. Douglas Bush (New York: Viking Penguin, 1977), 251.

500. Jean-Jacques Rousseau, *The Social Contract* (New York: Simon and Schuster, 1970), 9.

501. Rich, *Greatest Story Ever Sold*, 62.

502. Isikoff and Corn, *Hubris*, 81.

503. Bush, "President Visits Coffee Shop," White House press release, December 31, 2002.

504. Fallows, *Blind Into Baghdad*, 113.

505. Clarke, *Against All Enemies*, 244.

506. Peter Zimmerman, quoted in Isikoff and Corn, *Hubris*, 119. Zimmerman was Senate Foreign Relations Committee scientific adviser.

507. James Madison, *The Federalist Papers*, No. 41, ed. Clinton Rossiter (New York: Penguin, 1961), 260.

508. Thomas Paine, "The Crisis," in *The Works of Thomas Paine* (Philadelphia: E. Haskell, 1854), 3:20.

509. Woodward, *Plan of Attack*, 270.

510. Rich, *The Greatest Story Ever Sold*, 218 (emphasis added).

511. Risen, *State of War*, 3.

512. Walter Pincus and Dana Milbank, "Bush Clings To Dubious Allegations About Iraq," *Washington Post*, March 18, 2003.

513. "George Tenet: At the Center of the Storm," *60 Minutes*, CBS, April 29, 2007, http://www.cbsnews.com/stories/2007/04/25/60minutes/main2728375_page5.shtml.

514. Walter Pincus and Karen DeYoung, "Analysts' Warnings of Iraq Chaos Detailed," *Washington Post*, May 26, 2007.

515. Walter Cronkite and David Krieger, "Our Troops Must Leave Iraq," Common Dreams News Center, December 4, 2007, http://www.commondreams.org/archive/2007/12/04/5598/.

516. Fallows, *Blind Into Baghdad*, 47–48.

Chapter 7: Post-Invasion Iraq: The House of Cards Collapses

1.   Sen. Hiram Johnson, speech, U.S. Senate, February 3, 1917. See Tom Goldstein, *Journalism and Truth* (Evanston, IL: Northwestern University Press, 2007), 87.

2.   James Risen, *State of War: The Secret History of the CIA and the Bush Administration* (New York: Free Press, 2006), 123.

3.   George W. Bush, "Press Conference by the President," White House press release, October 25, 2006, http://georgewbush-whitehouse.archives.gov/news/releases/2006/10/20061025.html.

4.   "Senate committee approves Gates nomination," CNN, December 6, 2006, http://www.cnn.com/2006/POLITICS/12/05/gates.confirmation/index.html.

5.   James Madison, "Political Observations," in *Letters and Other Writings of James Madison* (Philadelphia: J. B. Lippincott, 1865), 4:491–492.

6.   Charles Duelfer, on *The Rachel Maddow Show*, MSNBC, February 27, 2009. Duelfer led the CIA weapons inspection team in Iraq after the war began.

7.   Juan Cole, "Civil war? What civil war?" *Salon*, March 23, 2006, http://www.salon.com/opinion/feature/2006/03/23/civil_war/index.html.

8.   George Orwell, *1984* (New York: Penguin, 1949), 215.

9.   Charles Duelfer, *Hide and Seek: The Search for Truth in Iraq* (New York: Public Affairs, 2009), 473.

10. Bush, quoted in "Bush: The Orwell Presidency," Daily Kos, March 1, 2006, http://www.dailykos.com/story/2006/3/1/151651/0701/352/190838.

11. Albert Einstein, *Einstein on Peace* (New York: Avnel, 1981), 397.

12. Edmund Burke, in *Speeches on the American War and Letters to the Sheriffs of Bristol* (Boston: D. C. Heath and Co., Boston, 1891), 183.

13. David Michael Green, "What Every American Should Know About Iraq," June 15, 2007, http://www.commondreams.org/archive/2007/06/15/1896/.

14. James Madison, *The Federalist on the New Constitution* (Glazier, Masters & co., 1831), 499–501.

15. Bush, declaring war on Iraq, March 16, 2003, White House press release, March 17, 2003, http://georgewbush-whitehouse.archives.gov/news/releases/2003/03/20030317-7.html.

16. Al Gore, *The Assault on Reason* (New York: Penguin, 2007), 104.

17. Green, "What Every American Should Know About Iraq."

18. Hans Blix, March 19, 2003, quoted in Frank Rich, "The Ides of March 2003," *New York Times*, March 18, 2007. Blix was chief weapons inspector for the United Nations.
19. John Locke, *An Essay Concerning Human Understanding* (London: Tegg, 1841), 522.
20. Bush, quoted in "The President's Address About Military Action in Iraq," The Miami Herald, March 20, 2003.
21. Martin Luther King Jr. *Strength to Love* (Philadelphia: Fortress Press, 1982), 14.
22. Gen. Anthony Zinni, quoted in Thomas E. Ricks, "Ex-Envoy Criticizes Bush's Postwar Policy," *Washington Post*, September 5, 2003.
23. James Fallows, *Blind Into Baghdad: America's War In Iraq* (New York, Vintage, 2006), 76.
24. David Margolick, "The Night of the Generals," *Vanity Fair*, April 2007, 276.
25. Gen. Anthony Zinni, on *Meet the Press*, NBC, April 15, 2007.
26. "Secretary Rumsfeld Remarks on ABC 'This Week with George Stephanopoulos,'" March 30, 2003, U.S. Department of Defense transcript, http://www.defenselink.mil/transcripts/transcript.aspx?transcriptid=2185.
27. Donald Rumsfeld, quoted in Michael Isikoff and David Corn, *Hubris: The Inside Story of Spin, Scandal, and the Selling of the Iraq War* (New York: Crown, 2006), 315. Rumsfeld had been asked to explain his assertion that "we know where the WMDs are."
28. Lt. Cmdr. Richard Riggs, quoted in Thomas E. Ricks, *Fiasco: The American Military Adventure in Iraq* (New York: Penguin, 2006), 377.
29. Bush, quoted in "Bush Warns of Iran's Influence over Iraq," FoxNews.com, August 29, 2007, http://www.foxnews.com/story/0,2933,294932,00.html.
30. Abraham Lincoln, in *Abraham Lincoln: Complete Works, Comprising His Speeches, Letters, State Papers, and Miscellaneous Writings* (New York: The Century Co., 1907), 112.
31. Maj. Gen. John Batiste, on *Countdown*, MSNBC, October 2, 2006.
32. Gen. Anthony Zinni, on *Meet the Press*, NBC, April 15, 2007.
33. Maj. Gen. John Batiste, on *Countdown*, MSNBC, October 2, 2006.
34. Fallows, *Blind Into Baghdad*, 104.
35. A senior planner, quoted in Seymour M. Hersh, *Chain of Command: The Road From 9/11 to Abu Ghraib* (New York: Harper Collins, 2004), 255.
36. Paul Rieckhoff, on *Countdown*, MSNBC, September 12, 2007. Rieckhoff is Executive Director of Veterans of Iraq & Afghanistan.
37. Richard Wolffe, on *Countdown*, MSNBC, September 11, 2007.
38. Maureen Dowd, "Reach Out and Touch No One," *New York Times*, January 7, 2006.
39. Maureen Dowd, "Father and Son Reunion," *New York Times*, May 10, 2006.
40. Lt. Gen. Greg Newbold (Ret.), "Why Iraq Was a Mistake," *Time*, April 9, 2006. Newbold was the Pentagon's top operations officer.
41. Conrad C. Crane and W. Andrew Terrill, "Reconstructing Iraq: Insights, Challenges, and Missions for Military Forces in a Post-Conflict Scenario," Strategic Studies Institute, February 2003, v–vi, http://www.strategicstudiesinstitute.army.mil/pdffiles/PUB182.pdf.
42. Dick Cheney, quoted in Isikoff and Corn, *Hubris*, 414.
43. Fallows, *Blind Into Baghdad*, 59–60.
44. Maureen Dowd, "Don't Become Them," *New York Times*, May 27, 2006.
45. Rumsfeld, quoted in Rupert Cornwell, "Rumsfeld Under Fire for 'Hillbilly Armour' Used to Defend Army," December 11, 2004, http://www.independent.co.uk/news/world/americas/rumsfeld-under-fire-for-hillbilly-armour-used-to-defend-army-683269.html. Rumsfeld was responding to an Iraq-bound National Guardsman.
46. Frank Rich, *The Greatest Story Ever Sold: The Decline and Fall of Truth From 9/11 to Katrina* (New York: Penguin, 2006), 157.
47. Maureen Dowd, "Teaching Remedial Decency," *New York Times*, June 3, 2006.
48. Frank Rich, "The Longer the War, the Larger the Lies," *New York Times*, September 17, 2006.
49. Edward Wong, "Iraqis Plan to Ring Baghdad With Trenches," *New York Times*, September 15, 2006.
50. Isikoff and Corn, *Hubris*, 363.
51. Gen. Anthony Zinni, quoted in Thomas Ricks, "For Vietnam Vet Anthony Zinni, Another War on Shaky Territory," *Washington Post*, December 23, 2003.
52. Newbold, "Why Iraq Was a Mistake."

53. Dwight D. Eisenhower, (speech, Columbia University National Bicentennial Dinner, New York City, May 31, 1954), http://www.presidency.ucsb.edu/ws/index.php?pid=9906&st=&st1.

54. John M. Broder, "Powell Tried to Warn Bush on Iraq, Book Says," *New York Times* October 1, 2006.

55. David S. Cloud, "Ex-Commander Says Iraq Effort Is 'a Nightmare,'" *New York Times*, October 13, 2007.

56. Lt. Gen. Ricardo S. Sanchez, quoted in ibid.

57. Isikoff and Corn, *Hubris*, 410. Emphasis in original.

58. Fallows, *Blind Into Baghdad*, 88.

59. Paul Wolfowitz, in Peter Slevin and Dana Priest, "Wolfowitz Concedes Iraq Errors," *Washington Post*, July 24, 2003. Wolfowitz was Deputy Secretary of Defense, 2001–2005.

60. Fallows, *Blind Into Baghdad*, 99.

61. Joby Warrick, "Lacking Biolabs, Trailers Carried Case for War: Administration Pushed Notion of Banned Iraqi Weapons Despite Evidence to Contrary," *Washington Post*, April 12, 2006.

62. Bush, "Interview of the President by TVP, Poland," White House press release, May 29, 2003, http://georgewbush-whitehouse.archives.gov/g8/interview5.html.

63. Bob Woodward, *State of Denial: Bush at War, Part III* (New York: Simon & Schuster, 2006), 210.

64. Green, "What Every American Should Know About Iraq."

65. Cullen Murphy and Todd S. Purdum, "Farewell to All That: An Oral History of the Bush White House," *Vanity Fair*, February 2009, 152.

66. Glenn Greenwald, *A Tragic Legacy: How a Good vs. Evil Mentality Destroyed the Bush Presidency* (New York: Crown, 2007), 9–10. Emphasis in original.

67. Green, "What Every American Should Know About Iraq."

68. Frank Rich, "Follow the Uranium," *New York Times*, July 17, 2005.

69. Bush, *Public Papers of the Presidents of the United States: George W. Bush, 2004, Book 2* (Washington, D.C.: National Archives and Records Administration, 2008), p. 1262.

70. Isikoff and Corn, *Hubris*, 364.

71. Frank Rich, "Has He Started Talking to the Walls?" *New York Times*, December 3, 2006.

72. "President Bush Appears on Meet the Press," February 8, 2004, http://www.msnbc.msn.com/id/4179618/.

73. Scott McClellan, *What Happened: Inside the Bush White House and Washington's Culture of Deception* (New York: Public Affairs, 2008), 203. McClellan was Bush press secretary, 2003–2006.

74. Dennis v. United States, 341 U.S. 494, 556 (1951).

75. Robert Draper, on *The Decider*, MSNBC, December 29, 2008. Draper is the author of *Dead Certain: The Presidency of George W. Bush.*

76. Richard Clarke, *Against All Enemies: Inside America's War on Terror* (New York: Free Press, 2004), 266.

77. Todd S. Purdum, "Inside Bush's Bunker," *Vanity Fair*, October 2007, 394.

78. Cheney, on *Larry King Live*, CNN, May 30, 2005. Since Cheney's statement until he left office, nearly 2,600 Americans died in Iraq. See Iraq Coalition Casualty Count, http://icasualties.org/.

79. Frank Rich, "Sunday in the Market With McCain," *New York Times*, April 8, 2007.

80. Bush, quoted in Rich Lowry, "The 'W' is not for 'Wobble,'" National Review, September 13, 2006, http://article.nationalreview.com/?q=NDdiZGNlMjgxMzUxYTI1OTDdmMWFiMTE4 ZmZiMzc2ZDM=.

81. Oliver Wendell Holmes, "Natural Law," 32 *Harvard Law Review* 40 (1918), 40–41.

82. Duelfer, *Hide and Seek*, xiii.

83. "No Progress Report," editorial, *New York Times*, July 13, 2007.

84. Bush, "The President's News Conference," December 15, 2003, http://www.presidency.ucsb.edu/ws/index.php?pid=753.

85. Bush, "The President's News Conference," April 13, 2004, http://www.presidency.ucsb.edu/ws/index.php?pid=62604.

86. Bush, "The President's News Conference with Prime Minister Tony Blair of the United Kingdom," April 16, 2004, http://www.presidency.ucsb.edu/ws/index.php?pid=64670.

87. Bush, "The President's News Conference with President Alvaro Uribe of Columbia in Crawford, Texas," August 4, 2005, http://www.presidency.ucsb.edu/ws/index.php?pid=73868.

88. Bush, "President Bush's Remarks Upon Arrival in Utah," White House press release, August 30, 2006, http://georgewbush-whitehouse.archives.gov/news/releases/2006/08/20060830-10.html.

89. Attribution is unclear. The line has been credited to both Benjamin Franklin and Albert Einstein.

90. Jonathan Alter, on *Countdown,* MSNBC, April 20, 2007.

91. Frank Rich, "'We Do Not Torture' and Other Funny Stories," *New York Times,* November 13, 2005.

92. Sen. Carl Levin, "Levin Says Newly Declassified Information Indicates Bush Administration's Use of Pre-War Intelligence Was Misleading," U.S. Senate press release, November 6, 2005, http://levin.senate.gov/issues/index.cfm?MainIssue=Iraq&SubIssue=IraqIntelligenceInquiry.

93. Rich, "'We Do Not Torture.'"

94. Keith Olbermann, commentary, *Countdown,* MSNBC, November 20, 2006.

95. Bush, "President Bush's Speech on Iraq," September 13, 2007, http://www.npr.org/templates/story/story.php?storyId=14406922.

96. "No Exit, No Strategy," editorial, *New York Times,* September 14, 2007.

97. Gen. Anthony Zinni, quoted in Ricks, *Fiasco,* 242.

98. James Glanz and Christian Miller, "Official History Spotlights Iraq Rebuilding Blunders," *New York Times,* December 14, 2008.

99. "The Intelligence Business," editorial, *New York Times,* May 7, 2006.

100. Ibid.

101. Rumsfeld, on "Rumsfeld Faces Tough Questions at Atlanta Event," CNN, May 4, 2006.

102. Bush, quoted in Deborah Orin, "'Complete Victory' Plan'—Bush: Let Iraqis Take Lead and We'll Pull Out," *New York Post,* December 1, 2005.

103. Michael Ware, quoted on *Anderson Cooper 360,* CNN, November 30, 2005. Ware was an embedded journalist working for *Time* magazine.

104. Bush, "Address by the President to the Nation on the Way Forward in Iraq," White House press release, September 13, 2007, http://georgewbush-whitehouse.archives.gov/news/releases/2007/09/20070913-2.html.

105. Bobby Ghosh, on *Hardball,* MSNBC, September 14, 2007. Ghosh is world editor for *Time.*

106. Anne E. Kornblut, "Bush Proclaims a Victory Success In Iraq Turns Tide In War On Terrorism, He Says," *Boston Globe,* May 2, 2003.

107. John W. Dean, *Worse Than Watergate: The Secret Presidency of George W. Bush* (New York: Warner, 2004), 74.

108. Keith Olbermann, on *Countdown,* MSNBC, May 1, 2007.

109. Bush, "Bush Makes Historic Speech Aboard Warship," CNN, May 1, 2003, http://www.cnn.com/2003/US/05/01/bush.transcript/.

110. Elisabeth Bumiller, "Keepers of Bush Image Lift Stagecraft to New Heights," *New York Times,* May 16, 2003.

111. "A Bitter Iraq War Anniversary," editorial, *Chattanooga Times Free Press,* March 21, 2006.

112. Bush, "Bush Makes Historic Speech Aboard Warship."

113. Ricks, *Fiasco,* 145.

114. "Empty Calories," editorial, *New York Times,* September 11, 2007.

115. Bush, "Bush Makes Historic Speech Aboard Warship."

116. Frank Rich, "Eight Days in July," *New York Times,* July 24, 2005.

117. Keith Olbermann, on *Countdown,* MSNBC, May 1, 2007.

118. Richard Perle, "Relax, Celebrate Victory," editorial, *USA Today,* May 2, 2003. Perle was chair of the Defense Policy Board Advisory Committee 2001–2003 and is a self-described neoconservative who strongly advocated regime change in Iraq.

119. Roger Cressey, on *Countdown,* MSNBC, April 6, 2007. Cressey is a former member of the National Security Council under presidents Clinton and Bush.

120. Frank Rich, "Dying to Save the GOP Congress," *New York Times,* October 29, 2006.

121. Ricks, *Fiasco,* 374–375.

122. Frank Rich, "The Vietnamization of Bush's Vacation," *New York Times,* August 28, 2005.

123. Bush, "President Bush Makes Remarks on the Emergency Supplemental," White House press release, April 3, 2007, http://www.globalsecurity.org/wmd/library/news/iraq/2007/04/iraq-070403-whitehouse01.htm.

124. Gates, "DOD Extends Active Army Tours To 15 Months," April 11, 2007, http://thegate.nationaljournal.com/2007/04/dod_extends_active_army_tours_1.php.

125. Robert Kagan, "Lowering Our Sights," editorial, *Washington Post*, May 2, 2004. Kagan is a senior associate at the Carnegie Endowment for International Peace.

126. Thomas L. Friedman, "Insulting Our Troops, and Our Intelligence," *New York Times*, November 3, 2006.

127. Frank Rich, "Why Libby's Pardon Is a Slam Dunk," *New York Times*, March 11, 2007.

128. Rich, *Greatest Story Ever Sold*, 109.

129. Aaron Brown, *CNN Newsnight*, CNN, April 23, 2004.

130. Lee Cowan, *CBS Evening News*, CBS, April 23, 2004.

131. "Ex-NFL star Tillman makes 'ultimate sacrifice,'"April 26, 2004, http://www.msnbc.msn.com/id/4815441.

132. Frank Rich, "All the President's Press," *New York Times*, April 29, 2007.

133. Thomas Paine, "Addressed to the Opposers of the Bank," in *The Complete Writings of Thomas Paine* (New York: Citadel Press, 1969), 2:434.

134. Scott Lindlaw, "After Tillman Death, Army Clamped Down," Associated Press, April 21, 2007.

135. "Gen. Tried to Warn Bush on Tillman Death," Associated Press, March 31, 2007, http://www.cbsnews.com/stories/2007/03/30/national/main2630912.shtml.

136. "Pat Tillman's 'Friendly Fire' Death: A Criminal Charade," editorial, *Arizona Republic*, March 27, 2007.

137. "Seeking the Truth About Pat Tillman," editorial, *New York Times*, July 27, 2007.

138. "What Really Happened to Pat Tillman," *60 Minutes*, CBS, May 4, 2008, http://www.cbsnews.com/stories/2008/05/01/60minutes/main4061656.shtml.

139. "Waiting for the Truth on Corporal Tillman," editorial, *New York Times*, August 4, 2007.

140. "Gen. Tried to Warn Bush on Tillman Death."

141. Rich, *Greatest Story Ever Sold*, 129.

142. John F. Kennedy, June 11, 1962, http://www.jfklibrary.org/Historical+Resources/Archives/Reference+Desk/Speeches/JFK/003POF03Yale06111962.htm.

143. "Pat Tillman's 'Friendly Fire Death: A Criminal Charade," editorial, *Arizona Republic*, March 27, 2007.

144. Lindlaw, "After Tillman Death."

145. Patrick Tillman, quoted in Rich, *Greatest Story Ever Sold*, 129. Patrick is Pat's father.

146. Nancy Gibbs, "Showdown: As Congress Tangles with the President Over Iraq, a Lesson on Truth," *Time*, May 7, 2007, 19.

147. Scott Lindlaw, "Tillman Family Wants Congressional Probe," Associated Press, March 27, 2007, http://today.msnbc.msn.com/id/17810007/ns/us_news-military/.

148. Rich, "All the President's Press."

149. Ibid.

150. "Daybook," *Washington Post*, April 2, 2003.

151. "Bush Applauds Dramatic Rescue of US Soldier," White House Bulletin, April 2, 2003.

152. John Kampfner, "The Truth About Jessica," *The Guardian*, May 15, 2003, http://www.guardian.co.uk/Iraq/Story/0,2763,956255,00.html.

153. Malcom Morford, "The Big Lie of Jessica Lynch," *San Francisco Chronicle*, September 5, 2003.

154. Thomas Paine, *The Political Writings of Thomas Paine* (Middletown, NJ: G. H. Evans, 1839), 1:88.

155. Frank Rich, "Truthiness 101: From Frey to Alito," *New York Times*, January 22, 2006.

156. Nancy Gibbs, "The Private Jessica Lynch," *Time*, November 3, 2003, http://www.time.com/time/magazine/article/0,9171,538846-1,00.html.

157. Kampfner, "The Truth About Jessica."

158. Steve Ludwig, "Lights, Camera, Rescue," editorial, *Seattle-Post Intelligencer*, May 30, 2003.

159. Rich, *Greatest Story Ever Sold*, 82.

160. Morford, "The Big Lie of Jessica Lynch."

161. Caitlin A. Johnson, "Jessica Lynch Sets Record Straight," CBS, April 25, 2007, http://www.cbsnews.com/stories/2007/04/25/earlyshow/main2725423.shtml.

162. Jessica Lynch, quoted in David Gardner, "U.S. Soldier Hailed for Bravery in Iraq says Pentagon Spin Doctors Made it All Up," *Daily Mail* (London), April 25, 2007, http://www.

google.com/imgres?imgurl=http://img.dailymail.co.uk/i/pix/2007/04_02/Kinsbed_468x441.
jpg&imgrefurl=http://www.dailymail.co.uk/pages/live/articles/news/news.html%3Fin_arti-
cle_id%3D450509%26in_page_id%3D1770&h=121&w=128&sz=70&tbnid=ZjRATSg1O
DoJ:&tbnh=121&tbnw=128&sa=X&oi=image_result&resnum=1&ct=image&cd=2.

163. Gardner, "U.S. Soldier Hailed for Bravery."
164. Maj. Gen. Paul Eaton (Ret.) U.S. Army, on *Hardball,* MSNBC, May 14, 2007.
165. Paul Krugman, "The Mensch Gap," *New York Times,* February 20, 2006.
166. Rumsfeld, quoted in Al Kamen, "Tent Rent," *Washington Post,* June 7, 2002.
167. Bush, "The President's Speech to the Nation," January 10, 2007, CBS News transcripts,
     http://www.cbsnews.com/stories/2007/01/10/iraq/main2349882.shtml.
168. "The Real Disaster," editorial, *New York Times,* January 11, 2007.
169. Thomas Paine, *The American Crisis* (Whitefish, MT: Kessinger Publishing, 2004), 64.
170. Frank Rich, "As the Iraqis Stand Down, We'll Stand Up," *New York Times,* September 9, 2007.
171. Karen DeYoung, "Experts Doubt Drop in Violence in Iraq," *Washington Post,* September 6, 2007.
172. "Bob Woodward: Bush Misleads on Iraq" CBS, October 1, 2006, http://www.cbsnews.com/
     stories/2006/09/28/60minutes/main2047607.shtml.
173. Rich, "As the Iraqis Stand Down."
174. Frank Rich, "Karl Rove Beats the Democrats Again," *New York Times,* June 18, 2006.
175. Bush, quoted in John F. Burns and Dexter Filkins, "Bush Makes Surprise Visit to Iraq to
     Press Leadership," *New York Times,* June 14, 2006. Bush was speaking to troops gathered in
     Baghdad.
176. Fouad Ajami, "Iraq May Survive, but the Dream is Dead," *New York Times,* May 26, 2004.
     Ajami is a Johns Hopkins University Mideast expert who had been in favor of the invasion.
177. Fareed Zakaria, "The Price of Arrogance," *Newsweek,* May 17, 2004, http://www.newsweek.
     com/id/105324.
178. John Lehman, "We're Not Winning This War," *Washington Post,* August 31, 2006. Lehman
     was secretary of the Navy in the Reagan administration and later served as a member of the
     September 11 Commission.
179. Frank Rich, "Is Condi Hiding the Smoking Gun?" *New York Times,* May 6, 2007.
180. George Stephanopoulos, on *This Week,* ABC, April 29, 2007.
181. Rich, "Is Condi Hiding the Smoking Gun?"
182. Bush, quoted on *Special Report with Brit Hume,* Fox News, May 2, 2007, http://www.foxnews.
     com/story/0,2933,269877,00.html.
183. Rich, "Is Condi Hiding the Smoking Gun?"
184. Bush, "President's Remarks at the United Nations General Assembly," White House press re-
     lease, September 12, 2002, http://georgewbush-whitehouse.archives.gov/news/releases/2002/
     09/20020912-1.html.
185. *The Iraq Study Group Report* (New York: Vintage, 2006), xiii.
186. Murphy and Purdum, "Farewell to All That," 157.
187. Lee Hamilton, quoted in ibid. Hamilton was co-chair of the Iraq Study Group and served in
     the U.S. House of Representatives, 1965–1999.
188. *Iraq Study Group Report,* 94–95.
189. Ibid., 95.
190. Frank Rich, "They'll Break the Bad News on 9/11," *New York Times,* June 24, 2007.
191. *Iraq Study Group Report,* 95.
192. Alan Simpson, quoted in Murphy and Purdum, "Farewell to All That," 157. Simpson is for-
     mer U.S. senator from Wyoming and was a member of the Iraq Study Group.
193. Bush, "The President's News Conference," July 12, 2007, http://www.presidency.ucsb.edu/ws/
     index.php?pid=75549.
194. Bruce Riedel, quoted in Michael R. Gordon and Jim Ruttenberg, "Bush Distorts Qaeda Links,
     Critics Assert," *New York Times,* July 13, 2007. Riedel is an expert at the Saban Center for
     Middle East Policy and a former CIA official.
195. Fallows, *Blind Into Baghdad,* 118–119.
196. "The Iraq War Debate: The Great Denier," editorial, *New York Times,* July 21, 2007.
197. Cheney, on *Meet the Press,* NBC, September 10, 2006, http://www.msnbc.msn.com/id/
     14720480/ns/meet_the_press_online_at_msnbc/.
198. Keith Olbermann, commentary, *Countdown,* MSNBC, September 11, 2006.

199. "Iraq Benchmark Report Card," Center for American Progress, January 24, 2008, http://www.americanprogress.org/issues/2008/01/benchmark.html.
200. Bush, "President's Address to the Nation," White House press release, Jan 10, 2007, http://georgewbush-whitehouse.archives.gov/news/releases/2007/01/20070110-7.html.
201. "Iraq Benchmark Report Card."
202. Rich, "They'll Break the Bad News."
203. Frank Rich, "Don't Laugh at Michael Chertoff," *New York Times*, July 15, 2007.
204. "War Without End," editorial, *New York Times*, May 27, 2007.
205. Scott Shane, "Senate Democrats Say Bush Ignored Spy Agencies' Prewar Warnings of Iraq Perils," *New York Times*, May 26, 2007.
206. Walter Pincus and Karen DeYoung, "Analysts' Warnings of Iraq Chaos Detailed," *Washington Post*, May 27, 2007.
207. Sen. John D. Rockefeller IV, quoted in ibid.
208. Fallows, *Blind Into Baghdad*, 102.
209. Rumsfeld, quoted in ibid., 101.
210. Thomas Paine, "Address to the People of France," in *The Writings of Thomas Paine* (New York: G. P. Putnam's Sons, 1895), 97.
211. Fallows, *Blind Into Baghdad*, 106.
212. Bush, "The President's News Conference," April 3, 2007, http://www.presidency.ucsb.edu/ws/index.php?pid=25014.
213. Frank Rich, "Oh What a Malleable War," *New York Times*, February 18, 2007.
214. Keith Olbermann, on *Countdown*, MSNBC, May 1, 2007.
215. George Orwell, *1984* (New York: Penguin, 1949), 198.
216. Martin Luther King Jr., *The Trumpet of Conscience* (San Francisco: Harper and Row Publishers, 1967), 33.
217. Frank Rich, on *Countdown*, MSNBC, May 1, 2007.
218. Jim Hoagland, "Bush's Vietnam Blunder," *Washington Post*, August 24, 2007.
219. Maureen Dowd, "Smoking Dutch Cleanser," *New York Times*, February 11, 2006.
220. Keith Olbermann, on *Countdown*, MSNBC, January 11, 2007.
221. "A Bitter Iraq War Anniversary," editorial, *Chattanooga Times Free Press*, March 21, 2006.
222. Keith Olbermann, on *Countdown*, MSNBC, January 11, 2007.
223. "A Bitter Iraq War Anniversary."
224. Keith Olbermann, on *Countdown*, MSNBC, January 11, 2007.
225. "A Bitter Iraq War Anniversary."
226. Paul Krugman, "Weapons of Math Destruction," *New York Times*, April 14, 2006.
227. Thomas Paine, *Age of Reason* (Whitefish, MT: Kessinger Publishing, 2004), 128.
228. Rich, "Oh What a Malleable War."
229. Naomi Wolf, on *Hardball*, MSNBC, August 17, 2007.
230. Sen. John Kerry, on *Hardball*, MSNBC, September 7, 2006.
231. Hersh, *Chain of Command*, 366.
232. Isikoff and Corn, *Hubris*, 338–339.
233. Bush, quoted in Dan Murphy, "Jobless Soldiers Fuel Anti-US Riots in Iraq," *Christian Science Monitor*, October 8, 2003.
234. Bush, "The President's News Conference With Prime Minister Ayad Allawi of Iraq," September 23, 2004, http://www.presidency.ucsb.edu/ws/index.php?pid=72762.
235. Julie Hirschfield Davis, "Bush Plan Cuts Social Security for Better-Off," *Baltimore Sun*, April 29, 2005.
236. Bush, "Remarks by President George W. Bush on the War on Terror," White House Briefing, October 28, 2005.
237. Bush, "Setting the Record Straight," White House press release, November 26, 2005.
238. Cheney, on *Fox News Sunday*, FOX, January 14, 2007, http://www.foxnews.com/story/0,2933,243632,00.html.
239. "The Great Divider" editorial, *New York Times*, November 2, 2006.
240. Bush, "Transcript of Debate Between Vice President Gore and Governor Bush," *New York Times*, October 4, 2000.
241. Keith Olbermann, on *Countdown*, MSNBC, January 10, 2007.
242. Cheney, on *Fox News Sunday*, FOX, January 14, 2007.

243. Rich, "Lying Like It's 2003," *New York Times*, January 21, 2007.
244. Bush, "Transcript: Bush Interview," *60 Minutes*, CBS, January 14, 2007, http://www.cbsnews.com/stories/2007/01/14/60minutes/main2359119_page4.shtml.
245. Greenwald, *A Tragic Legacy*, 16. Emphasis in original.
246. Richard Morin and Dan Balz, "Bush's Popularity Reaches New Low," *Washington Post*, November 4, 2005.
247. Mark Seibel, "Administration leaving out important details on Iraq," McClatchy Newspapers, January 14, 2007, http://www.mcclatchydc.com/iraq-intelligence/story/15384.html.
248. Mark Mazzetti, "Analysis Is Bleak on Iraq's Future," *New York Times*, February 3, 2007.
249. Cheney, on *The Situation Room*, CNN, January 24, 2007, http://i.a.cnn.net/cnn/2007/images/01/24/cheney.transcript.pdf.
250. Maureen Dowd, "No Way Out," *New York Times*, February 3, 2007.
251. Cheney, quoted in Mark Mazzetti, "Analysis Is Bleak on Iraq's Future."
252. "A Long Road Ahead in Iraq," editorial, *New York Times*, June 18, 2006.
253. Bush, "The President's News Conference," August 21, 2006, http://www.presidency.ucsb.edu/ws/index.php?pid=614.
254. David Corn, "At Press Conference, Bush Stays the Course," *The Nation*, August 21, 2006, http://www.thenation.com/blogs/capitalgames/114384.
255. Maureen Dowd, "A Wartime Love Story," *New York Times*, November 4, 2006.
256. Bob Herbert, "Other People's Blood," *New York Times*, June 8, 2006.
257. Frank Rich, "Iraq Is the Ultimate Aphrodisiac," *New York Times*, April 22, 2007.
258. Maureen Dowd, "Didn't See It Coming, Again," *New York Times*, February 1, 2006.
259. Gore, *Assault on Reason*, 63.
260. Clarke, *Against All Enemies*, 246.
261. Bush, "President Bush Participates in Joint Press Availability with Prime Minister Kevin Rudd of Australia," White House press release, March 28, 2008, http://georgewbush-whitehouse.archives.gov/news/releases/2008/03/images/20080328-3_p032808jb-0077-515h.html.
262. Frank Rich, "Tet Happened, and No One Cared," *New York Times*, April 6, 2008.
263. Clarke, *Against All Enemies*, 264.
264. Gore, *Assault on Reason*, 60.
265. James Fallows, *Blind Into Baghdad*, 114–115.
266. Bush, "Iraq Intelligence Failure My Biggest Regret: Bush," December 2, 2008, ABC News, http://www.abc.net.au/news/stories/2008/12/02/2435282.htm.
267. Frank Rich, "Two Cheers for Rod Blagojevich," *New York Times*, December 14, 2008.
268. "The Deluder in Chief," editorial, *New York Times*, December 7, 2008.
269. "President Bush Attends Saban Forum 2008," White House news release, December 5, 2008, http://georgewbush-whitehouse.archives.gov/news/releases/2008/12/20081205-8.html.
270. Mark Mazzetti, "Spy Agencies Say Iraq War Worsens Terrorism Threat," *New York Times*, September 24, 2006.
271. Bush, "President Bush Discusses National Security, Homeland Security and the Freedom Agenda at U.S. Army War College," White House news release, December 17, 2008, http://webcache.googleusercontent.com/search?q=cache:ZSS_jFPje40J:merln.ndu.edu/archivepdf/terrorism/wh/20081217-6.pdf+Bush,+%E2%80%9CPresident+Bush+Discusses+National+Security,+Homeland+Security+and+the+Freedom+Agenda+at+U.S.+Army+War+College,%E2%80%9D+White+House+news+release,+December+17,+2008&cd=1&hl=en&ct=clnk&gl=us&client=firefox-a.
272. "Afghan Attacks Rise as al-Qaeda Gains Strength: U.S. Report," CBS News, April 30, 2008, http://www.cbc.ca/world/story/2008/04/30/us-terrorreport.html.
273. Tom A. Peter, "Qaeda Stronger and a Threat to US homeland," Christian Science Monitor, July 19, 2007.
274. Jonathan Karl, "Al Qaeda's Strength 'Undiminished' in Iraq," ABC News, July 12, 2007, http://abcnews.go.com/International/Story?id=3366118&page=1.
275. Joschka Fischer, quoted in Murphy and Purdum, "Farewell to All That," 155. Fischer was German foreign minister and vice-chancellor.
276. Frank Rich, "Bring Back Warren Harding," *New York Times*, September 25, 2005.
277. Sen. Bob Graham, quoted in Murphy and Purdum, "Farewell to All That," 160. Graham, a Democratic senator from Florida, was chairman of the Senate Intelligence Committee.

Chapter 8: Torture and Rendition

1. Dick Cheney, "Vice President Dick Cheney Discusses the Attack on America and Response to Terrorism," on *Meet the Press*, NBC, September 16, 2001.
2. Jean-Jacques Rousseau, quoted in *Educational Ideas in America*, ed. S. Alexander Rippa (New York: D. McKay Co., 1969), 67.
3. George W. Bush, quoted on *Frontline*, PBS, June 20, 2006, http://www.pbs.org/wgbh/pages/frontline/darkside/themes/darkside.html.
4. Seymour M. Hersh, *Chain of Command: The Road From 9/11 to Abu Ghraib* (New York: Harper Collins, 2004), 21.
5. Cofer Black, quoted in Frank Davies, "'Americans Are Going to Die,' CIA Warned," *Miami Herald*, September. 27, 2002. Black headed the CIA's Counterterrorist Center.
6. Frederick A. O. Schwarz Jr. and Aziz Z. Huq, *Unchecked and Unbalanced: Presidential Power in a Time of Terror* (New York: New Press, 2007), 92.
7. Carrie Johnson, "Ex-Official Testifies About Efforts to Halt Harsh Tactics," *Washington Post*, May 14, 2009.
8. Cheney, on *Face the Nation*, CBS, May 10, 2009, http://www.cbsnews.com/htdocs/pdf/FTN_051009.pdf.
9. "The Torturers' Manifesto," editorial, *New York Times*, April 19, 2009.
10. Jonathan Turley, on *Countdown*, MSNBC, May 11, 2009. Turley is a constitutional law professor at George Washington University.
11. "On Torture and American Values," *New York Times*, October 7, 2007.
12. *Face the Nation*, CBS, May 10, 2009, http://www.cbsnews.com/htdocs/pdf/FTN_051009.pdf.
13. Jonathan Turley, on *Countdown*, MSNBC, April 10, 2008.
14. Bush, "Address Before a Joint Session of the Congress on the State of the Union," *January 28, 2003, http://www.presidency.ucsb.edu/ws/index.php?pid=29645*.
15. "On Torture and American Values," *New York Times*, October 7, 2007.
16. Anthony Lewis, "Making Torture Legal," *New York Review of Books*, July 15, 2004, http://www.nybooks.com/articles/article-preview?article_id=17230.
17. Condoleezza Rice, quoted in "Washington Digest," *Washington Post*, May 1, 2009.
18. Spencer Ackerman, "If the President Does It, It Isn't Torture: Did Rice Just Implicate Bush?" *Washington Independent*, April 30, 2009, http://washingtonindependent.com/41346/if-the-president-does-it-it-isnt-torture-did-rice-just-implicate-bush.
19. Jane Mayer, *The Dark Side: The Inside Story of How the War on Terror Turned Into a War on American Ideals* (New York: Doubleday, 2008), 79.
20. Gen. David Petraeus, quoted in "Inquiry into the Treatment of Detainees in U.S. Custody," U.S. Armed Services Committee report, xii, http://levin.senate.gov/newsroom/supporting/2009/SASC.DetaineeReport.042209.pdf.
21. Thomas Paine, "The Crisis," in *The Writings of Thomas Paine*, ed. Moncure Daniel Conway (New York: G. P. Putnam's Sons, 1894), 1:324.
22. Jonathan Turley, on *Countdown*, December 16, 2008.
23. Bush, "Leave Iraq Within 48 Hours," CNN, March 17, 2003, http://www.cnn.com/2003/WORLD/meast/03/17/sprj.irq.bush.transcript/.
24. Mayer, *The Dark Side*, 328.
25. Gene Healy and Timothy Lynch, "Power Surge: The Constitutional Record of George W. Bush," Cato Institute report, 2006, http://www.cato.org/pubs/wtpapers/powersurge_healy_lynch.pdf, 8.
26. Hersh, *Chain of Command*, 5.
27. Bush, "Text of order signed by President Bush on February 7, 2002, outlining treatment of al-Qaida and Taliban detainees," http://www.lawofwar.org/Bush_torture_memo.htm.
28. Schwarz and Huq, *Unchecked and Unbalanced*, 76.
29. Bush, "Text of order signed by President Bush on Feb. 7, 2002."
30. John Dean, on *Countdown*, MSNBC, October 4, 2007.
31. Julian E. Barnes, "Army Manual to Skip Geneva Detainee Rule," *Los Angeles Times*, June 5, 2006.
32. Healy and Lynch, "Power Surge," 9.
33. Sen. John Kerry, speech delivered April 22, 2006 http://blog.thedemocraticdaily.com/?p=2723.
34. Fredrich Nietzsche, *Beyond Good and Evil*, trans. Walter Kaufman (New York: Vintage, 1966),

89. Cheney, quoted in "White House Denies Cheney Endorsed 'Water Boarding,'" *USA Today*, October 27, 2006, http://www.usatoday.com/news/washington/2006-10-27-cheney_x.htm.

35. George W. Bush and Richard Wolffe, "Foreign Policy Questions Divert Bush Speech," NPR, Oct. 7, 2007, http://www.npr.org/templates/transcript/transcript.php?storyId=15377315

36. John Dean, on *Countdown*, MSNBC, October 4, 2007.

37. George Orwell, *1984* (New York: Penguin, 1949), 263.

38. Mayer, *The Dark Side*, 122.

39. Schwarz and Huq, *Unchecked and Unbalanced*, 66.

40. Bush, "Transcript: Presidents Bush 41 and 43" on *FOX News Sunday*, FOX, January 11, 2009, http://www.foxnews.com/story/0,2933,479174,00.html.

41. Schwarz and Huq, *Unchecked and Unbalanced*, 66–67.

42. Mayer, *The Dark Side*, 65.

43. "Transcript: Cheney Defends Hard Line Tactics," ABC News, December 16, 2008, http://abcnews.go.com/Politics/story?id=6464697&page=1.

44. Jonathan Turley, on *Countdown*, December 16, 2008.

45. Mayer, *The Dark Side*, 308.

46. Albert Einstein, in *The Collected Papers of Albert Einstein: The Early Years, 1879–1902*, trans. Anna Beck (Princeton: Princeton University Press, 1987), 1:177.

47. Donald Rumsfeld, "Pentagon Town Hall Meeting," CNN, April 17, 2003, http://transcripts.cnn.com/TRANSCRIPTS/0304/17/se.02.html.

48. Mayer, *The Dark Side*, 152.

49. Barton Gellman and Jo Becker, "A Different Understanding With the President," *Washington Post*, June 24, 2007.

50. Mayer, *The Dark Side*, 153.

51. Ibid., 47.

52. Gellman and Becker, "A Different Understanding With the President."

53. Mayer, *The Dark Side*, 8.

54. George Tenet, "George Tenet: At the Center of the Storm," *60 Minutes*, CBS, April 29, 2007. http://www.cbsnews.com/stories/2007/04/25/60minutes/main2728375_page3.shtml.

55. Michael Hayden, quoted in "Senate Dems Want Criminal Probe in Waterboarding Cases," *USA Today*, February 6, 2008, http://www.usatoday.com/news/washington/2008-02-05-terror-threat_N.htm.

56. Lara Jakes Jordan, "U.S. Acknowledges Use of Waterboarding," Associated Press, February 5, 2008, http://seattletimes.nwsource.com/html/politics/2004165892_apmukaseytorture05.html?syndication=rss.

57. Bradley S. Klapper, "U.N. Blasts White House on Waterboarding," Associated Press, February 6, 2008, http://www.newsvine.com/_news/2008/02/06/1282588-un-blasts-white-house-on-waterboarding.

58. "It's Torture; it's Illegal," editorial, *Los Angeles Times*, February 2, 2008.

59. Schwarz and Huq, *Unchecked and Unbalanced*, 69.

60. Al Gore, *The Assault on Reason* (New York: Penguin, 2007), 156.

61. Scott Shane, David Johnston, and James Risen, "Secret U.S. Endorsement of Severe Interrogations," *New York Times*, October 4, 2007.

62. William Glaberson, "Man Held by CIA Says He Was Tortured," *New York Times*, December 6, 2007.

63. Bush, "President Discusses Creation of Military Commissions to Try Suspected Terrorists," White House news release, September 6, 2006, http://georgewbush-whitehouse.archives.gov/news/releases/2006/09/20060906-3.html.

64. Mark Mazzetti and Scott Shane, "Interrogation Memos Detail Harsh Tactics by the CIA," *New York Times*, April 17, 2009.

65. Carrie Johnson and Julie Tate, "New Interrogation Details Emerge," *Washington Post*, April 17, 2009.

66. "The Torturers' Manifesto."

67. John Dean, on *Countdown*, MSNBC, April 16, 2009.

68. Johnson and Tate, "New Interrogation Details Emerge."

69. "The Torturers' Manifesto."

70. Frank Rich, "The Banality of Bush White House Evil," *New York Times*, April 26, 2009.

71. Jameel Jaffer, "Justice Department Releases Bush Administration Torture Memos," ACLU. org, April 16, 2009, http://www.aclu.org/safefree/torture/39393prs20090416.html. Jaffer is Director of the ACLU National Security Project.

72. David Cole, "Macabre and Excruciating Details," *New York Times*, April 16, 2009, http://roomfordebate.blogs.nytimes.com/2009/04/16/the-memos-torture-redefined/.

73. Mazzetti and Shane, "Interrogation Memos Detail Harsh Tactics."

74. Rich, "The Banality of Bush White House Evil."

75. Carl Jung, in *The Routledge Dictionary of Quotations*, ed. Robert Andrews (New York: Routledge, 1987), 266.

76. Mazzetti and Shane, "Interrogation Memos Detail Harsh Tactics."

77. Scott Shane, "Waterboarding Used 266 Times on 2 Suspects," *New York Times*, April 20, 2009.

78. Ron Suskind, on *The Rachel Maddow Show*, MSNBC, April 22, 2009.

79. "Report by the Senate Armed Services Committee on Detainee Treatment," Committee on Armed Services, U.S. Senate, http://documents.nytimes.com/report-by-the-senate-armed-services-committee-on-detainee-treatment. Burney was a U.S. Army psychiatrist.

80. Naomi Wolf, *The End of America: Letter of Warning to a Young Patriot* (White River Junction: VT: Chelsea Green Publishing, 2007), 71.

81. Ron Suskind, on *The Rachel Maddow Show*, MSNBC, April 22, 2009.

82. Rich, "The Banality of Bush White House Evil."

83. Jack Rice, on *Countdown,* MSNBC, December 11, 2007. Rice was a CIA agent.

84. Donald Rumsfeld, quoted in Andrew Chang, "Is Torture a Tool in the War on Terror?" ABC News, August 13, 2002, http://media.abcnews.com/International/story?id=79885&page=1.

85. Schwarz and Huq, *Unchecked and Unbalanced*, 77.

86. "The Torture Report," editorial, *New York Times*, December 17, 2008.

87. Eugene Robinson, "Closing Time at Guantanamo," *Washington Post*, June 20, 2006.

88. Cheney, quoted in Paul Richter, "Cheney Still Forecasts Collapse of Insurgency," *Los Angeles Times*, June 24, 2005.

89. Mayer, *The Dark Side*, 189.

90. Bush, "The President's News Conference with European Union Leaders," June 20, 2005, The American Presidency Project, http://www.presidency.ucsb.edu/ws/index.php?pid=63867.

91. Eugene Robinson, "The Heat is On Guantanamo" *Washington Post*, June 21, 2005.

92. Joe Margulies, quoted in Mayer, *The Dark Side*, 91. Margulies is a law professor at Northwestern University and author of *Guantanamo and the Abuse of Presidential Power*.

93. Mayer, *The Dark Side*, 230.

94. Andrew O. Selsky, "Ex-Bush Admin Official: Many at Gitmo are Innocent," Associated Press, March 19, 2009, http://www.commondreams.org/headline/2009/03/19-9.

95. Lawrence Wilkerson, quoted in Selsky, "Ex-Bush Admin Official: Many at Gitmo are Innocent." Wilkerson was a top aide and later chief of staff to Secretary of State Colin Powell.

96. Dave Becker, quoted in Mayer, *The Dark Side*, 195. Becker was chief of Guantanamo's "Interrogation Control Element."

97. Ron Suskind, on *The Rachel Maddow Show*, MSNBC, April 22, 2009.

98. Sen. Carl Levin, "Detainee Abuses and American Values," news release, April 24, 2009, http://levin.senate.gov/newsroom/release.cfm?id=311987.

99. Rich, "The Banality of Bush White House Evil."

100. Joint Personnel Recovery Agency memo attachment, quoted in Peter Finn and Joby Warrick, "In 2002, Military Agency Warned Against 'Torture,'" *Washington Post*, April 25, 2009.

101. Eugene Robinson, "Crimes That Deserve Punishment," *Washington Post*, April 10, 2009.

102. Voltaire, quoted in Rosemarie Jarski, *Words From the Wise* (New York: Skyhorse Publishing, 2007), 59.

103. Schwarz and Huq, *Unchecked and Unbalanced*, 147. Emphasis in original.

104. John W. Dean, *Worse Than Watergate: The Secret Presidency of George W. Bush* (New York: Warner, 2004), 216.

105. Olmstead v. United States, 277 U.S. 438, 485 (1928).

106. Eugene Fidell, quoted in Mark Mazzetti, "'03 Memo Approved Harsh Interrogations," *New York Times*, April 2, 2008. Fidell teaches military justice at Yale Law School and the Washington College of Law at American University.

107. "The Torture Sessions," editorial, *New York Times*, April 20, 2008.

108. John Kiriakou, on *Countdown,* MSNBC, December 11, 2007. Kiriakou is a former CIA officer.
109. Alberto Mora, quoted in Mayer, *The Dark Side*, 236. Mora was general counsel of the U.S. Navy.
110. Albert Camus, quoted in Jeffrey C. Isaac, *Arendt, Camus and Modern Rebellion* (New Haven: Yale University Press, 1992), 31.
111. Frank Rich, *The Greatest Story Ever Sold: The Decline and Fall of Truth From 9/11 to Katrina* (New York: Penguin, 2006), 39.
112. Bob Woodward, "Detainee Tortured, Says U.S. Official," *Washington Post*, January 14, 2009.
113. Susan J. Crawford, quoted in Woodward, ibid. Crawford is a retired judge and was the top Bush administration official in charge of deciding whether to bring Guantanamo Bay detainees to trial.
114. Lt. Cmdr. Charles Swift (Ret.), on *Countdown,* MSNBC, January 14, 2009. Swift was defense attorney for Salim Ahmed Hamdan in *Hamdan v. Rumsfeld*.
115. Bush, "President Discusses Creation of Military Commissions to Try Suspected Terrorists."
116. Stephen Kenny, quoted in Mayer, *The Dark Side*, 100. Kenney is a criminal defense lawyer.
117. Bush, "Transcript: Presidents Bush 41 and 43."
118. Scott Shane and Mark Mazzetti, "Report Blames Rumsfeld for Detainee Abuses," *New York Times*, December 11, 2008.
119. "The Torture Report."
120. Joby Warrick and Karen DeYoung, "Report on Detainee Abuse Blames Top Bush Officials," *Washington Post*, December 12, 2008.
121. "The Torture Report."
122. Jonathan Turley, on *Countdown,* December 16, 2008.
123. Warrick and DeYoung, "Report on Detainee Abuse Blames Top Bush Officials."
124. Matthew Alexander, "I'm Still Tortured by What I Saw in Iraq," *Washington Post*, November 30, 2008. Alexander led an interrogations team assigned to a Special Operations task force in Iraq in 2006. He writes under a pseudonym for security reasons.
125. Gen. David H. Petraeus, letter to all service personnel in Iraq, May 10, 2007, quoted in "Military Leaders: Ignore Bush Veto Threat, Ban Waterboarding," Huffington PostDec. 13, 2007 (http://www.huffingtonpost.com/2007/12/13/military-leaders-ignore-b_n_76656.html). Neal Katyal, on *Countdown,* MSNBC, October 4, 2007. Katyal was lead counsel in *Hamdan v. Rumsfeld*.
126. Sen. John Kerry, on *Hardball*, MSNBC, September 7, 2006.
127. Thomas Jefferson, "First Report of Conference Committee," December 4, 1777, in *The Writings of Thomas Jefferson: 1776–1781* ed. Paul Leicester Ford (New York: G. P. Putnam, 1893), 2:136.
128. Mayer, *The Dark Side*, 241.
129. Thomas E. Ricks, *Fiasco: The American Military Adventure in Iraq* (New York: Penguin, 2006), 290.
130. Carol Rosenberg, "U.S. Military Charges Six Soldiers with Assaulting Iraqi Prisoners," *Philadelphia Inquirer*, March 21, 2004.
131. Hersh, *Chain of Command*, 46.
132. Thomas L. Friedman, "Restoring Our Honor," *New York Times*, May 6, 2004.
133. "Rule of Lawlessness," editorial, *Washington Post*, May 2, 2004.
134. Esther Schrader and Patrick J. McDonnell, "Bush Denounces Troops' Treatment of Prisoners," *Los Angeles Times*, May 1, 2004.
135. Sen. Richard Durbin, quoted in Mayer, *The Dark Side*, 259.
136. Thom Shanker and Dexter Filkins, "Army Punishes 7 with Reprimands for Prison Abuse," *New York Times*, May 4, 2004.
137. Hersh, *Chain of Command*, 38.
138. Sen. Carl Levin, "Levin, McCain Release Executive Summary and Conclusions of Report on Treatment of Detainees in U.S. Custody," December 11, 2008, http://levin.senate.gov/newsroom/release.cfm?id=305735. Levin is chair of the Senate Armed Services committee.
139. Mayer, *The Dark Side*, 166.
140. Paul Wolfowitz, "Deputy Secretary Wolfowitz Interview on the Pentagon Channel," U.S. Department of Defense, May 4, 2004, http://www.defenselink.mil/transcripts/transcript.aspx?transcriptid=2970. Wolfowitz was Deputy Secretary of Defense, 2001–2005.

141. Sen. Carl Levin, "Detainee Abuses and American Values," news release, April 24, 2009, http://levin.senate.gov/newsroom/release.cfm?id=311987.

142. Gore, *Assault on Reason*, 60.

143. Lawrence Wilkerson, quoted in Jim Lobe, "Serious Lapses Taint Probes of Detainee Deaths," Common Dreams, Oct. 21, 2005 http://www.commondreams.org/headlines05/1021-01.htm.

144. Cheney, "Transcript of Dick Cheney's Remarks on National Security," CNN.com, May 21, 2009, http://www.cnn.com/2009/POLITICS/05/21/cheney.transcript/.

145. Hersh, *Chain of Command*, 362.

146. Gen. Janis Karpinski (Ret.), on *Countdown*, MSNBC, May 22, 2009. Karpinski was commander of U.S. prisons in Iraq.

147. Cheney, "Transcript of Dick Cheney's Remarks on National Security."

148. Gen. Janis Karpinski (Ret.), on *Countdown*, MSNBC, April 22, 2009.

149. Hersh, *Chain of Command*, 362.

150. Maj. Gen. John Batiste, U.S. Army (Ret.), on *Countdown*, MSNBC, April 24, 2009.

151. Mayer, *The Dark Side*, 258.

152. Sewell Chan and Michael Amon, "Prisoner Abuse Probe Widened," *Washington Post*, May 2, 2004.

153. "U.S., Britain Reeling Over Prisoner Abuse," *San Francisco Chronicle*, May 2, 2004.

154. Patrick J. McDonnell, "New Chief of Prisons Defends His Role in Iraq," *Los Angeles Times*, May 9, 2004.

155. Seymour M. Hersh, "The General's Report," *New Yorker*, June 25, 2007, 58.

156. Gen. Antonio Taguba (Ret.), quoted in Hersh, ibid. (referring to briefing of Defense Department executives on Abu Ghraib investigation

157. Schwarz and Huq, *Unchecked and Unbalanced*, 97.

158. Michael Duffy, "Letting the President Say," *Time*, October 9, 2006.

159. Bush, "President Discusses Creation of Military Commissions to Try Suspected Terrorists," White House news release, September 6, 2006, http://georgewbush-whitehouse.archives.gov/news/releases/2006/09/20060906-3.html.

160. Mazzetti and Shane, "Interrogation Memos Detail Harsh Tactics by the CIA"

161. James Risen, *State of War: The Secret History of the CIA and the Bush Administration* (New York: Free Press, 2006), 36–37.

162. Mayer, *The Dark Side*, 148.

163. R. Jeffrey Smith and Peter Finn, "Harsh Methods Approved as Early as Summer 2002," *Washington Post*, April 23, 2009.

164. Michael A. Fletcher, "Bush Defends CIA's Clandestine Prisons," *Washington Post*, November 8, 2005.

165. Mayer, *The Dark Side*, 325.

166. Bush, "President Discusses Creation of Military Commissions to Try Suspected Terrorists.".

167. Christopher Dickey, "The Constitution in Peril," *Newsweek*, October 8, 2007.

168. Schwarz and Huq, *Unchecked and Unbalanced*, 108.

169. Charlie Savage, *Takeover: The Return of the Imperial Presidency and the Subversion of American Democracy* (New York: Little Brown and Co., 2007), 213.

170. "Alberto Gonzales, The Sequel," editorial, *New York Times*, January 28, 2009.

171. Anonymous U.S. official, quoted in Dana Priest and Barton Gelman, "U.S. Decries Abuse but Defends Interrogations," *Washington Post*, December 26, 2002.

172. "The Torture Report."

173. "On Torture and American Values," editorial, *New York Times*, October 7, 2007.

174. Wolf, *End of America*, 46

175. Schwarz and Huq, *Unchecked and Unbalanced*, 105.

176. Alan Gomez, "CIA Destroyed Interrogation Tapes," *USA Today*, December 7, 2007, http://www.usatoday.com/news/washington/2007-12-06-cia-tapes-terror_N.htm.

177. Mark Mazzetti, "CIA Destroyed 2 Tapes Showing Interrogations," *New York Times*, December 7, 2007.

178. Sen. Christopher Dodd, on *Countdown*, MSNBC, December 18, 2007.

179. Nicholas D. Kristof, "Sami's Shame, and Ours," *New York Times*, October 17, 2006.

180. Oona A. Hathaway, quoted in Julian E. Barnes, "Army Manual to Skip Geneva Detainee Rule," *Los Angeles Times*, June, 5, 2006. Hathaway is an expert in international law at Yale Law School.

181. "Rendition, Torture and Accountability," editorial, *New York Times*, November 19, 2007.
182. Dana Priest, "CIA Holds Terror Suspects in Secret Prisons," *Washington Post*, November 2, 2005.
183. Mayer, *The Dark Side*, 148.
184. "Whose Privilege?" editorial, *New York Times*, April 18, 2008.
185. Paul Krugman, "King of Pain," *New York Times*, September 18, 2006.
186. "Rule of Lawlessness," editorial, *Washington Post*, May 2, 2004.
187. Rep. Henry Waxman, quoted in Mayer, *The Dark Side*, 326.
188. Ron Suskind, *The One Percent Doctrine: Deep Inside America's Pursuit of Its Enemies Since 9/11* (New York: Simon & Schuster, 2006), 229–230. Emphasis in original.
189. Sen. Jay Rockefeller, quoted in Mayer, *The Dark Side*, 330.
190. Mayer, *The Dark Side*, 327.
191. Dwight D. Eisenhower, in Peggy Anderson, *Great Quotes From Great Leaders* (Lombard, IL: Great Quotations Publishing Co., 1990), 131.

Afterword

1. Scott McClellan, *What Happened: Inside the Bush White House and Washington's Culture of Deception* (New York: Public Affairs, 2008), 291.
2. Maureen Dowd, "Delusion and Illusion Worthy of Dickens," *New York Times*, January 25, 2006.
3. Paul Krugman, "A Test of Our Character," *New York Times*, May 26, 2006.
4. Sen. Barbara Boxer, quoted in Margaret Kriz, "Vanishing Act," *National Journal*, April 12, 2008, http://www.nationaljournal.com/njmagazine/cs_20080412_9524.php. Boxer is the Senate Environment and Public Works Committee chairwoman.
5. Robert F. Kennedy Jr., "Texas Chainsaw Management," *Vanity Fair*, May 2007, http://www.vanityfair.com/politics/features/2007/05/revolvingdoor200705.
6. Larry West, "Federal Scientists Accuse Bush of Climate Science Censorship," http://environment.about.com/od/environmentallawpolicy/a/censorship_clim.htm.
7. Tim Dickinson, "Six Years of Deceit," *Rolling Stone*, June 28, 2007.
8. Ibid.
9. Mark Hertsgaard, "While Washington Slept," *Vanity Fair*, May 2006, 242.
10. "Press Briefing by Ari Fleischer," May 7, 2001, http://www.presidency.ucsb.edu/ws/index.php?pid=47520.
11. George W. Bush, "President Announces Clear Skies & Global Climate Change Initiatives," White House Press Release, Feb. 14, 2002, http://georgewbush-whitehouse.archives.gov/news/releases/2002/02/20020214-5.html.
12. "Lie By Lie: A Guide to President Bush's Calculated Deceptions on Global Warming," *Rolling Stone*, June 28, 2007, 59.
13. Charlie Savage, *Takeover: The Return of the Imperial Presidency and the Subversion of American Democracy* (New York: Little Brown and Co., 2007), 86.
14. Robert Winnett and Urmee Khan, "President George Bush: 'Goodbye From the World's Biggest Polluter,'" July 7, 2008, http://www.telegraph.co.uk/news/worldnews/2277298/President-George-Bush-Goodbye-from-the-worlds-biggest-polluter.html.

INDEX

ABOUT THE AUTHOR

Joseph Russomanno is an associate professor at the Walter Cronkite School of Journalism and Mass Communication at Arizona State University. He is the author of *Speaking Our Minds: Conversations with the People Behind Landmark Amendment Cases* (2002), coauthor of *The Law of Journalism and Mass Communication* (2007), and editor of *Defending the First: Commentary on First Amendment Issues and Cases* (2005). He lives in Chandler, Arizona.